Frommer's™

Best Hiking Trips in Northern California

My Northern California

by John McKinney

NORTHERN CALIFORNIA BECKONS THE HIKER WITH AN UNRIVALLED DIVERSITY of terrain and trails. Other parts of the planet have high peaks, deep canyons, great deserts, and long seashores—but only Northern California has all these grand landscapes in one place.

From the foggy headlands of San Francisco Bay to the snowy summits of the High Sierra, and from the golden hills of Wine Country to the towering redwood forests along the coast, this hiker's paradise is preserved in more than a dozen national parklands, more than a hundred state parks, and dozens of coastal preserves.

Walk among the redwoods, the tallest trees on earth, in Redwood National Park. Conquer Mt. Whitney, the highest peak in the continental United States. Follow in the footsteps of beloved naturalist John Muir en route to Yosemite's magnificent waterfalls, giant sequoia groves, granite domes, and peaks. Roam the wild coast of Point Reyes National Seashore and watch for elephant seals, tule elk, and hundreds of species of birds.

These natural treasures are reached by a remarkable network of pathways, built and maintained by dedicated hikers and government public land managers. Californians care passionately about protecting their land, and in 1969 founded "Trails Day" to encourage people to give their time and energy to building or rehabilitating footpaths—a program that has since spread to every state.

It gives this native Californian great pleasure to share some of the best hikes I've encountered in my many years exploring the Golden State. Hike on!

First page: top, ©Walter Bibikow / age fotostock; bottom, ©Paula Borchardt / age fotostock

©Dan Leffel / age fotostock

MUIR WOODS (left) Only 12 miles from the Golden Gate Bridge, this redwood preserve attracts more than a million visitors a year. Named for famed California naturalist John Muir, the park boasts gentle pathways meandering through the towering trees, the tallest of which is a 273-foot high Douglas fir.

Many of San Francisco's best hikes begin or end (or traverse) the **GOLDEN GATE BRIDGE (right)** and no wonder—on both sides of the bridge, hikers are treated to sights both wild and urban, and panoramic views of San Francisco Bay, which contains 90% of California's remaining coastal wetlands.

The coastline south of San Francisco boasts some wild and varied geography, beginning with the Santa Cruz mountains and the coastal panoramas of Big Sur. The **POINT LOBOS STATE RESERVE (below)** drew some of California's greatest landscape artists, including Francis McComas and Ansel Adams, to capture its rugged coastline and windswept cypress trees.

©iStockphoto.com

Some of the most rugged and sparsely populated parts of the state lie along its north coast, culminating in **REDWOOD NATIONAL PARK (left)**. The frequent fog often gives the place an other-worldly feel as you follow paths that wind among these giants, particularly in the natural cathedral of Tall Trees Grove.

Hiking need not mean physical hardship and a diet of trail mix. A few days wandering through the rolling hills of the Sonoma and the **NAPA VALLEY (below)** can be accompanied with a loaf of San Francisco sourdough and a strong cheese, along with, of course, a sample or two from one of Wine Country's hundreds of vineyards. This is particularly enticing during the fall, when the grapes are being harvested and the trees take on a beautiful golden hue.

©iStockphoto.com

Few national parks evoke the reverence that **YOSEMITE (below)** does among hikers of all abilities. It really does have it all—superbly maintained trails, postcard-perfect lakes and waterfalls, stunning aspens and sequoias, towering peaks, and iconic geography, including such household names as El Capitan and Half Dome (pictured here).

©iStockphoto.com

Thinking about the adjoining Sequoia and Kings Canyon National Parks, one word comes to mind—big. In the case of Sequoia, there is no better example of this than 14,494-foot high **MOUNT WHITNEY (above)**, the highest peak in the continental United States. The long hike to the top has lots of scenic viewpoints and resting places, such as the beautiful Lone Pine Lake pictured here.

They don't come any bigger than the **GENERAL SHERMAN TREE (right)** in Sequoia and Kings Canyon National Park. Measured as the world's largest living thing, its vital statistics are staggering—275 feet high, 102 feet in circumference, approximately 2,500 years old, and weighing an estimated 2.8 million pounds.

On the eastern edge of California, lies a boundary of blue—**LAKE TAHOE (below)**. With the pristine waters of the alpine lake (the largest in North America) matching the tint of the sky, there are many opportunities for peaceful contemplation as you walk. One of the best spots is the viewpoint over Emerald Bay; once you're done drinking in the vistas, you can walk down to enjoy a dip in the lake at one of Tahoe's best beaches.

©Charlie Borland / agefotostock

There are perhaps few other more alien landscapes on earth than those in **DEATH VALLEY NATIONAL PARK** (above). It is not often a place that first springs to mind for hikers, but its extremes draw them in: barren salt flats, sunlight-painted canyons, wildlife uniquely adapted to the harsh desert, and a severe topography that bedevils the imagination. It is truly a place like no other.

©Trish Drury

BANANA SLUG

Size: Up to about 10 inches long, although smaller ones are usually seen

Identifying features: Pale yellow, greenish-yellow, brownish-yellow, or bright yellow; sometimes with pale brown or black spots

Best sighting times: Cool, moist, overcast days from winter through mid-summer

Where to see them: Moist ground of coastal forests

Banana slugs look a bit like, well, bananas, with their yellow color and occasional dark spots. They are also very big—the second largest species of slug in the world—and very slimy. After you've picked one up—it's difficult not to—you'll discover how hard it is to remove the sticky slime from your fingers. This secretion helps keep the banana slug moist, aids it in gliding over surfaces, and offers some protection against predators.

From March through July, they are commonly seen on the ground, crossing trails or among low, moist vegetation, especially in or near redwood forests. Banana slugs become primarily nocturnal in August and into November, spending more time above the ground on shrubs and trees.

©Trish Drury

BRANDT'S CORMORANT

Size: 34 inches long

Identifying features: Black body, light-tan-colored throat has bright blue coloring during breeding season

Best sighting times: Sunny days from spring through early fall

Where to see them: Coastal areas; often on rocks near shore

Their long, skinny neck and black coloring make cormorants easy to identify. Brandt's is the most common in the area, but you may also see the double-crested cormorant, which looks very similar but has an orange throat. Although often floating or swimming on the ocean surface near shore, the Brandt's is easiest to spot when it's sitting on offshore rocks with its wings spread out to dry. Large groups of Brandt's cormorants will usually be seen together, flying along the coastline or settling on guano-covered rocks to roost at the end of the day. Like all cormorants, the Brandt's is a good swimmer, diving from the ocean surface to catch fish along the ocean bottom.

Cormorants breed on islands and coastal headlands from March to August, usually laying one to three eggs in round ground nests of seaweed and moss. Young begin to fly after 1 month.

CALIFORNIA QUAIL

Size: 10 inches long

Identifying features: Gray and brown with black face edged in white; black forward-curving topknot is distinctive

Best sighting times: Early morning and late afternoon in fall and winter

Where to see them: Grassy open space of oak-pine woodlands; usually in areas with water and scattered patches of dense brush for cover

©Trish Drury

One of the most recognizable sounds in the dry California foothills is the call of the California quail. A male lookout will perch on a shrub or rock and call "chi-cá-go" as a sign for the other quail to gather and feed. During midday, California quail often rest, hidden among brush. Walking along a trail and startling a group (or covey) of resting quail can be a heart-stopping experience as they suddenly burst into the air with a loud fluttering of wings before settling down again nearby. In the spring, quail form mated pairs, and 10 to 17 eggs are laid in a grass-lined ground nest. Family groups with several young quail may be seen crossing trails or other open areas during the late spring and early summer.

DOUGLAS' SQUIRREL

Size: Body 11 to 14 inches long; tail 4 to 6 inches long

Identifying features: Reddish or brownish gray on back, orange below; grayer in winter

Best sighting times: Late spring through early fall, except when it's raining

Where to see them: Coniferous forests

©iStockphoto.com

Look for these active little tree squirrels running up, down, and around the trunks of pine trees and other conifers or chattering noisily from tree branches. John Muir, the naturalist and writer, described the Douglas' squirrel as a "fiery, sputtering little bolt of life."

Also called pine squirrel or chickaree, Douglas' squirrels collect and hoard conifer cones in the autumn, storing them under downed logs or in hollow tree trunks. Some of these caches have hundreds of cones. The squirrels also eat the cone seeds while up in the trees, and you may notice a rain of cone scales falling from the branches as the squirrel pulls off each scale to get to the seed beneath.

Another commonly seen tree squirrel is the much larger western gray squirrel. They have gray backs with white undersides and are about twice the size of the Douglas' squirrel.

OCHRE SEA STAR

Size: 8 to 20 inches in diameter

Identifying features: Purple, orange, or brownish with white bumps called ossicles

Best sighting times: Periods of low tide

Where to see them: Rocky shores and pier pilings

Ochre sea stars are a colorful and easy-to-find coastal species. Look for them under rock overhangs, in rock crevices, and on pier pilings during low tide. The sea stars are especially common where goose barnacles and the bluish-black California mussel, their favorite food, also occur.

Often called "starfish," sea stars are not fish. Their undersides are covered with thousands of slender suction tube feet that move the animal over the surface of its underwater habitat and hold the sea star onto rocks in the pounding surf. These tube feet also grip the sides of mussels and other shellfish with enough constant force to pull the shells apart so the sea star can extend its stomach and digest the food.

Like other sea stars, the ochre sea star can regenerate any of the five arms (or rays) lost to their only natural predators, sea gulls and sea otters.

PACIFIC HARBOR SEAL

Size: 5 to 6 feet long

Identifying features: Gray or brownish with dark spots

Best sighting times: During low tide

Where to see them: In the water and on rocks of protected bays and harbors

Look offshore on flat rocky areas exposed at low tide. What may look like long, rounded rocks are probably Pacific harbor seals "hauled out" or resting. They also rest in the water during higher tides, floating vertically with just their heads visible. Mating occurs in the autumn, and pups are born in early spring.

These seals are exceptional swimmers and can stay underwater for up to 20 minutes. But they are clumsy on land and move with a jerky caterpillar-like motion, retreating to the water at the first sign of danger.

Harbor seals are fairly quiet animals. If you hear seals "barking" as you hike along a coastal trail, that's probably a group of California sea lions, the "trained seal" seen at marine shows and zoos. Sea lions are dark brown or tan and may be seen on coastal rocks from autumn through spring.

ROOSEVELT ELK

Size: About 5 feet tall and 8 feet long

Identifying features: Tan body with brown head, neck, and legs; whitish-tan rump

Best sighting times: In the morning or late afternoon

Where to see them: Meadows and forests

©Trish Drury

Roosevelt elk—named in honor of President Theodore Roosevelt—are the second-largest members of the deer family. Only moose are larger. The easiest place to spot elk is in a meadow or coastal prairie early in the morning or late in the afternoon. In Northern California, an elk herd is almost always present at Prairie Creek Redwoods State Park, often in the meadow adjacent to the park entrance.

During the fall rut (mating season), bulls make bugling calls as a challenge to other bulls, then use their antlers to fight for the dominance of harems and the herd. Only the bulls have antlers, which are lost after the rut. Observe elk cautiously and from a distance—they can be dangerous, especially during the rutting season and in the spring when calves are born.

STELLER'S JAY

Size: 12 inches long

Identifying features: Blue with black upper back, head, and crest

Best sighting times: Late morning through afternoon, especially spring through fall

Where to see them: Mountain conifer forests; also found in oak woodlands in the fall

©iStockphoto.com

The Steller's jay is a noisy, conspicuous bird commonly seen in mountain forests of pine and oak. The bird's blue color is evident as it flies across a trail or between nearby trees and the loud, raspy "shack, shack, shack" call can be heard for quite a distance. Related to crows and ravens, Steller's jays are smart birds and adapt quickly to the presence of people at picnic areas and campsites, often flying down to steal food left unattended. They are also excellent mimics of red-tailed hawks. You may find yourself searching the sky for the hawk before you again hear the call and realize it's coming from a Steller's jay on a nearby tree branch.

Another common jay is the blue and gray western scrub jay. Also noisy, it is found in the lower elevations of foothill woodlands and chaparral.

CALIFORNIA BLACK OAK

Size: 30 to 85 feet tall; 1- to 3-foot trunk diameter, up to 5 feet in older, mature trees; leaves 4 to 7 inches long

Identifying features: Large, flat, lobed leaves with pointed tips; dark brown bark on mature trees and dark green leaves that turn yellow, reddish, or brown in the autumn

Best sighting times: Late spring, when the leaves are new and bright green

Where to see them: Well-drained foothill and mountain areas with hot, dry summers and cool, moist winters; from 200- to 7,800 feet in elevation

The California black oak is the largest and most broadly distributed mountain oak in the region. It is especially common along the Sierra Nevada, where its large crown and broad base provide welcome shade. The dark color of the bark gives the tree its name, and large pointy-tipped, lobed leaves are distinct, aiding in identification. In areas with ponderosa pine and Douglas fir, California black oaks often act as nurse trees, sheltering seedlings until they become established.

The oak's acorns are an important food source for many animals. Black bear, mule deer, squirrels, and chipmunks eat them, and acorn woodpeckers drill holes in the oak's bark to store acorns for later.

COAST REDWOOD

Size: 200 to 325 feet tall; 10 to 15 feet in diameter; leaves ½ to 1 inch long; cones ½ to 1 inch long

Identifying features: Very tall tree with brown or grayish broadly-ridged bark, dark green leaves, and no branches for at least 100 feet above the ground

Best sighting times: Non-foggy days when you can look up to see the high branches

Where to see them: Moist, coastal forests within 20 miles of the ocean and between 100 and 2,500 feet in elevation

The upper branches of the coast redwoods are often lost in the mist that drifts in from the nearby coastline. But even on clear, sunny days, it's hard to see the tops of these tallest of trees. Huge brown or grayish trunks rise up from a forest floor often covered in western sword ferns *(Polystichum munitum)* and Pacific rhododendrons *(Rhododendron macrophyllum)*. The ground of redwood groves feels soft and spongy underfoot, and sounds seem muffled and hushed.

Mature coast redwoods can exceed 350 feet in height and may be over 2,000 years old. And, although redwood trees are still cut for lumber (96% of the old-growth redwood forests have been logged), most of the tallest and oldest redwoods are now protected in Redwood National and State parks.

DOUGLAS FIR

Size: 80 to 200 feet tall; 2 to 5 feet in diameter; cones 1½ to 3 inches long

Identifying characteristics: "Soft," light brown cones with three-pronged bracts sticking out from between the cone scales; grayish-brown bark; yellowish-green to dark bluish-green leaves

Best sighting times: Year round

Where to see them: Open areas in moist, well-drained coastal forests and in dry, inland mountain forests

©Trish Drury

Douglas fir is the second-tallest conifer (trees with cones) in California and the fourth-tallest tree species in the world. Short, stiff needles cover horizontal or slightly drooping branches, and the smooth grayish bark turns scaly, then deeply furrowed, as the tree ages. Fallen Douglas fir trees often become "nurse logs" for the western hemlock, whose seeds and seedlings find just the right amount of moisture and necessary fungi in the decaying wood.

The Douglas fir's common name is misleading because it is not a true fir. Early botanists noted its resemblance to pine, fir, spruce, yew, and hemlock. Then, in the mid-1800s, it was put into the genus *Pseudotsuga,* which means "false hemlock." The common name recognizes David Douglas, a Scottish botanist who found the tree in Oregon around 1820.

GIANT SEQUOIA

Size: 150 to 250 feet tall; 20 feet or more in diameter; leaves ⅛ to ½ inch long; cones 1¾ to 2¾ inches long

Identifying characteristics: Round branchlets covered in blue-green scale-like leaves; mature trees are extremely tall and wide with deeply furrowed reddish-brown bark

Best sighting times: Year round

Where to see them: Rocky soils in moist canyons or on moist slopes of the western Sierra Nevada, generally between 5,000 to 7,000 feet in elevation

©iStockphoto.com

Words or photos cannot fully prepare you for your first glimpse of a mature giant sequoia. Also called "Big Tree," many are massive. The General Sherman tree in Sequoia National Park (yes, some of the biggest sequoias have names) is just over 272 feet tall and about 30 feet in diameter near the base of the trunk. It is the single largest living thing on Earth, based on the volume of its trunk.

Giant sequoias are also long-lived. Estimates place the ages of many of the living trees at 2,000 to 3,000 years. Most eventually die by falling over, usually because fire and disease have damaged and weakened the roots and lower trunk.

You'll find giant sequoias in about 75 scattered groves, most of which are in California's national parks, state parks, or national forests.

©Trish Drury

LEOPARD LILY

Size: Plant 3 to 6 feet high; flowers 2 to 4 inches wide; leaves 3 to 5 inches long

Identifying features: Nodding (down-facing) flowers with petals curving back over the base of the flower; flowers are deep yellow to orangish-red with maroon spots; plant has light- to dark-green leaves

Best sighting times: May through August

Where to see them: Moist areas, such as stream banks and wet roadsides, from 3,000 to 6,000 feet in elevation

The leopard lily is one of several similar-looking native wildflowers that occur in the state's mountains and coastal areas. Many people refer to this group of flowers as tiger lilies. Most grow in moist habitats, although the Columbia lily and Humboldt's tiger lily are generally found in drier areas, such as open meadows and dry mountain forests.

The height of the leopard lily and its colorful flowers make it easy to spot, even in the relative darkness of dense forests. Growing from a bulb, this lily sometimes forms large colonies along streams and other wet areas. Leaves are usually narrow (wider in shady areas) and grow in a "whorl," fanning out in a circle from the same place on the stem.

Look for swallowtail butterflies, such as the western tiger swallowtail, and hummingbirds pollinating the flowers.

©Trish Drury

PACIFIC RHODODENDRON

Size: Commonly 6 to 12 feet tall; may get up to 25 feet tall

Identifying features: Large clusters of pink flowers from May to June; reddish-brown bark, deep green leaves, pink flowers (also white or purplish)

Best sighting times: Late spring

Where to find them: Moist forest understory

The Pacific rhododendron is often a medium-to-tall shrub with slender, curving branches ending in splays of elliptical-shaped evergreen leaves. In late spring, its huge clusters of pink flowers create a stunning display against the usual greens, browns, and grays of the misty coastal forests.

Common among the coast redwoods, these shrubs may also be found in some forests further inland.

On the ground near rhododendrons, look for flowering western trillium, whose three oval white petals turn pink with age. Beneath the three petals are three green petal-like sepals (parts of the flower head) and three broad, tapered leaves (*trillium* means "in threes"), all on a long stalk, making this early spring flower easy to identify.

PONDEROSA PINE

Size: 60 to 130 feet or more tall; 2 to 4 feet in diameter; needles up to 10 inches long; cones 2 to 6 inches long

Identifying features: Flaky jigsaw-puzzle pieces on plates of reddish-brown bark separated by dark furrows; bright yellow-green needles; light brown cones

Best sighting times: Year round

Where to find them: Mid-elevation dry mountain forests, from 3,000 to 6,000 feet in elevation

©iStockphoto.com

Ponderosa pines are probably the most common and widespread pine in California. They are often found in pure stands with the very similar Jeffrey pine at higher elevations. There are two ways to easily distinguish between ponderosa and Jeffrey pines. First, smell the bark. Ponderosa bark has little distinct smell, but Jeffrey bark smells like vanilla or pineapple. Then, close your hand over the pine cone. The ponderosa cones have scales with outward-curved prickly tips, while the tips of the Jeffrey cone curve inward; hence the saying "prickly ponderosa, gentle Jeffrey."

Protected by a thick bark, ponderosa pines rely on fire to clear the forest floor of accumulated pine needles and competing tree species.

The Scottish botanist David Douglas named this tree for its "ponderous" size.

WESTERN SWORD FERN

Size: Frond (leaf) 1 to 5 feet long

Identifying features: Large, round clumps of long, straight, green fronds, often with brown scales on the stems

Best sighting times: Late spring or early summer, when the new fronds have all unrolled

Where to find them: Moist coastal forest up to 2,500 feet in elevation; especially common in redwood forests

©Trish Drury

This fern blankets the forest floor beneath the coast redwoods. Its leaves grow mostly upright, creating a bouquet-like group of up to 100 fronds. Each leaf is long and narrow, wider at the middle, and tapering at both ends.

The western sword fern produces millions of wind-borne spores from early to mid-summer. Development and growth of subsequent new plants relies on the moderate temperature and moist environment found in the coastal forests of Northern California.

Western sword ferns are evergreen and provide food for Roosevelt elk, mule deer, and black bears. Although Native Americans have used sword ferns for food and medicine, today they are collected primarily for use in floral displays.

Frommer's™

Best Hiking Trips in Northern California

1st Edition

by John McKinney

Wildlife Guide by Marianne D. Wallace

Here's what the critics say about Frommer's:

"Amazingly easy to use. Very portable, very complete."
—BOOKLIST

"Detailed, accurate, and easy-to-read information for all price ranges."
—GLAMOUR MAGAZINE

"Hotel information is close to encyclopedic."
—DES MOINES SUNDAY REGISTER

"Frommer's Guides have a way of giving you a real feel for a place."
—KNIGHT RIDDER NEWSPAPERS

WILEY

John Wiley & Sons Canada, Ltd.

Published by:

JOHN WILEY & SONS CANADA, LTD.
6045 Freemont Blvd.
Mississauga, ON L5R 4J3

ISBN 978-0-470-15991-0

Editor: Gene Shannon
Development Editor: William Travis
Project Manager: Elizabeth McCurdy
Project Editor: Pauline Ricablanca
Editorial Assistant: Katie Wolsley
Project Coordinator: Lynsey Stanford
Cartographer: Lohnes+Wright
Mapping assistance: Edward Pultar & Indy Hurt
Vice President, Publishing Services: Karen Bryan
Production by Wiley Indianapolis Composition Services

Front cover photo: A hiker peers up at some of the tallest trees in the world in Redwood National Park.

SPECIAL SALES

For reseller information, including discounts and premium sales, please call our sales department: Tel. 416-646-7992. For press review copies, author interviews, or other publicity information, please contact our marketing department: Tel. 416-646-4584; Fax: 416-236-4448.

Wiley also publishes its books in a variety of electronic formats. Some content that appears in print may not be available in electronic formats.

Manufactured in the United States of America

1 2 3 4 5 RRD 14 13 12 11 10 09

CONTENTS

Table of Hikes

Hike	Distance
San Francisco Bay Area	
Lands End	6 miles round trip
San Francisco's Presidio	2 miles round trip
Golden Gate Promenade	7 miles round trip from Fort Mason to Golden Gate Bridge
Golden Gate Bridge	3 miles round trip across the Golden Gate from Fort Point to Vista Point
Angel Island State Park	5 miles round trip
Wildcat Regional Park	8 miles round trip to Jewel Lake; 11 miles round trip to Wildcat Peak
Mount Diablo	7 miles round trip
Tennessee Valley	4 miles round trip from Tennessee Valley to Tennessee Cove; 9 miles round trip to Tennessee Cove, Muir Beach
Muir Woods	6-mile loop from Muir Woods to Mount Tamalpais State Park
Mount Tamalpais	6 miles round trip from Mountain Home Inn to East Peak summit
Steep Ravine	7.2-mile loop from Stinson Beach to Pantoll Station
Palomarin & The Lakes District	8.2 miles round trip from Palomarin to Alamere Falls
Bear Valley & Arch Rock	8.8 miles round trip from Bear Valley Visitor Center to Divide Meadow
Mount Wittenberg	5.1 miles round trip to Mount Wittenberg; 6.6 miles round trip return via Old Pine Trail; 8.6 miles round trip return via Baldy Trail
Drakes Estero	8 miles round trip from Estero Trail head to Sunset Beach
Tomales Point	9.4 miles round trip from Upper Pierce Ranch to Tomales Point
Coast South of San Francisco	
Ano Nuevo State Reserve	4 miles round trip self-guided; 3 miles round trip on guided tour
Skyline to the Sea Trail	12 miles one way
Point Lobos State Reserve	75 miles round trip on Cypress Grove Trail; 3 miles or more round trip on North Shore Trail
Andrew Molera State Park's Beach & Backcountry	9.5 miles round trip
Pfeiffer Big Sur State Park	2 miles round trip from Big Sur Lodge to Pfeiffer Falls, Valley View

Difficulty	Best Time to Go	Star Rating	Page Number
Moderate	Late afternoon, year round		p. 35
Easy	Year round	★	p. 38
Moderate	Brisk winter or fall day		p. 41
Easy	Year round, especially at sunset	★★	p. 43
Moderate	During the day in the warmer months; ferry service is best on weekends	★★	p. 46
Moderate	Winter or spring, when Wildcat Creek is flowing		p. 49
Moderate	October to May	★	p. 51
Easy to moderate to Muir Beach	Year round	★★★	p. 54
Moderate	Year round, early morning or late afternoon	★★	p. 57
Moderate	Winter on a brisk clear day, spring after the rains fill the creeks	★	p. 60
Moderate	Spring, when wildflowers bloom and waterfalls cascade at full strength	★★	p. 63
Moderate	Alamere Falls is at full strength during winter and spring	★★	p. 65
Moderate	Year round		p. 68
Moderate	Clear fall or winter days	★	p. 70
Moderate	Winter, especially for the bird-watching	★★	p. 72
Moderate	Spring for wildflowers and fall for the tule elk		p. 75

Easy	December to April	★	p. 84
Moderate	Year round, especially on clear days	★★★	p. 87
Easy	Year round	★	p. 90
Moderate	Summer	★★	p. 92
Easy	Year round		p. 95

Table of Hikes

Hike	Distance
Coast North of San Francisco	
Sonoma Coast State Beach	7.6 miles round trip from Wright's Beach to Goat Rock
Fort Ross State Historic Park	.5 mile round trip to Fort Ross Cove; 4 miles round trip to Reef Campground & Day Use Area
Fern Canyon, Van Damme State Park	8 miles round trip to Pygmy Forest
Mendocino Headlands State Park	2.5 miles round trip
Humboldt Redwoods State Park	9-mile loop
Patrick's Point	4 miles round trip from Palmer's Point to Agate Beach Campground
Sinkyone Wilderness State Park	4.5 miles round trip to Whale Gulch
Gold Bluffs Beach	6 miles round trip to Ossagon Rocks
Redwood Creek	16.4 miles round trip to Tall Trees Grove
Del Norte Coast Redwoods State Park	4.5 miles round trip from Hwy. 101 to Damnation Cove
Wine Country & Gold Country	
Jack London State Historic Park	To lake is 2 miles round trip; to top of Sonoma Mountain is 8.25 miles round trip with 1,800-foot elevation gain
Sugarloaf Ridge State Park	6-mile loop through park with 700-foot elevation gain
Bothe-Napa Valley State Park	4.5 miles round trip with 900-foot elevation gain
Skyline Wilderness Park	To Lake Marie with return via Skyline Trail is 6 miles round trip with 600-foot elevation gain
Calaveras Big Trees State Park	South Grove Trail is 5 miles round trip with 400-foot elevation gain
Marshall Gold Discovery State Historic Park	4-mile loop
Empire Mine State Historic Park	2.4 miles round trip
Yosemite National Park	
Mariposa Grove	To Grizzly Giant is 1.6 miles round trip with 100-foot elevation gain or 4.8-mile loop with 1,000-foot elevation gain
Glacier Point & Four-Mile Trail	To Glacier Point is 9.2 miles round trip with 3,200-foot elevation gain
Yosemite Valley	5.5-mile loop
Vernal Fall and Nevada Fall	To Vernal Fall is 3 miles round trip with 1,000-foot elevation gain to Nevada Fall is 7 miles round trip with 2,000-foot elevation gain; add another 1.5 miles without shuttle bus

Difficulty	Best Time to Go	Star Rating	Page Number
Moderate	Year round		p. 102
Easy	Year round	★	p. 105
Moderate	April to October		p. 107
Easy	Year round	★	p. 109
Moderate	June to October; a seasonally installed footbridge over Eel River makes the loop trip easiest in summer	★★	p. 112
Easy	April to November	★	p. 115
Easy	May to November		p. 117
Moderate	May to October	★★	p. 120
Strenuous	Summer, when footbridges are in place	★	p. 123
Moderate	May to October		p. 126
Easy to lake, moderately strenuous to Sonoma Peak	Year round	★★	p. 134
Moderate	Spring and autumn		p. 137
Easy to moderate	Spring and autumn	★	p. 139
Moderate	Spring and autumn		p. 142
Easy to moderate	May to October	★★	p. 144
Easy	May to October		p. 147
Easy	May to October	★	p. 150
Easy to moderate	May to October	★	p. 159
Moderate to strenuous	May to October	★★	p. 162
Moderate	April to October	★	p. 165
Moderately strenuous to strenuous	March to November	★★	p. 168

Table of Hikes

Hike	Distance
Yosemite National Park (continued)	
Half Dome	From Happy Isles to Half Dome summit is 16.5 miles round trip with 4,800-foot elevation gain (14.2 miles round trip via Mist Trail)
Clouds Rest	From Tenaya Lake to Clouds Rest is 14 miles round trip with 2,300-foot elevation gain
Cathedral Lakes	To Lower Cathedral Lake is 7.5 miles round trip with 1,000-foot elevation gain
Lembert Dome	To Lembert Dome is 3.25 miles round trip with 900-foot elevation gain
Sequoia National Park	
Monarch Lakes & Crystal Lakes	To Monarch Lakes is 8.4 miles round trip with 2,600-foot elevation gain; to Crystal Lake is 9.8 miles round trip with 3,000-foot elevation gain
Giant Forest	Congress Trail is 2-mile loop; Trail of the Sequoias is 5.1-mile loop with 500-foot elevation gain
Heather & Pear Lakes	From Wolverton to Heather Lake is 8.4 miles round trip; to Emerald Lake is 10.5 miles round trip; to Pear Lake is 12.5 miles round trip with 2,200-foot elevation gain
Grant Grove & North Grove	General Grant Trail is 1 mile round trip; North Grove Loop Trail is 2.5 miles round trip with 300-foot elevation gain
Mount Whitney	From Whitney Portal to summit is 21.4 miles round trip with 6,100-foot elevation gain
Lake Tahoe	
D.L. Bliss & Emerald Bay State Parks	6 miles round trip from Rubicon Point to Emerald Point; 9 miles round trip to Vikingsholm
Sugar Pine Point State Park	4.5-mile loop to first bridge; 6.5 miles round trip to Lily Pond; 14 miles round trip to Duck Lake; 14.5 miles round trip to Lost Lake
Eagle Lake & Velma Lakes	2 miles round trip to Eagle Lake; 9 miles round trip to Middle Velma Lake
Grover Hot Springs & Burnside Lake	3 miles round trip to waterfall; 10 miles round trip to Burnside Lake
Death Valley National Park	
Ubehebe Peak	3 miles round trip to ridge crest
Death Valley Sand Dunes	2–4 miles round trip
Golden Canyon	2.8 miles round trip to Red Cathedral
Zabriskie Point & Gower Gulch	6.5-mile loop to Zabriskie Point with return via Gower Gulch
Telescope Peak	14 miles round trip to Telescope Peak

Difficulty	Best Time to Go	Star Rating	Page Number
Strenuous	Mid-May/early June to mid-October	★★★	p. 171
Strenuous	June to October	★★	p. 174
Moderate	June to October		p. 176
Moderate to strenuous, not for younger children	June to October	★	p. 180
Strenuous	June to October	★★	p. 188
Easy to moderate	April to November	★	p. 190
Moderately strenuous	June to October	★★	p. 193
Moderate	May to October	★	p. 195
Strenuous to say the least	June to October	★★★	p. 198
Moderate	June to October	★	p. 209
Moderate to strenuous	May to October		p. 212
Easy to strenuous	June to October	★	p. 216
Easy to strenuous	May to October	★	p. 218
Moderate	November to May	★	p. 227
Easy	November to May, in the morning or late afternoon		p. 229
Easy	November to April, at sunrise or sunset		p. 232
Moderate	November to April	★	p. 234
Strenuous	Mid-May to November	★★	p. 237

LIST OF MAPS

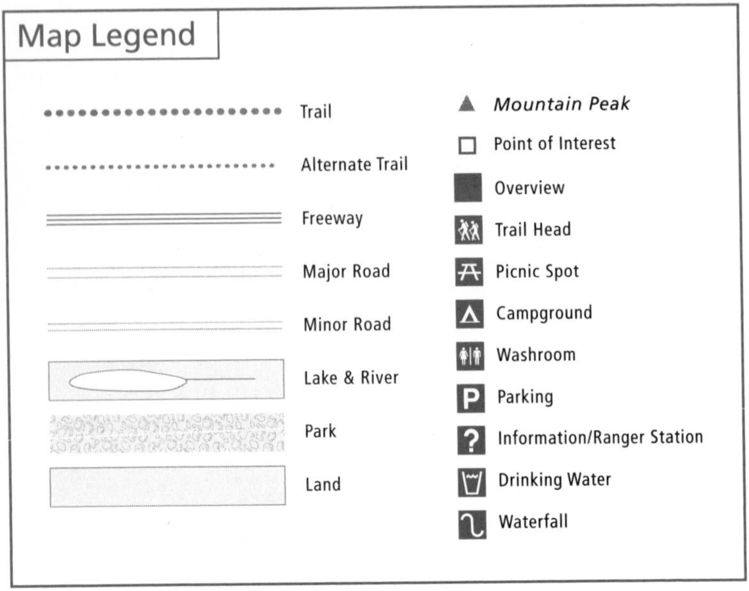

Map Legend
Trail
Alternate Trail
Freeway
Major Road
Minor Road
Lake & River
Park
Land
Mountain Peak
Point of Interest
Overview
Trail Head
Picnic Spot
Campground
Washroom
Parking
Information/Ranger Station
Drinking Water
Waterfall

ABOUT THE AUTHOR

John McKinney is the author of 20 books about hiking, parklands, and nature, including *The Hiker's Way* and *A Walk Along Land's End: Dispatches from the Edge of California on a 1,600-mile Hike from Mexico to Oregon.* For 18 years, McKinney, a.k.a. The Trailmaster, wrote a weekly hiking column for the *Los Angeles Times* and now writes articles and commentaries about nature and outdoor recreation for both print and online magazines. A passionate advocate for the environment and our need to reconnect to nature, McKinney also shares his expertise on radio, TV, and at www.TheTrailmaster.com.

ACKNOWLEDGMENTS

The author would like to express his sincere appreciation for the enthusiasm and expertise offered during the preparation of this guide by the California Department of Parks and Recreation field personnel. Another heartfelt thank you goes to all the National Park Service rangers who were unfailingly helpful and courteous during my visits to the parks detailed in this book. For considerable logistical help crucial to the completion of this work, a big thanks goes to the California Travel and Tourism Commission, particularly Amanda Moreland, Media Relations Manager. A tip of the hiker's cap goes to Cheri Rae for her substantial off-trail assistance. Many thanks to series editor Gene Shannon and the Frommer's editorial team; it was a pleasure working with you on this guide as well as helping to create this exciting new series for the traveling hiker.

AN INVITATION TO THE READER

In researching this book, we discovered many wonderful places—hotels, restaurants, shops, and more. We're sure you'll find others. Please tell us about them, so we can share the information with your fellow travelers in upcoming editions. If you were disappointed with a recommendation, we'd love to know that, too. Please write to:

Frommer's Best Hiking Trips in Northern California, 1st Edition
John Wiley & Sons Canada, Ltd. • 6045 Freemont Blvd. • Mississauga, ON L5R 4J3

AN ADDITIONAL NOTE

Please be advised that travel information is subject to change at any time—and this is especially true of prices. We therefore suggest that you write or call ahead for confirmation when making your travel plans. The authors, editors, and publisher cannot be held responsible for the experiences of readers while traveling. Your safety is important to us, however, so we encourage you to stay alert and be aware of your surroundings. Keep a close eye on cameras, purses, and wallets, all favorite targets of thieves and pickpockets.

FROMMER'S STAR RATINGS, ICONS & ABBREVIATIONS

Every hotel, restaurant, and attraction listing in this guide has been ranked for quality, value, service, amenities, and special features using a **star-rating system.** In country, state, and regional guides, we also rate towns and regions to help you narrow down your choices and budget your time accordingly. Hotels and restaurants are rated on a scale of zero (recommended) to three stars (exceptional). Attractions, shopping, nightlife, towns, and regions are rated according to the following scale: zero stars (recommended), one star (highly recommended), two stars (very highly recommended), and three stars (must-see).

In addition to the star-rating system, we also use **seven feature icons** that point you to the great deals, in-the-know advice, and unique experiences that separate travelers from tourists. Throughout the book, look for:

Finds	Special finds—those places only insiders know about
Fun Facts	Fun facts—details that make travelers more informed and their trips more fun
Kids	Best bets for kids and advice for the whole family
Moments	Special moments—those experiences that memories are made of
Overrated	Places or experiences not worth your time or money
Tips	Insider tips—great ways to save time and money
Value	Great values—where to get the best deals

The following **abbreviations** are used for credit cards:

AE	American Express	DISC	Discover	V	Visa
DC	Diners Club	MC	MasterCard		

FROMMERS.COM

Now that you have this guidebook to help you plan a great trip, visit our website at **www.frommers.com** for additional travel information on more than 4,000 destinations. We update features regularly to give you instant access to the most current trip-planning information available. At Frommers.com, you'll find scoops on the best airfares, lodging rates, and car rental bargains. You can even book your travel online through our reliable travel booking partners. Other popular features include:

- Online updates of our most popular guidebooks
- Vacation sweepstakes and contest giveaways
- Newsletters highlighting the hottest travel trends
- Podcasts, interactive maps, and up-to-the-minute events listings
- Opinionated blog entries by Arthur Frommer himself
- Online travel message boards with featured travel discussions

1

The Best of Hiking in Northern California

From the foggy shores of San Francisco to the icy summits of the Sierra Nevada, and from the towering redwoods of the north coast to the sun-kissed Wine Country, Northern California, in all its beauty and environmental diversity, is preserved in magnificent parks. These parks are accessible by trail systems as good or better than any found in parks across the nation or around the world.

Few other regions can boast of tall trees, high peaks, deep canyons, and long seashores, and can claim all these grand landscapes within its boundaries. This book collects and presents favorite hikes on trails in all these diverse kinds of wild lands.

This guide is your invitation to discover:

MOUNTAINS Climb Sequoia National Park's 14,495-foot Mount Whitney, California's highest peak, and the tallest summit in the U.S. outside Alaska. Explore the alpine peaks towering above Mineral King Valley in Sequoia National Park, as well as the vast backcountry of Yosemite National Park. Experience the greatest vertical rise in the lower 48 states by ascending Death Valley National Park's highest summit, 11,044-foot Telescope Peak, and gazing down at Badwater (282 ft. below sea level), the lowest point in North America.

LAKES Lake Tahoe is the crown jewel of the High Sierra and the largest alpine lake in North America. Lakes perched above the foggy shores of Point Reyes National Seashore are grouped together in a way that reminds some hikers of England's Lakes District. Trails lead to Monarch lakes and several more alt-hued jewels in the Mineral King area of Sequoia National Park.

WATERFALLS Yosemite National Park's world-famous cascades include Vernal, Nevada, and Yosemite Falls—the latter the highest in North America. Alamere Falls cascades from the high cliffs of Point Reyes into the sea—a spectacular sight to see. Excellent trails lead to waterfalls in Big Sur, the Wine Country, and the redwoods.

TREES Redwood and Sequoia national parks were preserved primarily for their namesake trees. Hike the Tall Trees Loop Trail to a 366-foot redwood, once considered the world's tallest tree. Walk to the world's largest living thing, the General Sherman Tree in Sequoia National Park's Giant Forest. Antiquarian oaks abound in the Gold Country and Wine Country.

THE COAST From Lands End in the heart of San Francisco to the northern limit of the redwoods at the border with Oregon, parks preserve notable segments of Northern California's shoreline. Walk over the Golden Gate Bridge to a park service vista point and behold dramatic panoramas of San Francisco Bay. Hike dramatic coastal trails along the beaches and bluffs of Big Sur, Point Reyes, and Mendocino.

1 THE BEST FAMILY HIKES

- **Golden Gate Bridge** (San Francisco): Kids love crossing "The Bridge at the End of the Continent" and one of the world's engineering marvels. It's a must-do, once-in-a-lifetime adventure. Adults will remember the views, kids will recall the spine-tingling feeling caused by the vehicle traffic on the bridge that seems to reverberate throughout one's entire being. Kids also like to watch the considerable ship traffic passing in and out of San Francisco Bay. See p. 43.
- **Steep Ravine** (Stinson Beach): Make this an easy, 3-mile long, one-way, mostly downhill jaunt by starting at Pantoll Station and descending Steep Ravine. Redwoods, ferns, and mosses add to the feeling of walking through a rainforest. Cascades, small waterfalls, footbridges, and even a ladder add zest and challenge to this favorite mountain path. Make the necessary transportation arrangements for a one-way hike; your family will thank you for it. See p. 62.
- **Pfeiffer Big Sur State Park** (Big Sur): The short trail leading from the Big Sur Lodge offers a great family-friendly intro to the delights of the state park. Begin with stately redwoods, add a creek-side meander and a walk in the tanbark oak woods, and conclude by beholding a handsome waterfall tumbling into a lovely grotto. And then there's even a great view: the Pacific Ocean pounding the Point Sur headlands and the Big Sur River Valley. See p. 95.
- **Fern Canyon** (Gold Bluffs Beach): The movie *Jurassic Park* wasn't filmed here, but it could have been. Fern Canyon is the forest primeval, and the kids will love it. They can splash in the creek and are taken into some mysterious world by the mist-wrapped redwoods and the profusion of five-finger, deer, lady, sworn, and chain ferns. See p. 107.
- **Yosemite Valley** (Yosemite National Park): Kids of all ages can't resist riding the shuttle bus just because it's a bus and because it puts most of Yosemite Valley's sights within easy hiking distance. Check out Yosemite Falls and El Capitan, pause for a picnic along the Merced River, hike a mile or two or three, then stop and ride the bus to conveniently located kid-friendly concessions such as a pizza place and ice cream parlor. See p. 164.
- **Death Valley Sand Dunes** (Death Valley National Park): It's family fun in a giant sandbox: a huge field of dunes bordered by some bizarre geology. These dunes look like the ones in the Middle East or North Africa, but are a whole lot less intimidating. Climbing the dunes is two-steps-forward-one-step-backward kind of hiking. What a blast to jump and roll down the dunes. See p. 227.

2 THE BEST HIKES FOR SEEING WILDLIFE

- **Bear Valley** (Point Reyes): The native black-tail deer and imported fallow deer wander the meadows near Bear Valley Visitor Center. The fallow deer appear in a variety of colors, from black to speckled to pure white. The National Park Service has met vociferous opposition by animal-loving groups with its policies to reduce (and sometimes shoot) the exotic deer population introduced by hunters to the area before it became a park. (Morgan horses certainly aren't wildlife, but admirers of these classic park service animals should check out the Park

Service's Morgan Horse Center near the Bear Valley Visitor Center.) See p. 67.

- **Drakes Estero** (Point Reyes): Every spring some 7,000 harbor seals, or 20% of the mainland California breeding population, haul out on the beaches of Point Reyes, and the estero (estuary) is a great place to observe them. The estero is also a birdwatcher's delight. Look for great blue herons, willets, godwits, and many more shorebirds feeding along the mudflats. Also try to spot such water birds as canvasbacks, ruddy ducks, and American wigeons. See p. 72.
- **Tomales Point** (Point Reyes): Be on the lookout for the tule elk herd that wanders the bluffs. A large elk population once roamed the Point Reyes area, but by the 1860s, hunters had eliminated the animals. In 1977, the National Park Service reintroduced the animals, and they have done extremely well on this terrain that resembles a Scottish moor or one of the Shetland Islands. Herds consist of a dominant bull, his "harem," and groups of bachelor bulls. See p. 75.
- **Ano Nuevo State Reserve** (north of Santa Cruz): Treat yourself to a wildlife drama that attracts visitors from around the world—a close-up look at the largest mainland population of elephant seals. To protect the elephant seals (and the humans who hike out to see them), parts of the reserve are open only through naturalist-guided tours from December through April. Also keep an eye out for Steller sea lions, California sea lions, and harbor seals. See p. 83.
- **Point Lobos State Reserve** (south of Monterey and Carmel): Look for black-tailed deer moving silently past the fog-wrapped cypress trees and then listen for the bark of sea lions, audible even over the sound of the sea thundering against the cliffs. Offshore are the rocky islands off Sea Lion Point. The Spaniards called the domain of these creatures Punto de los Lobos Marinos—Point of the Sea Wolves. You'll probably hear the barking of the sea lions before you see them. See p. 90.
- **Gold Bluffs Beach** (Prairie Creek Redwoods State Park): Both beach and bluffs are prime Roosevelt elk territory. The elk are enchanted-looking creatures with chocolate brown faces and necks, tan bodies, and dark legs. And they're big: a bull can tip the scales at 1,000 pounds. While nearby elk-viewing opportunities abound—particularly at namesake Elk Prairie up by Highway 101 and the Prairie Creek Visitor Center—the Roosevelts seem all the more majestic in a wilderness setting. See p. 120.

3 THE BEST HIKES INTO HISTORY

- **Angel Island** (in San Francisco Bay): For an island barely a square mile in size, Angel Island has an extremely diverse history. Over the last two centuries, the island has seen use as a Mexican land grant, Army artillery post, and an immigration station. The immigration part of the story is not a happy one, particularly for the many Asians who were detained and processed. New state park interpretive exhibits tell the story in a moving and painfully honest way. See p. 46.
- **Presidio** (near Golden Gate Bridge): Visit historic sites from the days when California was under the rule of Spanish soldiers, then the Civil War–era Main Post. Take a walk through architectural history, passing red brick barracks built in the Georgian style, and a theater and other buildings constructed in Spanish Revival style. Some experts

rate the Victorian-era homes along Funston Avenue among the best examples of that period in San Francisco. And don't miss historic Lovers Lane and the coastal military batteries. See p. 38 and 40.

- **Jack London State Historic Park** (Wine Country): The great writer's "Beauty Ranch" in the Sonoma Valley is preserved as a park. Visit the House of Happy Walls Museum, built by his wife Charmian London as a memorial to her husband's life and work; the cottage where London worked in his final years; and the "Pig Palace," London's hog pen deluxe. Hike the ranch grounds through the woods and over to London's little lake. This lovely scenery couldn't be more different than the harsh and freezing one London evoked in his novel *The Call of the Wild,* though both landscapes were much appreciated by the author. See p. 133.
- **Fort Ross State Historic Park** (Sonoma County Coast): Fort Ross, the last remnant of czarist Russia's foothold in California, is today a hiker's delight. Situated on a handsome, windswept bluff are a redwood stockade and a Russian Orthodox chapel. The high stockade, built entirely of hand-hewn redwood timber, looks particularly formidable. Before you hit the trail, stop at the Fort Ross Visitor Center, an excellent facility with Russian, Pomo, and natural history exhibits. See p. 105.
- **Marshall Gold Discovery State Historic Park** (Gold Country): It was here in 1848 James Marshall discovered gold; a year later, the world discovered California. Take a hike in the hills, then take a walk through the tiny village of Coloma, birthplace of the Gold Rush. Highlights include an operating replica of Sutter's Mill and the Gold Discovery Museum, with its mining exhibits and videos telling the story of Marshall's discovery. You can even visit Marshall Cabin, where Marshall, who benefited little from his great discovery, died bitter and penniless. See p. 146.
- **Empire Mine State Historic Park** (Gold Country): Empire Mine, one of California's richest, produced more than 6 million ounces of gold during its 100 years of operation. Take the Hardrock Trail, an interpretive path that visits mines, machinery, stamp mills, and much more while explaining hard-rock mining techniques. You should also tour Empire Cottage, the English manor-style home of the mine owner. Quite the "cottage"! See p. 149.

4 THE BEST HIKES FOR TREE-HUGGERS

- **Muir Woods** (north of San Francisco): Even the great naturalist gave his namesake grove a rave: "This is the best tree-lover's monument that could possibly be found in all the forests of the world." Sometimes, it seems all the peoples of the world come for a visit, but don't let the crowds dissuade you from a stroll through these cathedrals of redwoods that have a way of quieting even the most effusive visitor. See p. 57.
- **Humboldt Redwoods State Park** (near Weott): Thriving along Bull Creek is more than a redwood grove; it's truly a forest. This is matchless old-growth; for good reason, preserving it was a cause célèbre of early California conservationists. The spectacular redwoods are explored by a trail that not only stretches the legs, but the imagination, as well. See p. 112.

- **Tall Trees Grove** (Redwood National Park): First, there's the "World's Tallest Tree": Everyone wants to see this 366-foot giant, even though taller ones have been discovered since this was proclaimed "the tallest" back in 1963. Get a free permit and the combination to a locked gate from the park visitor center, then drive up to the grove's upper trail head. Take the Tall Trees Loop Trail and contemplate the third-largest and sixth-largest sempervirens, as well. See p. 124.
- **Calaveras Big Trees State Park** (Arnold, near Gold Country): The "Big Trees" in the park name is a tip-off: Two groves of giant sequoia redwoods are the highlights. The biggest trees are truly big—250 to 300 feet high and 25 to 30 feet across. And they're ancient—2,000 to 3,000 years old. Visit grand specimens such as Abraham Lincoln, Empire State, or Father of the Forest in South Grove, or hit the trail in the far less visited and remote North Grove. See p. 143.
- **Giant Forest** (Sequoia National Park): No visit to Sequoia would be complete without a look at the General Sherman Tree—275 feet high. Perhaps 2,700 years old, it's the world's largest living thing in Mariposa Grove. Congress Trail visits groups of trees named for presidents and assorted famous personages. For a longer tour of Giant Forest, follow the Trail of the Sequoias. See p. 189.
- **Mariposa Grove** (Yosemite National Park): By far the largest of Yosemite's three groves of giant sequoias, a walk among the world's largest living things in Mariposa Grove is one to remember. These magnificent trees, along with Yosemite Valley, inspired creation of the entire national park system. Grizzly Giant, a 200-foot-tall behemoth that measures 30 feet in diameter, is estimated to have sprouted some 2,700 years ago; it's believed to be the oldest sequoia in the grove. See p. 158.

5 THE BEST EASY HIKES

- **Golden Gate Promenade** (San Francisco): You could turn the promenade into a power-walk by hurrying along, but with so many sights to see, this is really a waterfront stroll that lends itself to poking along. Don't miss the mother of all tourist attractions, Fisherman's Wharf, and the far-less-discovered San Francisco Maritime Museum, with its small fleet of old ships that you can step aboard. You can also enjoy a bit of the natural scene—a beach and some low sand dunes—on this easy shoreline excursion. See p. 41.
- **Mendocino Headlands State Park** (Mendocino): The headlands are laced with paths that offer postcard views of wave tunnels and tide pools, beaches, and blowholes. This is an easy hike around the fringes of Mendocino, which resembles a New England village, no doubt by design of its founders. A summer or weekend walk allows you to escape the crowds, while a winter walk, perhaps when a storm is brewing offshore, is a special experience indeed. See p. 109.
- **Patrick's Point State Park** (north of San Francisco): Roam the park's rocky promontories amidst a mixed forest of Sitka spruce, Douglas fir, and red alder. Rim Trail leads to rocky points that jut out into the Pacific and offer commanding views. Descend to Agate Beach, a wide swath where beachcombers find agates, a nearly transparent variety of quartz polished by sand and the restless sea. See p. 115.
- **Grant Grove** (Kings Canyon): General Grant Tree is big in popularity. It was

the showpiece of General Grant National Park, forerunner of Kings Canyon, and is designated "The Nation's Christmas Tree." An easy walk leads to the world's third-largest tree (and number one in base diameter), as well as to many other grand specimens, including the awesome Fallen Monarch. See p. 194.

- **Grover Hot Springs State Park** (south of Lake Tahoe): Nothing like a soothing soak in a hot spring after a hike. While it's true you can take off on a serious High Sierra hike, a much easier alternative is to wander across a meadow and into the woods to a small waterfall. Reward yourself for this modest effort with a soak in the park's hot springs. Mellow out in a hot pool (102°F/39°C) fed by six mineral springs. See p. 217.
- **Golden Canyon** (Death Valley National Park): Golden Canyon Trail is a self-guided interpretive trail. Even the most casual student of earth science, even those who disdain nature trails, will gain an appreciation of the complex geology and the millions of years required to sculpt and color Golden Canyon. Both sunrise and sunset—when the light is magical and fellow hikers are few—are particularly good times to walk the canyon. See p. 230.

6 THE BEST MEDIUM HIKES

- **Skyline to the Sea** (Big Basin Redwoods State Park): This trail may be moderate, but it's epic in the experience offered. Hike (mostly) downhill one-way from the crest of the Santa Cruz Mountains through the redwoods to the Pacific Ocean. The path travels through redwood canyons and past waterfalls in Big Basin Redwoods State Park, California's very first state park. See p. 87.
- **Andrew Molera State Park** (south of Monterey): Mountains, meadows, and the mouth of the Big Sur River are the highlights of a medium-length tour in this gem of a state park. Hike along bluffs overlooking 3 miles of beach and climb through meadows and oak woodland. At the river mouth are a shallow lagoon and beautiful sandy beach. Splendid scenic diversity available for modest effort. See p. 92.
- **Sugarloaf Ridge** (Wine Country): Wildflower-splashed grassy meadows, woodlands of oak and Douglas fir, and even a handsome waterfall are some of the attractions of this Wine Country retreat. Reward for climbing the distinguished looking Sugarloaf Ridge to the top of Bald Mountain is a terrific view stretching from the Napa Valley vineyards to the snowy peaks of the High Sierra. See p. 136.
- **Cathedral Lakes** (Yosemite National Park): Sample a fine length of the John Muir Trail, which extends some 210 miles through what some hikers consider the most scenic high country in the U.S. The two Cathedral lakes and the lofty spires of Cathedral Peak comprise a glorious mountain sanctuary. Find out why John Muir's effusive descriptions of the High Sierra have a spiritual tone, and refer to landscapes as sanctuaries, temples, and cathedrals. See p. 175.
- **D. L. Bliss and Emerald Bay State Parks** (Lake Tahoe): Hike a superb shoreline pathway by what Native Americans called "The Lake of the Sky." Meander among stately stands of red and white fir, Jeffrey pine, and incense cedar. Traipse slopes splashed with monkeyflower, columbine, lupine, and leopard lily to Vikingsholm and tour a replica of a 9th-century Norse Castle, complete with turrets, towers, and 38 rooms. Sunbathe or go for a (very cold)

swim at Emerald Bay, one of Tahoe's best beaches. See p. 208.

- **Zabriskie Point** (Death Valley National Park): Before sunrise, photographers set up their tripods at the point and aim their cameras at Golden Canyon and the great expanse of Death Valley. Magnificent indeed, as is getting right into deeply furrowed Golden Canyon itself and hiking up to Zabriskie Point for the great view. You don't have to be a geologist to appreciate the amazing sights: Red Cathedral, white outcroppings of borax, the mudstone hills, and much more. See p. 232.

7 THE BEST STRENUOUS HIKES

- **Half Dome** (Yosemite National Park): To the non-hiker of yesteryear, and even today, Half Dome seems impossible to ascend. Really, though, it's not impossible, but definitely challenging. The very long day hike begins in Happy Isles, where the John Muir Trail begins. Past Vernal Falls and Nevada Falls you climb, then on through Little Yosemite Valley. The final assault on the summit requires climbing at an almost 45-degree angle up slick granite with the help of cables that hikers grip to haul themselves to the top. See p. 170.
- **Clouds Rest** (Yosemite National Park): While an easier hike than the one up Half Dome, Clouds Rest Trail is far from easy. The final part of the climb is steep, an ascent over a narrow ridge with a steep drop-off on either side. From atop Clouds Rest (9,926 ft. high in the sky), Yosemite's largest granite face, savor a jaw-dropping panorama of rounded domes and sharp ridges. See p. 173.
- **Heather and Pear Lakes** (Sequoia National Park): Lakes Trail leads to little lakes called tarns resting in rock bowls that were scoured by glaciers long ago. Two more challenging trails must be surmounted to get to the lakes, though. Hiking over The Watchtower, an awesome granite formation, is a hike along the edge of the world—or at least along the edge of a precipitous cliff. And then there's Hump Trail, which rises every bit as steeply as its name suggests. See p. 192.
- **Monarch and Crystal Lakes** (Mineral King, Sequoia National Park): Rewards for this strenuous outing are two superb sets of high-country lakes. "High" is the operative word here; lung-popping ascents through thin air are required to reach the lakes. The lakes are nestled in rocky bowls below awesome peaks. A no-nonsense trail leads across marmot-populated Groundhog Meadow, then over foxtail pine-spiked ridges and rocky slopes to the cobalt-hued lakes. See p. 187.
- **Mount Whitney** (Eastern Sierra): You can't get any higher than the 14,491-foot summit of Whitney, highest of all peaks in the continental U.S. and a once-in-a-lifetime (at least!) hiking experience. Over the years, the trail has had several makeovers, and it stands today—graded switchbacks hewn out of granite walls—as one of the finest examples in America of the trail builder's art. Heed the many precautions, make the many arrangements, prepare yourself to the best of your ability, and go for it. See p. 197.
- **Telescope Peak** (Death Valley National Park): Sure, you can look up at the peak from Badwater, 282 feet below sea level, and marvel at the greatest vertical rise in the lower 48 states. For the serious hiker, however, the challenge of climbing 11,404-foot Telescope Peak and looking down at Death Valley will prove irresistible. Views from dogged and dramatic Telescope Peak Trail include Badwater, low point of the continental U.S., and Mount Whitney, the continental high point. See p. 235.

8 THE BEST HIKER-ORIENTED LODGES

- **Point Reyes Seashore Lodge** (Point Reyes National Seashore; ✆ **415/663-9000**): All comfort and beauty in this pleasant spot offering all-natural amenities: views, songbirds, and gardens. Lovely rooms located just steps—literally—from national parkland. Cross a bridge over a bubbling brook and follow a footpath across a meadow to Bear Valley Visitor Center. See p. 79.
- **Big Sur Lodge** (Big Sur; ✆ **800/424-4787**): Hike all day, sleep all night. It's the perfect getaway in the perfect spot; take advantage of reduced winter rates. Spacious, rustic private cabins feature decks and porches with breathtaking views; some with fireplaces and kitchens. Restaurant and grocery store on the premises for meals, trail snacks, and hiking supplies. See p. 97.
- **Little River Inn** (Mendocino; ✆ **888/488-5683**): Eight decades of hospitality, and better than ever. Rooms, suites, and cottages with Jacuzzis and fireplaces, and furnished in rustic country charm. Llamas roam the scenic gardens of this family-owned, eco-conscious retreat. A hiking trail leads from the inn to Van Damme State Park. Sample the finest in local seafood, grilled meats, and fresh produce at the Inn's standout restaurant with a view. See p. 128.
- **Benbow Inn** (Garberville; ✆ **800/355-3301**): Long ago and faraway. That's the feeling imparted by this elegant National Historic Landmark, all elegance and history located just steps from the state park. The onetime set for Hollywood films, you'll feel like a star in these fine accommodations and amenities, once enjoyed by luminaries like Clark Gable and Spencer Tracy. See p. 128.
- **Yosemite Lodge at the Falls** (Yosemite National Park; ✆ **559/252-4848**): The prime attractions are the location near the falls and the abundance of wildlife that gather here. Pleasant rooms in a variety of sizes and shapes, most with patios or balconies from which to enjoy nature's ever-changing scene. The lodge includes restaurants and a lounge, an outdoor pool, bicycle rentals, child-care and programs, a general store, and an ice cream counter. See p. 181.
- **John Muir Lodge** (Sequoia & Kings Canyon National Parks; ✆ **866/522-6966**): Located in an idyllic forest, with stunning views, this classic national park lodge was built from logs in 1998. Complete with modern amenities, all but one room offers two queen beds (the other has a queen bed and a queen sleeper sofa). See p. 202.
- **Sunnyside Lodge** (Lake Tahoe; ✆ **800/822-2754**): This lodge is the stuff of dreams: a historic (1908) home transformed into a great, woodsy lodge with stone fireplaces and modern comforts, plus just steps from a gravel beach, water activities, and marina. The Sunnyside Restaurant occupies the ground floor; room service is also available. Lakefront rooms are a real treat with views and privacy. See p. 220.

9 THE BEST HIKER-SATISFYING RESTAURANTS

- **Olema Farm House Restaurant** (Point Reyes National Seashore; ✆ **415/663-8615**): Serving hungry visitors since 1865, this farm-friendly establishment offers natural goodness in a setting filled with historic charm. Do not miss the burger with Point Reyes Blue Cheese—a standout selection among lunch choices that include excellent sandwiches, soups, and salads. Sample the local ales and be sure to try the local oysters. See p. 80.

- **Pelican Inn Restaurant** (Muir Beach; ✆ **415/383-6000**): Jolly Old England in an unexpected location. Sample the best in English specialties, including hearty shepherd's pie, and bangers and mash. Hikers who have conquered the Cotswolds in the heart of the English countryside will feel right at home with a pub lunch, washed down with a fine draught ale. See p. 81.
- **Kevah Café** (Big Sur; ✆ **831/667-2345**): A deck with a view to die for, and a great selection of creative and healthy fare, espresso drinks, grilled seafood, chicken, and delicious omelets. Try the tasty homemade granola. It gets cold here when the fog rolls in; bring a jacket and your wallet, and enjoy the natural show. See p. 99.
- **North Coast Brewing Company** (Fort Bragg; ✆ **707/964-3400**): A wonderful historic building houses this fun-filled, award-winning brewpub that serves really great beers, and then some. A free brewery tour and shopping opportunities are part of the menu—in addition to basic pub grub and upscale specialties. Try the sumptuous, glazed roast Cornish game hen for a memorable treat. See p. 129.
- **Samoa Cookhouse** (Samoa; ✆ **707/442-1659**): A historic cookhouse that once served the hungry lumberjacks who toiled in nearby forests. Bring your appetite, and leave your finicky health-food concerns at home. Heavy-duty breakfasts, lunches, and dinners stick to the ribs—if not the hips. Red-checked tablecloths and memorabilia on the walls complete the picture of this relic from days gone by. See p. 129.
- **Wolf House** (Glen Ellen; ✆ **707/996-4401**): Eclectic elegance in dining with a clubby atmosphere, memorable meals, and a location par excellence, right on the shaded shores of Sonoma Creek. Local gourmet touches to traditional lunch favorites (the burger with blue cheese from Point Reyes is great!); dinnertime specialties topped off with your choice of fine local wines. See p. 153.

2

Planning Your Trip to Northern California

Northern California has an enormous amount of excellent hiking trails, and I have picked some of the best routes amidst the most beautiful and interesting parts of the country. The countryside is so varied—from woods and low hills to rugged mountains—that there are hikes to suit everyone.

This chapter will provide you with essential information, helpful tips, and advice for the more common challenges that visitors may encounter while vacationing in the northern half of the Golden State.

For additional help in planning your trip and for more on-the-ground resources in Northern California, please turn to the "Fast Facts, Toll-Free Numbers & Websites" appendix on p. 241.

1 BEFORE YOU GO

VISITOR INFORMATION

For information on the state as a whole, log onto the **California Tourism** website at www.visitcalifornia.com. U.S. and Canadian residents can receive free travel planning information by phone (✆ **800/862-2543**). Most cities and towns also have a tourist bureau or chamber of commerce that distributes information on the area. These are listed in the following chapters, organized geographically.

To learn more about California's national parks, contact the **Pacific West Region Information Center,** National Park Service, 1111 Jackson St., Ste. 700, Oakland, CA 94607 (✆ **510/817-1300;** www.nps.gov). You can make reservations at national park campsites—including Yosemite (✆ **877/444-6777** in the U.S., 001-518/885-3639 outside the U.S.; www.recreation.gov).

For information on state parks, contact the **Department of Parks and Recreation**, P.O. Box 942896, Sacramento, CA 94296-0001 (✆ **800/777-0369;** www.parks.ca.gov). Thousands of campsites are on the department's reservation system and can be booked in advance by contacting **ReserveAmerica** (✆ **800/444-7275;** www.reserveamerica.com).

Plan Before You Hike at Frommers.com

Want to make your hiking vacation as smooth and enjoyable as possible? We've added lots of valuable information about how to plan the perfect trip on our website at www.frommers.com/go/hiking. You'll find tips on how to get fit before your trip, suggestions on how best to plan your route, and useful packing tips.

Tips What to Bring: The Hiker's Checklist

Day pack	Water bottle
Boots	Food
Socks	First aid kit
Underwear	Map and compass
Pants and shorts	Sunglasses
Long-sleeved shirt or sweater	Sun block
Parka or windbreaker	Insect repellant
Waterproof jacket and pants	Matches and fire starter
Hat	Plastic bags

Also consider these items:

- **Camera,** battery charger, extra memory card.
- **Trekking pole(s),** the collapsible, telescoping variety.
- **A bandana** has many uses. Soak one in water and tie around your neck for an instant pick-me-up in hot weather; tie around your head for a sweatband; or use as a mask tied below your eyes to protect from wind and dust.
- **Heart-rate monitor** to wear on your wrist to track target heart rate, particularly if you have any physical infirmities that would require paying particular attention to over-exertion, especially on strenuous hikes at altitude or in extreme weather.
- **A good book** for after the hike or to enjoy during a break on the trail. A paperback is lighter to carry around.

Complete information on what to bring on your hiking vacation can be found at www.frommers.com, including tips on day packs, clothing, and equipment to pack, and recommendations for other things to bring with you.

HELPFUL WEBSITES

To read blogs about travel within California, try www.gocalifornia.about.com. There are numerous national travel blogs that cover the state, including:

- www.gridskipper.com
- http://travelblog.com
- www.travelblog.org
- www.worldhum.com
- www.writtenroad.com

PASSPORTS

For an up-to-date, country-by-country listing of passport requirements around the world, go to the "Foreign Entry Requirement" Web page of the U.S. State Department at http://travel.state.gov. International visitors can obtain a visa application at the same website. ***Note:*** Children are required to present a passport when entering the United States at airports. More information on obtaining a passport for a minor can be found at http://travel.state.gov.

CUSTOMS

What You Can Bring into the U.S.

Every visitor more than 21 years of age may bring in, free of duty, the following: (1) 1 liter of wine or hard liquor; (2) 200 cigarettes, 100 cigars (but not from Cuba), or 3 pounds of smoking tobacco; and (3) $100 worth of gifts. These exemptions are offered to travelers who spend at least 72 hours in the United States and who have not claimed them within the preceding 6 months. It is forbidden to bring into the country almost any meat products (including canned, fresh, and dried meat products such as bouillon, soup mixes, and so forth). Generally, condiments (including vinegars, oils, spices, coffee, and tea), and some cheeses and baked goods, are permitted. Avoid rice products, as rice can often harbor insects. Bringing fruits and vegetables is not advised, though not prohibited. Customs will allow produce, depending on where you got it and where you're going after you arrive in the U.S. Foreign tourists may carry in or out up to $10,000 in U.S. or foreign currency with no formalities; larger sums must be declared to U.S. Customs on entering or leaving, which includes filing form CM 4790. For details regarding U.S. Customs and Border Protection, consult your nearest U.S. embassy or consulate, or **U.S. Customs** (www.cbp.gov).

What You Can Take Home from California

Canadian citizens: For a clear summary of Canadian rules, write for the booklet *I Declare,* issued by the Canada Border Services Agency (✆ **800/461-9999** in Canada, or 204/983-3500; www.cbsa-asfc.gc.ca).

U.K. citizens: For information, contact **HM Revenue & Customs** at ✆ **084/5010-9000** (from outside the U.K., 020/8929-0152), or consult their website at www.hmrc.gov.uk.

Australian citizens: A helpful brochure available from Australian consulates or Customs offices is *Know Before You Go.* For more information, call the **Australian Customs Service** at ✆ **13/0036-3263** or log on to www.customs.gov.au.

New Zealand citizens: Most questions are answered in a free pamphlet available at New Zealand consulates and Customs offices: *New Zealand Customs Guide for Travellers, Notice no. 4.* For more information, contact **New Zealand Customs,** The Customhouse, 17–21 Whitmore St., Box 2218, Wellington (✆ **04/473-6099** or 0800/428-786; www.customs.govt.nz).

2 WHEN TO GO

CLIMATE

Northern California's climate is quite varied, and it's a challenge to generalize about the state.

San Francisco's temperate marine climate means relatively mild weather year-round. In summer, temperatures rarely top 70°F (21°C; pack sweaters, even in Aug), and the city's famous fog rolls in most mornings and evenings. In winter, the mercury seldom falls below freezing, and snow is almost unheard of. Because of the fog, summer rarely sees more than a few hot days in a row. Head a few miles inland, though, and it's likely to be clear and hot.

The **Coast south of San Francisco** shares San Francisco's climate, although it gets warmer as you get farther south. The **Coast north of San Francisco** is rainier and foggier; winters tend to be mild but wet.

Summers are pleasant around **Lake Tahoe** and in **Yosemite and Sequoia national parks.** The climate is ideal for hiking, camping, and other outdoor activities, making these regions popular with residents of the state's sweltering deserts and valleys.

The deserts, including **Death Valley National Park,** are sizzling hot in summer; temperatures regularly top 100°F (38°C). Winter is the time to visit the desert (and remember, it gets surprisingly cold at night in the desert).

Average Daytime Temperature (°F & °C) & Rainfall (inches) in San Francisco

	Jan	Feb	Mar	Apr	May	June	July	Aug	Sep	Oct	Nov	Dec
Temp (°F)	50	53	55	55	56	58	59	59	63	62	58	53
Temp (°C)	10	11	13	13	13	14	15	15	17	17	14	11
Rainfall (in.)	2.2	1.6	1.9	1.5	2.0	2.0	2.5	2.7	2.5	2.4	2.5	2.4

AVOIDING THE CROWDS

Given California's pleasant summer weather (with relatively low humidity), the time between Memorial Day and Labor Day is the height of the tourism season virtually everywhere—except for desert areas such as Death Valley, where sizzling temperatures daunt all but the hardiest bargain hunters. Naturally, prices are highest at this time, and they can drop dramatically before and after that period.

Insider tip: Many Californians think the best time to travel the state is autumn. From late September to early December, crowds drop off, "shoulder season" rates kick in, and winter rains have yet to start looming on the horizon.

3 GETTING THERE & GETTING AROUND

GETTING TO CALIFORNIA

By Plane

All major U.S. carriers serve the San Francisco (SFO), Oakland (OAK), Sacramento (SMF), and San Jose (SJC) airports. They include **American** (✆ 800/433-7300; www.aa.com), **America West** (✆ 800/235-9292; www.americawest.com), **Continental** (✆ 800/525-0280; www.continental.com), **Delta** (✆ 800/221-1212; www.delta.com), **JetBlue** (✆ 800/538-2583; www.jetblue.com), **Northwest** (✆ 800/225-2525; www.nwa.com), **Southwest** (✆ 800/435-9792; www.southwest.com), **United** (✆ 800/241-6522; www.united.com), and **US Airways** (✆ 800/428-4322; www.usairways.com). The lowest round-trip fares to the West Coast from New York fluctuate between about $450 and $700; from Chicago, they range from $350 to $450. For details on air travel within California, see "Getting Around," below.

ARRIVING AT THE AIRPORT International visitors arriving by air, no matter what the port of entry, should cultivate patience and resignation before setting foot on U.S. soil. U.S. airports have considerably beefed up security clearances in the years since the terrorist attacks of September 11, 2001, and clearing **Customs and Immigration** can take as long as 2 hours.

By Car

If you are driving and aren't already a member, it's worth joining the **American Automobile Association** (AAA; ✆ **800/922-8228;** www.csaa.com). It charges $49 to $79 per year (with an additional one-time joining fee), depending on where you join, and provides free roadside assistance and a wealth of free travel information, including maps, to motorists. **BP Motor Club** (✆ **800/334-3300;** www.bpmotorclub.com) is another recommended choice. Also, many hotels and attractions throughout California offer discounts to AAA members—always ask. Call ✆ **800/922-8228** or visit www.aaa.com for membership details.

For listings of the major car rental agencies in California, please see "Toll-Free Numbers & Websites," in the appendix (p. 250).

By Train

Amtrak (✆ **800/USA-RAIL;** www.amtrak.com) connects California with about 500 American cities. The Sunset Limited is Amtrak's regularly scheduled transcontinental service, originating in Florida and making 52 stops along the way as it passes through Alabama, Mississippi, Louisiana, Texas, New Mexico, and Arizona, before arriving in Los Angeles 2 days later. The train, which runs three times weekly, features reclining seats, a sightseeing car with large windows, and a full-service dining car. Round-trip coach fares begin at around $350; several varieties of sleeping compartments are also available for an extra charge.

GETTING AROUND

By Car

Unless you plan to spend the bulk of your vacation in a city where hiking is the best way to get around, the most cost-effective way to travel is by car.

If you're visiting from abroad and plan to rent a car in the United States, you probably won't need the services of an additional automobile organization. If you're planning to buy or borrow a car, automobile-association membership is recommended. The **American Automobile Association,** better known as **AAA** (✆ **800/222-4357;** http://travel.aaa.com), is the country's largest motor club and supplies its members with maps, insurance, and emergency road service. ***Note:*** Foreign driver's licenses are usually recognized in the U.S., but you should get an international one if your home license is not in English. Check out **Breezenet.com** (www.bnm.com), which offers U.S. car-rental discounts with some of the most competitive rates around. Also worth visiting are **Orbitz.com, Hotwire.com, Travelocity.com,** and **Priceline.com,** all of which offer competitive online car-rental rates from major national car rental agencies.

California's freeway signs often indicate direction by naming a town rather than a point on the compass. If you've never heard of Canoga Park, you might be in trouble—unless you have a map. The best state road guide is the comprehensive ***Thomas Guide California Road Atlas,*** a 300-plus-page book of maps with schematics of towns and cities statewide. It costs about $25, a good investment if you plan to do a lot of exploring. Smaller, accordion-style maps are handy for the entire state or for individual cities and regions; you'll find a useful one in the back of this book.

DRIVING RULES California law requires both drivers and passengers to wear seat belts, and that a safety seat must be used for children under the age of 6 or less than 60 pounds. Motorcyclists must wear helmets at all times. Auto insurance is mandatory; the car's registration and proof of insurance must stay in the car.

You can turn right at a red light, unless otherwise indicated—but be sure to come to a complete stop.

Many California freeways have designated carpool lanes, also known as high-occupancy vehicle (HOV) lanes or "diamond" lanes. Some require two passengers, others three. Most on-ramps are metered during even light congestion to regulate the flow of traffic onto the freeway; cars in HOV lanes can pass the signal without stopping. All other drivers are required to observe the stoplights—fines begin at around $270.

DEMYSTIFYING RENTER'S INSURANCE Before you drive off in a rental car, be sure you're insured. Hasty assumptions about your personal auto insurance or a rental agency's additional coverage could end up costing you tens of thousands of dollars—even if you're involved in an accident that was clearly the fault of another driver.

If you already have **private auto insurance,** you are most likely covered in the

U.S. for loss of or damage to a rental car, and liability in case of injury to any other party in an accident. Be sure to find out whether you're covered in the area you're visiting, whether your policy extends to all persons who will be driving the rental car, how much liability is covered in case an outside party is injured in an accident, and whether the type of vehicle you are renting is included under your contract. (Rental trucks, sport-utility vehicles, and luxury vehicles or sports cars may not be covered.)

Most **major credit cards** provide some coverage, as well, if they were used to pay for the rental. Terms vary widely, however, so be sure to call your credit card company directly before you rent.

If you're **uninsured,** your credit card may provide primary coverage as long as you decline the rental agency's insurance. This means that the credit card may cover damage or theft of a rental car for the full cost of the vehicle. (In a few states, however, theft is not covered.) If you already have insurance, your credit card may provide secondary coverage—which basically covers your deductible.

Credit cards will not cover liability or the cost of injury to an outside party or damage to his or her vehicle. If you do not hold an insurance policy, you may want to consider purchasing additional liability insurance from your rental company. Be sure to check the terms, however: Some rental agencies cover liability only if the renter is not at fault.

The basic insurance coverage offered by most car-rental companies, known as the **Loss/Damage Waiver (LDW)** or **Collision Damage Waiver (CDW),** can cost as much as $20 per day. It usually covers the full value of the vehicle with no deductible if an outside party causes an accident or other damage to the rental car. Liability coverage varies according to the company policy and state law, but the minimum is usually at least $15,000. If you are at fault in an accident, however, you will be covered for the full replacement value of the car but not for liability. In California, you can buy additional liability coverage for such cases. Most rental companies will require a police report in order to process any claims you file, but your private insurer will not be notified of the accident.

By Train

Amtrak (✆ **800/USA-RAIL;** www.amtrak.com) operates up and down the California coast, connecting San Diego, Los Angeles, San Francisco, and points in between. Multiple trains depart each day, and rates fluctuate according to season and special promotions. One-way fares for the most popular segments can range from $22 (L.A.–Santa Barbara) to $39 (L.A.–San Diego), and from $52 to $84 (San Francisco–L.A.).

International visitors can buy a **USA Rail Pass,** good for 15 or 30 days of unlimited travel on **Amtrak** (✆ **800/USA-RAIL;** www.amtrak.com). The pass is available online or through many overseas travel agents. See Amtrak's website for the cost of travel within the western, eastern, or northwestern United States. Reservations are generally required and should be made as early as possible. Regional rail passes are also available.

By Bus

Bus travel is often the most economical form of public transit for short hops between U.S. cities, but it's certainly not an option for everyone (particularly when Amtrak, which is far more luxurious, offers similar rates). **Greyhound** (✆ **800/231-2222;** www.greyhound.com) is the sole nationwide bus line. International visitors can obtain information about the **Greyhound North American Discovery Pass.** The pass can be obtained from foreign travel agents or through www.discoverypass.com for unlimited travel and stopovers in the U.S. and Canada.

4 CHOOSING A HIKE

For such a rich and diverse hiking destination, there are obviously thousands of different hikes you could take—so what makes these the best? While any choice is going to be subjective, I've used my years of experience to choose the best hikes for all kinds of interests: the best hikes for spectacular views, the best to see wildlife, the best forest hikes, the best coastal routes, the best challenges, and the best to see places to explore the culture while you hike. Above all, I've strived to provide routes that show you something unique about Northern California that you won't likely find where you've come from.

ELEMENTS OF A FROMMER'S "BEST HIKING TRIP"

At the beginning of each review, there is a lot of information to help you decide if a particular hike is right for you. Keeping in mind what kind of vacation experience you want, use these tools to help you plan and get the most out of your vacation.

Star Ratings & Icons

Located in the title bar at the beginning of the hike review, these ratings are the quickest way to see which hikes I believe are "the best of the best."

All routes in this book have been carefully recommended and make for an excellent hiking experience; however, a few routes are so exceptional that they deserve special attention. For these, I've awarded a star (or two or three stars) for easy identification.

Likewise, some hikes have special qualities that deserve recognition:

Finds Lesser-known hikes that don't have the crowds of some of the more popular routes—the hidden treasures.

Kids These choices are ones best suited for doing with young families, with easier terrain and lots to see and do to keep children engaged.

Moments These routes contain experiences that are so special they will leave lasting memories—something you may never have seen before, but will never forget.

Difficulty Rating

A trail's **degree of difficulty** greatly affects the time needed to complete the hike. Park agencies and guidebook writers rate the degree of challenge a trail presents to the average traveler. Of course the "average" hiker varies widely, as do skills, experience, and conditioning; assessing "degree of difficulty" is inevitably subjective.

A path's elevation gain and loss, exposure to elements, steepness, climatic conditions, and the natural obstacles a person encounters along the way (for example, a boulder field or several creek crossings) figure prominently in determining the route's difficulty rating.

In this book, hikes are rated with an Easy-Moderate-Strenuous system. The rating in brief is:

- **Easy:** Less than 5 miles with an elevation gain of less than 700 to 800 feet. These are easy day trails suitable for beginners and children.
- **Moderate:** Between 5 and 10 miles, with less than a 2,000-foot elevation gain. You should be reasonably fit for these.
- **Strenuous:** Hikes over 10 miles, and those with more than a 2,000-foot elevation gain. These are not suitable for children or people of questionable fitness.

Pets in the Parks

National parks, as well as other federal lands administered by the National Park Service, are not pet-friendly, and those planning to visit the parks should consider leaving their pets at home. **Pets are almost always prohibited on hiking trails, in the backcountry, and in buildings, and they must always be on a leash.** Essentially, this means that if you take your dogs or cats into the parks, they can be with you in the campgrounds and inside your vehicle, and you can walk them in parking areas, but that's about all. It's no fun for you or your pet.

Aside from regulations, you need to be concerned with your pet's well-being. Pets should never be left in closed vehicles, where temperatures can soar to over 120°F (49°C) in minutes, resulting in brain damage or death. No punishment is too severe for the human who subjects a dog or cat to that torture.

Those who do decide to take pets with them, despite these warnings, should take the pets' leashes, of course; carry plenty of water (pet shops sell clever little travel water bowls that won't spill in a moving vehicle); and bring proof that the dogs or cats have been vaccinated against rabies. Flea and tick spray or powder is also important, since fleas that may carry bubonic plague have been found on prairie dogs and other rodents in some parks.

Distance

Distance is expressed in miles and includes the complete distance to hike, beginning at the trail head. The routes in this guide range from 2 to 16 miles round trip. I also indicate whether the walk is a loop trail, out-and-back route, or one-way path (where another means of transport returns you to the trail head).

Estimated Time

Estimated time needed to complete the hikes in this guidebook is based on the expected performance of a person in average physical and aerobic condition, traveling at a moderate pace. Age, fitness, and trail experience vary widely among people, and the estimated time may be far too long for some, far too short for others. The estimate also includes recommended amounts of time for taking breaks along the route.

Elevation Gain

Elevation gain measures the net gain from the trail head to the route's highest point. Overall gain (or gross gain) on a trail with rolling terrain that climbs and loses elevation could be substantially more. The elevation chart that appears with the trail map for each hike will show the route's topography.

Costs & Permits

Though fees have increased in the past few years, visiting a national park is still a bargain—a steal compared to the prices you'd pay for a theme park or even a movie. Entry fees, ranging from nothing to $25, are usually charged per private vehicle (for up to 1 week), regardless of how many visitors you stuff inside. Those arriving on foot or by bicycle usually pay lower per-person fees. Some parks offer passes good for unlimited visits to the same park for 12 months.

Tips It's Easy Being Green

Here are a few simple ways you can help conserve fuel and energy when you travel:

- Each time you take a flight or drive a car, greenhouse gases release into the atmosphere. You can help neutralize this danger to the planet through "carbon offsetting"—paying someone to invest your money in programs that reduce greenhouse gas emissions by the same amount you've added. Before buying carbon-offset credits, just make sure that you're using a reputable company, one with a proven program that invests in renewable energy. Reliable carbon offset companies include **Carbonfund.org** (www.carbonfund.org), **TerraPass** (www.terrapass.org), and **Carbon Neutral** (www.carbonneutral.com).
- Whenever possible, choose nonstop flights; they generally require less fuel than indirect flights that stop and take off again. Try to fly during the day—some scientists estimate that nighttime flights are twice as harmful to the environment. And pack light—each 15 pounds of luggage on a 5,000-mile flight adds up to 50 pounds of carbon dioxide emitted.
- Where you stay during your travels can have a major environmental impact. To determine the green credentials of a property, ask about trash disposal and recycling, water conservation, and energy use; also, question whether sustainable materials were used in the construction of the property. The website **www.greenhotels.com** recommends green-rated member hotels around the world that fulfill the company's stringent environmental requirements. Also consult **www.environmentallyfriendlyhotels.com** for more green accommodations ratings.
- At hotels, request that your sheets and towels not be changed daily. (Many hotels already have programs like this in place.) Turn off the lights and air-conditioner (or heater) when you leave your room.
- Use public transport where possible—trains, buses, and even taxis are more energy-efficient forms of transport than driving. Even better is to walk or cycle; you'll produce zero emissions and stay fit and healthy on your travels.
- If renting a car is necessary, ask the rental agent for a hybrid, or rent the most fuel-efficient car available. You'll use less gas and save money at the tank.
- Eat at locally owned and operated restaurants that use produce grown in the area. This contributes to the local economy and cuts down on greenhouse-gas emissions by supporting restaurants where the food is not flown or trucked in across long distances.

SPECIAL PASSES Those who enjoy vacationing at national parks, national forests, and other federal lands have a new annual pass, but for most of us, it will cost more than the old passes that have now been phased out.

The ***America the Beautiful–National Parks and Federal Recreational Lands Pass,*** which went on sale in 2007 for $80, provides free admission for the pass holder and those in his or her vehicle to recreation sites that charge vehicle entrance fees. These include lands administered by the National Park Service, U.S. Forest Service, U.S. Fish and Wildlife Service, Bureau of Land Management, and Bureau of Reclamation. At areas that charge per person fees, the passes are good for the pass holder, plus three additional adults. Children under 16 are admitted free.

The pass, which is valid for 1 year from the date of purchase, replaces the National Parks Pass, which was limited to only properties administered by the National Park Service, and the Golden Eagle Passport, which provided free entry to all the federal lands covered by the new pass. The new passes are also available for U.S. citizens and permanent residents 62 and older for a lifetime fee of $10 (same as the former Golden Age passports), and are free for U.S. residents and permanent residents with permanent disabilities (also the same as the former Golden Access passports).

The passes can be purchased at all national parks. For information, call ✆ **888/275-8747,** ext. 1 or go to www.nps.gov.

Best Time to Go

I have suggested the best time period to take a particular hike. Northern California offers four-season hiking, but some climatic restrictions must be heeded. You can hike some of the trails in this guide all of the time, all of the trails some of the time, but not necessarily all of the trails all of the time.

The suggested times are intended to show the best time for maximum enjoyment of the trail, but almost all of the hikes are also accessible outside the suggested time period.

Website

The suggested website is the best place to go to get further information on the trail and surrounding area.

Recommended Map

I've listed my favorite trail maps, those that are reasonably easy for the traveler to obtain. These will likely provide additional detail to the map provided in this guide.

Trail Head GPS

We've listed the GPS coordinates for where the recommended trail begins. The intent is to get you to the start of your route easily, by entering the coordinates into a handheld or automotive GPS device, GPS-enabled mobile phone, or online mapping program.

Trail Head Directions

Directions to the hike's starting point are given from the nearest highway or major road to the parking area for the trail head. For trails having two desirable trail heads, directions to both are given. A few trails can be hiked one-way with the possibility of a public transport or a car shuttle. Suggested car shuttle points are noted.

NAVIGATION ASSISTANCE

Maps

Each trail in this guide has a map. Familiarize yourself with the map legend. To follow the map easily, first look for the north. Then, find the trail head and follow the directions given to each waypoint.

Several companies produce smaller-scale maps that are useful for seeing the bigger picture and for traveling around the country. An online source of such maps is www.mapsworldwide.com.

Google Maps (www.maps.google.com) is particularly useful for finding your way to hikes. Google Maps provide highly specific driving directions from Point A to Point B—that is to say, from the city to the country and from one hike to another.

Google Maps provides road maps and, in some cases, also shows tracks used by hikes. A more specific Terrain map view displays a topographic view. In addition, the Satellite view shows terrain in a more three-dimensional way. You can create and edit Google maps on your home computer before your trip or download them to a wireless device.

MapQuest (www.mapquest.com) has excellent mapmaking capabilities and will enable you to get maps and directions to towns and trail heads. The company also offers a product called MapQuest Navigator 5.0 that provides GPS car navigation on your phone without the need to buy another navigation device.

Reading GPS Coordinates

In North America, GPS coordinates normally reflect a measurement of longitude and latitude given in "degrees."

Walks can be broken up with waypoints, or stops along the way. These waypoints can guide you back to the trail head if you are lost, by checking the coordinates for where you are and aiming yourself towards the coordinates of the nearest waypoint.

Having a GPS reading of the trail head and of certain trail waypoints can be both helpful and confusing. Such readings can be particularly helpful as a supplement to a map for finding obscure trail heads, unsigned junctions, or going off-trail—situations you will rarely encounter while hiking any of the high-quality trails in this guide.

Where a GPS reading can be confusing to the less-experienced hiker and GPS user has to do with the fact that a GPS device shows direction or gives distance only "as the crow flies," meaning in a straight line. But hikers are not crows! Most trails don't take a straight line from Point A to Point B, so be sure to consult the map included with the hike description, along with your GPS readings.

5 HIKING SAFETY

Don't venture off on any extensive hike, even a day hike, without the following gear: a compass, a topographical map, bug repellent, a whistle, and a watch. In many Western parks, sunglasses, sunscreen, and wide-brimmed hats are also considered essential.

To be on the safe side, you should keep a **first-aid kit** in your car or luggage, and have it handy when hiking. At a minimum, it should contain butterfly bandages, sterile gauze pads, adhesive tape, antibiotic ointment, pain relievers, alcohol pads, and a knife with scissors and tweezers.

TRAIL HEAD SAFETY & PARKING PRECAUTIONS

Returning to the trail head after a joyful day on the trail to find a car window smashed and valuables missing can ruin your vacation. Thieves are known to target car parks that attract lots of tourists, as their cars may contain cameras, money, and other valuables.

A few simple steps can minimize the likelihood of your car being broken into: Don't leave valuables in the car (best idea) or lock valuables in the trunk (second best idea); bring your wallet and keys with you, rather than hiding them in your vehicle.

PLANNING YOUR HIKE

It's equally important for your safety to know your limitations, to understand the environment, and to take the proper equipment when exploring the park. Always stop at the visitor center before you set out on a hike. Park staff there can offer advice on your hiking plans and supply you with pamphlets, maps, and

Frommers.com: The Complete Travel Resource

Planning a trip or just returned? Head to **Frommers.com,** voted Best Travel Site by *PC Magazine.* We think you'll find our site indispensable before, during, and after your travels—with expert advice and tips; independent reviews of hotels, restaurants, attractions, and preferred shopping and nightlife venues; vacation giveaways; and an online booking tool. We publish the complete contents of over 135 travel guides in our **Destinations** section, covering over 4,000 places worldwide. Each weekday, we publish original articles that report on **deals and news** via our free **Frommers.com Newsletters.** What's more, **Arthur Frommer** himself blogs 5 days a week, with cutting opinions about the state of travel in the modern world. We're betting you'll find our **Events** listings an invaluable resource; it's an up-to-the-minute roster of what's happening in cities everywhere—including concerts, festivals, lectures, and more. We've also added weekly **podcasts, interactive maps,** and hundreds of new images across the site. Finally, don't forget to visit our **Message Boards,** where you can join in conversations with thousands of fellow Frommer's travelers and post your trip report once you return.

information on weather conditions or any dangers, such as bear activity or flash flood possibilities on canyon hikes. Once out on the trail, hikers should always carry sufficient water and, just as important, remember to drink it. Wear sturdy shoes with good ankle support and rock-gripping soles. Always keep a close eye on any children in your group and never let them run ahead.

COMMON AILMENTS

Since many park visitors live at or near sea level, one of the most common health hazards is **altitude sickness,** caused by the high elevations of many of the parks in this book. Symptoms include headache, fatigue, nausea, loss of appetite, muscle pain, and lightheadedness. Doctors recommend that until you are acclimated—which can take several days—you should consume light meals and drink lots of liquids, avoiding those with caffeine or alcohol. It's a good idea to take frequent sips of water, as well.

One proven method of minimizing the effects of high altitudes is to work up to them. For instance, go to a lower-elevation park for a day or two before heading to the higher mountains.

A waterborne hazard is *Giardia,* a **parasite** that wreaks havoc on the human digestive system. If you pick up this pesky hanger-on, it may accompany you on your trip home. The best solution is to carry all the water you'll need (usually a gallon a day). If you need additional water from the parks' lakes and streams, it should be boiled for 3 to 6 minutes before consumption.

ENCOUNTERING WILDLIFE

When out on the trails, even for a day hike, keep safety in mind. The wild, untouched nature of these parks is what makes them so exciting and breathtakingly beautiful—but along with wildness comes risk. The national parks are neither playgrounds nor zoos. The animals here are truly untamed and sometimes dangerous. This doesn't mean that disaster could strike at any time, but it does mean that visitors should exercise basic caution and common sense at all times, respecting the wilderness around them and always following the rules of the park.

Never feed, bother, or approach animals. Even the smallest among them can carry harmful, sometimes deadly, diseases, and feeding them is dangerous not only to yourself but also to the animals, who (like us) will happily eat what their bodies can't handle. In addition, wild animals' dependence on human handouts can lead to unpleasant confrontations, which often result in rangers' having to relocate or kill the animal. As the Park Service reminds us, "A fed bear is a dead bear."

In some parks where there are bears and mountain lions, it's often a good idea to make noise as you hike, to make sure you don't accidentally stumble upon and frighten an animal into aggression. Also, follow park rules on food storage when in bear country. Photographers should always keep a safe distance when taking pictures of wildlife—the best photos are shot with a telephoto lens.

6 PROTECTING THE ENVIRONMENT

Not long ago, the rule of thumb was to "leave only footprints"; these days, we're trying to do better and not leave even footprints. It's relatively easy to be a good outdoor citizen—just use common sense. Pack up all trash; stay on designated trails; be especially careful not to pollute water; don't disturb plants, wildlife, or archaeological resources; don't pick flowers or collect rocks; and, in general, do your best to have as little impact on the environment as possible. Some hikers go further, carrying a small trash bag to pick up what others may have left. As the Park Service likes to remind us, protecting our national parks is everyone's responsibility.

Suggested Itineraries

Northern California parks showcase a fabulous array of nature's handiwork: ancient sequoias, giant redwoods, soaring alpine peaks, and the most scenic of shorelines. The parks also preserve a cross-section of Golden State ecology, from the mist-covered coast to the summit of Mount Whitney, the highest peak in the continental U.S. While it's tempting to want to experience—and hike—this multitude of environments in one trip, it's far more enjoyable to sample them one or two at a time. Thus, for your hiking pleasure as well as for your peace of mind and spirit, consider planning your Northern California sojourn with the help of the following suggested itineraries.

1 THE NORTH COAST IN ONE WEEK

The 350-plus miles of the California coast, north of San Francisco, is sparsely populated and little developed. As you travel north, you pass from rolling, grass-covered hillsides to steep cliffs and densely forested coastal mountains. California's coastline rises to a magnificent crescendo at Redwood National and State parks, where hikers can visit the tallest trees on Earth. Follow this tour for hikes that explore the Golden State's wildest and most inspiring coast.

Day 1: Driving North

Leave San Francisco by heading north on Hwy. 101 and drive across the **Golden Gate Bridge** (p. 43). Stop at Vista Point at the north end of the bridge to bid adieu to the Bay Area and perhaps to walk a bit of the bridge. Follow 101 for an hour to Santa Rosa, then take Hwys. 12 and 116 for the drive (34 miles) west to the coast at **Sonoma Coast State Beach** (p. 102). Enjoy a walk over the coastal bluffs here and/or the bluffs a bit north at **Fort Ross State Historic Park** (p. 105). Pick up a snack or picnic supplies at one of the small stores located along Hwy. 1 (from south to north: Jenner, Sea Ranch, and Gualala). If you're traveling in spring, stop for a short stroll amongst the pale pink blossoms of the California rhododendrons in Kruse Rhododendron State Reserve, located a few miles north of Fort Ross. Stop for the night at **Little River Inn** (p. 128), located a few miles south of Mendocino. Have dinner at the inn.

Days 2 & 3: Mendecino

After breakfast, walk out the door of the inn and follow the trail to **Van Damme State Park** (p. 107). Hike along the Little River to Fern Canyon and perhaps continue all the way to the Pygmy Forest. Fortify yourself with lunch at the deli located in Little River across Hwy. 1 from the inn and drive a few miles north to Big River, where there is a big estuary and big trees (redwoods). Explore Big River State Park on a riverside walking trail, or rent a canoe or kayak and paddle the river and estuary. Reward yourself with a dinner out at the **Bay View Café** (p. 129) in Mendocino.

The next day, head into Mendocino, find a scarce parking space, and walk past the grand Victorians and simple New England saltboxes into a Maine-village-like downtown of fascinating 19th-century buildings. Be sure to check out the historic Ford House perched above the bay on the south side of town. Inside the house are nature and history exhibits and headquarters for **Mendocino Headlands State Park** (p. 109). Walk the dramatic bluffs, then drive north 5 miles on Hwy. 1 to the curious Jug Handle State Reserve, home to some weird plant communities stacked in an "ecological staircase," as well as the Mendocino Pygmy Forest with its 5-foot-high pine and cypress. Continue 5 more miles to Fort Bragg, walk the former lumber town's small downtown, then dine at **North Coast Brewing Company** (p. 129).

Day ❹: Humbolt Redwoods State Park

From Mendocino, follow Hwy. 1 north 40 miles to junction Hwy. 101, continuing north another 20 miles to the **Benbow Inn** (p. 128). Check in here or stay at one of the numerous modest motels in nearby Garberville. Continue north a short distance farther and exit Hwy. 101 onto Avenue of the Giants, a 32-mile parkway parallel to the main highway that runs the length of **Humboldt Redwoods State Park** (p. 112). Hike the Bull Creek Flats Loop Trail through an awesome redwood forest, then return to overnight in Benbow/Garberville.

Days ❺ & ❻: Redwood National Park, Crescent City

Take Hwy. 101 north and begin a morning of touring some special towns. Make your first stop Ferndale, a quaint, handsomely restored 1890s Victorian village with some fine art galleries, museums, shops, and B&Bs. You can pick up a brochure that details a walking tour from any of the shops on Main Street. Continue north on 101 and, if you're *really* hungry, stop for a meal in the lumber town of Samoa at the **Samoa Cookhouse** (p. 129) or perhaps in the college town of Arcata at the **Plaza Grill** (p. 129). Continue north into the redwoods and take the turnoff for **Prairie Creek Redwoods State Park** (p. 120). Watch for the enchanting Roosevelt elk as you hike Gold Bluffs Beach and Fern Canyon. Drive north to Crescent City to overnight in **Curly Redwood Lodge** (p. 128), a modest motel, and eat a tasty seafood dinner at the **Beachcomber** (p. 129).

The next day, pack a picnic lunch and head south on Hwy. 1 to the Redwood Information Center near the hamlet of Orick and learn about the history of Redwood National Park. Pick up a permit and the combination lock numbers for the gate across Bald Hills Road, then make the 17 mile drive to the **Tall Trees** trail head. (p. 124). Visit what was once considered the world's tallest tree via this route. Next, head north on Hwy. 101 to **Del Norte Coast Redwoods State Park** (p. 126), where magnificent old-growth redwoods and an impressive coastline are accessed via Damnation Creek Trail and Last Chance Trail. Return to Crescent City.

Day ❼: Patrick's Point State Park

Break up the long drive south to San Francisco with a stop at **Patrick's Point State Park** (p. 115) and a hike along cliffs, forested with Sitka spruce, to Agate Beach. If it's a warm day, stop back in Benbow for a swim in the Eel River at Benbow State Recreation Area or pause for a dip in the river at nearby Richardson Grove State Park.

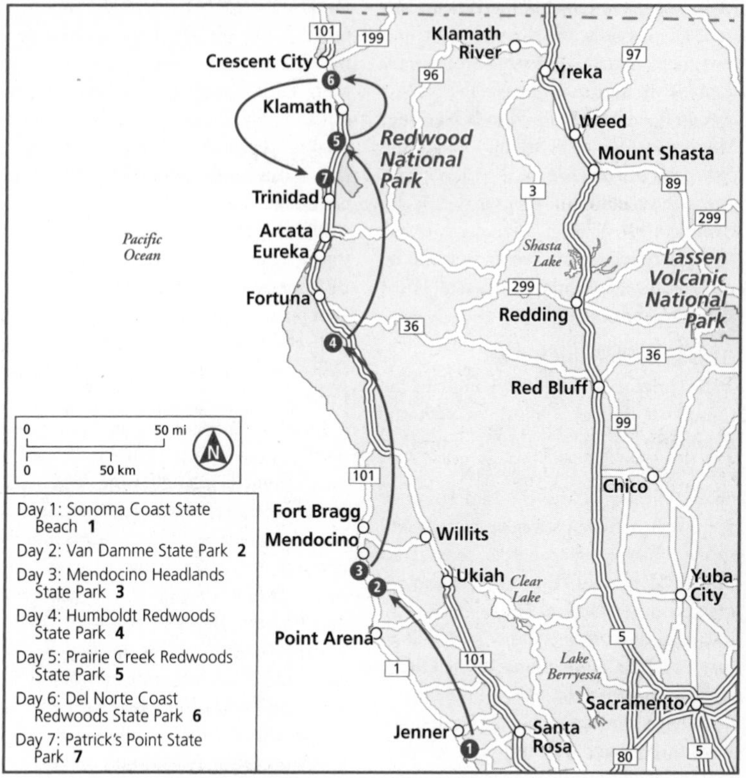

2 NORTH BAY & WINE COUNTRY IN ONE WEEK

You could walk for a week in the parklands north of the Golden Gate and in the Wine Country with one of those upscale walking vacation companies. Or do it yourself at your own pace with the tour described below for half the cost. The magnificent trails meandering through Point Reyes National Seashore beckon the hiker to explore wide grasslands, Douglas fir forest, sage-cloaked coastal ridges, and windswept beaches. Then, leave the fog-bound coast for the sun-kissed Wine Country and a splendid mix of vineyards and vagabonding.

Day 1: North of Golden Gate

From San Francisco, follow Hwy. 101 over the **Golden Gate Bridge** (p. 43) into Marin County. Exit on Hwy. 1, soon turning off this highway onto Tennessee Valley Road and reaching the trail head for the hike to **Tennessee Valley and Muir Beach** (p. 54). Hike the stirring Coast Trail to Muir Beach and lunch at the **Pelican Inn** (p. 81), an authentic English pub and restaurant. Retrace your steps on the trail, then drive north on Hwy. 1 to Muir Woods Road and **Muir Woods National Monument** (p. 57). Hike through the cathedrals of redwoods with visitors from across the nation and around the world. Return to Hwy. 1 and drive north to the town of Olema and the warm, welcoming, and for the hiker, ideally situated **Point Reyes Seashore Lodge** (p. 79).

Days ❷ & ❸: Point Reyes

Today, drive south on Hwy. 1 and take the turnoff to Bolinas. On the way to the **Palomarin** trail head (p. 65), stop off at the Point Reyes Bird Observatory and observe firsthand why the bird count in the diverse national seashore exceeds 430 species. Take a hike on the **Coast Trail** through the "Lake District" to cascading-into-the-sea **Alamere Falls.** Return to Olema and the lodge, and enjoy the local oysters, local ale, and dinner at the **Olema Farm House** (p. 80).

The next morning, with a picnic lunch in your day pack, walk out the back door of the lodge and take the trail across a meadow to the national seashore's Bear Valley Visitor Center. After learning all about the San Andreas Fault and earthquakes that have shaped this land and the fascinating natural attractions of Point Reyes, take the hike through **Bear Valley** (p. 67). Hike the valley all the way to the ocean and/or ascend **Mount Wittenberg** (1,407 ft.) (p. 70), high point of the national seashore, for panoramic views. Treat yourself to a hearty dinner at **Rosie's Cowboy Cookhouse** (p. 81) in Point Reyes Station.

Days ❹ & ❺: Drakes Beach & Tomales Bay

Follow Hwy. 1 north a short distance and connect with Sir Francis Drake Boulevard, which angles north and west, and delivers you to the trail head for the hike to **Drakes Estero** (p. 72). Keep your field glasses handy for the abundant wildlife at the estuary: harbor seals, shore birds, and water birds. After your hike, continue south on Sir Francis Drake Boulevard to Drakes Beach, and lunch or snack at the Drakes Beach Café. Back on Sir Francis Drake Boulevard, continue south to road's end at the Point Reyes Lighthouse (open Thurs–Mon, weather permitting). By some accounts, Point Reyes is the foggiest point on the Pacific Coast. After your chilly visit, return to Point Reyes Station and a hot dinner at the **Station House Café** (p. 81).

On Day 5, pack a picnic and drive north on Sir Francis Drake Boulevard to Pierce Point Road, following it to road's end at the trail head for the path to **Tomales Point** (p. 75). Roam across the dew-dampened grasslands with the tule elk to the north end of the point and grand island-like views of a lot of Pacific Ocean and a lot of Tomales Bay. Retrace your steps and the route of your drive, stopping if you choose to take a walk on the Pacific side of the peninsula at Kehoe Beach or on the bayside at romantic little Hearts Desire Beach in Tomales Bay State Park. Back at Point Reyes Station, stop for a meal or snack at the superb deli at the Palace Market, which also carries a large selection of local cheeses. Thus fortified, head briefly north on Hwy. 1 to Point Reyes–Petaluma Road and motor east on this scenic byway to Petaluma. Join Hwy. 116 and continue east to the Sonoma Valley. Head north on Hwy. 12 to Sonoma. Stop for the night at the **Best Western Sonoma Valley Inn** (p. 152), located just steps from the historic Sonoma Plaza.

Day ❻: Sonoma Valley

From Sonoma, drive north on Hwy. 12 and take the turnoff to the town of Glen Ellen and **Jack London State Park**

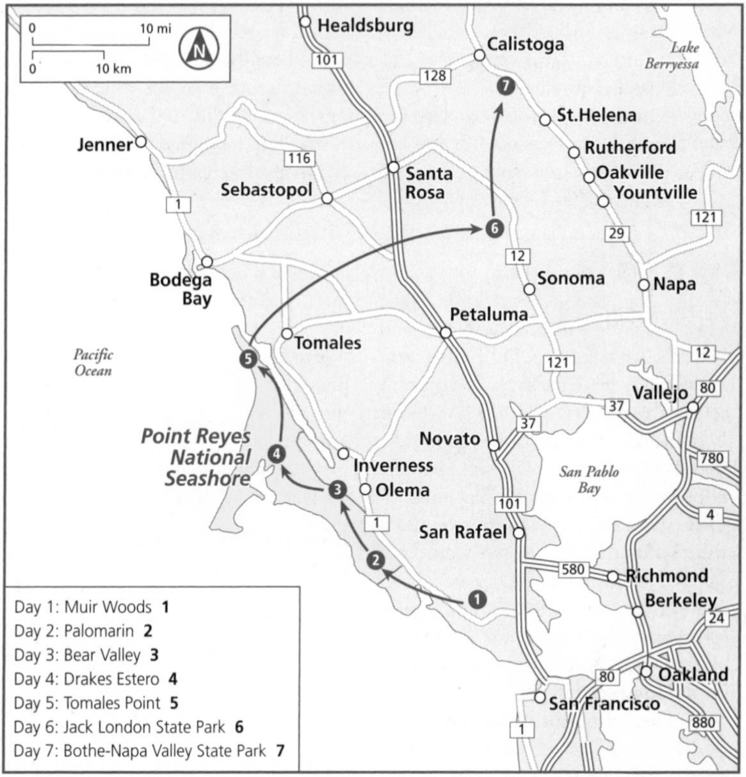

(p. 133). Heed the *Call of the Wild* and hike the great author's Beauty Ranch in the lovely Valley of the Moon. Stop in Glen Ellen for lunch at **Wolf House** (p. 153), located on the shaded shores of Sonoma Creek. Continue north on Hwy. 12 to **Sugarloaf Ridge State Park.** Enjoy a hillside ramble and ridge-top views of the Wine Country. Enjoy a post-hike wine tasting at one of the many wineries located in the Sonoma Valley on your way back to the town of Sonoma.

Day 7: Napa Valley

Head north on Hwy. 12 to Trinity Road for the drive eastward up and over the hills to the Napa Valley and the town of Oakville. Stop at the **Oakville Grocery Co.** (p. 153) and select picnic items from a dazzling array of gourmet foodstuffs. Drive north on Hwy. 29 to **Bothe-Napa Valley State Park** for a great hike (redwoods, views, and much more) and place to picnic. Relax away any remaining cares at the hot springs in Calistoga, located north of the park, then hit the wine trail as you drive south along Hwy. 29. Meander through St. Helena, Rutherford, Yountville, Napa, then all too soon, you're back to I-80, the bustling East Bay, and over the San Francisco–Oakland Bay Bridge back to San Francisco.

3 HIGH SIERRA PARK IN ONE WEEK

Many hikers feel strongly that the High Sierra offers the very best hiking in the Golden State. The rugged "Range of Light" is a magnificent backdrop for Lake Tahoe, as well as the parks and trails along its shore. Surely, hikers and everyone else have run out of superlatives to describe Yosemite, known for its great granite cliffs and domes, enormous waterfalls, and giant sequoia. Far less known than other more popular parks, Sequoia National Park, with its mighty trees and stunning alpine backcountry, may surprise—and delight—the traveling hiker.

Days 1 & 2: Lake Tahoe

Get up close and personal with Tahoe right away with a hike on Rubicon Trail along the lakeshore in **D.L. Bliss and Emerald Bay State parks** (p. 208). Reach the parks by following Hwy. 89 north for 11 miles from the town of South Lake Tahoe. Sunbathe or swim (if you like chilly water) at Emerald Bay, one of Tahoe's best beaches. Get a great sandwich at the **Yellow Sub** (p. 221) in South Lake Tahoe. If you're up for a little more hiking, follow Hwy. 89 north 9 miles to the parking area for the **Desolation Wilderness** (p. 215). The 2-mile hike to Eagle Lake is just the way to end the day. In South Lake Tahoe, spend the night at **Camp Richardson Resort** (p. 219), which offers a range of rooms and cabins, as well as on-site dining options.

On Day 2, stoke up on a massive pre-hike breakfast at **Ernie's Coffee Shop** (p. 221) in South Lake Tahoe, then drive south on Hwys. 50 and 89 to the turnoff for **Grover Hot Springs State Park** (p. 217). Here, you can take a hike to a waterfall and "take the cure" at the soothing hot springs. Continue on 89 to a junction with Hwy. 395 and head south. Stop at curious Mono Lake, a super-saline environment that attracts abundant birdlife. At the hamlet of Lee Vining, head west, cresting the High Sierra at Tioga Pass (9,945 ft.), and enter **Yosemite National Park.** Stop at the Tuolumne Meadows Visitor Center to learn about this splendid area of the national park and then stroll through **Tuolumne Meadows** (p. 176), one of the world's most beautiful and beloved alpine meadows. Stop for the night at **Tuolumne Meadows Lodge** (p. 181), really a group of tent cabins, with a prime location near some of the park's best hiking trails. Enjoy a hearty dinner at the edge of the lodge (p. 183).

Days 3, 4 & 5: Yosemite National Park

Drive the short distance on Tioga Road to the trail head for **Cathedral Lakes** (p. 175), where you can then hike the John Muir Trail to these picturesque lakes. After your hike, drive west on Tioga Road, stopping often to see the sights, including Tenaya Lake and Olmsted Point. When you reach Big Oak Flat Road, head southeast, following the signs to Yosemite Valley. Pass through a tunnel through the mountains, stop to regard the valley from aptly named Valley View, and make another stop soon thereafter to check out impressive Bridalveil Fall, reached by a short trail. Check into **Yosemite Lodge at the Falls** (p. 181) and eat dinner next door at the **Yosemite Lodge Food Court** (p. 183).

On Day 4, getting to know Yosemite Valley is on the top of your agenda. Take some or all of the **Yosemite Valley** hike (p. 164). Marvel at Lower Yosemite Fall, amble along the Merced River, and check out the rock-climbers on El Capitan. Use the free shuttle bus to assist in your valley sightseeing tour and to get oriented to the

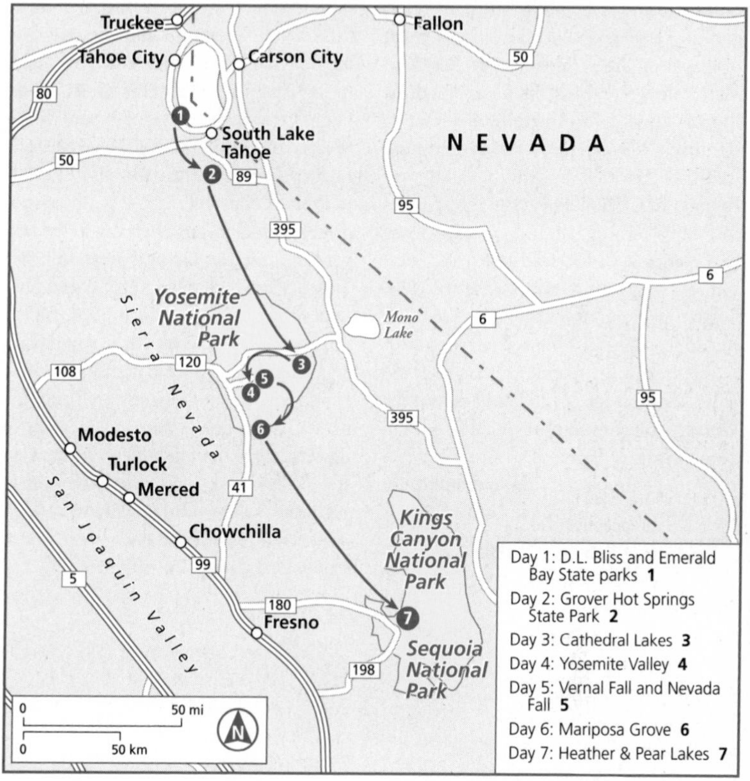

landscape and trail heads. Stop for lunch at **Degnan's Deli** (p. 183), then stroll the Ansel Adams Gallery in Yosemite Village. Learn about the natural attractions and history of Yosemite at the Valley Visitor Center and Yosemite Museum, also in Yosemite Village. Have a great dinner with a view to match at the **Mountain Room Restaurant** (p. 183) near Yosemite Lodge.

On Day 5, take the shuttle bus to Curry Village, load up on the big buffet-style breakfast at **Curry Village Pavilion** (p. 182), then walk or take the shuttle bus over to the stop for the Nature Center at Happy Isles and the trail head for the hike to **Vernal Fall and Nevada Fall** (p. 168). Ascend to these two waterfalls of uncommon beauty via two fabulous footpaths—well-named Mist Trail and famed John Muir Trail. Dig into a post-hike pizza at the **Curry Village Pizza Patio** (p. 183).

Spend the rest of the afternoon catching up on any sights to see in Yosemite Valley or drive (rather than hike) up to **Glacier Point** (p. 161) for superb panoramic vistas of the valley.

Days 6 & 7: Sequoia National Park

Begin what could be called "A Big Day with Big Trees" by driving west through Yosemite and through another tunnel to join Wawona Road, which leads south. At the park's South Entrance, take the road to **Mariposa Grove** (p. 158), by far the largest of Yosemite's groves of giant sequoias and an inspiration to hike. It was these magnificent trees, along with Yosemite Valley, that prompted President Abraham Lincoln to set aside Yosemite as a reserve. Return to Wawona Road, which continues south as Hwy. 41. Drive 60 miles to Fresno, then follow Hwy. 180 for 52 miles to the Big Stump Entrance of Kings Canyon National Park. Head north to Grant Grove Village and **Grant Grove** (p. 194). Take a hike among outstanding sequoias, including General Grant Tree, the third-largest tree in the world. Overnight at the **John Muir Lodge** (p. 202) and dine at the **Grant Grove Restaurant** (p. 204), both in Grant Grove Village.

From Grant Grove Village, motor south on Generals Highway into Sequoia National Park. Stop at the Lodgepole Visitor Center to learn more about the park, and pick up a snack or trail lunch at the **Lodgepole Market** (p. 204). Travel a short distance down the highway to the turnoff for Wolverton and the trail head for the trail to **Heather and Pear Lakes** (p. 192). The Lakes Trail is an all-day High Sierra classic. Overnight and dine at **Wuksachi Lodge** (p. 202), located in the Lodgepole area of the park.

From Lodgepole, drive south a short distance on Generals Highway to the large parking area for **Giant Forest** (p. 189). Take a short hike to see the General Sherman Tree, 275 feet high, 2.8 million pounds, 2,700 years old—the world's largest living thing. As time permits, see more giant sequoias on Congress Trail and Trail of the Sequoias. When you're ready to descend from the High Sierra to the Central Valley and meet the state's major highways, follow Generals Highway (Hwy. 198) south out of the park, then west to Visalia and a junction with Hwy. 99.

San Francisco Bay Area

San Francisco is a city of walkers. And many of the city's best walks are hikes along the bay and ocean shores of the Golden Gate National Recreation Area. GGNRA, as it's known, extends across the Golden Gate Bridge and protects the wild headlands of Marin County.

From the "Bridge at the Edge of the Continent," walkers are treated to splendid views of San Francisco Bay, which contains 90% of California's remaining coastal wetlands. Other great bay views—and great hikes—can be had from Angel Island, Mount Tamalpais, and the Marin Headlands north of the Golden Gate Bridge.

By some accounts, the 76,000-acre Golden Gate National Recreation Area is the largest urban park in the world. In addition to its San Francisco shoreline, the park also includes coastal wild lands north and south of the bridge. Hiking GGNRA offers an urban-rural-wilderness collage; natural history and social history are often part of the same walk. From the forested ridges, take in San Francisco's skyline; from the city, look toward the bold Marin Headlands.

While San Francisco's shore is every bit a part of one of America's most beloved cities, it also offers a feeling of remoteness. Preserving the waterfront as public domain during the real estate go-go years of the 1970s and 1980s provided San Francisco with a terrific greenbelt sprinkled with historical and cultural attractions.

North of the GGNRA is Point Reyes National Seashore—with its densely forested ridges, wild and open coastal bluffs, and deserted beaches—an unforgettable place to ramble. With its moors, weirs, glens, and vales, Point Reyes Peninsula calls to mind the seacoast of Great Britain. When fog settles over the dew-dampened grasslands of Tomales Point, walkers can easily imagine that they're stepping onto a Scottish moor or wandering one of the Shetland Islands.

When hiking, the awesome forces that shaped this land are often evident. You can hike along the earthquake rift zone, tramp along creeks flowing through the peninsula's fissures, and look down from the ridges at Olema Valley, the 1906 quake's epicenter.

Along with the earthquake-displaced land, the Pacific Ocean is an overwhelming presence here. Point Reyes is bounded on three sides by more than 50 miles of bay and ocean frontage. The point, described as hammer-headed—or wing-shaped by the more poetic—literally and figuratively sticks out and stands out from California's fairly straight-trending coast north of San Francisco.

Point Reyes is also a haven for birds; not surprisingly, the seashore makes *Audubon* magazine's "Top Ten National Seashores" list. A diversity of habitats—seashore, forest, chaparral, and more—is one reason the bird count exceeds 430 species. Because Point Reyes thrusts 10 miles into the Pacific, it lures many winter migrants. Limantour and Drake *esteros* (estuaries) are resting and feeding areas for many species of shorebirds and waterfowl.

Other wildlife-watching opportunities abound. A resident tule elk herd roams the Tomales Point area. Point Reyes Lighthouse is a premier spot for winter whale-watching, when migrating California gray whales swim close to the point.

More than 100 miles of trail meandering through the national seashore beckon the hiker to explore wide grasslands, Bishop pine and Douglas fir forests, chaparral-cloaked coastal ridges, and windswept beaches. The paths range from easy beach walks and nature hikes to rugged mountain rambles.

ESSENTIALS

GETTING THERE

By Air

The northern Bay Area has two major airports: San Francisco International and Oakland International.

SAN FRANCISCO INTERNATIONAL AIRPORT Almost four dozen major scheduled carriers serve **San Francisco International Airport** or **SFO** (✆ **650/821-8211;** www.flysfo.com), 14 miles directly south of downtown on U.S. 101.

The fastest and cheapest way to get from SFO to the city is to take **BART** (Bay Area Rapid Transit; ✆ **415/989-2278;** www.bart.gov), which offers numerous stops within downtown San Francisco. This route, which takes about 35 minutes, avoids traffic on the way and costs a heck of a lot less than taxis or shuttles (about $6 each way, depending on exactly where you're going). Just jump on the airport's free shuttle bus to the International terminal, enter the BART station there, and you're on your way to San Francisco. Trains leave approximately every 15 minutes.

Travel time to downtown during commuter rush hour is about 40 minutes; at other times, it's about 20 to 25 minutes. For up-to-the-minute information about public transportation and traffic, call ✆ **511** or visit www.511.org.

A **cab** from the airport to downtown costs $35 to $40, plus tip, and takes about 30 minutes, traffic permitting.

SuperShuttle (✆ **800/BLUE-VAN** or 415/558-8500; www.supershuttle.com) is a private shuttle company that provides door-to-door airport service, in which you share a van with a few other passengers. They will take you anywhere in the city, charging $15 per person to a residence or business. On the return trip, add $8 to $15 for each additional person, depending on whether you're traveling from a hotel or a residence. The shuttle stops at least every 20 minutes, sometimes sooner, and picks up passengers from the marked areas outside the terminals' upper levels. Reservations are required for the return trip to the airport only and should be made 1 day before departure. These shuttles often demand they pick you up 2 hours before your domestic flight and 3 hours before international flights and during holidays. Keep in mind that you could be the first one on and the last one off, so this trip could take a while; you might want to ask before getting in. For $65, you can either charter the entire van for up to seven people or an Execucar private sedan for up to four people. For more info on the Execucar, call ✆ **800/410-4444.**

The San Mateo County Transit system, **SamTrans** (✆ **800/660-4287** or 650/508-6200; www.samtrans.com) runs two buses between the San Francisco Airport and the Transbay Terminal at First and Mission streets. Bus no. 292 costs $1.50 and makes the trip in about 55 minutes. The KX bus costs $4 and takes just 35 minutes, but it permits only one carry-on bag. Both buses run daily. The no. 292 starts Monday through Friday

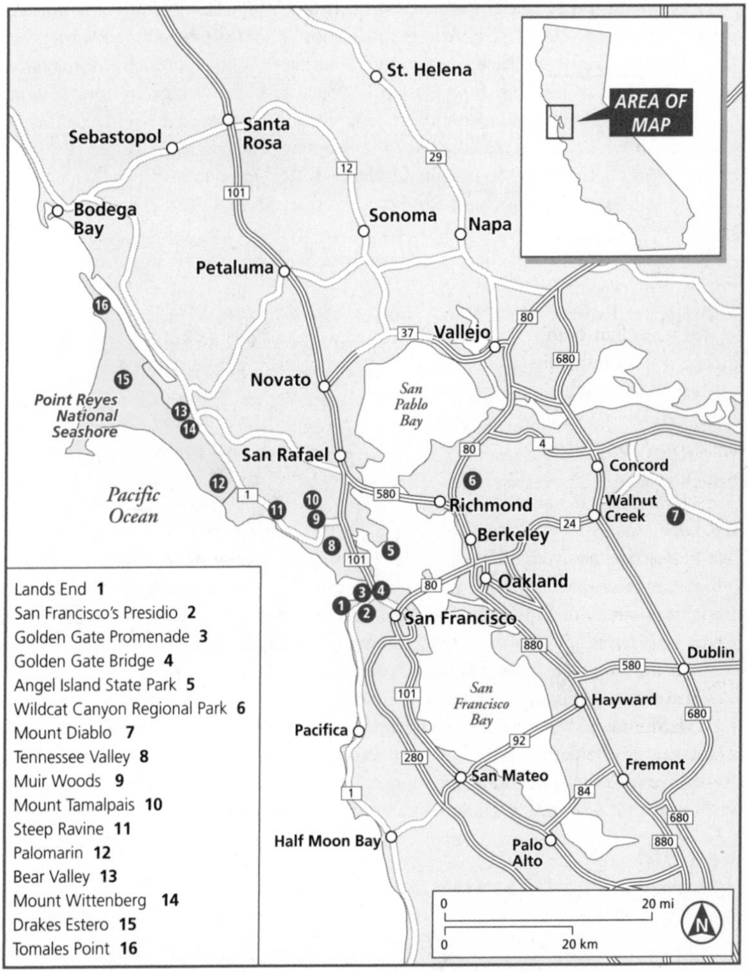

at 5:25am and on weekends at 5:30am; it continues daily until 1am and runs every half-hour until 7:30pm, when it runs hourly. The KX starts at 5:53am and ends at 10:37pm Monday through Friday. On weekends, service runs from 7:19am to 9:30pm, runs every half-hour until 6:30pm, and then changes to an hourly schedule.

OAKLAND INTERNATIONAL AIRPORT About 5 miles south of downtown Oakland, at the Hegenberger Road exit of CA. 17 (U.S. 880; if coming from the south, take 98th Ave.), **Oakland International Airport** or **OAK** (© **800/247-6255** or 510/563-3300; www.oaklandairport.com) primarily serves passengers with East Bay destinations. Some San Franciscans prefer this less-crowded, more accessible airport. Travel time to downtown San Francisco takes about half an hour (traffic permitting). The airport is also accessible by BART via a shuttle bus.

The cheapest way to reach downtown San Francisco is to take the shuttle bus from the Oakland Airport to **BART** (Bay Area Rapid Transit; © **510/464-6000;** www.bart.gov). The AirBART shuttle bus runs about every 15 minutes Monday through Saturday from 5am to 12:05am and Sunday from 8am to 12:05am. It makes pickups in front of terminals 1 and 2 near the ground transportation signs. Tickets must be purchased at the Oakland Airport's vending machines prior to boarding. The cost is $2 for the 10-minute ride to BART's Coliseum Station in Oakland. BART fares vary, depending on your destination; the trip to downtown San Francisco costs $3.15 and takes 15 minutes once you're on board. The entire excursion should take around 45 minutes.

Taxis from the Oakland Airport to downtown San Francisco are expensive—approximately $50, plus tip.

Bayporter Express (© **877/467-1800** or 415/467-1800; www.bayporter.com) is a shuttle service that charges $26 for the first person and $12 for each additional person for the ride from the Oakland Airport to downtown San Francisco. Children under 12 pay $7. The fare for outer areas of San Francisco is higher. The service accepts advance reservations. To the right of the Oakland Airport exit, there are usually shuttles that take you to San Francisco for around $20 per person. The shuttles in this fleet are independently owned, and prices vary.

By Car

San Francisco is easily accessible by major highways: **I-5,** from the north, and **U.S. 101,** which cuts south-north through the peninsula from San Jose and across the Golden Gate Bridge to points north. If you drive from Los Angeles, you can take the longer coastal route (437 miles) or the inland route (389 miles). From Mendocino, it's 156 miles; from Sacramento, 88 miles; from Yosemite, 210 miles.

Point Reyes National Seashore is 30 miles northwest of San Francisco, but it takes at least 90 minutes to reach by car (the small towns slow you down). The easiest route is Sir Francis Drake Boulevard from U.S. 101 south of San Rafael; it takes its time to Point Reyes, but it's without detours. For a longer, more scenic route, take the Stinson Beach/Hwy. 1 exit off U.S. 101 south of Sausalito onto Hwy. 1 north.

By Train

Traveling by train takes a long time and usually costs as much as, or more than, flying. Still, if you want to take a leisurely ride across America, rail may be a good option.

San Francisco–bound **Amtrak** (© **800/872-7245** or 800/USA-RAIL; www.amtrak.com) trains leave from New York and cross the country via Chicago. The journey takes about 3½ days, and seats sell quickly. At this writing, the lowest round-trip fare costs about $300 from New York and $270 from Chicago. Round-trip tickets from Los Angeles range from $120 to as much as $200. Trains arrive in Emeryville, just north of Oakland, and connect with regularly scheduled buses to San Francisco's Ferry Building and the Caltrain Station in downtown San Francisco.

VISITOR INFORMATION

The **San Francisco Visitor Information Center,** on the lower level of Hallidie Plaza, 900 Market St., at Powell Street (© **415/391-2000;** www.onlyinsanfrancisco.com), is the best source of specialized information about the city. Even if you don't have a specific question, you might want to request the free *Visitors Planning Guide* and the *San Francisco Visitors* kit. The kit includes a 6-month calendar of events; a city history; shopping and dining information; several good, clear maps; plus lodging information. The bureau highlights only its members' establishments, so if it doesn't have what you're looking for, that doesn't mean it's nonexistent.

You can also get the latest on San Francisco at the following online addresses:

The *Bay Guardian,* the city's free weekly paper: **www.sfbg.com**
SF Gate, the city's *Chronicle* newspaper: **www.sfgate.com**
CitySearch: **http://sanfrancisco.citysearch.com**

If you're traveling to Point Reyes, stop at the **Bear Valley Visitor Center** (✆ **415/464-5100;** www.nps.gov/pore) on Bear Valley Road (look for the small sign just north of Olema on Hwy. 1) and pick up a free Point Reyes trail map. The rangers are helpful and can answer your questions about the national seashore. Be sure to check out the great natural history and cultural displays, as well. It's open Monday through Friday from 9am to 5pm; Saturday, Sunday, and holidays from 8am to 5pm. Websites with information about Point Reyes include www.pointreyes.net and www.pointreyes.org.

LANDS END

Difficulty rating: Moderate

Distance: 8 miles round-trip from Cliff House to Golden Gate Bridge

Estimated time: 2½ hr.

Elevation gain: Minimal

Cost/permits: None

Best time to go: Late afternoon, year round

Website: www.nps.gov/goga

Recommended map: National Park Service Golden Gate National Recreation Area

Trail head GPS: N37 46.644, W 122 30.559

Trail head directions: From Hwy. 101 (Van Ness Blvd.) in the city, turn west on Geary Blvd. and follow it to its end. As the road turns south toward Ocean Beach, you'll see Cliff House on your right.

This coastal hike, a scenic and historic journey from Cliff House to the Golden Gate, is the wildest natural place in San Francisco. Hikers will encounter awesome panoramic vistas from three publicly accessible observation decks. Seal Rocks, frequented by seals and noisy sea lions; the Marin Headlands; and the wide blue Pacific are all part of the stunning views.

Today's Cliff House, perched above Ocean Beach, is the fourth structure erected on this site. In 1863, the first roadhouse was built; it catered to the wealthy, high-toned carriage crowd. Along came millionaire and philanthropist Adolph Sutro, who had moved to San Francisco after making his fortune as an engineer during Nevada's silver-strike era. Sutro thought that the city's working-class residents would enjoy a seaside diversion of public pools. Thus, not only did he build the pools, he also built a steam railway from downtown to the coast; the ride to Cliff House cost a nickel.

After the original Cliff House, called Seal Rock House, burned down, Sutro replaced it with a six-story gingerbread-style Victorian mansion. This, too, burned to the ground in 1907. Sutro again rebuilt, this time constructing a rather utilitarian structure.

After many years of planning and 2 years of renovation, the latest incarnation of Cliff house re-opened in 2004. This new and greatly updated Cliff House boasts two bars, two restaurants, and a terrace available for sunset wedding ceremonies and other private parties. Architectural elements from the 1909 design, as well as some inspiration from the old Sutro Baths, were incorporated into Cliff House IV.

After you've enjoyed the many attractions of Cliff House, walk northeast a short distance to the Greco-Roman-like ruins of the Sutro Baths. Here, six saltwater swimming pools and a freshwater plunge were once heated by a complex series of pipes and canals. Museums, galleries, and restaurants were also part of the complex built by Adolph Sutro in 1890. The popularity of public spas gradually waned and, in 1966, fire destroyed all but the cement foundations of the baths.

❶ Coastal Trail Wander north over to the Merrie Way parking area and join Coastal Trail. For a time, you'll be walking on the abandoned bed of the old Cliff House and Ferries Railroad. The trail winds through cypress and coastal sage, and hugs the cliffs below El Camino del Mar.

Coastal Trail leads along the Lincoln Park Bluffs. If it's low tide when you look down at the shoreline, you might be able to spot the wreckage of some of the ships that have been dashed to pieces on the rocks below. This rocky, precipitous stretch of coast is known as Lands End.

❷ Lands End You'll get great views from the Eagle Point Lookout, then briefly join El Camino Del Mar through the wealthy Seacliff residential area. A quarter-mile of travel (keep bearing left) brings you to sandy China Beach, the site of an encampment for Chinese fishermen a century ago. The beach is also known as James Phelan Beach for the politician/philanthropist who left part of his fortune to help California writers and artists.

❸ Baker Beach Backtrack to Sea Cliff Avenue, following the westernmost lanes of this fancy residential area, and continue north a short half-mile to expansive Baker Beach. At the south end of the beach is the outlet of Lobos Creek.

In his autobiography, Ansel Adams recalled the many delightful days he spent as a child exploring Lobos Creek. These childhood adventures were the great nature photographer's first contact with the natural world.

At the north end of Baker Beach is Battery Chamberlain, a former coastal defense site, complete with a "disappearing" 95,000-pound cannon. Occasionally, park interpreters demonstrate how the cannon could be cranked into its cement, tree-hidden bunker.

Follow the beach service road up through the cypress to Lincoln Boulevard. Coastal Trail is a bit sketchy as it follows the boulevard's guard rail for a half-mile of contouring along the cliffs. The trail meanders among cypress and passes more military installations—Batteries Crosby, Dynamite, and Marcus Miller.

❹ Golden Gate Bridge Beyond the last battery, Coastal Trail leads under the Golden Gate Bridge. Just after the trail passes under the bridge, you can follow a path to historic Fort Point.

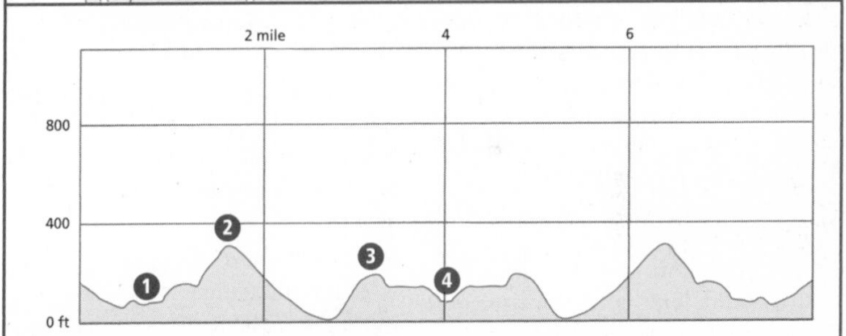

N 37 46.644, W 122 30.559: Trail head

❶ N 37 46.867, W 122 30.705 (0.7 miles): Join Coastal Trail at Merrie Way parking area

❷ N 37 47.273, W 122 30.344 (1.7 miles): Eagle Point lookout

❸ N 37 47.490, W 122 29.088 (3.3 miles): Follow Sea Cliff Ave. to Baker Beach

❹ N 37 48.631, W 122 28.616 (4.0 miles): Trail passes under Golden Gate Bridge

SAN FRANCISCO'S PRESIDIO ★ Kids

Difficulty rating: Easy

Distance: 2 miles round-trip

Estimated time: 1 hr.

Elevation gain: 300 ft.

Cost/permits: None

Best time to go: Year round

Websites: www.nps.gov/goga; www.presidio.gov; www.nps.gov/prsf

Recommended map: National Park Service Golden Gate National Recreation Area

Trail head GPS: N 37 47.531, W 122 27.495

Trail head directions: From the Presidio's Arguello Gate entrance, just north of Arguello Blvd. and Jackson St., drive a few hundred yards to the paved parking area on the right, at Inspiration Point. The trail head is on the east side.

The Presidio, a historic military post turned parkland, inhabits some 1,600 acres of real estate in one of America's most desirable cities. This loop trail explores architecture and military history, and also offers a nice walk in the woods.

After a century and a half of use, the U.S. Army transferred ownership of San Francisco's historic Presidio to the National Park Service in 1994. Of the many Army bases across the U.S. shut down during a decade of such closures, the Presidio was the only military installation to become part of the park system.

The Park Service manages the Presidio in partnership with the Presidio Trust, a federal government corporation. With the trust managing the interior and the majority of the buildings, and the Park Service responsible for the coastal areas, the agencies team to enhance natural areas, renovate and maintain buildings, upgrade the Presidio trail system, and offer visitor programs.

The Park Service and the Presidio Trust aim to rehabilitate the best of the Presidio's historic buildings, as well as to restore the woodlands and native dune vegetation. The Presidio hosts an astonishing number (280) species of native plants. More than 200 species of birds have been sighted in this urban refuge, which offers habitat to a variety of mammals and reptiles.The best place to begin a hiking tour of the Presidio is near Inspiration Point, at the southeastern corner of the Presidio, on the Ecology Trail. If you have young ones in tow, pick up a copy of "Kids on Trails," a free children's tour guide to activities along the Ecology Trail.

From the parking area, walk down a set of wooden steps and turn left to join Ecology Trail, a wide dirt trail (fire road). After passing Inspiration Point, you'll make a gradual descent through groves of Monterey pine and eucalyptus. The buildings of the Main Post lie ahead.

❶ Main Post The Presidio's oldest existing structures, dating back to 1861 and the Civil War, are found on Main Post, as is the Visitor Center, located in the former Presidio Officers' Club.

Now, the path is paved. Pass Pershing Hall—a bachelor officers' quarters—and continue along the sidewalk on Funston Avenue. Officers' Quarters, a splendid row of Victorians that housed officers and their families, is another historic area on Funston Avenue.

❷ Lover's Lane Turn right at Presidio Avenue and continue over a footbridge. Cross MacArthur and continue on to paved Lovers' Lane. The lane has been a favorite of romantic walkers ever since the 1860s, when it was used by off-duty soldiers to walk into town to meet their sweethearts.

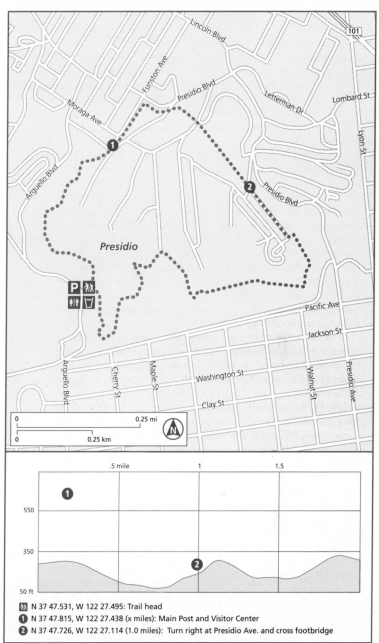

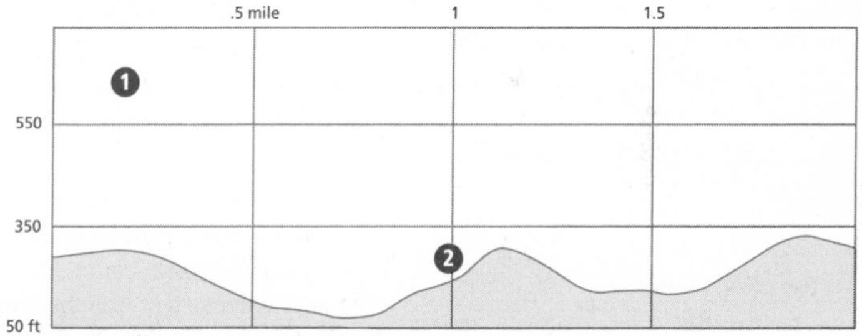

N 37 47.531, W 122 27.495: Trail head

1 N 37 47.815, W 122 27.438 (x miles): Main Post and Visitor Center

2 N 37 47.726, W 122 27.114 (1.0 miles): Turn right at Presidio Ave. and cross footbridge

The Presidio

A little more than a decade after its formation, the urban national park reached a milestone: It began to pay for itself. Some 2,500 residents rent housing ranging from converted barracks to renovated officers quarters. A free shuttle system connects residents from the Presidio's 21 neighborhoods to nearby public transit.

The Presidio is home to a significant number of quality profit-making and non-profit enterprises. Filmmaker George Lucas' Letterman Digital Arts Center opened for business in 2005 on the site of an old army hospital. The Thoreau Center for Sustainability houses 50 community and environmental organizations.

Not everyone is altogether pleased by such developments, though most of the local citizenry and visitors seem to be taking the Presidio's extreme makeover in stride. As buildings are restored, so too are landscapes, including hiking trails, wildlife habitat, and the unique urban forest.

Several periods of architecture are represented in the Presidio, ranging from red brick barracks (circa 1895) built in the Georgian style to a Spanish Revival–style theater. Some experts rate the Victorian-era officers' homes along Funston Avenue among the best examples of that period in San Francisco.

Environmentally conscious before his time, Army Major W.A. Jones is credited with initiating a forestry program in the 1880s that transformed the forlorn, windswept sand dunes into the wooded preserve it is today. Thousands of trees, native and not, were planted under the direction of the Army Corps of Engineers: Acacia, eucalyptus, Monterey pine, redwood, madrone, and many more species. Some areas were planted in straight rows and now appear like companies of soldiers standing in formation.

Once landscaped, the Presidio proved to be one of the most highly desirable stateside locations for a soldier's assignment. Although the base was used mainly as a medical facility and administration center, during World War II, its coastal batteries were activated in order to defend the Golden Gate Bridge against possible enemy attack.

Even before the Presidio became part of Golden Gate National Recreation Area, San Franciscans in the know enjoyed limited public access. Now, the walker can wander at will over a network of paved roads, sidewalks, and footpaths.

The Visitor Center, located at the former Officers' Club (Building 50 at Moraga Ave.), is your source for Presidio information, including books, free maps, and brochures. It's open daily 9am to 5pm.

A gradual uphill grade leads near the historic site of El Polin Springs, used by Spanish soldiers more than 200 years ago. During the summer, archaeology students conduct ongoing excavations of the site.

The slope above the springs is serpentine grasslands, and is home to many rare or threatened plants, including the endangered Presidio clarkia. More than two dozen varieties of trees can be seen along the trail. Continue up the trail to the base of Inspiration Point and follow your route back to the parking lot.

Extend your walk by joining the 11 miles of hiking trails that cross the Presidio, including portions of the Coastal Trail, Bay Area Ridge Trail, Bay Trail, and Anza National Historic Trail.

GOLDEN GATE PROMENADE

Difficulty rating: Moderate

Distance: 7 miles round-trip from Fort Mason to Golden Gate Bridge

Estimated time: 4 hr.

Elevation gain: None

Cost/permits: None

Best time to go: Brisk winter or fall day

Website: www.nps.gov/goga

Recommended map: National Park Service Golden Gate National Recreation Area

Trail head GPS: N 37 48.649, W 122 28.601

Trail head directions: Fort Mason and parking lots maintained by the Golden Gate National Recreation Area are free. Enter Fort Mason at Franklin and Bay sts. If you happen to snag a parking space near Fisherman's Wharf, keep it and begin walking the promenade from that famed attraction.

Surely, one of the most memorable shore walks in San Francisco is along Golden Gate Promenade. Along the 4-mile path extending from Aquatic Park to Golden Gate Bridge is a rich diversity of historical, architectural, and cultural attractions complemented by a sandy beach, vast waterfront green, and inspiring vistas of the Golden Gate Bridge and Marin Headlands.

You can't miss Golden Gate Promenade. Just look for its logo: a blue and white sailboat emblem. On a stroll along the promenade, you can see several periods of military history from the early airfield at Crissy Field to that Civil War–era brick fortress, Fort Point.

Fort Mason (well worth a walk all by itself) has evolved into the north shore's culture capital. The piers and warehouses of Fort Mason Center host theater performances, live radio shows, environmental education seminars, and many kinds of recreational activities. Golden Gate National Recreation Area headquarters is at Fort Mason, too. Obtain a map from the white, three-story structure, one of many historic buildings at Fort Mason.

❶ Marina Green From Fort Mason, you may walk along Marina Boulevard or across Marina Green, but the paved pathway along the bay shore is the best way to go. Sunbathers enjoy snuggling into one of the hollows of grassy Marina Green to get out of the wind, which is considerable—to the delight of kite fliers.

At St. Francis Yacht Harbor, notice the sea wall, which offers a great stroll; at its end is a wave organ, which when the tide is right, serenades walkers with the sounds of San Francisco Bay.

The promenade joins Marina Boulevard for a time, passing some Mediterranean-style haciendas and nearing that glorious reminder of the 1915 Panama Pacific Exposition—the Palace of Fine Arts and its superb, hands-on science exhibits in the Exploratorium.

❷ Crissy Field Resuming a more bayside route, Golden Gate Promenade leads along Crissy Field, an airfield used by the U.S. Army from 1921 until 1936 and named to honor Major Dana Crissy. Besides nostalgia for the early days of aviation, Crissy Field also boasts San Francisco's north shore's most pristine stretch of beach. The low dunes bordering the beach are dotted with native grasses.

A spectacular transformation occurred on the once-degraded 100 acres of Crissy Field shoreline. Now a restored salt marsh, the walking and biking paths, and native

Golden Gate Promenade

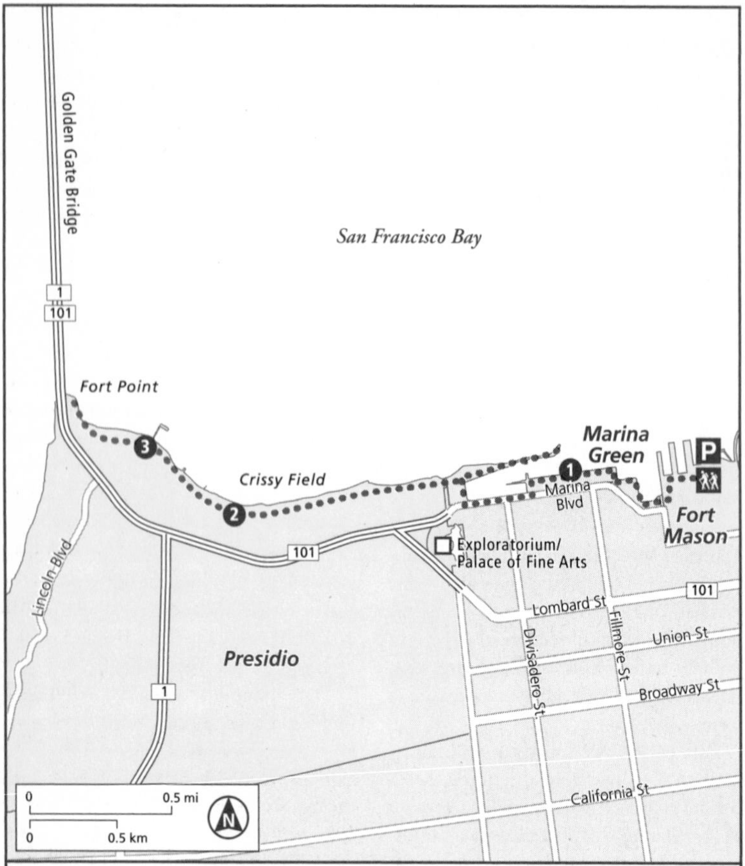

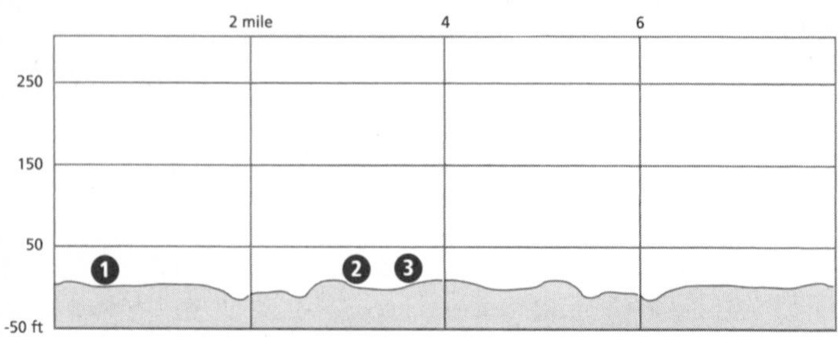

N 37 48.649, W 122 28.601: Trail head

❶ N 37 48.426, W 122 26.351 (0.6 miles): Follow paved pathway along the bay shore

❷ N 37 48.275, W 122 27.842 (3.0 miles): Crissy Field

❸ N 37 48.505, W 122 28.242 (3.6 miles): Warming hut at west end of Crissy Field, near fishing pier

plants, extend from Marina Green to the foot of the Golden Gate Bridge. A world-class board-sailing area borders Crissy Field. Between 1998 and 2000, individuals and groups from schools, corporations, and civic organizations planted more than 100,000 native plants in an area formerly occupied by military buildings and asphalt.

The promenade is a popular place to exercise. San Franciscans jog, walk, run, and triathlon here. Some stop at the exercise stations en route. Rare is the time when the area isn't filled with athletic Bay Area residents pursuing their aerobic conditioning.

Located near the fishing pier at the west end of Crissy Field is the warm and welcoming **Warming Hut,** a café and bookstore. Enjoy excellent hot coffee and cocoa, as well as soups and sandwiches, at this hospitable refuge from the often-bracing and sometimes-biting cold.

❸ **Fort Point** Continue past the Warming Hut towards Fort Point ahead. Join the Coastal Trail on a short climb to Battery East, one of many such Bay Area batteries, part of the historic coastal defense system. Make another easy ascent to the parking area of the south viewpoint at the Golden Gate Bridge. Continue on the Coastal Trail, enjoying excellent vistas of the Civil War–era Fort Point, to the toll plaza at the San Francisco end of the Golden Gate Bridge.

With so much to see, your return route will be as fascinating as the first half of your walk. If you take this walk on a late (fog-free) afternoon, you might view a glorious sunset behind the Golden Gate Bridge and the bright lights of the city as you return.

Once back at Fort Mason, don't miss the opportunity to walk the shoreline east to Aquatic Park, which has benches, lawns, and a sandy beach on the bay.

Near the park stands—well, floats—another national park system attraction off the promenade: San Francisco Maritime National Historic Park. Once part of the Golden Gate National Recreation Area, it's now an independent unit that includes a museum and a collection of historic ships.

The maritime museum is housed in a onetime 1930s bathhouse, built in the form of a luxury ocean liner. Stainless steel railings and portholes add to the nautical look of the structure. Inside are exhibits interpreting a century and a half of California seafaring—from the ships that carried gold-seeking 49ers to whaling boats, yachts, and ferries.

Park visitors can step aboard (admission fee) a half-dozen historic vessels, including the 1895 schooner *C.A. Thayer* and the 1907 steam tug *Hercules.*

And don't miss—not that you could—Fisherman's Wharf, San Francisco's most popular destination, known for its delicious seafood, historic waterfront, and grand views of San Francisco Bay.

GOLDEN GATE BRIDGE ★★ Kids

Difficulty rating: Easy

Distance: 3 miles round-trip across the Golden Gate from Fort Point to Vista Point

Estimated time: 1½ hr.

Elevation gain: None

Cost/permits: None

Best time to go: Year round, especially at sunset

Website: www.nps.gov/goga

Recommended map: National Park Service Golden Gate National Recreation Area

Trail head GPS: N 37 48.649, W 122 28.600

Trail head directions: Parking is available in the parking lot on the southeast side of the bridge. Northbound travelers should take the last San Francisco exit off Hwy. 101. ***Warning:*** First-time visitors often miss the viewpoint parking area just south of the toll plaza, and before they know it, they end up in Sausalito. Fort Point's parking lot is one good place to leave your vehicle, as are otherparking lots along the bay.

It's known as one of the world's engineering marvels, the proud emblem of a proud city, and "The Bridge at the End of the Continent." The Golden Gate is all of this—and a great walk: It is one of those must-do-once-in-a-lifetime adventures. For all its utilitarian value, the bridge is an artistic triumph. As you walk the bridge, try to remember how many set-in–San Francisco movies and television shows have opened with an establishing shot of the bridge.

Guarding the Golden Gate is Fort Point, a huge Civil War–era structure built of red brick. The fort, similar in design to Fort Sumter in South Carolina, was built for the then-astronomical cost of $2.8 million and was intended to ensure California's loyalty to the union.

❶ Fort Point Begin at Fort Point, part of Golden Gate National Recreation Area. The fort boasts several fine military exhibits, including one emphasizing the contributions of African-American soldiers. Visitors enjoy prowling the three-story fort's many corridors and stairwells. From 1933 to 1937, the fort was the coordinating center for the bridge construction.

From Fort Point, a gravel, then paved, road leads up to a statue of visionary engineer Joseph Strauss, who persuaded a doubting populace to build the bridge. If you want to make a souvenir stop and get that Golden Gate Bridge towel set, tote bag, fridge magnet, mouse pad, or whatever, detour over to the Gift Center, located in the historic "Roundhouse" building on the southeast side of the Golden Gate Bridge Toll Plaza. Designed in 1938, the Roundhouse was originally a restaurant for passing motorists.

> As you start walking along the bridge's east sidewalk, you'll get a great view of Fort Point located far below. Pause frequently to watch the ship traffic: yachts, tankers, tug boats, ferries, and passenger liners. Literally everything necessary for modern life, from California almonds to Japanese cars, passes in and out of the bay by freighter.

❷ Crossing the Bridge While the walk across the bridge is unique and the clear-day views grand, the trip can also be wearing on the nerves. A bone-chilling wind often buffets bridge walkers, and traffic vibrating the bridge also seems to vibrate one's very being. Judging by the number of pedestrians who walk near the traffic lanes, rather than by the bridge rails, most of the people who cross the Golden Gate on foot are likely afraid of heights.

The technically-inclined revel in the bridge's vital statistics: its 8,981-foot length, cables that support 200 million pounds, twin towers the height of 65-story buildings. Statisticians have calculated everything from the number of gallons of International Orange paint required to cover 10 million square feet of bridge to

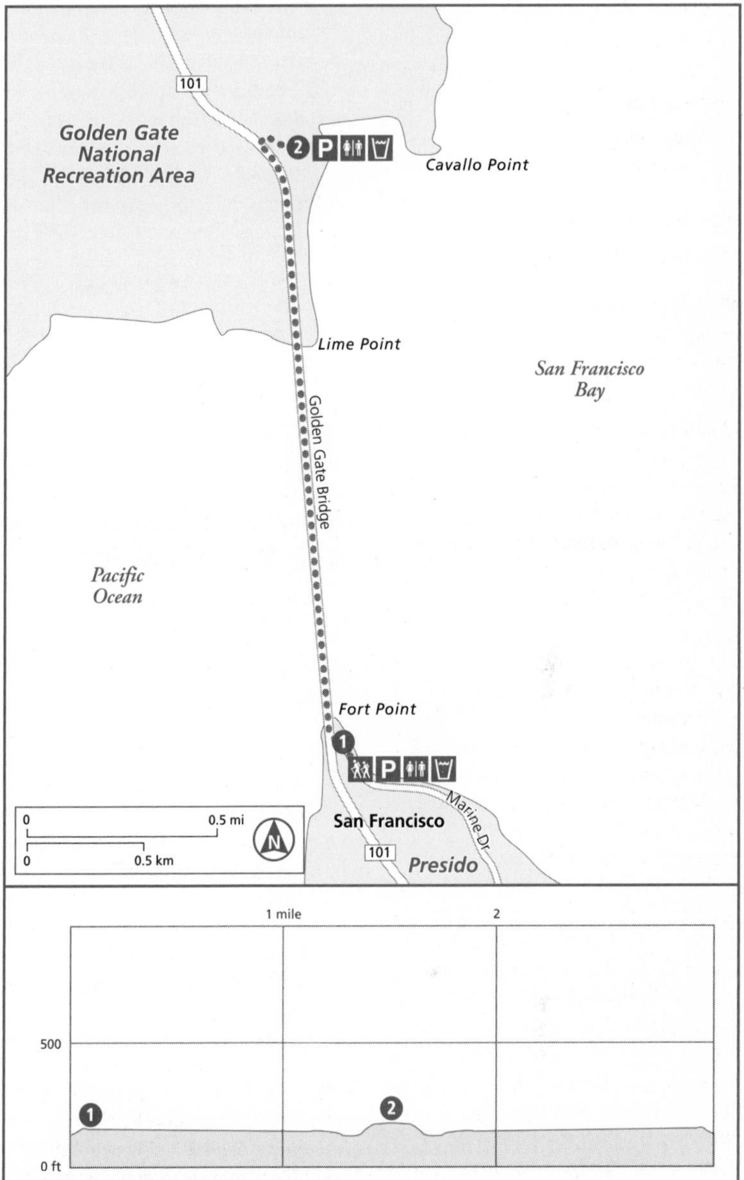

N 37 48.649, W 122 28.600: Trail head
❶ N 37 48.639, W 122 28.618 (0.1 miles): Follow road to statue of Joseph Strauss
❷ N 37 49.948, W 122 28.767 (1.5 miles): Retrace your steps when you reach Vista point

the number of star-crossed lovers who have leaped from bridge to bay.

The bridge spans 400 square miles of San Francisco Bay, which is really three bays—San Francisco and the smaller San Pablo and Suisun bays to the north and northeast. Geographers describe the bay as the drowned mouth and floodplain of the Sacramento–San Joaquin Rivers.

Ninety percent of California's remaining coastal wetlands are contained in San Francisco Bay and its estuaries. Shoreline development and industrial pollutants have damaged fish, shellfish, and bird populations; fortunately, a great many people care about the bay and are working hard to save and rehabilitate one of the state's most important natural resources.

For centuries, high mountains and heavy fogs concealed one of the world's great natural anchorages from passing European ships. It was a coast walker—Sergeant Jose Francisco Ortega, of the 1769 Portola overland expedition—who first sighted San Francisco Bay.

The bridge's second high tower marks the beginning of Marin County. Splendorous clear-day views include the cities of the East Bay and the bold headlands of Marin, which form the more rural part of Golden Gate National Recreation Area. You'll spot Treasure, Alcatraz, and Angel islands and, of course, the San Francisco skyline.

3 Vista Point Vista Point is the end of your bridge walk. Here, you'll witness tourists from around the world photographing each other and proclaiming their admiration for the Golden Gate in a dozen languages.

ANGEL ISLAND STATE PARK ★★ Kids

Difficulty rating: Moderate

Distance: 5 miles round-trip

Estimated time: 2½ hr.

Elevation gain: 350 ft.

Cost/permits: Ferry service (see below)

Best time to go: During the day in the warmer months; ferry service is best on weekends

Website: www.parks.ca.gov; www.angelisland.org

Recommended map: Tom Harrison Maps Angel Island

Trail head GPS: N 37 52.136, W 122 26.072

Trail head directions: For information about ferry service to the island from Tiburon, call the Angel Island–Tiburon Ferry (✆ **415/435-2131;** www.angelislandferry.com). Roundtrip fares are $14 for adults, $12 for children, and include state park admission fee.

There is also limited ferry service from San Francisco's Pier 41 via Blue and Gold Fleet (✆ **415/705-8200;** www.blueandgoldfleet.com), $21 for adults, $15 for children. The ferries land at Ayala Cove on the northwest side of the island. Park your car—for a fee—in one of Tiburon's parking lots near the waterfront or attempt to find some of the scarce free parking.

From Tiburon, just north of the Golden Gate Bridge, take a 10-minute ferry ride to Angel Island State Park, the "Jewel of San Francisco Bay." For an island barely a square mile in size, Angel Island has an extremely diverse history. Rocky coves and sandy beaches, grassy slopes and forested ridges, plus a fine trail network add up to a walker's delight.

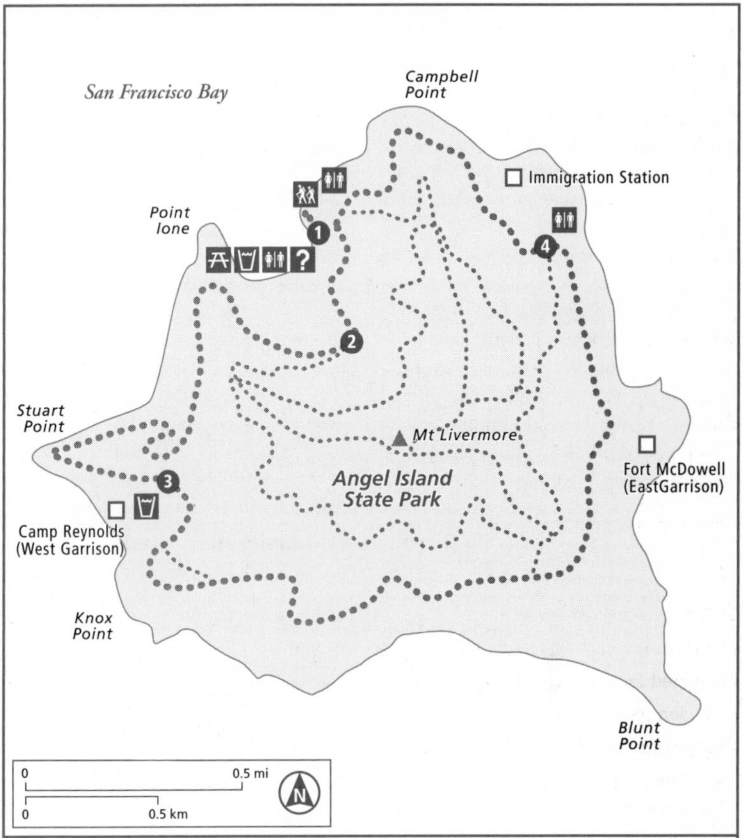

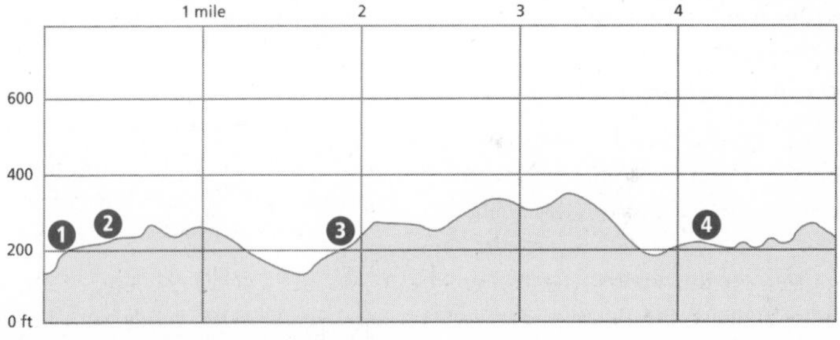

- N 37 52.135, W 122 26.071: Trail head
- ❶ N 37 52.105, W 122 26.068 (0.1 miles): Visitor Center
- ❷ N 37 51.871, W 122 25.966 (0.4 miles): Junction to Sunset trail head.
- ❸ N 37 51.613, W 122 26.431 (1.9 miles): Side road to Camp Reynolds
- ❹ N 37 52.050, W 122 25.458 (4.2 miles): Immigration Station

Over the last two centuries, the island has seen use as a pirate's supply station, a Mexican land grant, an Army artillery emplacement, and an immigrant detention center. Now, it's a state park, attracting hikers, history buffs, and islo-philes of all persuasions.

Perimeter Road takes the walker on a 5-mile tour of the island and offers a different bay view from every turn. From atop Mount Livermore, a terrific 360-degree panorama unfolds of San Francisco Bay and the Golden Gate.

When you disembark from the ferry, head for the park visitor center, located in a white building that once served as bachelor quarters for unmarried officers assigned to the U.S. Quarantine Station that operated here from 1892 to 1949. At that time, Ayala Cove was named Hospital Cove. At the visitor center, you can check out the interpretive exhibits and pick up a park map.

❶ Visitor Center A hundred years of U.S. military occupation began in 1863, when the first gun batteries were installed. The military used the island until 1962, when its Nike Missile Station was deactivated. During wartime periods, particularly during the Spanish–American War, Angel Island was one of the busiest outposts in America. The island served as a processing center for men about to be dispatched to the Philippines and as a reception/quarantine center for soldiers who returned with tropical diseases.

❷ Sunset Trailhead Walk uphill on the road to the left of the visitor center. You'll intersect Perimeter Road and the Sunset Trailhead at the top of the hill. (Sunset Trail switchbacks up steep, coastal-scrub-covered slopes, to the top of 781-foot Mount Caroline Livermore. Picnic tables have replaced the helicopter pad and radio antennae that once stood on the summit. Views of Ayala Cove, Tiburon, and the Golden Gate are memorable.)

❸ Camp Reynolds Continuing right (west) on Perimeter Road, you'll soon overlook Camp Reynolds (West Garrison). A side road leads down to the island's first military fortifications. You can walk the parade ground and see the brick hospital built in 1908. Still standing are the chapel, mule barn, barracks, and several more structures. Some of the buildings are being restored.

Perimeter Road turns eastward, contouring around chaparral-covered slopes and offering a view down to Point Blunt. You may hear and see the seals gathered around the point. The road curves north and soon arrives at East Garrison, where a collection of utilitarian-looking buildings are a reminder of the many thousands of men who were processed here. East Garrison trained about 30,000 men a year for overseas duty. The hospital, barracks, mess hall, and officers' homes still stand.

❹ Immigration Station Continue north. You'll soon come to the Immigration Station. Much recent work has been done to preserve and rehabilitate Angel Island's historic Immigration Station, named "one of America's most endangered historic places" by the National Trust for Historical Preservation.

Wrongly characterized as the "Ellis Island of the West," the station was designed mostly to process Chinese immigrants, whose entry was restricted by the Chinese Exclusion Act of 1882. More accurately called a detention facility, the station became the point of entry for some 175,000 Chinese immigrants who came to the U.S. from 1910, when the station opened, to 1943, when it closed. More than 97% of immigrants processed on Angel Island were Chinese. Processing and interrogating new arrivals took weeks, months, even a year, and many were denied entrance and returned home.

Restoration efforts focus on poems etched by the would-be Chinese immigrants into the wooden walls of the detention center. The poems, written in traditional styles, are testimony as to the reason why the immigrants came, their excitement about the new land, and their frustration and anger at long detention and difficult conditions.

Perimeter Road rounds Point Campbell, northernmost part of the island, and you'll get a glimpse of the Richmond–San Rafael Bridge and then a view of Tiburon before the road descends to Ayala Cove.

WILDCAT CANYON REGIONAL PARK

Difficulty rating: Moderate

Distance: 8 miles round-trip to Jewel Lake; 11 miles round-trip to Wildcat Peak

Estimated time: 4–5 hr.

Elevation gain: 900 ft.

Cost/permits: None

Best time to go: Winter or spring, when Wildcat Creek is flowing

Website: www.ebparks.org/parks/wildcat

Recommended map: East Bay Regional Parks District Wildcat Regional Park

Trail head GPS: N 37 57.057, W 122 18.856

Trail head directions: From east-bound I-80 in Richmond, take the Amador/Solano exit and head east on Amador St. At the second stop sign, turn right on McBryde, continuing to a stop sign and the entrance to Alvarado Park. Continue straight onto Park Ave. and travel 1/4 mile to the Wildcat Canyon parking and trail head.

Wildcat is the flip side of adjacent Tilden Park, its quiet neighbor. Wildcat is far less developed and far less visited—a park for hikers. Trails offer the only access to its oak woodlands, wide meadows, and remote canyons. A climb to the park's high points provides stellar views of the Bay Area's treasures: Mount Tamalpais, the Marin Headlands, the San Francisco skyline, the Golden Gate Bridge, lots of San Francisco Bay, and Mount Diablo.

Begin hiking along Wildcat Creek Trail, at first a wide road lined with oak, eucalyptus, and toyon.

❶ **Trail Junction** In a half mile, you'll reach a junction with Belgum Trail. If you're only up for a short hike today, hoof it 3/4 mile up Belgum Trail to a vista point. Before you return the way you came, survey the great San Francisco Bay panorama.

Continue along with one of the more handsome sections of Wildcat Creek Trail. It's the little trailside sights you remember about Wildcat Canyon: a banana slug crawling over a mossy log, a newt slithering across the trail, frogs croaking, and a variety of songbirds maintaining a subdued but steady calling from their perches in the trees.

Under one of the region's frequent blankets of fog that seals off the park from all sight and sound of civilization, hikers imagine they are trekking in a remote wilderness, rather than a canyon located less than a mile as the red-tail hawk flies from I-80 and the city of Richmond.

❷ **Junction with Mezue Trail** At the 2-mile mark, the trail passes a junction with Mezue Trail, a path that climbs from the canyon to San Pablo Ridge. After another 1/4 mile, the trail crosses a bridge over Wildcat Creek and soon thereafter climbs very briefly to a three-way intersection.

❸ **Tilden Regional Park** Stick with Wildcat Creek Trail and hike another 1.2 miles and cross the boundary into Tilden Regional Park.

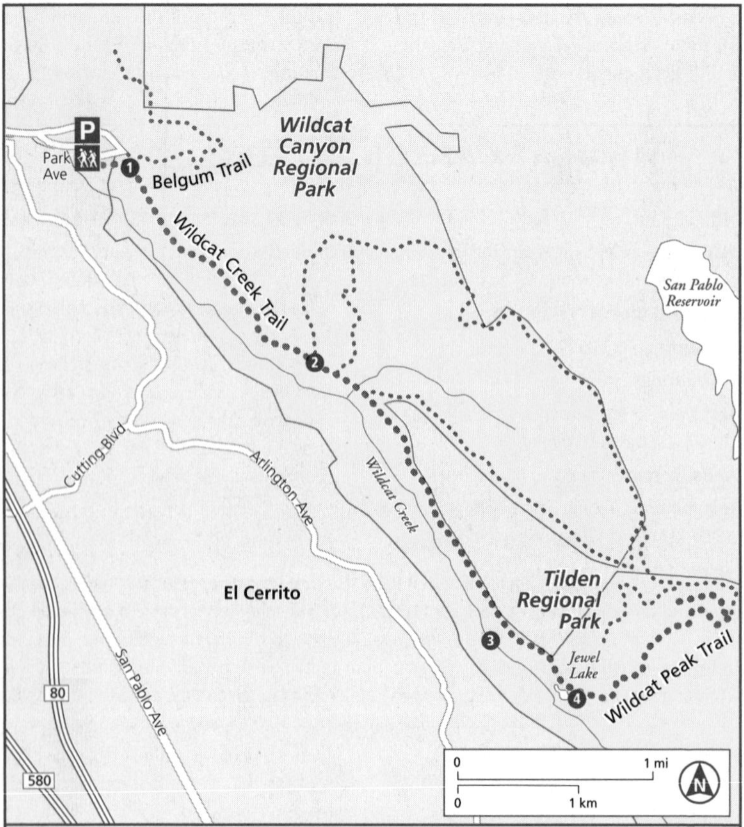

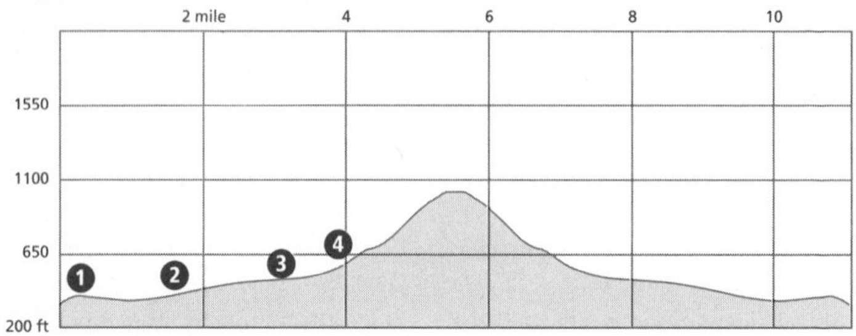

N 37 57.057, W 122 18.856: Trail head

1. N 37 57.046, W 122 18.657 (0.3 miles): Stay on Wildcat Creek Trail at junction with Belgum
2. N 37 56.124, W 122 17.532 (1.8 miles): Pass junction with Mezue Trail, then cross bridge over creek after ¼ mile
3. N 37 55.234, W 122 16.682 (3.2 miles): Cross boundary into Tilden Regional Park
4. N 37 54.744, W 122 16.108 (4.0 miles): Join Wildcat Peak Trail

Tilden Regional Park and its wilder neighbor, Wildcat Canyon Regional Park, form a microcosm of the country's most pedestrian-friendly local park systems—the East Bay Regional Park District.

Mention "Tilden Park" to an East Bay resident, past or present, and it invariably brings forth a pleasant memory: the antique merry-go-round, the Botanic Garden, the golf course, or Lake Anza with its popular beach.

Hikers have a good time in Tilden, too. The experience is usually more social than solitary because the hiker often shares the trail with joggers and dog-walkers.

Tilden is tucked in a valley, bounded by San Pablo Ridge to the east and Berkeley Hills to the west. Shading trails and picnic areas are native forests of oak and bay, as well as planted stands of eucalyptus and Monterey pine. The park is full of contrasts: wild, brushy slopes and irrigated lawns, seasonal creeks, and artificial lakes. Tilden is no wilderness, but it does promote ecological values and learning with classes and exhibits at the Environmental Education Center. The center is also the trail head for several family-friendly nature trails and the terminus or starting point for the 4.5-mile one-way hike through Wildcat Canyon.

From the Wildcat-Tilden border, another 3/4-mile of travel on Wildcat Creek Trail leads to Jewel Lake (rather a grandiose name for a duck pond). A mile-long, self-guided nature trail loops around Jewel Lake

❹ Wildcat Peak Trail At the lake, the trail meets signed Wildcat Peak Trail. Ascend 1 1/2 miles amidst eucalyptus groves and brush to Wildcat Peak, the park's 1,250-foot high point.

> Excellent vistas reward the hiker from Wildcat Peak: Mount Tamalpais, the San Francisco skyline, the Golden Gate Bridge, lots of San Francisco Bay, and Mount Diablo. Near the summit is a grove of sequoias that honor the world's peacemakers.

MOUNT DIABLO ★

Difficulty rating: Moderate

Distance: 7 miles round-trip

Estimated time: 4 hr.

Elevation gain: 1,300 ft.

Cost/permits: $6 California State Park entry fee

Best time to go: October to May

Website: www.parks.ca.gov

Recommended map: California State Parks Mount Diablo State Park

Trail head GPS: N 37 53.711, W 121 55.444

Trail head directions: Follow I-680 north from the Pleasanton/Dublin area. Exit on Diablo Blvd. in Danville, traveling to the east. Diablo Rd. makes several turns en route to Mount Diablo Scenic Dr. Continue on Diablo Rd. past a fire station on the right until you reach Mount Diablo Scenic Dr. Turn left and follow this road into the park. To reach the summit, turn right on Summit Rd. at the Junction Ranger office.

From the Golden Gate to the Farallon Islands, from the High Sierra to the Central Valley—this is the sweeping panorama you can savor from atop Mount Diablo. Geographers claim that hikers can see more of the Earth's surface from the top of Mount Diablo than from any other peak in the world with only one exception: Africa's legendary 19,340-foot Mount Kilimanjaro.

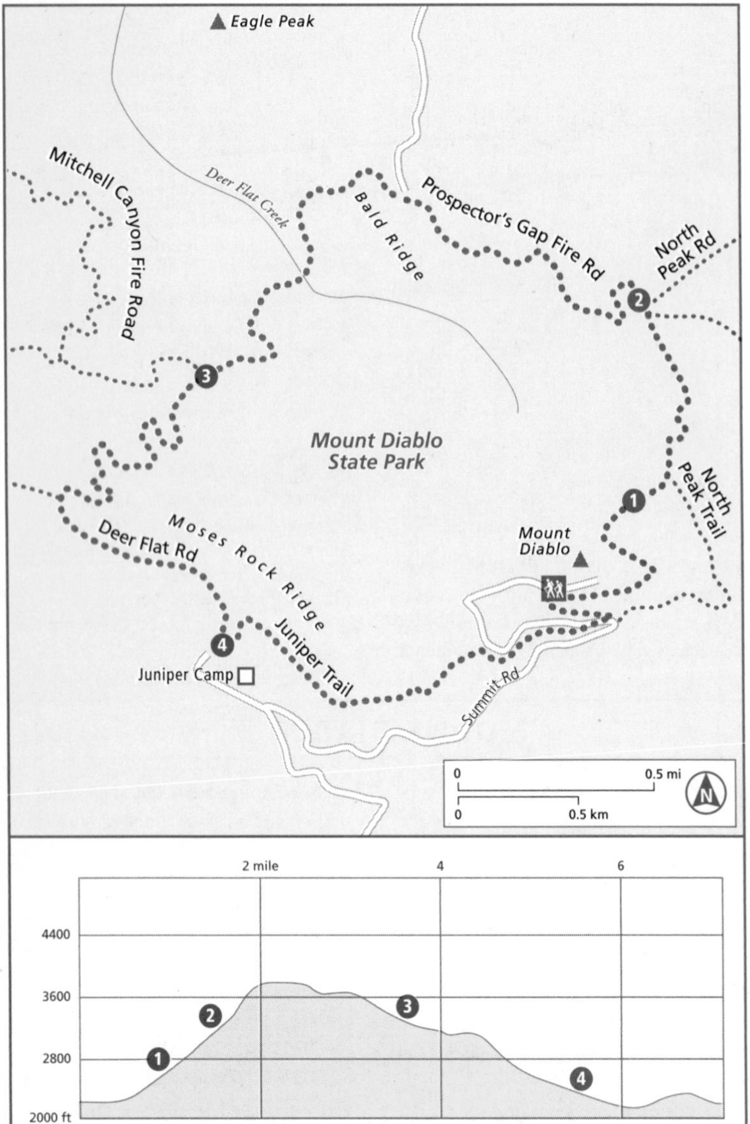

N 37 53.710, W 121 55.443: Trail head

1. N 37 53.052, W 121 54.788 (1.0 miles): Join the North Peak Trail
2. N 37 53.479, W 121 54.796 (1.6 miles): At 4-way junction, take Prospector's Gap Fire Road west
3. N 37 53.322, W 121 56.024 (3.8 miles): Join Deer Flat Road and bear left
4. N 37 52.713, W 121 55.986 (5.5 miles): Juniper Picnic Area

Mount Diablo

Several colorful yarns describe how the mountain got its name. The most popular account supposedly arose from an 1806 expedition of Spanish soldiers from San Francisco Presidio who marched into the area to do battle with the local Indians. In the midst of the fighting, a shaman clad in striking plumage appeared on the mountain. The Spaniards were convinced they saw Diablo—the Devil—and quickly retreated.

In 1851, Mount Diablo's summit, long a landmark for California explorers, was established as the official base point for California land surveys. Even today, Mount Diablo's base line and meridian lines are used in legal descriptions of much California real estate.

Toll roads up the mountain were opened in the 1870s, and a fancy hotel was built. In order to make their California holiday complete, tourists of the time just *had* to climb Mount Diablo and take in the majestic view.

In 1931, the upper slopes of Mount Diablo were preserved as a state park. In more recent years, the lower slopes were added to the park, thanks in a large measure to the efforts of Save Mount Diablo, a local conservation organization.

Today, Mount Diablo State Park consists of some 19,000 acres of oak woodland, grassland, and chaparral. Stands of knobcone and Coulter pine, as well as scattered gray pine, are found all over the mountain.

A great way to tour the park is to follow what park rangers call "The Grand Loop," a 7-mile circuit that connects several trails and fire roads and offers views of—and from—Diablo in every direction.

Plan to spend some time on Mount Diablo's summit, partaking of the view. Locator maps help you identify cities and natural features near and far. The far-reaching panorama from Mount Diablo is all the more impressive, considering the mountain's relatively short (elevation 3,849 ft.) height. Two reasons for the grand views: 1) the mountain rises abruptly from its surroundings, and 2) the land surrounding the mountain—the San Francisco Bay and Central Valley—is nearly flat.

Mount Diablo boasts some fine trails, but even the most ardent hiker will admit the state park is primarily oriented to the automobile. Something of the majesty of conquering Diablo is lost for hikers when they're joined at the top by dozens of visitors stepping from their cars.

Still, there are plenty of places on Diablo's flanks where cars can't go, as we shall soon see.

After taking in the view, join Summit Trail, descending from the southeast side of the lower lot, which in a quarter mile, meets North Peak Trail, also located by the paved road.

❶ **North Peak Trail** Summit Trail heads southwest down the mountain, but you join the eastward-trending trail to North Peak.

Enjoy the awesome view of the Central Valley as you march over a rocky, juniper-dotted slope. The red-brown rock formation above looks more than a little diabolical; the most prominent rock formation is known as Devil's Pulpit.

❷ **Prospector's Gap** North Peak Trail descends to a distinct saddle, Prospectors Gap, and a four-way junction, $1^1/_2$ miles from the trail head. Take signed Prospector's Gap Fire Road west to an intersection with northbound Donner Creek Fire Road, whereupon the route continues west as Meridian Ridge Fire Road.

Passing a junction with Eagle Peak Trail, the fire road bends south, crosses Deer Flat Creek, and reaches Deer Flat, a pleasant rest stop shaded by blue oak, located at about the 4-mile mark of this hike.

3 Deer Flat Road Begin a moderately steep mile-long ascent to reach Deer Flat Road and bear left (southeast), savoring the views and (in springtime) wildflowers.

> Botanists say Mount Diablo's slopes support one of the Bay Area's greatest numbers of flowering plants. In springtime, meadows blossom with buttercups, blue-eyed grass, and blue dicks. Other common blooms include Indian paintbrush, clarkia, larkspur, and California fuchsia. The keen-eyed wildflower lover might even spot the rare Mount Diablo globe lily, a squat yellow flower with a blossom shaped like a small lantern; it grows only on and around the mountain.

Consider, as you ascend, that geologically speaking, Mount Diablo is an odd duck indeed. The hiker climbs over successively older and older rocks on the way to the summit; this is exactly the opposite of the usual progression. Much of Diablo's sedimentary rock, which long ago formed an ancient sea bed, has been tilted, turned upside down and pushed up by a plug of hard red Franciscan rock.

4 Juniper Campground Another mile of hiking brings you to Juniper Picnic Area and Campground. From the campground, join Juniper Trail, which climbs a ridge cloaked with oak and chaparral to reach Summit Road and a short path leading to the lower parking lot.

TENNESSEE VALLEY ★★★

Difficulty rating: Easy to Tennessee Cove, moderate to Muir Beach

Distance: 4 miles round-trip from Tennessee Valley to Tennessee Cove; 9 miles round-trip to Muir Beach

Estimated time: 1½–2 hr. to Tennessee Cove; 4–5 hr. to Muir Beach

Elevation gain: 550 ft.

Cost/permits: None

Best time to go: Year round

Website: www.nps.gov/goga

Recommended map: National Park Service Golden Gate National Recreation Area

Trail head GPS: N 37 51.623, W 122 32.178

Trail head directions: From Hwy. 101 north of the Golden Gate Bridge, take the Hwy. 1 exit. Follow the highway a half-mile, turn left on Tennessee Valley Rd., and follow this road to the trail head and parking area.

The walk through Tennessee Valley to the shore is suitable for the whole family. More intrepid walkers will join Coastal Trail for an up-and-down journey to Muir Beach, a wide windswept beach and a hamlet highlighted by the Pelican Inn. Make lunch at the inn part of your intinerary—you'll think you're back in Merry Olde England.

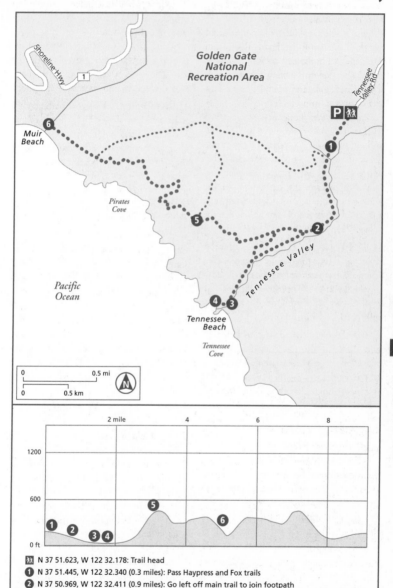

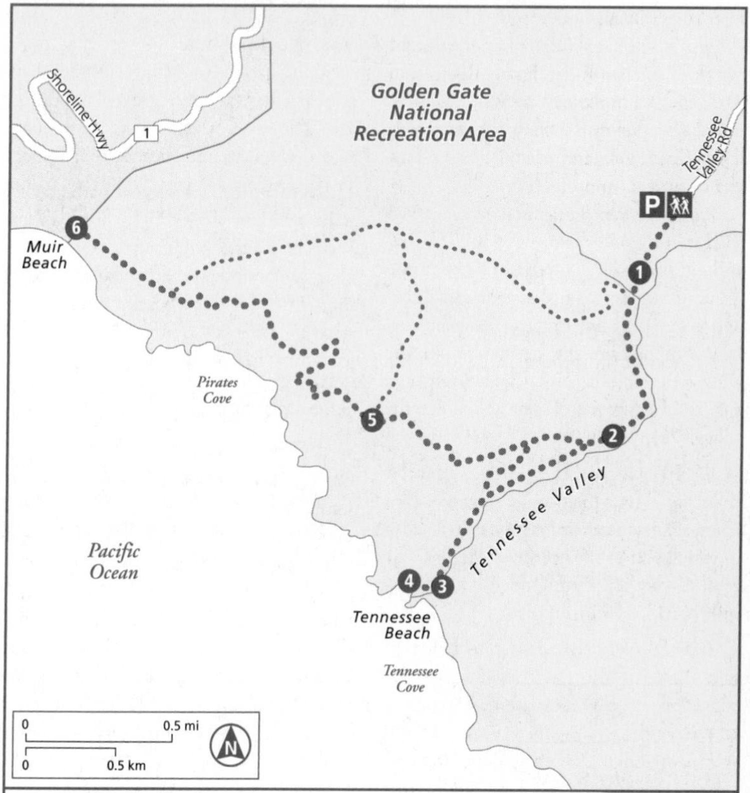

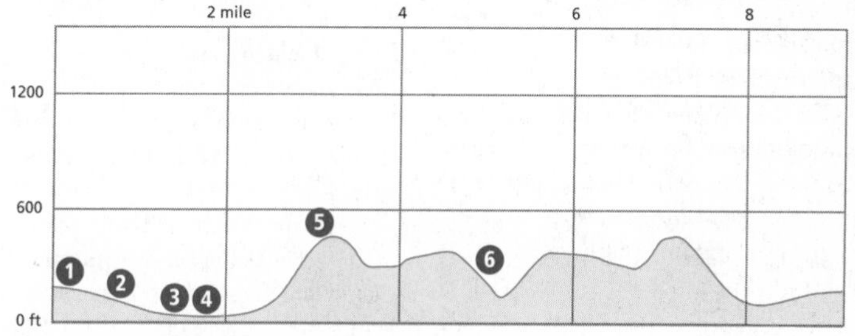

🥾 N 37 51.623, W 122 32.178: Trail head

1. N 37 51.445, W 122 32.340 (0.3 miles): Pass Haypress and Fox trails
2. N 37 50.969, W 122 32.411 (0.9 miles): Go left off main trail to join footpath
3. N 37 50.521, W 122 33.112 (1.7 miles): Follow edge of creek to Tennessee Beach
4. N 37 50.525, W 122 33.178 (1.8 miles): Climb stairs to vista point next to military bunker
5. N 37 50.999, W 122 33.386 (3.2 miles): At junction, follow footpath along the coast
6. N 37 51.552, W 122 34.519 (5.0 miles): Pass junction with Coyote Ridge trail, descend to Muir Beach

Although only a few miles north of San Francisco, Tennessee Valley, walled in by high ridges, seems quite isolated from the world. Until 1976, when it became part of the Golden Gate National Recreation Area, the valley was part of Witter Ranch. Tennessee Valley Trail junctions with Coast Trail, about a half-mile from Tennessee Beach.

Tennessee Valley Trail begins as a paved road (farther on, it becomes gravel; farther still, it becomes a footpath). The route descends moderately alongside a willow- and eucalyptus-lined creek. Great-horned owls can occasionally be spotted in the eucalyptus, and the American kestrel and a variety of hawk patrol the skies above the valley.

❶ Trail junctions After a quarter mile, you'll pass the trail to Haypress Trail Camp and soon thereafter, Fox Trail, both of which veer to the northwest (right). The road reaches a private residence at the 3/4-mile mark and turns to dirt.

❷ Hikers-only footpath A mile out, take the left-forking trail, which is a seasonal (hikers only) footpath that wends its way around a willow-lined marshy area. If this path looks like it's too wet for easy travel, continue with the drier and higher main Tennessee Valley Trail. The main path passes a pine-shaded porta-potty and intersects Coastal Trail.

The seasonal footpath and the main Tennessee Valley Trail reunite about a half-mile from Tennessee Cove. Continue to the western end of the marshland and follow the creek draining into the Pacific to Tennessee Beach.

❸ Tennessee Beach It was a dark and stormy night when the side-wheel steamship *Tennessee,* with 600 passengers aboard, overshot the Golden Gate and ran aground off this isolated Marin County cove. No lives were lost on that foggy night of March 6, 1853, but the abandoned ship was soon broken up by the surf. The vessel is remembered by a point, a cove, a valley, and a beach.

❹ Vista Point A narrow path ascends stairs and the steep slopes north of the beach to a vista point adjacent to a onetime military bunker. After you've explored the 300-yard long beach, retrace your steps on the main Tennessee Valley Trail, this time forking left and ascending to meet Coastal Trail. As you ascend north on Coastal Trail, pause to look behind at Tennessee Valley.

❺ Coastal Trail Divides Atop a knoll, Coastal Trail splits into a fire road that turns inland and a footpath that continues closer to the coast. I highly recommend taking the footpath. Coastal Trail (the footpath) flattens out a bit, then descends to Pirate's Cove. The trail marches up and down the coastal bluffs and passes a junction with Coyote Ridge Trail. You'll get grand views of Muir Beach and Green Gulch.

❻ Muir Beach From this junction, you'll descend rather steeply down to Muir Beach. Golden Gate National Recreation Area boasts two major beaches in Marin—Stinson and Muir, the latter a wide, semicircular strand enclosed by a forested cove.

From the beach, you can walk a dirt road 3/4 mile to the Pelican Inn, an authentic-looking English pub that serves shepherd's pie, bangers and mash, fish and chips, and a great selection of ales.

MUIR WOODS ★★

Difficulty rating: Moderate

Distance: 6-mile loop from Muir Woods to Mount Tamalpais State Park

Estimated time: 2½–3½ hr.

Elevation gain: 1,000 ft.

Cost/permits: $5 National Park entry fee

Best time to go: Year round, early morning or late afternoon

Website: www.nps.gov/muwo

Recommended map: Golden Gate National Parks Conservancy Muir Woods National Monument

Trail head GPS: N 37 53.629, W 122 34.392

Trail head directions: Muir Woods is 12 miles from the Golden Gate Bridge. From Hwy. 101 northbound in Mill Valley, take the Hwy. 1/Stinson Beach exit. After exiting, stay in the right lane as you go under Hwy. 101. You are now on Shoreline Highway (Hwy. 1). Head west 2¾ miles to Panoramic Highway, turn right, and drive ¾ mile to Muir Woods Rd. Turn left and proceed 1½ miles to the main parking area for Muir Woods on your right. If the main parking lot is full, there is another one located about 100 yd. southeast.

"This is the best tree-lover's monument that could possibly be found in all the forests of the world," wrote John Muir upon learning a redwood preserve was dedicated in his name. Most of the million-plus visitors a year who walk in the woods would agree with the great naturalist. Without a doubt, the national monument is a must-see for visitors from around the state and around the world. Muir Woods is linked by trail to Mount Tamalpais State Park; this hike is a grand tour of the redwoods.

From the parking area, walk north to the information kiosk and Visitor Center. Pay the small entrance fee and join the paved, well-traveled trail along Redwood Creek. Several bridges over Redwood Creek enable the casual walker to make several loops.

You pass the Visitor Center, café, and gift shop on the right and Bridge 1 over Redwood Creek on your left. Reflect that your journey up-creek appears to be much easier than that of the wintertime passage of steelhead and salmon struggling upstream to spawn.

Muir Woods definitely draws an international crowd. While walking the trails, expect to hear a half-dozen languages praising the tall trees—though something about these cathedrals of redwoods quiets even the most effusive visitors.

❶ Memorial You'll pass a memorial to pioneer forester Gifford Pinchot, a conservationist in his own right but an extremely utilitarian one, who was often philosophically at odds with the visionary John Muir. Look right for signed Ocean View Trail. If you have a second day to hike in Muir Woods, consider taking this 1.6-mile-long path up to Panoramic Highway, the Mountain Home Inn, and the trail head for the hike to Mount Tamalpais. (See the Mount Tam hike description on p. 60.)

❷ Cathedral Grove A nature trail with numbered stops and keyed to a park brochure begins at Bridge 2. Continue along the main trail to Bridge 3 and Cathedral Grove. Shortly after President Franklin Roosevelt died in 1945, representatives of the fledgling United Nations (then headquartered in San Francisco) met in this solemn grove of redwoods to honor America's 31st president.

❸ William Kent Memorial Tree At a junction with right-forking Fern Creek

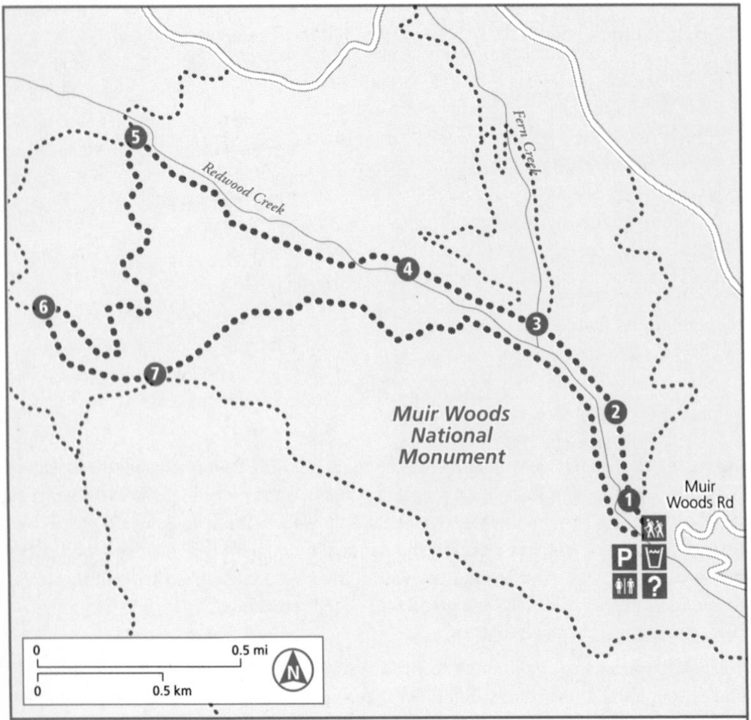

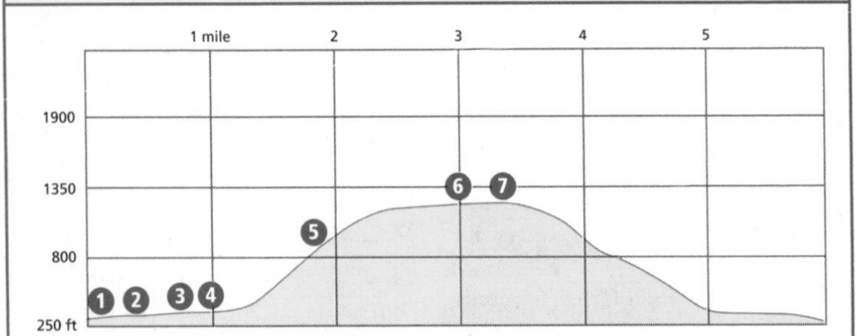

N 37 53.629, W 122 34.392: Trail head
1. N 37 53.656, W 122 34.483 (0.1 miles): Memorial to Gifford Pinchot
2. N 37 53.856, W 122 34.495 (0.4 miles): Follow nature trail to Cathedral Grove
3. N 37 54.042, W 122 34.708 (0.7 miles): Turn right at junction to view tallest tree in Muir Woods
4. N 37 54.168, W 122 35.073 (1.0 miles): Join Bootjack Trail at Bridge #4
5. N 37 54.478, W 122 35.851 (1.9 miles): Go left at Junction with TCC Trail
6. N 37 54.085, W 122 36.132 (3.0 miles): Turn left to join Stapelveldt Trail, and go left again to stay on trail
7. N 37 53.944, W 122 35.801 (3.3 miles): Join Ben Johnson Trail

Finds Stinson Beach: The Bay Area's Best

One of Northern California's most popular beaches, this 3-mile-wide stretch of sand, at the western foot of Mount Tamalpais, is packed with Bay Area residents (and their dogs) on those rare, fog-free summer weekends. Granted, it lacks Southern California's hard bodies and soft golden sand, but it still makes for an enjoyable day trip via the scenic drive on Highway 1. Swimming is allowed, with lifeguards on duty from May to mid-September, but notices about riptides and the cold water usually discourage beachgoers from venturing into the surf. Adjoining the beach is the small town of Stinson Beach, where you can have an enjoyable alfresco lunch at the numerous cafes along Highway 1. To reach Stinson Beach from San Francisco, cross the Golden Gate Bridge heading north on U.S. 101, take the Stinson Beach/Highway 1 exit heading west, and follow the signs (it's a winding 20 miles). The beach is free, open daily from 9am to 10pm. For more information, log onto **www.stinsonbeachonline.com**.

Trail, step off the main trail to visit the William Kent Memorial Tree, which to most visitor's surprise, is not a redwood but a sky-scraping 273-foot-high Douglas fir—the tallest tree in Muir Woods. The great naturalist John Muir may have provided the inspiration for setting aside these redwoods, but it was Congressman William Kent who provided the necessary funds and political juice. In 1905, Kent purchased 300 acres of virgin redwoods, just in time to save them from the loggers' axes. He then persuaded President Theodore Roosevelt to declare the grove a national monument and name it for Muir. In later years, Kent donated more acreage, improved roads, and brought a branch line of the Mount Tamalpais Railroad to the woods.

4 Bootjack Trail A mile of walking from the trail head is all that it takes to leave 98% of the crowds behind. At Bridge 4, join Bootjack Trail and continue along Redwood Creek. The footpath ascends more steeply amidst ferns and occasional big-leaf maple, leaving the creek for a time, then returning to it. The path climbs more aggressively to a spectacular footbridge over Redwood Creek (photo op!).

Look over the redwood forest. Listen to the cascading creek, which originates high on the west shoulder of Mt. Tam. Breathe deeply, taking in the sweet, moist air. Seclusion. Serenity. A moment of Zen.

5 Van Wyck Meadow and Junction with TCC Trail From the bridge, the path ascends fairly steeply to diminutive Van Wyck Meadow (perhaps amidst the towering redwoods and Douglas fir, any patch of grassland is deserving of the "meadow" name) and intersects signed TCC Trail, $2^{1}/_{3}$ miles from the trail head.

Bear left on the historic World War I–era TCC (Tamalpais Conservation Club) Trail and enjoy a mellow, fairly flat $1^{1}/_{3}$-mile amble through the woods and a meeting with Stapelveldt Trail.

6 Junction with Stapelveldt Trail Make two left turns to join and stay on Stapelveldt Trail. Hike a half mile to two redwoods that suggest an archway and a signed intersection with Ben Johnson Trail.

7 Meet Ben Johnson Trail Join this path and descend a mile to meet Hillside

Trail. Hillside Trail brings you to Bohemian Grove, where California's premiere men's club retreated in the 1890s. The Bohemians considered building a rough-it-deluxe camp here but opted for the more temperate environs along the Russian River. Follow this path (blessedly far less traveled than Main Trail on the other side of Redwood Creek) 3/4 mile to Bridge 1. Cross the bridge to Main Trail at a point near the café, gift shop, and park entrance.

MOUNT TAMALPAIS ★

Difficulty rating: Moderate

Distance: 6 miles round-trip from Mountain Home Inn to East Peak summit

Estimated time: 2 1/2–3 1/2 hr.

Elevation gain: 1,300 ft.

Cost/permits: None

Best time to go: Winter on a brisk clear day, spring after the rains fill the creeks

Website: www.parks.ca.gov

Recommended map: California State Parks Mount Tamalpais State Park

Trail head GPS: N 37 54.641, W 122 34.635

Trail head directions: From Hwy. 1 in Mill Valley, veer right on Panoramic Highway, ascending a few miles to Mountain Home Inn and a parking area. The trail begins across Panoramic Highway.

Two words from the native tongue of the Coast Miwok were combined to name the summit: *tamal,* meaning coast, and *pais,* meaning mountain. From the 2,571-foot summit of the "coast mountain," fabulous panoramas of the Pacific and San Francisco Bay coastlines, including the city of San Francisco, unfold. Getting to the summit is more than half the fun, particularly on trails like Railroad Grade and Fern Creek, which offer a little bit of everything: dense stands of laurel, open grassland, oak-dotted knolls, a canyon full of redwoods, and ferns.

Tam is a mountain of many moods. The great nature photographer Galen Rowell, who climbed and photographed the mountains of all seven continents, seemed particularly able to capture the spirit of this natural landmark. The longtime Bay Area resident (who perished in a tragic plane crash near Bishop, California) did some of his best work on this mountain near his home.

Thanks to the early trail-building efforts of the Tamalpais Conservation Club, as well as later efforts by the CCC during the 1930s, more than 50 miles of trails explore the state park that, thanks to continued conservation efforts, now exceeds 6,300 acres. Park trails connect to 200 (!) more miles of trail that lead through the wooded watershed of the Marin Municipal Water District, and over to Muir Woods National Monument and Golden Gate National Recreation Area.

Begin your steady ascent (7% grade all the way) on the Old Railroad Grade. An occasional view opens up among the brush.

The Mount Tamalpais and Muir Woods Railroad, known as "the crookedest railroad in the world," was constructed in 1896; it brought passengers from Mill Valley to the summit via 281 curves. Atop Mount Tam, the Tavern of Tamalpais welcomed diners and dancers.

➊ Junction with East Fork of Fern Canyon Trail Almost 2 miles out, you'll reach a junction with the east fork of Fern Canyon. Take this very steep shortcut 3/4 mile to Ridecrest Boulevard just below the East Peak parking lot.

Dogged railroad buffs will ignore such shortcuts and stay on the Railroad Grade,

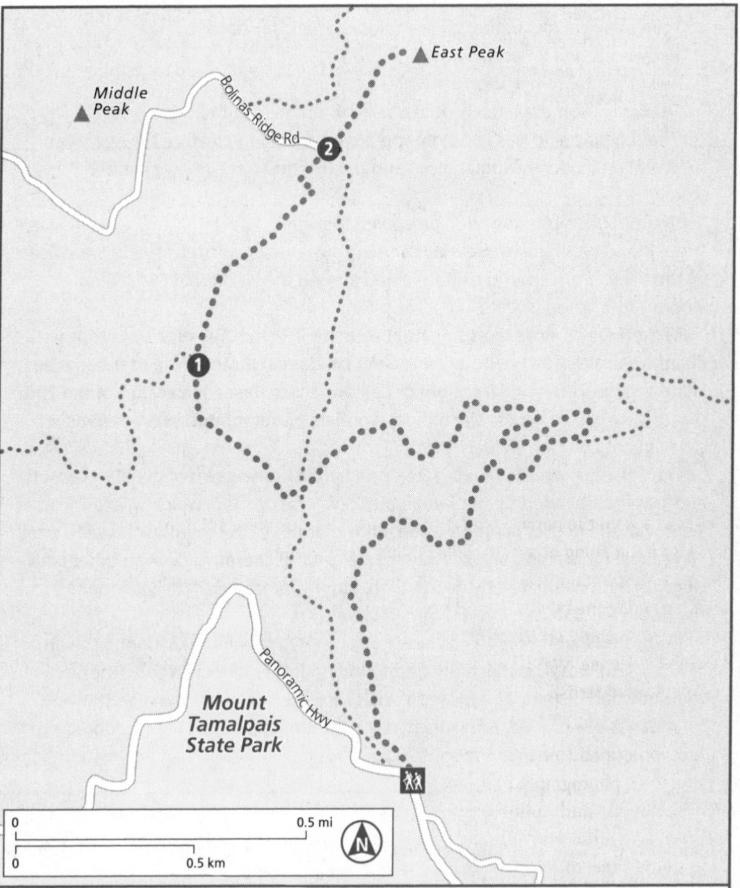

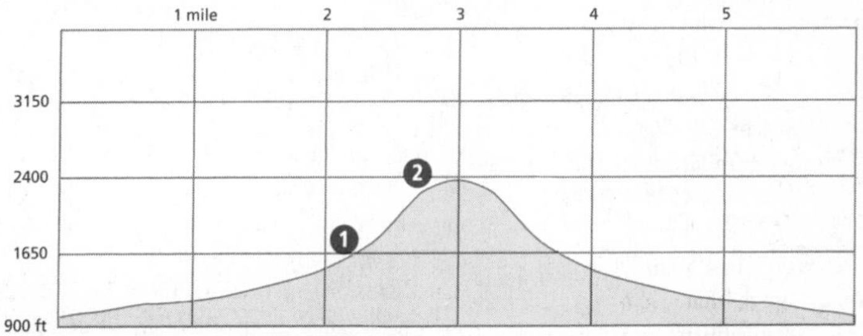

[Trailhead] N 37 54.641, W 122 34.635: Trail head

1 N 37 55.264, W 122 35.086 (2.1 miles): Go left at junction with Fern Canyon Trail

2 N 37 55.638, W 122 34.776 (2.7 miles): Join summit trail at parking area

Mount Tamalpais

"I can't believe this mountain is so close to San Francisco."

"Redwoods *and* an ocean view!"

"Tell us again, Tam is short for what?"

"Seriously? Someone really built a railroad up this mountain?"

"That banana slug has got to be the grossest looking creature I've ever seen."

"We've only been hiking an hour and the weather has already changed three times."

"Thank God, this is in a park, preserved forever."

These are some of the impressions and enthusiastic expressions I've heard voiced by the hikers from around California and around the world that I've met on Mount Tam's trails.

As much as or more than any other state park, Mount Tamalpais is a triumphant example of the value of protecting parklands located close to urban areas. Thanks to the vision and foresight of Californians in the early decades of the 20th century, we can delight in the natural wonders of this mountain that seems to stand guard over the Golden Gate.

The fight to preserve Mount Tamalpais began at the dawn of the 20th century and was spearheaded by the Tamalpais Conservation Club, which was founded in 1912 with the goal of creating a park on the slopes of the mountain. Finally, after 18 years of fundraising and preservation efforts, in coordination with other activist organizations such as the Sierra Club, Mount Tamalpais State Park opened to the public in 1930.

Dedicated Marin County conservationist (not to mention U.S. Congressman) William Kent was a guiding light and founding father of Muir Woods, the Save-the-Redwood League, and Mount Tamalpais State Park. Kent donated the land for Muir Woods in 1908 and launched Mount Tamalpais State Park by donating redwood-filled Steep Ravine in 1928.

which visits the West Point Inn, originally built by the railroad and now owned by the Marin Water District and run by the West Point Inn Association.

Hikers may pause on the veranda and buy some refreshment (tea, soda, and energy bars). This haven for hikers, complete with chairs on the veranda and nearby picnic tables, offers grand vistas of San Francisco, the East Bay, and the Golden Gate.

You'll circle clockwise around West Point, heading north another two miles up the Railroad Grade. If you want to stay on the Railroad Grade all the way to the top of Mount Tam, add $2\frac{1}{2}$ miles to the ascent, plus $2\frac{1}{2}$ miles to the descent.

2 Summit Parking Area Once you reach the summit parking lot and picnic area, catch your breath and join the $\frac{1}{3}$-mile summit trail to the top of Mount Tam. Alas, because motorists can drive close to the top, there could be crowd at the summit.

With its fenced-off fire lookout tower, the summit itself is not as grand as the top-of-the-world view it offers.

Lucky hikers might experience what locals call a "Farallons Day"—one of those clear days when visibility is greater than 25 miles, thus allowing a glimpse of the sharp peaks of the Farallon Islands.

STEEP RAVINE ★★

Difficulty rating: Moderate

Distance: 7.2-mile loop from Stinson Beach to Pantoll Station

Estimated time: 4 hr.

Elevation gain: 1,600 ft.

Cost/permits: None

Best time to go: Spring, when wildflowers bloom and waterfalls cascade at full strength

Website: www.parks.ca.gov

Recommended map: California State Parks Mount Tamalpais State Park

Trail head GPS: N 37 54.263, W 122 36.238

Trail head directions: From Hwy. 1 in Stinson Beach, turn inland at the fire station on Belvedere Ave. and travel 1/4 mile to the trail head and parking on the left side of the street.

Matt Davis, Steep Ravine, and Dipsea trails are each in their own way wonderfully scenic and masterpieces of the trail-builders art. Together, this trio of Mount Tam's best trails combine to offer a spectacular hiking experience. Matt Davis Trail wanders in and out of the forest and climbs the great mountain; Steep Ravine is a steep creek-side descent, accompanied by stair steps and even a ladder in one place, through a redwood forest; the historic Dipsea, most famous of them all, also bestows brilliant views.

Matt Davis Trail crosses a creek on a bridge and travels in the shade of alder and California bay. At a quarter mile, ignore an unsigned path branching right to Panoramic Highway and begin your long ascent. The trail crosses the creek again on a bridge and continues climbing via short switchbacks into a coastal sage community of sage, toyon, and (beware) poison oak. The path returns to the shade (past some particularly fetching big-leaf maple) and crosses the creek again on another bridge.

Now, you start to climb in earnest, up some stone steps known as the Bischof Steps and ascending to the top of Table Rock, a massive boulder that's a great rest/picnic stop.

❶ Table Rock From Table Rock, the path continues to climb, switchbacking over onto a grassy western slope and intersecting with Coastal Trail at the 2 1/2-mile mark.

❷ Intersection with Coastal Trail From this junction, Matt Davis Trail leaves behind a wooded canyon and in a quarter-mile comes to another junction, this one with two side trails that climb to viewpoints. Actually, the view from the trail intersection is pretty darn good, with panoramas to San Francisco and the Golden Gate.

Leave behind the grassy slopes and enter a Douglas fir–dominated woodland that also has an eclectic mix of trees, including oak, bay, and a few redwoods.

❸ Traffic Noise As the path nears Pantoll and Panoramic Highway (you'll begin hearing the sound of auto traffic and, worse, tranquility-shattering motorcycles), the trail levels out.

❹ Pantoll Station Carefully cross Panoramic Highway to the Pantoll Station parking area. Having traveled 4 1/4 miles from the trail head and accomplished all the elevation gain, take a break here.

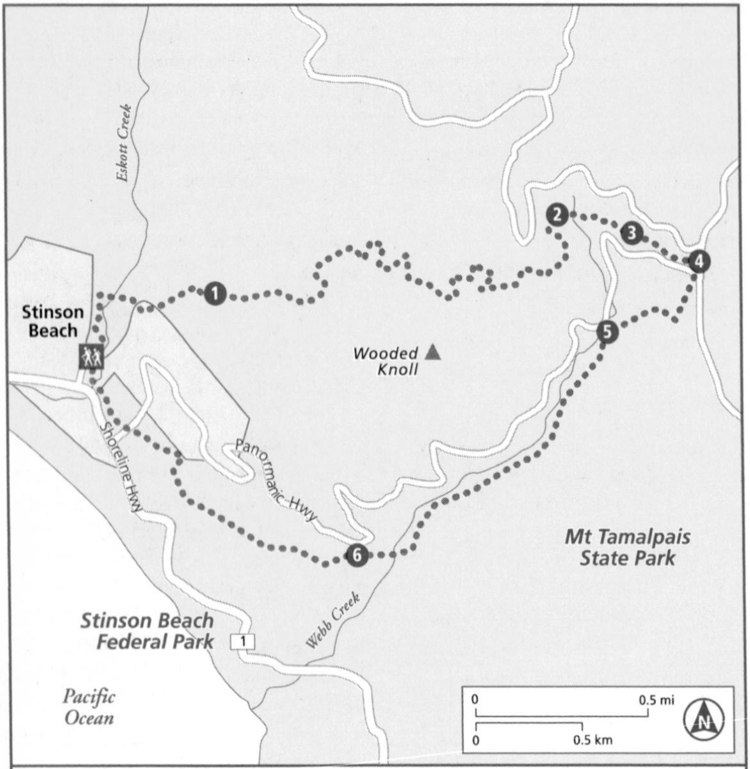

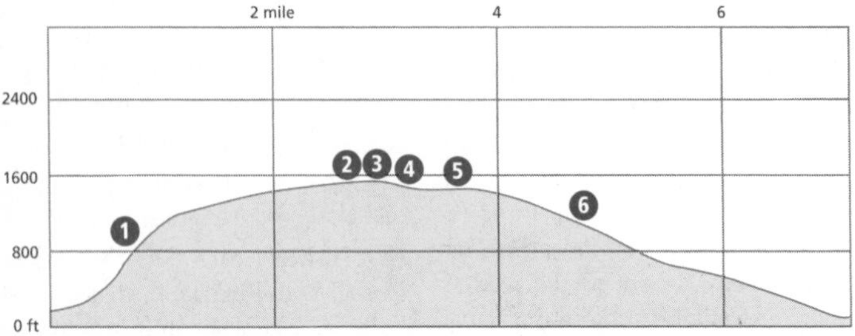

Trail head: N 37 53.986, W 122 38.250: Trail head

1. N 37 54.133, W 122 37.839 (0.7 miles): Pass the massive boulder at Table Rock
2. N 37 54.330, W 122 36.723 (2.7 miles): Pass intersection with Coastal Trail
3. N 37 54.287, W 122 36.471 (3.0 miles): Trail levels out as you begin to hear traffic noise
4. N 37 54.218, W 122 36.253 (3.2 miles): Cross Panoramic Highway to the Pantoll Station parking area, join Steep Ravine Trail
5. N 37 54.047, W 122 36.558 (3.8 miles): Trail meets Webb Creek
6. N 37 53.485, W 122 37.385 (4.8 miles): Turn right on Dipsea Trail

Pantoll offers an information board, picnic area, and restrooms.

Signed Steep Ravine Trail is located by a paved service road off the upper parking lot. The trail heads south, descending a series of switchbacks through redwood, Douglas fir, and huckleberry.

5 Webb Creek In a half-mile, the trail reaches Webb Creek and begins descending Steep Ravine. Wet, shaded, remote—no wonder Steep Ravine Trail is a favorite of Bay Area hikers. Redwoods, ferns, and mosses add to the feeling of walking through a rainforest.

Wood ferns, sword ferns, and five-finger ferns line the trail, which passes under solemn redwoods. You descend a ladder, originally built by the Civilian Conservation Corps of the 1930s, and cross the creek a couple of times on footbridges. The route along Webb Creek, when swollen by winter rains, becomes a quite vigorous watercourse, complete with waterfalls.

6 Junction with Dipsea Trail About $1\frac{3}{4}$ miles from Pantoll and about 6 miles into the hike, Steep Ravine Trail is joined by Dipsea Trail, coming from the east over a footbridge. (Steep Ravine Trail continues to Hwy. 1, then descends to the Steep Ravine Cabins, built in the 1930s as a family retreat for Congressman William Kent, who was instrumental in preserving Mount Tam and Muir Woods.)

Keep right on Dipsea Trail and head for the town of Stinson Beach.

> The path traverses an open slope seasonally splashed with California poppies, and blue and purple lupine, before cresting a low hillock and serving up jaw-dropping vistas of the coastline.

The trail dips into a moist little area, travels a bit of boardwalk, and reaches Panoramic Highway at the $7\frac{1}{4}$-mile mark. Cross (carefully) and continue on a final quarter-mile of the Dipsea Trail to meet Coast Hwy. 1. Walk the highway shoulder north a short distance into Stinson Beach, the town. Enjoy a meal or beverage at one of the town's cafés, or purchase some picnic items at the store and head for Stinson State Beach, a long sand strand.

PALOMARIN & THE LAKES DISTRICT ★★

Difficulty rating: Moderate

Distance: 8.2 miles round-trip from Palomarin to Alamere Falls

Estimated time: 4–5 hr.

Elevation gain: 300 ft.

Cost/permits: None

Best time to go: Alamere Falls is at full strength during winter and spring

Website: www.nps.gov/pore

Recommended map: Tom Harrison Maps Point Reyes National Seashore

Trail head GPS: N 37 56.059, W 122 44.824

Trail head directions: From Stinson Beach, drive $4\frac{1}{2}$ miles north and take the turnoff (Olema-Bolinas Rd.) to Bolinas. (This turnoff is rarely signed; Bolinas residents remove it.) At Mesa Rd., turn right and travel $4\frac{1}{2}$ miles to the large trail head parking area at road's end.

For the homesick Brit or Scot, Point Reyes peninsula has more than a passing resemblance to the homeland. Along with its United Kingdom–like moors, weirs, glens, and vales, Point Reyes has its "Lakes District." Five lakes—Bass, Pelican, Crystal, Ocean, and Wildcat—were created in part by movement along the nearby San Andreas Fault. Earth slippage sealed off passage of spring-fed waterways, thus forming the little lakes. The

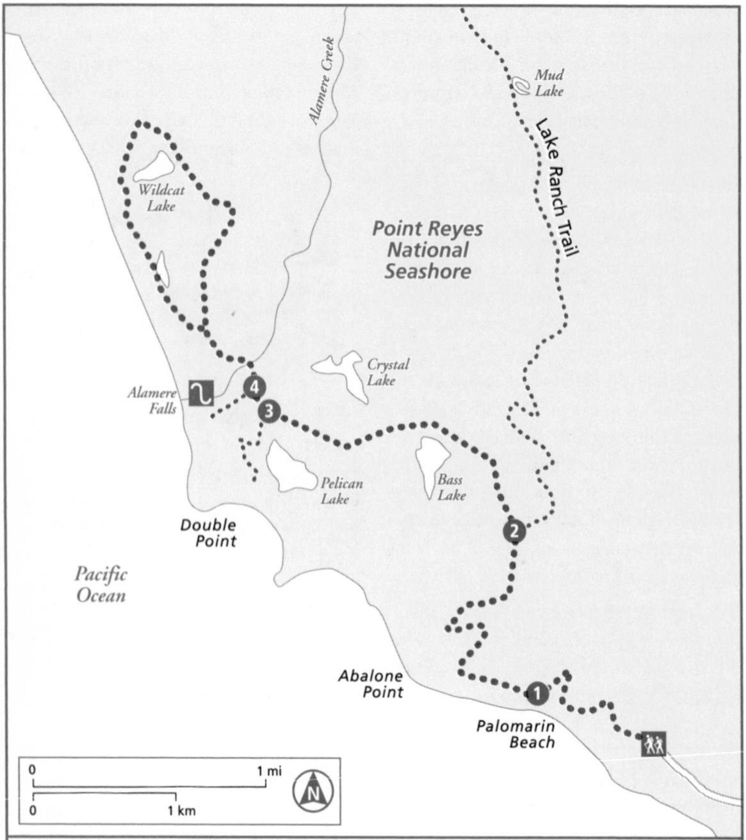

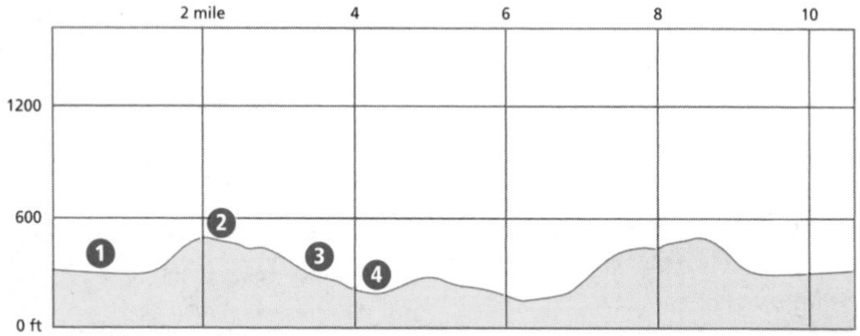

- N 37 56.059, W 122 44.824: Trail head
- ❶ N 37 56.212, W 122 45.324 (0.8 miles): Take side trail heading west to Palomarin Beach
- ❷ N 37 56.802, W 122 45.439 (2.2 miles): Intersection with Lake Ranch Trail
- ❸ N 37 57.222, W 122 46.667 (3.6 miles): Side trail to Double Point
- ❹ N 37 57.257, W 122 46.726 (4.2 miles): Trail to Alamere Falls

trail zigzags and roller-coasters along as it serves up ocean vistas and leads to Alamere Falls that cascades in spectacular fashion 50 feet over the coastal cliffs to the beach below.

From the parking lot, you'll climb a staircase and join Coast Trail, an old farm road that turns north and ascends into a mature stand of eucalyptus.

❶ Trail Junction After a quarter mile, Coast Trail junctions a westward-branching side trail leading to Palomarin Beach. Contouring out onto the cliff edge, the trail here, and in the miles to follow, is lined with coastal scrub—coyote bush, black sage, coffee berry.

In springtime, the route is brightened by wildflowers: foxgloves (causing nostalgic sighs from our British friends), lupine, morning glory, cow parsnip, and paintbrush.

After a mile of tracing the edge of the bluff-tops, the trail turns inland, descends into a gully, then climbs again back to the bluff-tops. Coast Trail soon repeats this maneuver, this time climbing in and out of a larger gully.

❷ Junction with Lake Ranch Trail About $2\frac{1}{4}$ miles from the trail head, Coast Trail intersects Lake Ranch Trail, which leads (among other places) to Five Brooks Trailhead off Hwy. 1. Hike another $\frac{3}{4}$ mile past a couple of ponds to Bass Lake, a tranquil spot shaded by Douglas fir. A quarter-mile more of hiking leads to another junction and the opportunity to take Crystal Lake Trail to another lake in the "Lakes District."

Continue on Coast Trail, which descends from the woods to more open scrub community and serves up a view of triangular-shaped Pelican Lake, perched on a bluff-top. This is the next lake visited by Coast Trail, which descends to an unsigned junction about $3\frac{1}{2}$ miles from the trail head.

❸ Side Trail A half-mile side trail leads coastward to overlook Double Point, two shale outcroppings that enclose a small bay. Seals often haul out on the bay's small beach. Offshore stand Stormy Stacks, where California brown pelicans and cormorants roost.

❹ Junction with Alamere Falls Trail Just beyond this junction is another signed one for Alamere Falls. The brush-crowded path (watch for poison oak) parallels willow-lined Alamere Creek, which is to the north (right) of the trail. Keep descending to the eroded bluffs near the top of the falls.

> Many hikers are content to contemplate the falls from a rocky platform adjacent to the cascade and watch it tumble to the beach. If you insist on a bottom-up view of the falls, you can cross Alamere Creek (do not attempt this at times of high water), and carefully pick your way down the cliffs to the beach.

Either way you look at it, Alamere Creek comes to a spectacular end in the form of the falls cascading over the coastal bluffs. Few California creeks make it to the ocean, and rare indeed is the creek that arrives with sufficient vigor as to propel a waterfall hurtling over the cliffs to the shore.

Double-back to Coastal Trail. Return the same way or consider adding about $2\frac{1}{2}$ more miles to the journey by heading north. After crossing Alamere Creek, the trail forks: the left fork, Wildcat Trail, and the right fork, a continuation of Coast Trail, both lead a bit over a mile to Wildcat Camp. The two trails skirt Ocean Lake and Wildcat Lake, and form a handy loop. From the camp, there's easy access to Wildcat Beach.

BEAR VALLEY & ARCH ROCK

Difficulty rating: Moderate

Distance: 8.8 miles round-trip from Bear Valley Visitor Center to Divide Meadow

Estimated time: 4 hr.

Elevation gain: 400 ft.

Cost/permits: None

Best time to go: Year round

Website: www.nps.gov/pore

Recommended map: Tom Harrison Maps Point Reyes National Seashore

Trail head GPS: N 38 02.348, W 122 47.986

Trail head directions: Bear Valley Visitor Center is located just outside the town of Olema, 35 slow and curving miles north of San Francisco on Hwy. 1. A quicker route is by Hwy. 101, exiting on Sir Francis Drake Blvd. and traveling 20 miles to Olema. Turn right on Coast Hwy. 1, proceed 1/4 mile, then turn left on Bear Valley Rd., which leads 1/2 mile to parking for the Point Reyes National Seashore Visitor Center and the trail head.

Bear Valley, one of the most popular paths in the national seashore, is the busy hub of Point Reyes National Seashore. From the park visitor center, more than 40 miles of trail thread through the valley, and to the ridges and beaches beyond. It passes through a very low gap in Inverness Ridge and follows a nearly-level route to the ocean. What's not to like about a fairly flat footpath that leads through lovely forest, across wide meadows, and ends at a drop-dead gorgeous overlook above the ocean?

Begin at the National Park Service's Bear Valley Visitor Center, a friendly place full of excellent history and natural history exhibits. Film screenings, a seismograph, and dioramas tell the story behind the seashore's scenery.

Outside the visitor center, there is much to see, including a traditional Coast Miwok village. The family dwellings, sweat lodge, and other structures were built using traditional native methods. Near the visitor center is the Morgan Horse Ranch, where park service animals are raised and trained.

Two park interpretive trails are well worth a stroll. Woodpecker Trail is a self-guided nature trail that introduces walkers to the tremendous diversity of the region's native flora. Earthquake Trail uses old photographs and other displays to explain the seismic forces unleashed by the great 1906 San Francisco earthquake. This well-done and entertaining geology lesson is particularly relevant because most of the land west of the San Andreas Fault Zone is within boundaries of Point Reyes National Seashore.

Bear Valley Trail, an old ranch road, heads through an open meadow and, after 1/4 mile, passes a junction with Mount Wittenberg Trail, which ascends Mount Wittenberg (see p. 70). Beyond this junction, the trail enters a forest of Bishop pine and Douglas fir. Your path is alongside Bear Valley Creek.

Notice that the creek flows north, in the opposite direction of Coast Creek, which you'll soon be following from Divide Meadow to the sea. This strange drainage pattern is one more example of how the mighty San Andreas Fault can shape the land.

❶ Divide Meadow A half-mile along, you'll pass a second trail, Meadow Trail, and after almost another mile of travel, arrive at Divide Meadow, 1 1/2 miles from the trail head. A hunt club, visited by Presidents William Howard Taft and Theodore Roosevelt, once stood here. During the early part of this century, meadows

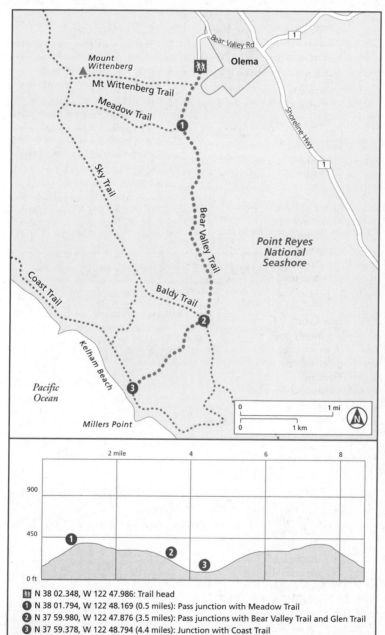

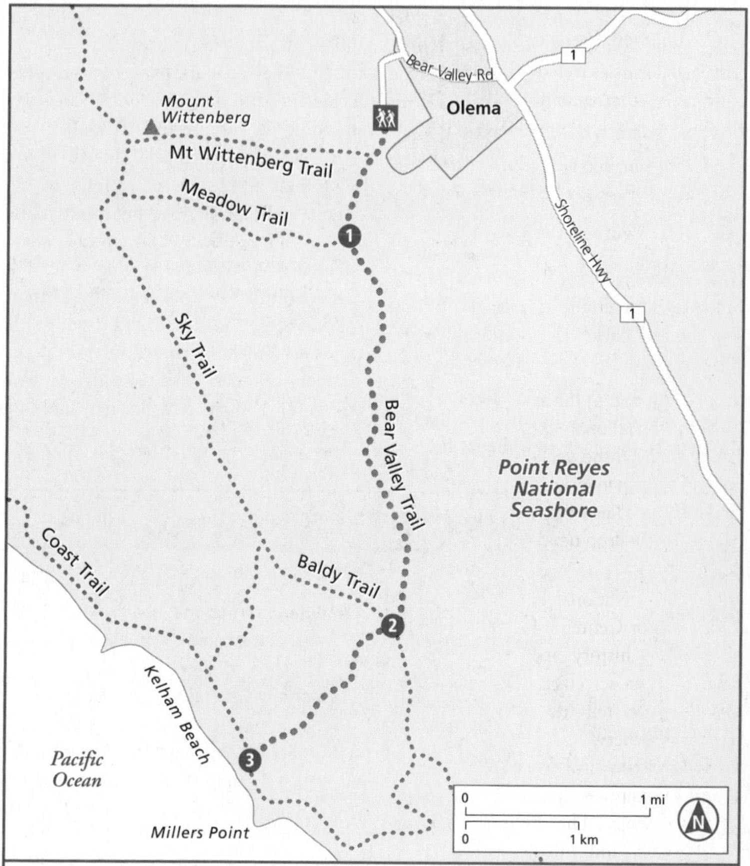

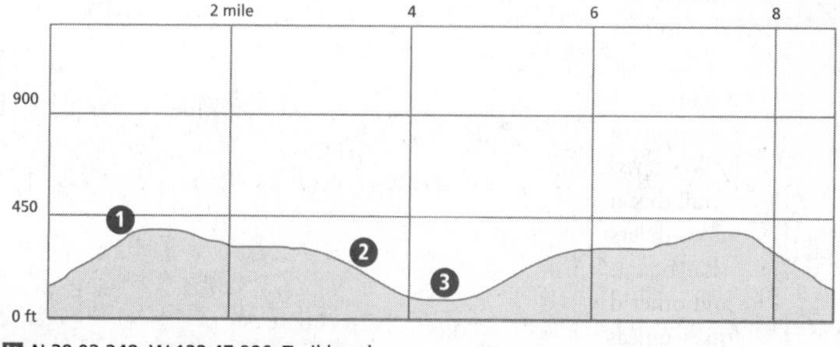

N 38 02.348, W 122 47.986: Trail head

1 N 38 01.794, W 122 48.169 (0.5 miles): Pass junction with Meadow Trail

2 N 37 59.980, W 122 47.876 (3.5 miles): Pass junctions with Bear Valley Trail and Glen Trail

3 N 37 59.378, W 122 48.794 (4.4 miles): Junction with Coast Trail

and nearby forested ridges abounded with deer, bear, mountain lion, and game birds.

Well-named Divide Meadow divides Bear Valley Creek from Coast Creek, which you'll soon be following when you continue on Bear Valley Trail. Divide Meadow, bordered by Douglas fir, is a fine place for a picnic, as well as being a popular destination/turnaround point for many hikers.

❷ Junction with Baldy Trail Shady Bear Valley Trail continues another 1½ miles to a junction with Baldy Trail (a northbound path that ascends Inverness Ridge to the Sky Trail) and with southbound Glen Trail. Bear Valley Trail narrows from road to footpath, heading for the coast in the shade of Douglas fir.

❸ Junction with Coast Trail Four miles along, the trail ends at a junction with Coast Trail. Join Coast Trail, then follow the signs to Arch Rock.

Near the ocean, the path crosses through coastal scrub and arrives at an open meadow on the precipitous bluffs above Arch Rock. Unpack your lunch, unfold your map, and plan a return route by way of one of Bear Valley's many scenic trails.

On your return, if you want to "see it all in one day," consider legging it up Old Pine Trail to Sky Trail, ascending Mount Wittenberg, and descending back to the visitor center and trail head via Mount Wittenberg Trail. This would add 4 or more miles to the day, but it would be a memorable day, indeed.

MOUNT WITTENBERG ★

Difficulty rating: Moderate

Distance: 5.1 miles round-trip to Mount Wittenberg; 6.6 miles round-trip return via Old Pine Trail; 8.6 miles round-trip return via Baldy Trail

Estimated time: 2½–3½ hr.

Elevation gain: 1,300 ft.

Cost/permits: None

Best time to go: Clear fall or winter days

Website: www.nps.gov/pore

Recommended map: Tom Harrison Maps Point Reyes National Seashore

Trail head GPS: N 38 02.348, W 122 47.986

Trail head directions: Bear Valley Visitor Center is located just outside the town of Olema, 35 slow and curving miles north of San Francisco on Hwy. 1. A quicker route is by Hwy. 101, exiting on Sir Francis Drake Blvd. and traveling 20 miles to Olema. Turn right on Coast Hwy. 1, proceed ¼ mile, then turn left on Bear Valley Rd., which leads ½ mile to parking for the Point Reyes National Seashore Visitor Center and the trail head.

The highest summit on Point Reyes National Seashore, 1,407-foot Mount Wittenberg offers sweeping vistas of the entire Point Reyes Peninsula: Tomales Bay, Olema Valley, and Bolinas Ridge. On clear days, look for distant Mount St. Helena and Mount Diablo.

Mount Wittenberg Trail is surely the least-used of the paths that begin from the seashore's busy headquarters. I'm guessing the trail's stiff ascent scares off most hikers. No need to be scared, although it is a serious workout to walk Wittenberg. Rewards for the ascent include the aforementioned views and Sky Camp, an excellent picnic spot. Once you've gained the summit, you can join Sky Trail along Inverness Ridge, then choose one of a couple different trails to return to Bear Valley.

Begin on Bear Valley Trail and, in ¼ mile, reach a right-forking junction at a large bay tree with signed Mount Wittenberg Trail.

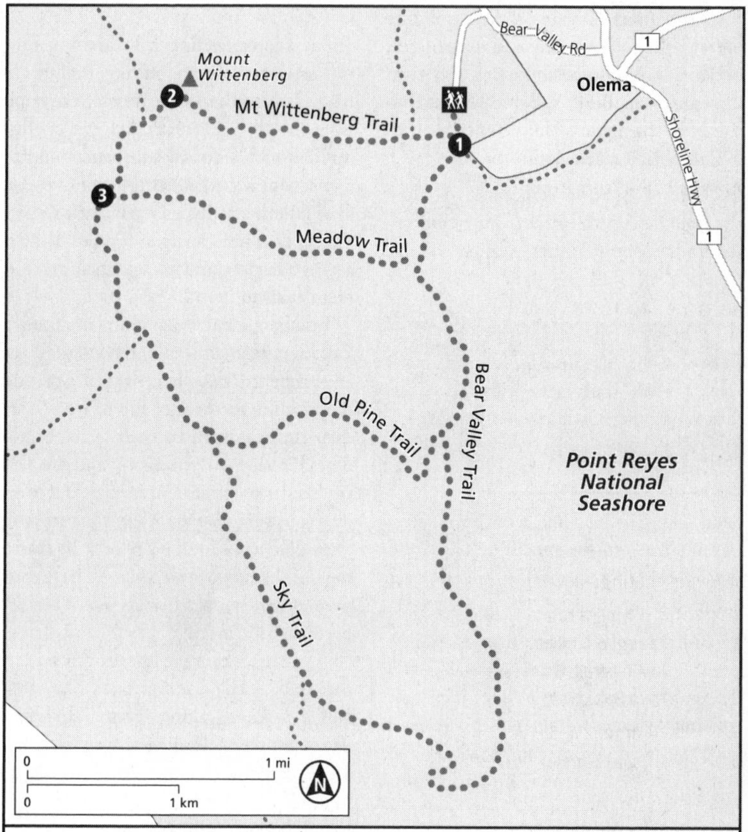

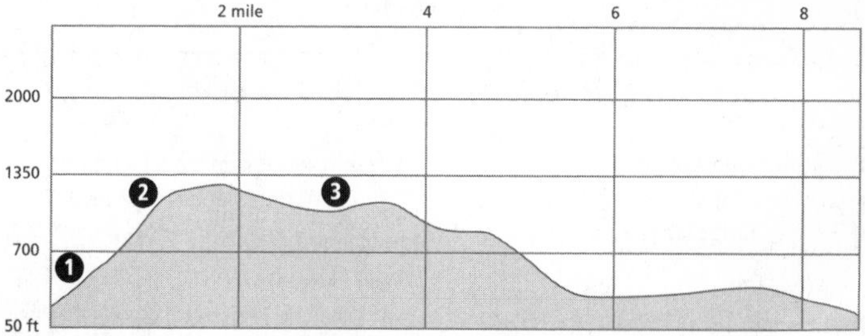

N 38 02.348, W 122 47.986: Trail head

❶ N 38 02.221, W 122 47.995 (0.2 miles): Turn right on to Mount Wittenberg trail

❷ N 38 02.366, W 122 49.307 (2.0 miles): Turn right on to Z-ranch trail and climb to summit of Mount Wittenberg

❸ N 38 02.015, W 122 49.582 (3.1 miles): At junction choose which route to take back to your starting point

❶ **Mount Wittenberg Trail** Bear right and begin your march toward Inverness Ridge. With sword ferns pointing the way, the path climbs past a mixed forest of tanbark oak and Douglas fir. After gaining more than 1,000 feet in elevation, you reach the ridge crest and a junction with Z-Ranch Trail at the 2-mile mark.

❷ **Top of Mount Wittenberg** Join the rightward path for a ¼-mile climb to the top of Mount Wittenberg.

> Clear-day views south and east on the top of Mount Wittenberg include plenty of Point Reyes and Mount Tamalpais; alas, trees on the summit screen the views north and west.

After taking in the vista, retrace your steps ¼ mile back to the junction. This time, you'll head left and travel ½ mile to reach a four-way junction.

❸ **Junction with Sky and Meadow trails** For a somewhat mellow 1½-mile descent back to Bear Valley, join east-trending Meadow Trail, which crosses a wide meadow. From the meadow, look across the peninsula to mighty Mount Tam. The path drops rapidly off Inverness Ridge, descending past bay trees and Douglas fir to a footbridge crossing Bear Valley Creek and a junction with Bear Valley Trail

For a longer return from the junction, continue the journey on Sky Trail, a dirt road. Look west at the forest recovering from the 1995 Vision Fire. Travel south 1 mile through a Douglas fir forest and past a variety of berry bushes to meet Old Pine Trail, another fairly easy way back to Bear Valley. This trail descends 2 miles through a long meadow and past a small grove of mature Bishop pine.

Bishop pine, along with its similar-looking piney cousins, the Monterey and knobcone, are known as fire pines because they require the heat of fire to crack open their cones and release their seeds. Bishop pines are slow to propagate, and are relatively rare in coastal California. The surest way to distinguish a Bishop pine from its look-alike, the Monterey pine, is by counting the needles: Monterey pines have three needles to a bunch, Bishop pine have two needles to a cluster.

If you're seeking the longest way back to the trail head, continue on Sky Trail, which descends along forested Inverness Ridge another 1½ miles to face "Baldy," a 1,034-foot rock knob. Baldy Trail drops a mile to Bear Valley; it's then 3 miles of hiking back to the trail head.

DRAKES ESTERO ★★

Difficulty rating: Moderate

Distance: 8 miles round-trip from Estero Trailhead to Sunset Beach

Estimated time: 4 hr.

Elevation gain: 240 ft.

Cost/permits: None

Best time to go: Winter, especially for the bird-watching

Website: www.nps.gov/pore

Recommended map: Tom Harrison Maps Point Reyes National Seashore

Trail head GPS: N 38 04.923, W 122 54.846

Trail head directions: From Hwy. 1 in Olema (where there's a well-marked turnoff for the Point Reyes National Seashore Bear Valley Visitor Center), proceed 2 miles north and veer left onto Sir Francis Drake Blvd. Follow the highway 7½ miles to Estero Rd. Turn left and drive 1 mile to the Estero parking area and signed trail head.

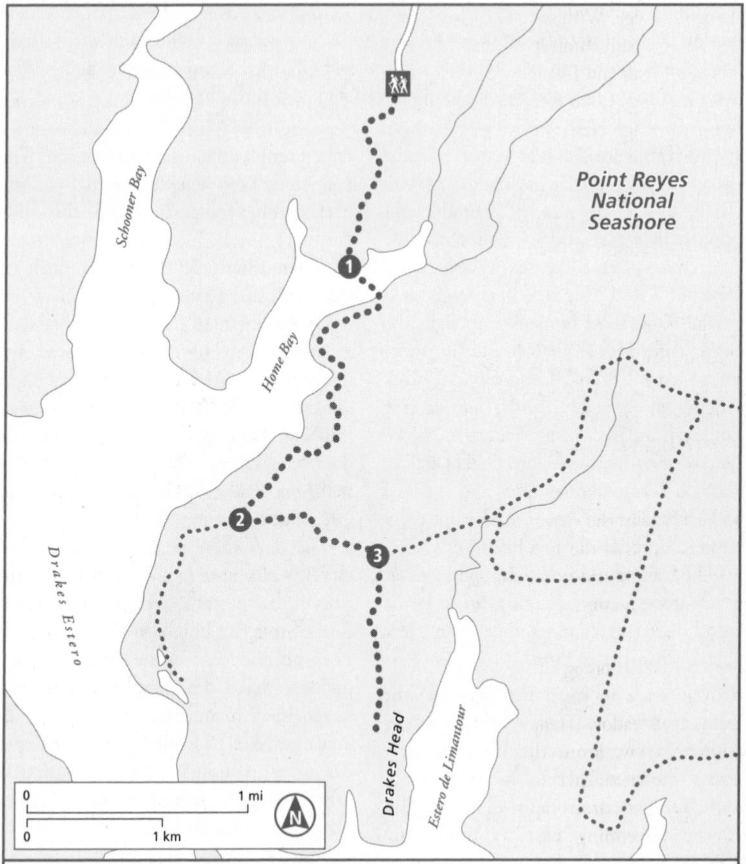

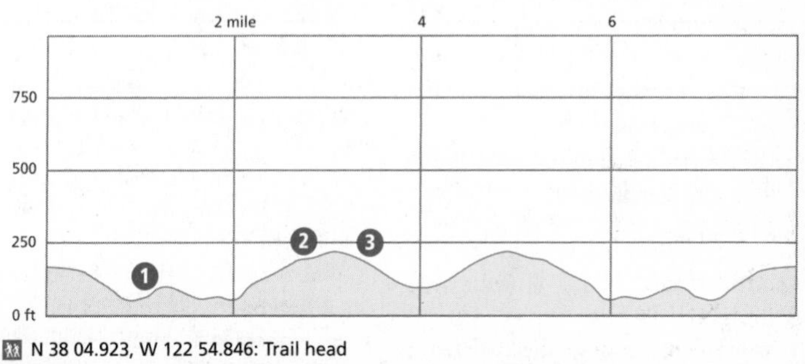

N 38 04.923, W 122 54.846: Trail head

1 N 38 04.183, W 122 55.087 (1.0 miles): Trail crosses causeway

2 N 38 03.259, W 122 55.675 (2.7 miles): Option to follow Sunset Beach trail

3 N 38 03.122, W 122 54.956 (3.4 miles): At junction choose which route to take to end of hike

This memorable coastal hike over old ranch roads on the western slope of Inverness Ridge will keep you glued to your field glasses. No, the route of dramatic Estero Trail isn't difficult to follow; you'll want the field glasses to help you observe the abundant wildlife around Drakes *Estero*, Spanish for estuary. Great blue herons, willets, godwits, sanderlings, sandpipers, and many, many more shorebirds feed along the mudflats. Harbor seals and sea lions often swim into the *estero* and bask on its beaches.

Estero Trail, an old ranch road, climbs gently across pastoral grasslands. As you climb, look over your left shoulder and admire Inverness Ridge, highlighted by, from west to east, Mount Vision, Point Reyes Hill, and Mount Wittenberg.

You won't need binoculars to sight the most common animal found in these parts—cows. Both Herefords and Black Angus graze the headlands. This is cow country, and has been since the 1850s. Schooners maneuvered into Drakes Estero, took on a cargo of fine butter, and returned to San Francisco, a ready market for dairy products produced on Point Reyes.

The trail turns to the left, and at about a half mile from the trail head, passes a stand of Monterey pine, once the nucleus of a Christmas tree farm.

❶ Causeway In another half mile, the path crosses a causeway, which divides Home Bay from a pond. Even the most casual birder will sight large numbers of shorebirds in the mudflats of Home Bay. The many fingers of Drakes Estero, Marin County's largest lagoon, are patrolled by canvasbacks, ruddy ducks, and American wigeons. For the hiker's wildlife-watching convenience, benches are built into the bridge.

The trail ascends lupine-dotted slopes and offers good views of Home Bay shores and its many habitués. You might see deer, either the native black-tailed or the "imported" white fallow, browsing the grassy ridges.

About $2^1/_2$ miles from the trail head, you come to a signed junction.

❷ Junction with Sunset Beach Trail Sunset Beach Trail heads straight (southwest) well above the *estero* for more than a mile before dropping to a gate. The path ends at a couple of small ponds, backed by Drakes Bay and the wide Pacific.

Drakes Estero, Beach, and Overlook are named for that pirate/explorer in the service of Queen Elizabeth I, Sir Francis Drake.

Californians have long debated the question: Did Sir Francis in June of 1579 sail his *Golden Hinde* into Drakes Bay or into San Francisco Bay? Is he really the discoverer of San Francisco Bay, or does that honor fall to other sailors, more than 200 years earlier?

The bay where Drake set anchor had chalky cliffs and reminded the Englishman of the cliffs of Dover. Drake's description of this bay points to Drakes Bay. To mark his discovery, Drake left a brass plate nailed to a post. This plate was supposedly found in 1936 and was originally considered genuine. Metallurgical tests later called in question it authenticity, and in 2003 the plate was confirmed to be a hoax, an elaborate and playful scheme dreamed up by local historians.

For an excellent overview of the great Drake debate, check out the exhibits at the Ken C. Patrick Visitor Center, housed in a handsome redwood building perched above Drakes Beach. The Park Service does an excellent job of discussing Drake's voyage in its many cultural and political manifestations.

Whether you're a Drakes Bay believer or not (or even if you couldn't give a whit about something 5 centuries removed from the present), you'll enjoy sauntering a mile or two along Drakes Beach. Enjoy a post-hike meal at the excellent Drakes Beach Café, located by the Visitor Center.

Finds Drake's Bay Oyster Farm

If you want to escape the crowds and enjoy some man-made entertainment, head to **Drake's Bay Oyster Farm.** On the edge of Drakes Estero (a uniquely pristine and nutrient-rich saltwater lagoon on the Point Reyes peninsula that produces some of the finest oysters in the world), the oyster farm doesn't look like much—just a cluster of wooden shacks and oyster tanks surrounded by piles of oyster shells—but California has no better place to buy delicious fresh-out-of-the-water oysters by the sack full. The owner is very friendly and doles out all the information you'll ever want to know about the bivalves, including a lesson on how to properly shuck them. They also have picnic tables and bottled oyster sauce, so you can enjoy your recently purchased bivalves immediately (though I prefer to drive down to Point Reyes Beach), but bring your own oyster knife. Drake's Bay Oyster Farm is located at 17171 Sir Francis Drake Blvd., about 6 miles west(ish) of Inverness on the way to the Point Reyes Lighthouse. It's open daily 8am to 4:30pm (✆ **415/669-1149;** www.drakesbayfamilyfarms.com).

❸ Junction with Drakes Head Trail Estero Trail swings east and, after 3/4 mile, comes to a junction. If you're not up for one of the longer hikes to Sunset Beach or Drakes Estero, I recommend going as far as this junction to partake of the fabulous views offered of Drakes Bay. You may head south on Drakes Head Trail down to Limantour Estero, or you may follow Estero Trail all the way to Limantour Beach.

TOMALES POINT

Difficulty rating: Strenuous

Distance: 9.4 miles round-trip from Upper Pierce Ranch to Tomales Point

Estimated time: 4–5 hr.

Elevation gain: 300 ft.

Cost/permits: None

Best time to go: Spring for wildflowers and fall for the tule elk

Website: www.nps.gov/pore

Recommended map: Tom Harrison Maps Point Reyes National Seashore

Trail head GPS: N 38 11.305, W 122 57.230

Trail head directions: Drive north on Sir Francis Drake Blvd. past the town of Inverness. Shortly after Sir Francis turns west, bear right (north) on Pierce Point Rd. and follow this road 9 miles to its end at Upper Pierce Point Ranch. Tomales Point Trail shares a trail head with the half-mile-long path leading to McClures Beach.

Tomales Point, solid granite carved by restless waves into bold cliffs, is quite the contrast to the softer slopes that comprise most of the California coast. Tomales Point Trail, an old ranch road, wanders over the green hillocks that top the 4-mile-long finger of land thrusting northwesterly into the Pacific. Be on the lookout for the tule elk herd that wanders the bluffs. Dramatic views of the Point Reyes area are available from Tomales Point, the northernmost boundary of Marin County and Point Reyes National Seashore.

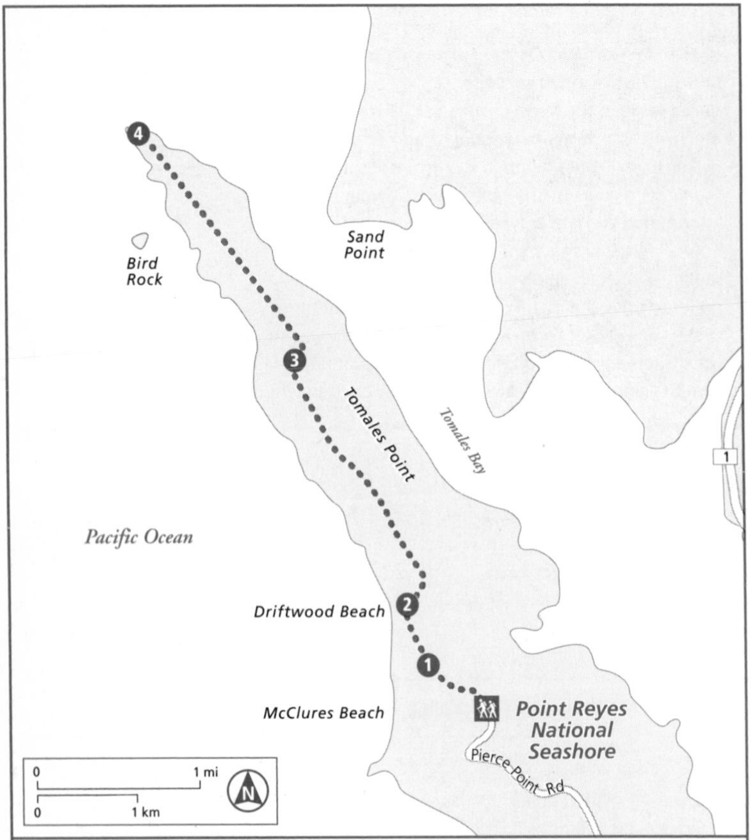

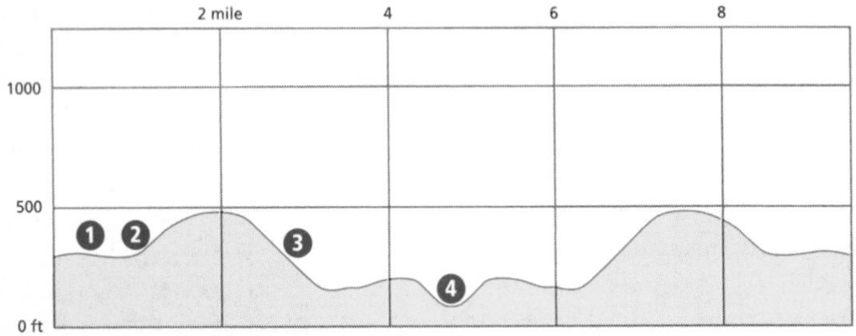

- Trail head icon: N 38 11.305, W 122 57.229: Trail head
- ❶ N 38 11.529, W 122 57.686 (0.6 miles): Views of McClure Beach from top of first hillock
- ❷ N 38 11.867, W 122 57.804 (1.0 miles): Path descends to Windy Gap
- ❸ N 38 13.158, W 122 58.621 (2.7 miles): Lower Pierce Ranch
- ❹ N 38 14.437, W 122 59.721 (4.6 miles): Tomales Point

Begin the hike from the signed trail head near the old dairy buildings at Upper Pierce Ranch. The point's rich pasture caught the eye of Solomon Pierce, who began a dairy in 1858. Pierce and his son Abram produced fine butter, which was shipped to San Francisco from a wharf they built on Tomales Bay. For 7 decades, the point remained in the Pierce family. Upper Pierce Ranch, where the family house, barn, and outbuildings are, is now maintained by the park service.

The wide path passes near a wind-battered windbreak of Monterey cypress and traverses grasslands dotted with coyote brush and two lovely lupines—ground-hugging blue lupine and showy, fragrant, yellow-flowered coastal bush lupine.

1 McClure's Beach The trail climbs north across the coastal prairie and offers superb views of the beach and surf. From the first hillock, look down at McClures Beach and Elephant Rock at its southern end.

> McClure's Beach is positively theatrical: great granite cliffs, enormous rocks, and huge waves. Exposed to the full fury of the Pacific, the beach resounds with waves like rolling thunder that strike the rocks and sea stacks at land's end and toss great plumes of spray skyward.

Margaret McClure, whose family owned a dairy, was one of the first property owners to permit public access to a Point Reyes–area beach. She donated the beach and a portion of the nearby bluffs to the public for parkland back in the 1940s.

You can walk down to the beach from the Tomales Point trail head or from the signed parking for McClures Beach on the west side of Pierce Point Road. Join the sandy, creek-side trail for the brief descent to the beach. Look offshore for the unusual sea scoter, a small, black sea duck with a bright orange and white bill that surfs the waves. Pelicans, cormorants, and murres are among the many seabirds that perch on the rocks near shore.

The most intriguing part of the $^{3}/_{4}$-mile-long beach is the south end. Head toward the sea stacks, sculpted from McClures' cliffs by the relentless surf. At low tide, you can squeeze through a narrow rock passageway and emerge at a dramatic little pocket beach.

Keep an eye out for tule elk. A large elk population once roamed the Point Reyes area, but by the 1860s, hunters had eliminated the animals. In 1977, the National Park Service relocated some elk onto Tomales Point from the Owens Valley. The tule elk are usually found in two different groups—a bull and his harem, and in a congregation of bachelor bulls.

2 Windy Gap A mile out, you'll descend into aptly named Windy Gap and look down at also well-named Driftwood Beach. The wide path climbs and descends at a moderate rate. As you crest the ridge and drift over to its eastern side, you'll begin to get a view of Tomales Bay, as well as Hog Island and the village of Dillon Beach. At about the 2-mile mark, you'll reach the hike's high point.

3 Lower Pierce Ranch Three miles out, the old ranch road descends to the site of Lower Pierce Ranch, the site identified by a pond and eucalyptus grove. Soon, the road becomes a trail and, about $^{1}/_{2}$ mile past the ranch, arrives at a high vista point that looks down on Bird Rock. The rock is occupied by cormorants and white pelicans.

When the fog settles over the dew-dampened grasslands of Tomales Point, hikers can easily imagine that they're stepping onto a Scottish moor or wandering one of the Shetland Islands. The point is seasonally sprinkled with yellow poppies and tidy tips, orange fiddleneck, and purple iris.

❹ **Tomales Point** A faint path, and some cross-country travel, will take you to the very tip of Tomales Point, a rocky perch about 30 feet above the Pacific. Watch your footing! Stirring views of Bodega Head and Tomales Bay are the reward for reaching land's end.

SLEEPING & EATING

ACCOMMODATIONS

San Francisco

★ **Hostelling International San Francisco—Fisherman's Wharf** Unbelievable but true—you can get front-row bay views for a mere $23 a night. This hostel, on national park property, provides dorm-style accommodations and offers easy access to the Marina's shops and restaurants. Rooms sleep 2 to 12 people, and there are 10 private rooms available; communal space includes a fireplace, kitchen, dining room, coffee bar, pool table, and foosball table. The breakfast alone practically makes it worth the price. Make reservations well in advance.

240 Building, Fort Mason, San Francisco, CA 94123. ✆ **415/771-7277.** www.sfhostels.com. 150 beds. $23–$29 adults; $15–$17 children. Rates include breakfast. MC, V. **Close to:** All San Francisco hikes.

★★ **Hotel Bijou** Although it's on the periphery of the gritty Tenderloin (just 3 blocks off Union Sq.), once inside this gussied-up 1911 hotel, all's cheery, bright, and perfect for budget travelers who want a little style with their savings. Rooms, named after locally made films, are small, clean, and colorful. Considering the price and perks, you can't go wrong here.

111 Mason St., Union Square, San Francisco, CA 94102. ✆ **800/771-1022** or 415/771-1200. www.hotelbijou.com. 65 units. $99–$159 double. Rates include continental breakfast. AE, DC, DISC, MC, V. **Close to:** All San Francisco hikes.

Hotel Drisco Located on one of the most sought-after blocks of residential property in all of San Francisco, the Drisco, built in 1903, is one of the city's best small hotels. As in the neighboring mansions, traditional antique furnishings and thick, luxurious fabrics abound here. The hotel's comfy beds will make you want to loll late into the morning before primping in the large marble bathrooms, complete with robes and slippers.

2901 Pacific Ave. (at Broderick St.), San Francisco, CA 94115. ✆ **800/634-7277** or 415/346-2880. www.hoteldrisco.com. 48 rooms. $249 double; $369–$399 suite. Rates include buffet breakfast and evening wine hour. AE, DC, DISC, MC, V. **Close to:** All San Francisco hikes.

★★ **King George Hotel** The location of this boutique hotel—surrounded by cable car lines, the Theater District, Union Square, and dozens of restaurants—is superb. The guest rooms can be very small (in the smallest rooms, it can be difficult for two people to maneuver at the same time), but they still manage to find room for writing desks, private bathrooms, and king or queen pillow-top beds with down comforters.

334 Mason St. (between Geary and O'Farrell sts.), San Francisco, CA 94102. ✆ **800/288-6005** or 415/781-5050. www.kinggeorge.com. 153 units. $175 double; $195 suite. MC, V. **Close to:** All San Francisco hikes.

★ **Laurel Inn** Tucked just beyond the southernmost tip of the Presidio and Pacific Heights, the outside is nothing impressive—just another motor inn. Inside, the decor is *très* chic and modern, with Zen-like influences. The rooms, some of which have excellent city views, are smartly designed and decorated in the style of a contemporary studio apartment.

444 Presidio Ave. (at California Ave.), San Francisco, CA 94115. ✆ **800/552-8735** or 415/567-8467. www.thelaurelinn.com. 49 units. $169–$209 double. Rates include continental breakfast, and afternoon lemonade and cookies. AE, DC, DISC, MC, V. **Close to:** All San Francisco hikes.

Marina Inn Each guest room in the 1924 four-story Victorian looks like something from a country furnishings catalog, complete with rustic pinewood furniture and a four-poster bed with silky-soft comforter. Combine that with such amenities as free Wi-Fi and an armada of shops and restaurants within easy walking distance, and you have one of the best values in San Francisco.

3110 Octavia St. (at Lombard St.), San Francisco, CA 94123. ✆ **800/274-1420** or 415/928-1000. 40 units. Nov–Feb $75–$115 double; Mar–May $85–$135 double; June–Oct $95–$145 double. Rates include continental breakfast. AE, DC, DISC, MC, V. **Close to:** All San Francisco hikes.

Point Reyes

Inns of Marin (✆ **800/887-2880** or 415/663-2000; www.innsofmarin.com), **Point Reyes Lodging Association** (✆ **800/539-1872** or 415/663-1872; www.ptreyes.com), and **West Marin Network** (✆ **415/663-9543**) are reputable services that will help you find accommodations, from one-room cottages to inns and vacation homes. The **West Marin Chamber of Commerce** (✆ **415/663-9232;** www.pointreyes.org) is also a good source for lodging and visitor information. Keep in mind that many places here require a 2-night minimum stay, but in slow season, they may make exceptions. They'll also refer you to restaurants, hiking trails, and other attractions in the area.

★ **Motel Inverness** Who cares where you sleep when you spend most of your trip hiking in the great outdoors? This pleasant and comfortable motel offers everything you need and nothing you don't. Fun for the family, with a huge lawn and great room with fireplace, suites, cottages, and guest rooms—all non-smoking.

12718 Sir Francis Drake Blvd., Inverness, CA 94937. ✆ **888/669-6909** or 415/669-1081. www.motelinverness.com. 7 units. 1 cottage. $99–$175 double; $225–$275 suite; $500 cottage. MC, V. **Close to:** Drakes Estero.

★ **Point Reyes Seashore Lodge** All comfort and beauty in this pleasant spot offering all-natural amenities: views, songbirds, gardens, and a magnificent lawn. Private rooms and cottages located on 3 lush acres just steps—literally—from the National Park. Cross a plank bridge over a bubbling book and follow a footpath across a meadow to Bear Valley Visitor Center. Breakfast and afternoon snacks included.

10021 Hwy. 1, Olema, CA 94950. ✆ **800/404-5634** or 415/663-9000. www.pointreyesseashore.com. 23 units. 2 cottages. $135–$245 double. AE, D, MC, V, AE. **Close to:** Muir Woods.

Steep Ravine Environmental Cabins Five can stay for $15 apiece—it doesn't get any better. Staying in these rustic cabins—with sleeping platforms, wood-burning stoves, running water, and yes, outhouses—puts you close to magnificent trails and Stinson Beach. Bring your sleeping bag and an adventurous spirit. The cabins are very popular, so reserve one as far in advance as possible (you can book them up to 7 months prior).

Mount Tamalpais State Park, Mill Valley, CA 94941 ✆ **415/388-2070.** Reservations ✆ **800/444-7275.** www.reserveamerica.com. 6 campsites, 10 cabins, $15–$75 double. **Close to:** Mount Tamalpais and Steep Ravine.

San Francisco

★★ **Andalé Taqueria** MEXICAN Andalé (Spanish for "hurry up") offers *muy bueno* high-end fast food for the health-conscious and the just plain hungry. As the long menu explains, this small California chain prides itself on its fresh ingredients and low-cal options. Andalé favors salad dressings made with double virgin olive oil, whole vegetarian beans (not refried), skinless chicken, salsas and *aguas frescas* made from fresh fruits and veggies, and mesquite-grilled meats. Cafeteria-style service keeps prices low.

2150 Chestnut St. (between Steiner and Pierce sts.), San Francisco, CA 94123. ✆ **415/749-0506.** Reservations not accepted. Main courses $4–$11. MC, V. Daily 10am–10pm. **Close to:** All San Francisco hikes.

Barney's Gourmet Hamburgers AMERICAN If you're on a perpetual quest for the best burger in America, a mandatory stop is Barney's Gourmet Hamburgers. You're bombarded by a mind-boggling menu of beef, chicken, turkey, and vegetarian burgers to choose from, as well as sandwiches and salads. The ultimate combo is a humungous basket of fries (enough for a party of three), ¹/₃-pound burger, and thick shake. Be sure to dine alfresco in the hidden courtyard in back.

3344 Steiner St. (between Chestnut and Lombard sts.), San Francisco, CA 94114. ✆ **415/563-0307.** www.barneyshamburgers.com. Main courses $5–$8. No credit cards. Mon–Thurs 11am–9:30pm; Fri–Sat 11am–10pm; Sun 11am–9pm. **Close to:** All San Francisco hikes.

★★★ **Beach Chalet Brewery & Restaurant** AMERICAN While Cliff House has more historical character and better ocean views, the Beach Chalet down the road has far better food, drinks, and atmosphere (ergo, it's where the locals go). Dinner is pricey, and the ocean view disappears with the sun, so come for lunch or an early dinner when you can eat your hamburger, buttermilk fried calamari, or grilled Atlantic salmon with one of the best vistas around. In the evening, it's a more local crowd, especially on Tuesday through Sunday evenings, when live bands accompany the cocktails and house-brewed ales. Breakfast is served here, as well. The adjoining Park Chalet serves more casual fare.

1000 Great Hwy. (at west end of Golden Gate Park, near Fulton St.), San Francisco, CA 94121. ✆ **415/386-8439.** www.beachchalet.com. Breakfast $8–$17; lunch/dinner $11–$27. AE, MC, V. Beach Chalet: daily 9am–10pm. Park Chalet: Mon–Thurs noon–9pm; Fri noon–11pm; Sat–Sun 11am–2pm and 5pm–11pm. **Close to:** All San Francisco hikes.

★★ **Cliff House California** SEAFOOD The revamped San Francisco landmark caters mostly to tourists who arrive to gander at the Sutro Baths remains next door or dine at the two remodeled restaurants. The more formal (and pricey) Sutro's has contemporary decor, spectacular panoramic views, and a fancy seafood-influenced American menu that showcases local ingredients. The same spectacular views can be found at the Bistro, which serves big salads, sandwiches, burgers, and other soul-satisfiers.

1090 Point Lobos (at Merrie Way), San Francisco, CA 94121. ✆ **415/386-3330.** www.cliffhouse.com. Bistro main courses $9–$26, Sutro main courses $18–$30; 3-course prix-fixe lunch $25, dinner $35 (Mon–Fri only). AE, DC, DISC, MC, V. Bistro: Mon–Sat 9am–9:30pm; Sat–Sun 9am–10pm. Sutro: daily 11:30am–3:30pm and 5–9:30pm; brunch Sun 10am–2pm. **Close to:** All San Francisco hikes.

Greens Restaurant VEGETARIAN In an old waterfront warehouse, with enormous windows overlooking the bridge, boats, and bay, Greens is one of the most renowned vegetarian restaurants in the country. Executive chef Annie Somerville (author of *Fields of Greens*) cooks with the seasons, using produce from local organic farms. The adjacent Greens To Go sells sandwiches, soups, salads, and pastries.

Building A, Fort Mason (enter Fort Mason opposite the Safeway at Buchanan and Marina sts.), San Francisco, CA 94123. ✆ **415/771-6222.** www.greensrestaurant.com. Reservations recommended. Main courses $9.50–$20. AE, DISC, MC, V. Mon–Sat noon–2:30pm and 5:30–9pm; Sun 10:30am–9pm. Greens To Go: Mon–Thurs 8am–8pm; Fri–Sat 8am–5pm; Sun 10:30am–4pm. **Close to:** All San Francisco hikes.

★ **Home Plate** CAFE Many Marina residents kick off their hectic weekends by carbo-loading here on big piles of buttermilk pancakes and waffles smothered with fresh fruit, or hefty omelets stuffed with everything from apple wood-smoked ham to spinach. You'll always start off with a coveted plate of freshly baked scones, best eaten with a bit of butter and a dab of jam. And as every fan of this tiny cafe knows, it's best to call ahead and ask to have your name put on the waiting list before you slide into Home Plate.

2274 Lombard St. (at Pierce St.), San Francisco, CA 94123. ✆ **415/922-4663.** Reservations recommended. Main courses $3.95–$7. DC, DISC, MC, V. Daily 7am–4pm. **Close to:** All San Francisco hikes.

Point Reyes

★ **Olema Farm House Restaurant** Deli Serving hungry visitors since 1865, this farm-friendly establishment offers natural goodness in a setting filled with historic charm. Do not miss the burger with Point Reyes Blue Cheese—a standout selection among lunch choices that include excellent sandwiches, soups, and salads. Sample the local ales and be sure to try the local oysters.

10005 State Hwy. 1, Olema, CA 94950. ✆ **415/663-8615.** www.olemafarmhouse.com. Main courses $9–$20. AE, D, MC, V. **Close to:** Muir Woods.

★★ **Pelican Inn** PUB Jolly Old England in an unexpected location. Sample the best in English specialties, including hearty shepherd's pie, and bangers and mash. Hikers who have conquered the Cotswolds in the heart of the English countryside will feel right at home with a pub lunch, accompanied by a fine ale on tap.

10 Pacific Way, Muir Beach, CA 94965. ✆ **415/383-6000.** www.pelicaninn.com. Main courses $9–$20. AE, MC, V. Daily 11:30am–3:00pm and 5:30–9pm. **Close to:** Tennessee Valley.

Rosie's Cowboy Cookhouse MEXICAN/AMERICAN Tex-Mex as good as it gets—with plenty of local, free-range, and organic ingredients thrown in. Long a favorite destination, where a famed *taqueria* once stood, the new incarnation retains much of the flavor, as well as the popularity, of its forerunner. Homemade dishes to savor include tasty chili and tamales.

11285 Hwy. 1 (at 3rd and Main sts.), Point Reyes Station, CA 94956. ✆ **415/663-8868.** Main courses $7–$15. No credit cards. Wed–Mon 11am–9pm. **Close to:** Bear Valley & Arch Rock.

Station House Café AMERICAN Visitors to Point Reyes return time and again to this landmark eatery that's been around for more than 20 years. Comfortable and casual are the watchwords—add delicious and local to describe the food; tasty and tantalizing to describe the wines and beers. Enjoy live music and outdoor dining when weather permits.

11180 Main St., Point Reyes Station, CA 94956. ✆ **415/663-1515.** www.stationhousecafe.com. Main courses $6–$27. AE, DISC, MC, V. Sun–Tues and Thurs 8am–9pm; Fri–Sat 8am–10pm (bar open until 11pm). Closed Wed. **Close to:** Bear Valley & Arch Rock.

5

Coast South of San Francisco

The Coast south of San Francisco is full of surprises: wildflower-covered bluffs, silver crescents of sand, tall dunes, rich estuaries, and two long coastal ranges—the Santa Cruz Mountains and Santa Lucia Mountains, which offer the hiker excellent trails and fabulous coastal vistas.

The Santa Cruz Mountains extend some 80 miles along the coast from a bit south of San Francisco to the Pajaro River on the Santa Cruz/Monterey county border. Lower and narrower in the northern reaches, the range is higher, wider, and wilder in the south. The young, geologically active mountains support impressive redwood groves. The delights of hiking the Santa Cruz Mountains include deep, Douglas fir– and redwood-lined canyons, view-filled ridges, and tranquil canyons.

What is popularly known as Big Sur is really the Santa Lucia Mountains, a range extending 90 miles from the Carmel Valley in the north to San Simeon in San Luis Obispo. Trails probe the headwaters of the Arroyo Seco, Little Sur, and Big Sur rivers, which originate in the Ventana Wilderness. In these mountains is the southernmost limit of the natural range of the magnificent coastal redwoods. Fern-lined canyons, oak-studded potreros, and meadows smothered with colorful Douglas iris, pink owl's clover, and California poppies greet the backcountry traveler.

The wild geography of Point Lobos, a highlight of coast south's diverse landscape, moved landscape artist Francis McComas to call it "the greatest meeting of land and sea in the world." And, indeed, you'll discover many such spectacular meetings of shore and sea along the coast south of San Francisco. You might even meet up with a colony of boisterous elephant seals at Point Ano Nuevo, or find inspiration in the redwoods of the Santa Cruz Mountains and Big Sur. The coast south shares some of the north's weather—generous rains, frequent fogs—as well as some of the sunshine and temperate breezes more typical of the coast in Central and Southern California.

Many of the parks in the Santa Cruz Mountains have excellent trails. The superb Skyline to the Sea Trail links Big Basin Redwoods State Park with mountaintop preserves and Pacific beaches. This trail—and many local volunteers—made history when the first Trails Day ever was held in 1969 to restore the trail.

The Big Sur Coast offers some of California's most striking coastline—hidden beaches, rocky coves, and bluffs carpeted with native wildflowers and introduced ice plant. Another lure is wonderful wildlife watching. Sea otters and sea lions bask on the rocks just offshore. Seabirds, such as oystercatchers and cormorants, glide over the waves. The bluffs are excellent vantage points from which to observe California gray whales on their annual winter migration.

Give yourself at least 3 days to get a fair sampling of the coast south of San Francisco: a day in Santa Cruz and the Santa Cruz Mountains, a day visiting parks along the Monterey Bay, and a day in Big Sur. Monterey, located 116 miles south of San Francisco and 45 miles south of Santa Cruz, is a pleasant seaside community with magnificent vistas, historic architecture, and a variety of lodging options. More important, Monterey offers easy access to the 90-mile-long Big Sur coastline.

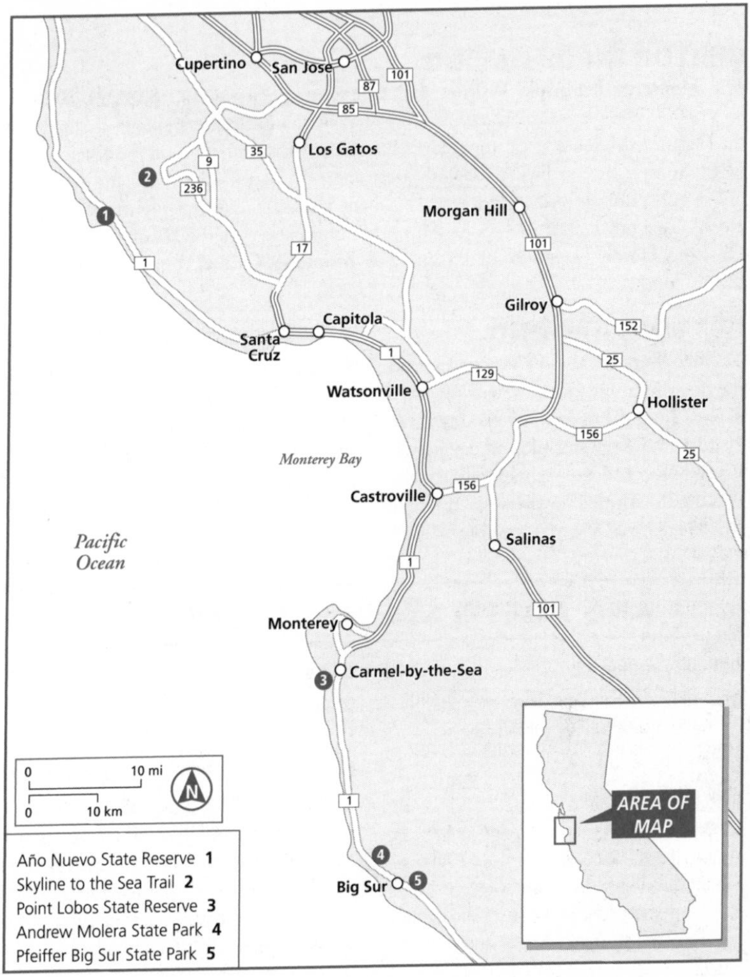

ESSENTIALS

GETTING THERE

By Air

The region's most convenient airport, the **Monterey Peninsula Airport** (**© 831/648-7000;** www.montereyairport.com), is 3 miles east of Monterey on Hwy. 68. American Eagle, Northwest, United, and US Airways run daily flights in and out of Monterey. Several national car-rental companies have airport locations, including **Dollar** (**© 800/800-3665;** www.dollar.com) and **Hertz** (**© 800/654-3131;** www.hertz.com).

By Car

Monterey is located 45 miles south of Santa Cruz and 116 miles south of San Francisco.

VISITOR INFORMATION

The **Monterey Peninsula Visitors and Convention Bureau** (✆ **888/221-1010** or 831/649-1770; www.seemontereyinfo.com) has two visitor centers: one in the lobby of the Maritime Museum at Custom House Plaza near Fisherman's Wharf, the other at Lake El Estero on Camino El Estero. Both locations, open daily, offer maps and free pamphlets and publications, including an excellent visitors' guide and the magazine *Coast Weekly.* Two other good sources for Monterey information are the **Monterey Peninsula On-Line Guide** (www.monterey.com) and **Monterey-Carmel.com** (www.monterey-carmel.com).

GETTING AROUND

The free **Waterfront Area Visitor Express (WAVE)** shuttle takes passengers to and from the aquarium and other waterfront attractions from Memorial Day to Labor Day. It departs from the downtown parking garages at Tyler Street and Del Monte Avenue every 10 to 12 minutes and runs all day between 9am and 6pm. Other WAVE stops include many hotels and motels in Monterey and Pacific Grove, which eliminates the stress of parking in crowded downtown. For further information, call **Monterey Salinas Transit** (✆ **831/899-2555;** www.mst.org).

ANO NUEVO STATE RESERVE ★ Kids

Difficulty rating: Easy

Distance: 4 miles round-trip self-guided; 3 miles round-trip on guided tour

Estimated time: 2 hr.

Elevation gain: Minimal

Costs/permits: $6 state park entry fee; permit (free) required Apr–Nov to hike preserve. Guided tours (Dec–Mar) cost $7 per person. Reservations for the guided walks are strongly recommended.

Best time to go: December to April

Website: www.parks.ca.gov; www.reserveamerica.com (for reservations)

Recommended map: California State Parks Ano Nuevo State Reserve

Trail head GPS: N 37 07.189, W 122 18.432

Trail head directions: Ano Nuevo State Reserve is located just west of Hwy. 1, 22 miles north of Santa Cruz and 30 miles south of Half Moon Badeey.

If you take a winter trip to Ano Nuevo State Reserve, you'll be treated to a wildlife drama that attracts visitors from all over the world—a close-up look at the largest mainland population of elephant seals. From December through March, a colony of these huge creatures visits the reserve to breed and bear young. To protect the elephant seals (and the humans who hike out to see them), the reserve is open only through naturalist-guided tours during these months. At other times, hikers may obtain a permit to hike the preserve's trails. North of the restricted access around Ano Nuevo Point is a splendid coastline of rocky coves, low dunes, and wildflower-strewn meadowland.

Elephant Seals and Their Reserve

Slaughtered for their oil-rich blubber, the elephant seal population numbered fewer than 100 by the early 1900s. Placed under government protection, the huge mammals rebounded rapidly from the brink of extinction. Ano Nuevo State Reserve was created in 1958 to protect the seals.

Male elephant seals, some reaching lengths of 16 feet and weighing 3 tons, arrive in December and begin battling for dominance. Only a very small percentage of males actually get to inseminate a female; most remain lifelong bachelors. The females, relatively svelte at 1,200 to 2,000 pounds, come ashore in January and join the harems of the dominant males.

La Punta De Ano Nuevo (The Point of the New Year) was named by the Spanish explorer Sebastian Vizcaino on January 3, 1603. It's one of the oldest place names in California.

At the time of its discovery, the Point was occupied by the Ohlone, who lived off the bounty of the sea. Judging from kitchen midden sites—shell mounds—found in the nearby dunes, it was a rich bounty, indeed.

The Ano Nuevo area later hosted a variety of enterprises. From the 1850s to 1920, redwood cut from the slopes of the nearby Santa Cruz Mountains was shipped from Ano Nuevo Bay. A dairy industry flourished on the coastal bluffs. The reserve's visitor center is a restored early 20th-century dairy barn.

While the elephant seals are clearly the main attraction when they come ashore during the winter to breed and during the spring and summer to molt, the reserve is just as fascinating when the big creatures are not in residence.

Bird-watchers may glimpse a cliff swallow, Western gull, red-tailed hawk, and many other inland and shore birds. Beach grass, morning glory, and extensive patches of beach strawberry cover the beautiful sand dunes.

At the parking area, you join Ano Nuevo Point Trail, which soon (in 100 ft.) junctions left-branching Pond Loop Trail.

Stay right, curving inland past clumps of poison oak and blackberry, and over a grassland. At 3/4 mile, the path encounters Pond Loop Trail once again.

1 Wildlife Protection area Continue a quarter mile along the wide, flat Ano Nuevo Point Trail to the official border of the wildlife protection area and a small building with exhibits highlighting the various species of seals and sea lions. During the winter months, this is where the docent-led tours begin. Other months, in possession of a wildlife permit, you may continue on Ano Nuevo Point Trail.

Bordered by guide-wires and coastal brush, the path heads up-coast and offers great views of Ano Nuevo Island with its thriving populations of birds and seals. The trail crosses sandy terrain and approaches some dunes, colorfully dotted with yellow sand verbena, morning glory, and beach strawberry. Archaeologists have discovered evidence—chipped tools and mounds of seashells—of a lengthy occupation here by native peoples.

2 Observation Points Spur trails lead to a trio of observation points: South Beach Overlook, Bight Beach Overlook, and North Beach Overlook. Often, docents are present to discuss the elephant seals and the rich natural history of this special coast.

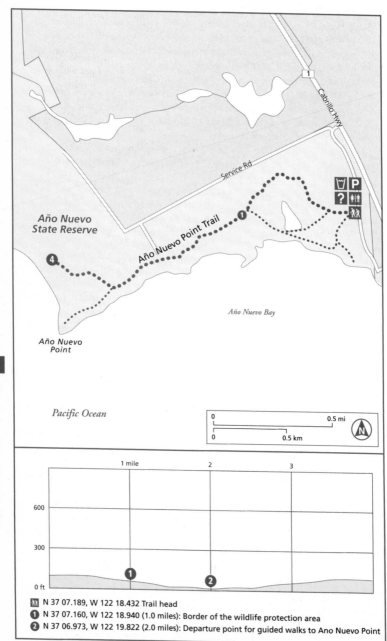

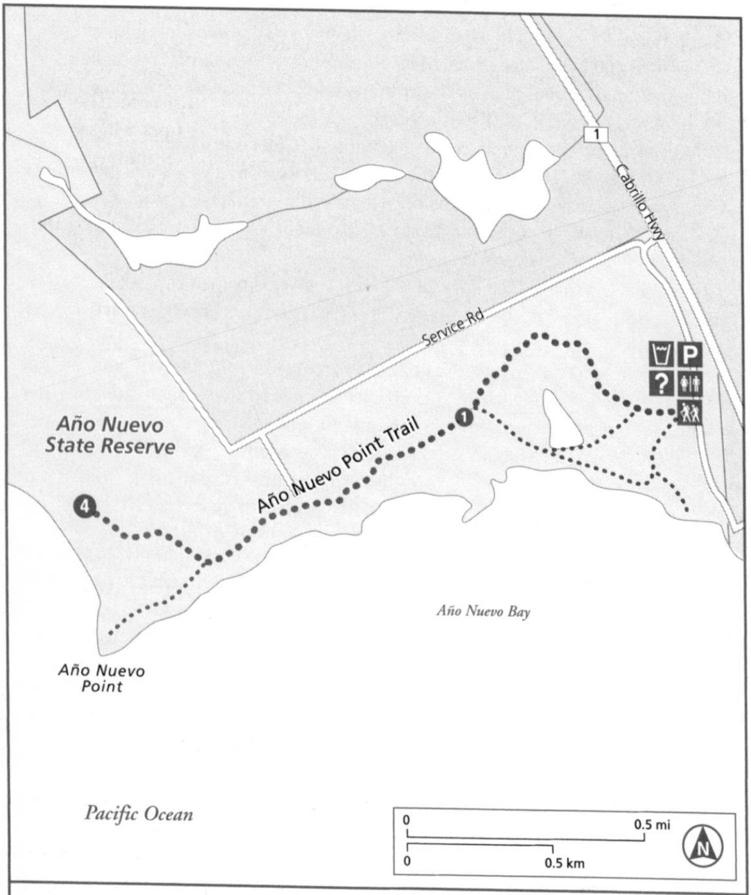

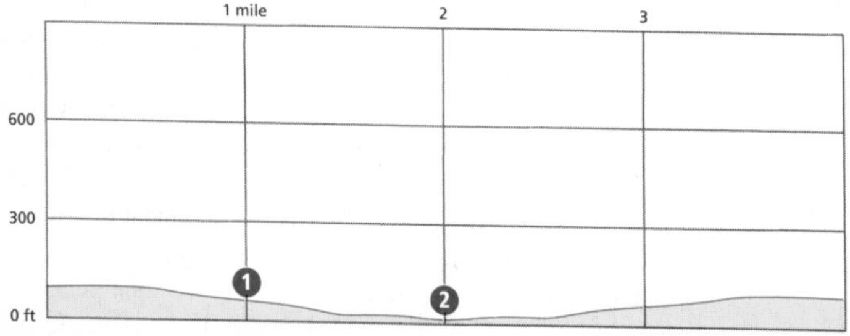

N 37 07.189, W 122 18.432 Trail head

1 N 37 07.160, W 122 18.940 (1.0 miles): Border of the wildlife protection area

2 N 37 06.973, W 122 19.822 (2.0 miles): Departure point for guided walks to Ano Nuevo Point

Retrace your steps back to the junction with Pond Loop Trail. Bear right on this path, passing a junction with Cove Beach Trail and a pond that's a favorite hangout for pelicans, then returning to meet Ano Nuevo Point Trail and the nearby trail head.

Joining the elephant seals on Ano Nuevo Island are Steller sea lions, California sea lions, and harbor seals. Seals inhabit Ano Nuevo year-round. Viewing is great on the beaches in the spring and summer months. Autumn brings 1- to 3-year-old "yearling" seals ashore to rest on the beaches.

The new Marine Education Center, which creatively uses three landmark structures from the historic Steele Dairy Ranch, provides much-needed interpretive and educational facilities without intruding into the domain of the elephant seals. The center supports the efforts of the more than 200 docents who give guided tours. Web-cam technology gives visitors close-up views of the elephant seals on Ano Nuevo Island.

SKYLINE TO THE SEA TRAIL ★★★

Difficulty rating: Moderate

Distance: 12 miles one way

Estimated time: 7 hr.

Elevation loss: 1,100 ft.

Costs/permits: $6 state park entry fee

Best time to go: Year round, especially on clear days

Website: www.bigbasin.org; www.parks.ca.gov

Recommended map: California State Parks Big Basin Redwoods State Park

Trail head GPS: N 37 10.296, W 122 13.232

Trail head directions: From Santa Cruz, drive 12 miles north on Hwy. 9. Turn west on Hwy. 236 and proceed 9 miles to Big Basin Redwoods State Park. Locate the trail head across the road from park headquarters at the large Redwood Trail marker. If you're hiking from Big Basin to the sea, you'll need to arrange a car shuttle. Waddell Beach, at trail's end, is 18 miles up-coast from Santa Cruz on Hwy. 1. Santa Cruz Metropolitan Transit District (✆ **408/425-8600;** www.scmtd.com) provides bus service to Waddel Beach and Big Basin. Rte. 35 offers weekend seasonal (spring/summer) service from Santa Cruz to Big Basin. Rte. 40 travels Hwy. 1 and transports the hiker from trail's end at Waddell Beach back to Santa Cruz. Leave your car at the Santa Cruz bus station (920 Pacific Ave.) and take the 7:45am bus bound for the state park. You'll arrive about 9am. Hit the trail and take the 5:15pm bus from Waddell Beach back to Santa Cruz.

Without a doubt, Skyline to the Sea Trail is one of the gems of the state's trail system. As its name suggests, the path drops from the crest of the Santa Cruz Mountains to the Pacific Ocean. Views from the Skyline—redwood-forested slopes, fern-smothered canyons, and the great blue Pacific—are superb. And if further enticement be needed, the trail runs mostly downhill on its scenic journey.

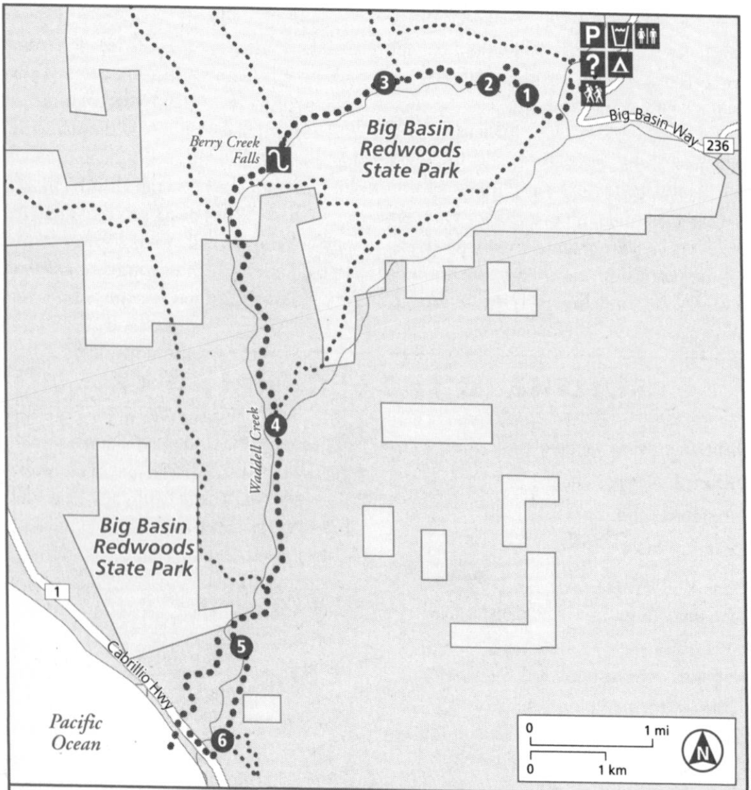

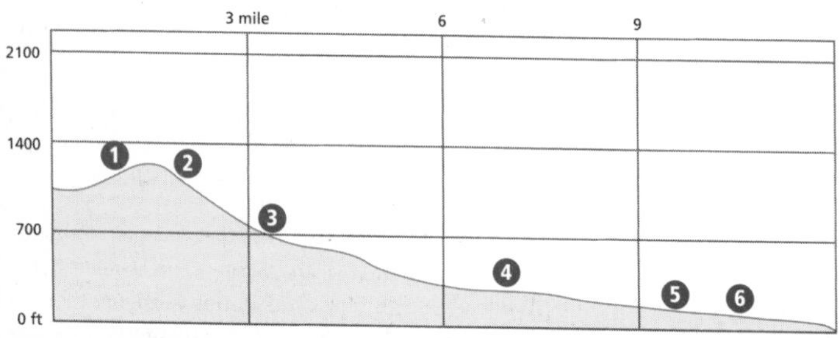

N 37 10.296, W 122 13.232 Trail head
1 N 37 10.278, W 122 13.798 (1.3 miles): Stay on trail past junction with Middle Ridge Road
2 N 37 10.324, W 122 14.134 (2.0 miles): Cross footbridge over Kelly Creek
3 N 37 10.329, W 122 15.012 (3.2 miles): Detour on Berry Creek Falls Trail to viewing platform
4 N 37 08.037, W 122 16.042 (7.3 miles): Twin Redwoods Trail Camp
5 N 37 06.540, W 122 16.387 (9.4 miles): Follow narrow footpath where trail splits
6 N 37 05.801, W 122 16.559 (10.6 miles): Trail passes freshwater marsh

The wildest and most beautiful part of the 35-mile long trail extends from state park headquarters in Big Basin to Waddell Creek Beach. It winds through deep woods and explores the moist environments of Waddell and Berry creeks.

The hike begins in the nucleus of the park on Opal Creek flatlands at the bottom of the basin. From park headquarters, you join Redwood Trail, which crosses a bridge and travels a few hundred yards to a signed junction with Skyline to the Sea Trail. You'll turn toward the sea and begin a vigorous climb out of the basin.

❶ Junction with Middle Ridge Road The first part of the trail takes you through very tall redwoods, then climbs over a ridge (and past a junction with Middle Ridge Rd.), and then returns to the redwoods.

❷ Kelly Creek footbridge Two miles out, you'll cross the Kelly Creek footbridge, sticking with Skyline Trail and passing junctions with other park trails.

After climbing, the trail descends through deep and dark woods, first with Kelly Creek, then along the west fork of Waddell Creek. Ferns and mushrooms, salamanders and banana slugs, occupy the wet world of the trail.

This is a hike for all seasons—great on a clear winter day. Spring, when the creeks are frothy torrents and Berry Creek Falls cascades at full vigor, is a particularly dramatic time to walk the trail. During summer, the cool redwood canyons are great places to beat the heat.

❸ Junction with Berry Creek Falls Trail Some 4 miles from the trail head, just short of the confluence of Waddell Creek and Berry Creek, you'll intersect Berry Creek Falls Trail.

> The Berry Creek Falls cascade over fern-covered cliffs into a frothy pool. Walk up Berry Creek Falls Trail $\frac{1}{4}$ mile to a viewing platform and wooden benches—a perfect lunch stop.

Skyline to the Sea Trail descends with Waddell Creek and passes through the heart of the beautiful Waddell Valley. Rancho del Oso, "Ranch of the Bears," as this region is known, has second-generation redwoods, Douglas fir, and Monterey pine, as well as lush meadows.

❹ Twin Redwoods Trail Camp, Alder Trail Camp About $3\frac{1}{4}$ miles from the sea, you'll pass the signed junction with McCrary Ridge Trail and continue along Waddell Creek. A mile and a half from the ocean, you'll reach Twin Redwoods Trail Camp and then Alder Trail Camp.

❺ Hiker's Route Just beyond Alder Trail Camp, the trail splits. The wide dirt road (horse trail/bicycle route) continues on a mellow descent with Waddell Creek. The hiker's route (a footpath) climbs the canyon wall above the creek and offers great views of the valley. After meandering up and around more than most hikers would like at this point in what was supposed to be an all downhill hike, the path eventually touches down on the valley floor, passing by a ranger station and a self-registration board for campers. The last $\frac{1}{3}$ mile is paved road.

❻ Freshwater Marsh Near trail's end is a freshwater marsh, a favorite stopping place for migratory birds on the Pacific flyway. A wildlife sanctuary, Theodore J. Hoover Natural Preserve, in the heart of the marsh area, serves more than 200 kinds of native and migratory birds.

The trail ends at Hwy. 1. West of the highway is a bus stop and windswept Waddell Beach.

Trails Day

By some hikers' reckoning, Trails Days, at least how we think of them now, began in California's Santa Cruz Mountains. Skyline to the Sea Trail needed some maintenance and, as it turned out, this gem of a trail had many friends.

During one weekend in 1969, dedicated members of the Sempervirens Fund and the Santa Cruz Trails Association turned out more than 2,000 volunteers to dig, clear, prune, and improve the path. Area volunteers put together an annual Trails Day that became a model for trails organization through the state and planted the seed for a National Trails Day, an annual celebration held each June with some 3,000 events across the U.S. to encourage hikers and newcomers to appreciate, preserve, and maintain their local trails.

POINT LOBOS STATE RESERVE ★ Kids

Difficulty rating: Easy

Distance: 0.75 mile round-trip on Cypress Grove Trail; 3 miles round-trip on North Shore Trail

Estimated time: 2 hr.

Elevation gain: 50 ft.

Costs/permits: $6 state park entry fee

Best time to go: Year round

Website: www.parks.ca.gov

Recommended map: California State Parks Point Lobos State Reserve

Trail head GPS: N 36 31.143, W 121 56.976

Trail head directions: Point Lobos State Reserve is located 3 miles south of Carmel just off Hwy. 1. There is a state park day-use fee. Both Cypress Grove Trail and North Shore Trail depart from the northwest end of Cypress Grove parking area.

A visit to Point Lobos State Reserve, in good weather and bad, is always memorable. Maybe it's the tranquil moments at Point Lobos: black-tailed deer moving through the forest, the fog-wrapped cypress trees. Or maybe it's peeking at nature's more boisterous moments: the bark of sea lions at Sea Lion Point, the sea thundering against the cliffs.

Some of photographer Ansel Adams' greatest work was inspired by the reserve's wind-sculpted cypress, lonely sentinels perched at the edge of the continent. Landscape artist Francis McComas called Point Lobos "the greatest meeting of land and water in the world."

❶ Allan Memorial Grove The first stop along the Cypress Grove Trail is Allan Memorial Grove, which honors A.M. Allan who, in the early years of the 20th century, helped preserve Point Lobos from resort developers. When Point Lobos became a reserve in 1933, Allan's family gave the cypress grove to the state.

At Point Lobos, the Monterey cypress makes a last stand. Botanists believe that during Pleistocene times, some half-million years ago, when the climate was wetter and cooler than it is now, huge forests of cypress grew along the coast—indeed, throughout North America. When the world's climate warmed, the cypress retreated to a few damp spots. Nowadays, the grove at Point Lobos and another across Carmel Bay at Cypress Point are the only two native stands in existence.

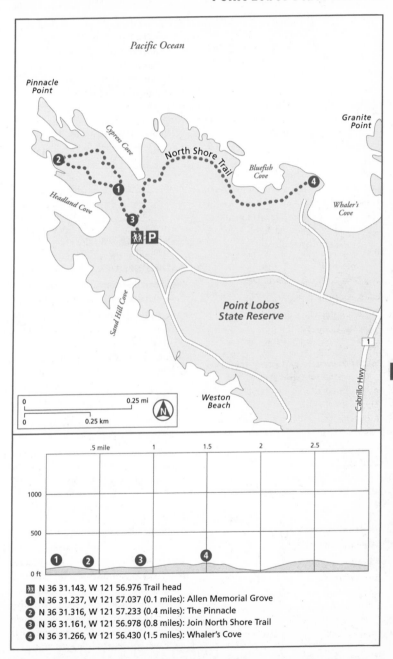

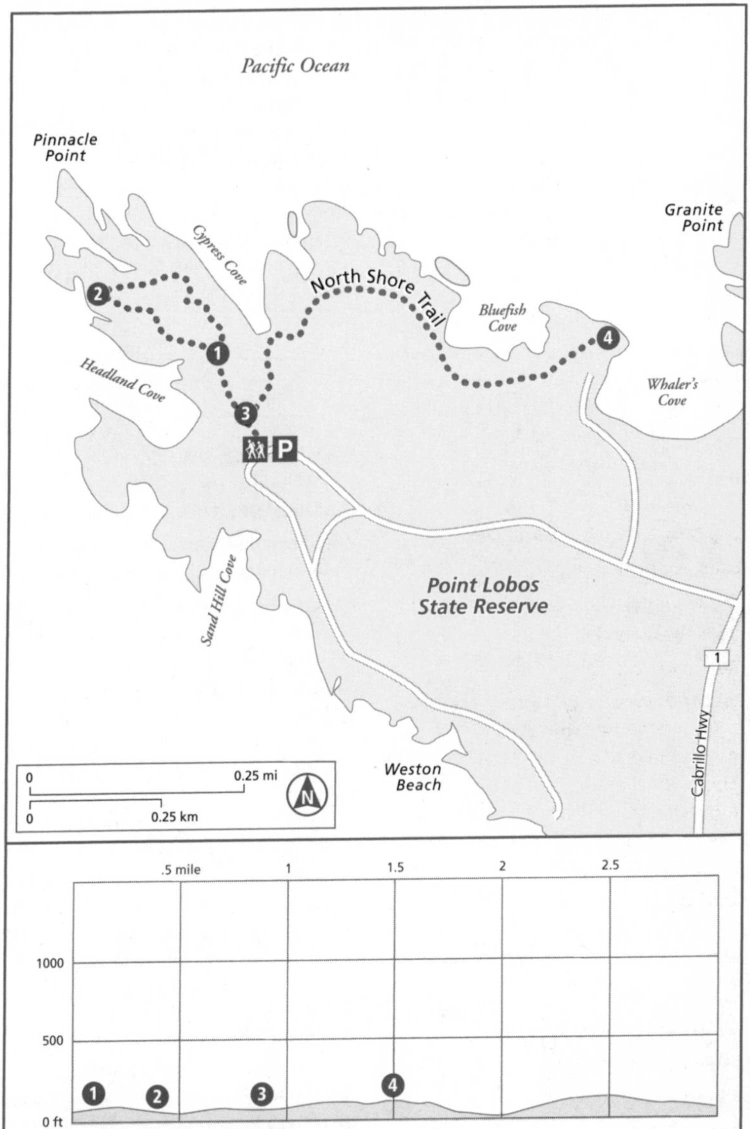

N 36 31.143, W 121 56.976 Trail head
1. N 36 31.237, W 121 57.037 (0.1 miles): Allen Memorial Grove
2. N 36 31.316, W 121 57.233 (0.4 miles): The Pinnacle
3. N 36 31.161, W 121 56.978 (0.8 miles): Join North Shore Trail
4. N 36 31.266, W 121 56.430 (1.5 miles): Whaler's Cove

The Monterey cypress, with the help of humans, can cross hot and dry regions and become established in cool areas elsewhere. In fact, this rare conifer is easily grown from seed and has been successfully distributed all over the world, so it's puzzling why the trees natural range is so restricted.

❷ The Pinnacle The trail passes near The Pinnacle, the northernmost point in the reserve. Winds off the Pacific really batter this point and the exposed trees. To combat the wind, the trees adopt a survival response called buttressing: a narrow part of the trunk faces the wind while the trunk grows thicker on the other side in order to brace itself. The wind-sculpted trunks and wind-shaped foliage give the cypress their fantastic shapes.

Cypress Grove Trail offers great tree-framed views of Carmel Bay and Monterey peninsula. Offshore are the rocky islands off Sea Lion Point. The Spaniards called the domain of these creatures *Punto de los Lobos Marinos*—Point of the Sea Wolves. You'll probably hear the barking of the sea lions before you see them.

❸ North Shore Trail Upon returning from Cypress Grove Trail, you will join the North Shore Trail, which meanders through groves of Monterey pine, less celebrated than the Monterey cypress, but nearly as rare. Native stands of the fog-loving, three-needled pine grow in only a few places in California.

North Shore Trail wanders through the pines and provides terrific coastal panoramas. Admirers of spooky beauty will appreciate the shrouds of pale green lichen hanging from the dead branches of the Monterey pines. Lichen, which conducts the business of life as a limited partnership of algae and fungi, is not a parasite and does not hurt the tree. It's believed that the presence of lichen is an indication of extremely good air quality.

The trail also gives a bird's-eye-view of Guillemot Island, where a variety of birds, including pigeon guillemots and cormorants, nest atop its large offshore rocks.

❹ Whalers Cove As you hike by Whalers Cove, you'll probably see divers entering the Point Lobos Underwater Reserve, America's first such reserve set aside in 1960. Divers explore the 100-foot-high kelp forests in Whalers and Blue Fish Cove. Mineral-rich waters from the nearby 1,000-foot-deep Carmel Submarine Canyon upwell to join the more shallow waters of the coves.

ANDREW MOLERA STATE PARK ★★

Difficulty rating: Moderate

Distance: 9.5 miles round-trip

Estimated time: 5 hr.

Elevation gain: 1,150 ft.

Costs/permits: $6 state park entry fee

Best time to go: Summer

Website: www.parks.ca.gov

Recommended map: California State Parks Andrew Molera State Park

Trail head GPS: N 36 17.179, W 121 50.568

Trail head directions: Andrew Molera State Park is just off CA 1, some 21 miles south of Carmel.

Mountains, meadows, and the mouth of Big Sur River are some of the highlights of a hike through Andrew Molera State Park, the largest park (4,800 acres) along the Big Sur coast. My favorite hike leads along the bluffs overlooking 3 miles of beach, then traverses meadows and oak woodland. At the mouth of the Big Sur River are a shallow lagoon and a beautiful sandy beach. The Big Sur River, the bluffs above Molera Beach, and steep grassy ridge tops that afford vistas of the coast as well as Ventana Wilderness peaks provide a memorable experience.

From the parking lot, cross the Big Sur River on the seasonal footbridge. Walk 100 yards or so along a broad path that soon splits. Bear right onto Beach Trail. (The left fork joins Creamery Meadow Trail, a substitute for beach trail if the river bridges are not in place or the water level is too high for safe crossing.) The trail stays near the river and banks crowded with thimbleberry and blackberry, honeysuckle vines, willow, and bay laurel.

❶ Campground At $^1/_3$ mile, you'll pass through the park's campground, popular with young people from across the country and around the world. A side trail leads to Cooper Cabin, an 1861 redwood structure that's the oldest building on Big Sur's coast.

❷ Mouth of Big Sur River At the river mouth is a small beach and shallow lagoon, frequented by sanderlings, willets, and many more shorebirds. A short path (Headlands Trail) leads above the beach to Molera Point, where you can watch for whales (Jan–Apr) or passing ships. The beach to the south is walk-able at low tide.

In 1855, Yankee fur trader Juan Bautista Roger Cooper acquired this land, formerly part of the Mexican land grant Rancho El Sur. Acquaintances of his day—and historians of today—speculate that Cooper used his "Ranch of the South" as a landing spot, bringing cargo ashore at the Big Sur River mouth to avoid the high custom fees of Monterey Harbor.

Grandson Andrew Molera, who inherited the ranch, had a successful dairy operation. His Monterey Jack cheese was particularly prized. He was a hospitable fellow, popular with neighbors who camped along the river while awaiting shipments of supplies from San Francisco.

Cross the summer footbridge over the Big Sur River to follow the upper part of the beach, then climb the bluffs and head south to a junction with Bluff Trail and Ridge Trail.

❸ Junction with Bluff Trail Join wide Bluff Trail, an old road, and head south over the almost-level bluffs, a marine terrace cloaked in grasses and coastal scrub. Summer-blooming lizard-tail blankets the terrace in yellow.

> Bluff Trail reaches a junction with Spring Trail, which offers a quarter-mile route to Molera Beach. Stop here for a picnic on the beach. (A return to the trail head from here would add up to a 6-mile round-trip hike.)

❹ Panorama Trail About $1^3/_4$ miles from the mouth of the Big Sur River, Bluff Trail gives way to Panorama Trail, a much more rigorous path that soon dips into a deep gully, then climbs steeply up a ridge, where wind-stunted redwoods cling to life. The trail climbs toward the southern boundary of the park and ascends to a junction with Ridge Trail at about $5^1/_2$ miles from the trail head.

❺ Junction with Ridge Trail A bench here offers a place to take it easy and eat your lunch. Your rewards for gaining about 900 feet in elevation are great views

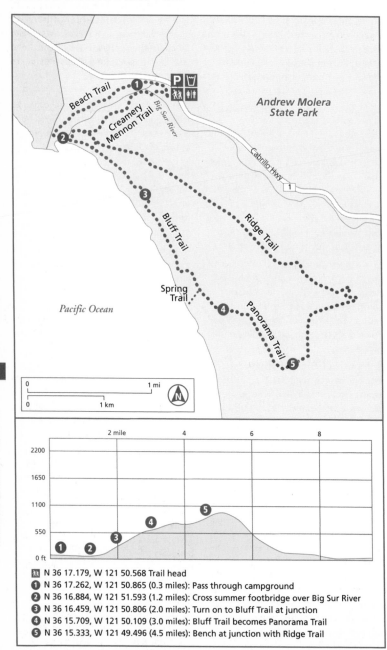

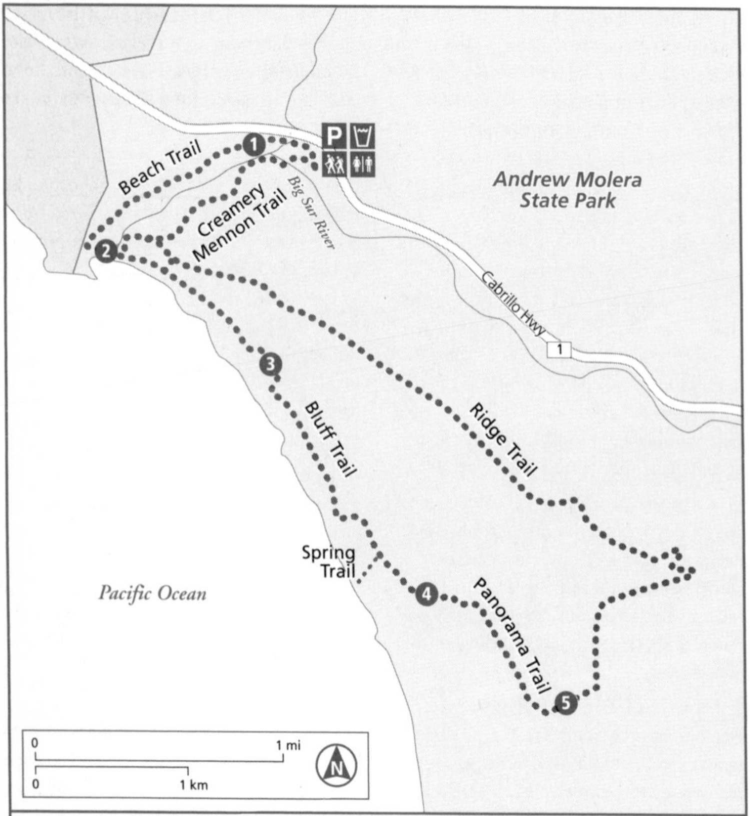

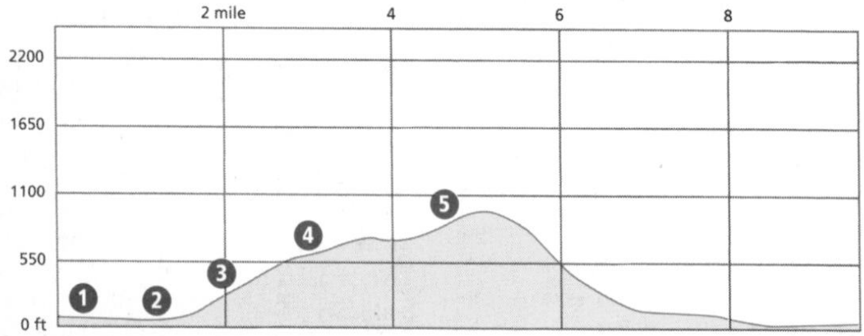

N 36 17.179, W 121 50.568 Trail head
1 N 36 17.262, W 121 50.865 (0.3 miles): Pass through campground
2 N 36 16.884, W 121 51.593 (1.2 miles): Cross summer footbridge over Big Sur River
3 N 36 16.459, W 121 50.806 (2.0 miles): Turn on to Bluff Trail at junction
4 N 36 15.709, W 121 50.109 (3.0 miles): Bluff Trail becomes Panorama Trail
5 N 36 15.333, W 121 49.496 (4.5 miles): Bench at junction with Ridge Trail

of the state park, the coast to the south, and the triangular-shaped Cone Peak, one of the high points of the Santa Lucia Mountains.

Ridge Trail begins its long (nearly 4-mile) descent northwest along the park's main ridge. You'll pass through an oak grove, then a tanoak and redwood forest, soon emerging onto the trail's more characteristic open, grassy slopes.

Ridge Trail continues back toward the coast, whereupon you can retrace your steps by taking Beach Trail to the trail head or return via River Trail on the south side of the Big Sur River.

PFEIFFER BIG SUR STATE PARK (Kids)

Difficulty rating: Easy

Distance: 2 miles round-trip from Big Sur Lodge to Pfeiffer Falls, Valley View

Estimated time: 1 hr.

Elevation gain: 400 ft.

Costs/permits: $5 state park entry fee

Best time to go: Year round

Website: www.parks.ca.gov

Recommended map: Pfeiffer Big Sur State Park map

Trail head GPS: N 36 15.139, W 121 47.038

Trail head directions: Pfeiffer Big Sur State Park is located off Hwy. 1, 26 miles south of Carmel and 2 miles south of the hamlet of Big Sur. Beyond the entry booth (fee required), turn left at the stop sign, then veer right (uphill) for day-use parking. A much larger parking area is located near the store and restaurant at the bottom of the hill.

Big Sur in a small package. This hike along Pfeiffer Falls Trail and Valley View Trail is an easy hike that visits Pfeiffer Falls and provides a good introduction to the delights of the state park, including some lovely redwoods.

John Pfeiffer, for whom the park was named, homesteaded 160 acres of mountainous terrain between Sycamore Canyon and the Big Sur River. In 1884, he moved into a cabin perched above the Big Sur River Gorge. John Pfeiffer sold and donated some of his ranchland to the state in the 1930s, and it became the nucleus of the state park, one of the most noteworthy in the California system.

Big Sur means different things to different people. To hardy hikers, it's the challenging Ventana Wilderness backcountry. To others, it's the hamlet of Big Sur with its post office, roadside businesses and campgrounds, lodging, and information station. For big-city dwellers to the north and south, Big Sur offers romantic weekends and a great escape.

Unfortunately, Big Sur is often associated with big fires, which in the summer of 2008 burned 162,818 acres and cost more than $77 million to fight. It was the third-largest wildfire in California history and scorched many of the trails in Los Padres National Forest, as well as in several state parks. However, most of the visitor facilities in Pfeiffer Big Sur State Park, including the campground, lodge, and the main trail to Pfeiffer Falls were spared.

For the motorist, Coast Highway from Carmel to the Monterey/San Luis Obispo county line has long been regarded as one of the world's great drives. In 1965, this stretch of Hwy. 1 was designated California's first scenic highway.

But the highway, noble engineering feat that it was, great road that it is, only gets you so close to Big Sur coast.

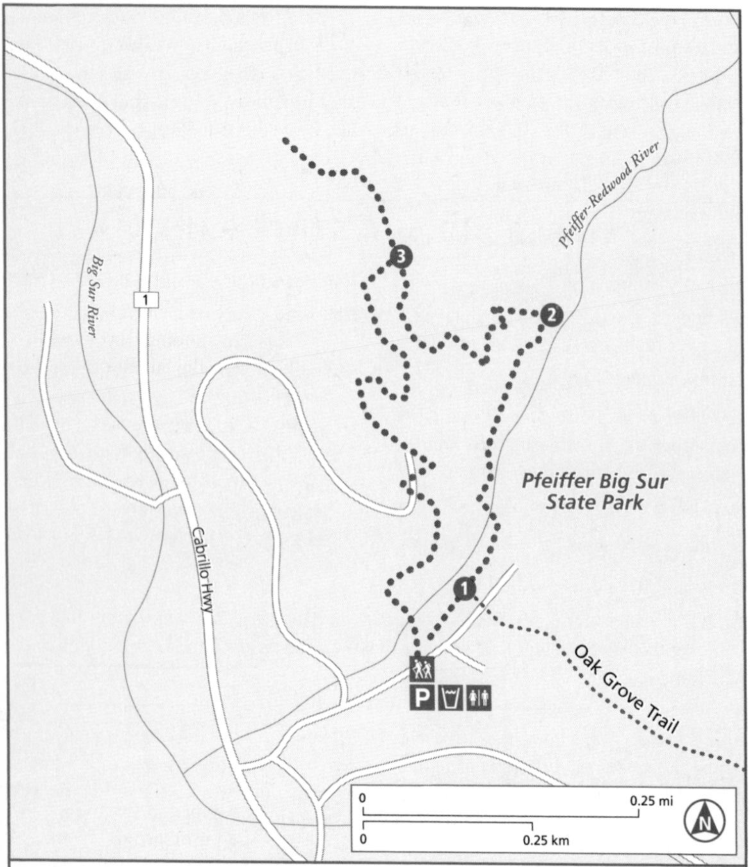

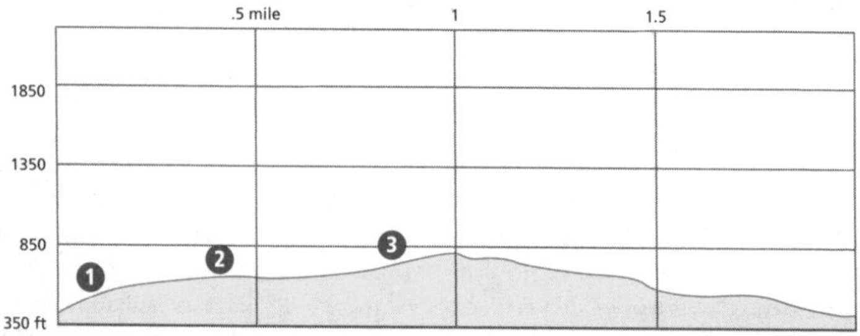

N 36 15.139, W 121 47.038 Trail head

❶ N 36 15.189, W 121 46.988 (0.1 miles): Stay left at junction with Oak Grove Trail

❷ N 36 15.397, W 121 46.881 (0.4 miles): Take right on to Valley View Trail

❸ N 36 15.439, W 121 47.052 (0.8 miles): Turn right at signed junction for lookout

For nature-oriented visitors, "Big Sur" means Pfeiffer Big Sur State Park, the best-known park on the Big Sur Coast. The state park—and its brief but popular trail system—is dominated by the Big Sur River, which meanders through redwood groves on its way to the Pacific Ocean, 5 miles away.

From the signed trail head, follow the trail to Pfeiffer Falls. Very shortly, on your left, you'll spot a trail heading left to Valley View; this will be your return path. The walk continues under stately redwoods and meanders along with Pfeiffer–Redwood Creek.

❶ **Oak Grove Trail Junction** You'll soon ascend a redwood stairway to a junction with Oak Grove Trail, which leads rightward 1½ miles through oak and madrone woodland over to the Mount Manuel Trail. Stay left at this junction and follow Pfeiffer Falls Trail through the forest and past a second branch of the Valley View Trail.

❷ **Pfeiffer Falls** A stairway leads to an observation platform at the base of the falls. Pfeiffer–Redwood Creek cascades over a 40-foot precipice to a small grotto.

❸ **Valley View Trail** After enjoying the falls, descend the stairway and bear right on the Valley View Trail, which leaves behind the redwoods and ascends into a tanbark oak and coast live oak woodland.

❹ **Side trail to lookout** At a signed junction, turn right and follow the pathway along a minor ridge to a lookout. The Pacific Ocean pounding the Point Sur headlands and the Big Sur River Valley are part of the fine view.

Backtrack along Valley View Trail and, at the first junction, stay right and descend on Pfeiffer Falls Trail back to Pfeiffer–Redwood Canyon. Another right at the canyon bottom brings you back to the trail head.

SLEEPING & EATING

ACCOMMODATIONS

★★★ **Big Sur Lodge** Hike all day, sleep all night. It's the perfect getaway in the perfect spot; take advantage of reduced winter rates. Spacious, rustic private cabins feature decks and porches with breathtaking views; some have fireplaces and kitchens. There's a restaurant and grocery store on the premises for meals, trail snacks, and hiking supplies.

47225 Hwy. 1, in Pfeiffer–Big Sur State Park, Big Sur, CA 93920. ✆ **800/424-4787** or 831/667-3100. www.bigsurlodge.com. 61 cottages. $199–$249 cottage; $259–$319 kitchen suite; $289–$359 kitchen suite with fireplace. Park entrance fee included. AE, MC, V. From Carmel, take Hwy. 1 south 26 miles. **Close to:** Pfeiffer–Big Sur State Park.

★ **Del Monte Beach Inn** A sweet deal if you don't insist on en-suite. Location and history are part of the attraction of this European-style inn with shared baths; it feels far removed from the tourist-y traps, although it's located within easy walking distance. Some rooms have ocean views; television is available in the pleasant communal library.

1110 Del Monte Ave, Monterey, CA 93940. ✆ **831/649-4410.** 19 units. Winter $60–$76 double; summer $76–$109 double. Rates include continental breakfast. MC, V. **Close to:** Point Lobos State Park.

★★ **Edgewater Beach Motel** It's like stepping into a fully furnished Hollywood set for a 1960s family flick. The kids will enjoy the heated pool; mom and dad will appreciate the clean rooms, convenient kitchenettes, and reasonable rates. Located within walking distance of the historic Santa Cruz Boardwalk, it's just the place for an inexpensive off-season getaway.

525 Second St., Santa Cruz, CA 95060. ✆ **888/809-6767** or 831/423-0440. www.edgewaterbeachmotel.com. 17 units. Winter $85–$219 double; summer $139–$299 double. AE, DC, DISC, MC, V. **Close to:** Skyline to the Sea Trail.

Fern River Resort Lots of resort-y activities, in addition to hiking along the nearby extensive trails at Henry Cowell State Park. Cabins nestled in the woods, in the gardens, or on the river provide privacy and quiet for resting and relaxing. Kitchens are available, but bring your own cooking utensils. Enjoy the spa-tub and small beach.

5250 Hwy. 9, Felton, CA 95018. ✆ **831/335-4412.** www.fernriver.com. 16 units. Summer $90–$155 double; winter $94–$142 double. AE, MC, V. **Close to:** Ano Nuevo State Park.

Spindrift Inn An oasis of class and luxury amid the hustle-bustle of Cannery Row. Elegant touches include canopy beds, down comforters, hardwood floors, marble, brass, and wood-burning fireplaces. Snuggle into a comfy terry robe (provided for your stay); enjoy the ocean view from the window seat or private balcony—and just relax.

652 Cannery Row, Monterey, CA 93940. ✆ **800/841-1879** or 831/646-8900. www.spindriftinn.com. 42 units. $209–$339 double with Cannery Row view; $339–$469 double with ocean view. Rates include continental breakfast delivered to your room and afternoon wine and cheese. AE, DC, DISC, MC, V. **Close to:** Point Lobos State Park.

★ **Ventana Inn and Spa** Sprawled on more than 200 acres of classic Big Sur mountain and waterfront, the wooden structures of this inn are appointed with luxurious décor and plenty of privacy. A hike through the property offers serenity and utter retreat away from it all. A stay here renews and refreshes like no other.

Hwy. 1, Big Sur, CA 93920. ✆ **800/628-6500** or 831/667-2331. www.ventanainn.com. 62 units, 2 cottages. $450–$1,100 double; from $850 cottage. Rates include continental breakfast and afternoon wine and cheese. AE, DC, DISC, MC, V. **Close to:** Pfeiffer–Big Sur State Park.

RESTAURANTS

★★ **Big Sur River Inn California** AMERICAN Hang out next to—or in—the Big Sur River and enjoy your breakfast, lunch, or dinner; cocktails or beers from the bar; and the most interesting clientele around. Espresso drinks, sports on the big-screen, and all the down-home favorites—and ambience—you could ever want.

On Hwy. 1, 2 miles north of Pfeiffer–Big Sur State Park, Big Sur, CA 93920. ✆ **831/667-2700.** www.bigsurriverinn.com. Main courses $6–$12 breakfast, $8.75–$15 lunch, $8.95–$28 dinner. AE, DC, MC, V. Daily spring–fall 8am–10pm; winter 8am–9pm. **Close to:** Pfeiffer–Big Sur State Park.

★ **The Crepe Place** ECLECTIC For well over 3 decades, this popular eatery has served up a variety of inspired crepes, as well as other sumptuous homemade specialties, in its warm and lovely dining room and beautiful garden. Open late, it's popular with locals in-the-know. Brunch is served on weekends.

1134 Soquel Ave., at Seabright Ave., Santa Cruz, CA 95060. ✆ **831/429-6994.** www.thecrepeplace.com. Main courses $5–$14. AE, MC, V. Mon–Thurs 11am–midnight; Fri–Sun 10am–1am. **Close to:** Skyline to the Sea Trail.

★ **The Fishwife at Asilomar Beach** SEAFOOD Maybe the term "fishwife" isn't the most complimentary, but don't let that keep you from entering this historic location where you'll enjoy the best Boston clam chowder around. The price is right, the atmosphere inviting, and the entire family is welcome at this tasty place where seafood is king—or queen.

1996½ Sunset Dr., at Asilomar Beach, Monterey, CA 93940. ✆ **831/375-7107.** www.fishwife.com. Main courses $9.50–$18. AE, DISC, MC, V. Mon–Sat 11am–10pm; Sun 10am–10pm. From Hwy. 1, take the Pacific Grove exit (Hwy. 68) and stay left until it becomes Sunset Dr.; the restaurant will be on your left about 1 mile ahead as you approach Asilomar Beach. **Close to:** Point Lobos State Park.

★★ **Kevah Café Southwest** CALIFORNIA A deck with a view to die for, and a great selection of creative and healthy fare, espresso drinks, grilled seafood, chicken, and delicious omelets. Try the tasty homemade granola. It gets cold here when the fog rolls in; bring a jacket and your wallet, and enjoy the natural show.

On Hwy. 1, 29 miles south of Carmel (5 miles south of the River Inn), Big Sur, CA 93920. ✆ **831/667-2345.** www.nepenthebigsur.com. Appetizers $6–$12; main courses $11–$18. AE, MC, V. Daily 9am–4pm. Closes when it rains. **Close to:** Pfeiffer–Big Sur State Park.

Neilsen Brothers Market DELI Stock up on picnic supplies for your day at the beach or your time on the trail. Choose from a fine selection of deli favorites, including sandwiches, burgers, salads, chicken, and ribs. Plan ahead to save time; call your order in, especially at lunchtime when it can get crowded around here.

San Carlos (at 7th), Carmel, CA 93921. ✆ **831/624-6263** (deli); 831/624-6441 (market). Picnic items $3–$5. MC, V. Mon–Sat 8am–8pm; Sun 10am–7pm. **Close to:** Point Lobos State Park.

★ **Papá Chano's Taqueria** MEXICAN Don't be put off by the lack of atmosphere that characterizes this place; the Mexican specialties are authentic, delicious, and very fresh. And that's what you'll return for time after time. Cozy, you can get in lots of places, but *platillos especiales* as tasty as these are rare, indeed.

462 Alvarado St., at Bonifacio Place near Franklin, Monterey, CA 93940. ✆ **831/646-9587.** Mexican plates $4–$8. No credit cards. Daily 10am–10pm. **Close to:** Point Lobos State Park.

6

Coast North of San Francisco

North of Marin County is the sparsely populated and little-developed coastline of Sonoma and Mendocino counties. As you travel north, you pass from rolling, grass-covered hillsides to steep cliffs and densely forested coastal mountains.

The names on Sonoma's shore are intriguing: Blind Beach, Schoolhouse Beach, Arched Rock, Goat Rock, Penny Island, and Bodega Head. These colorfully named locales are the highlight of Sonoma Coast State Beach, which is not one beach, but many.

Few coastal locales are as photographed as the town of Mendocino and its bold headlands. The town itself, which lies just north of the mouth of Big River, resembles a New England village. Now protected by a state park, the Mendocino Headlands are laced with trails that offer postcard views of wave tunnels and tide pools, beaches, and blowholes.

Sinkyone Wilderness State Park and King Range National Conservation Area are part of California's famed Lost Coast. So rugged is this country, highway engineers were forced to route Hwy. 1 many miles inland; as a result, the region has remained sparsely settled and unspoiled. Its magnificent vistas and varied terrain—dense forests, prairies, and black sand beaches—reward the hearty explorer.

California's coastline rises to a magnificent crescendo at Redwood National Park. Redwood Creek Trail travels through the heart of the national park to Tall Trees Grove, site of what was once considered the world's tallest tree. The redwoods seem most at home in places like Gold Bluffs in Prairie Creek State Park. Dim and quiet, wrapped in mist and silence, the redwoods roof a moist and mysterious world.

Many beautiful "fern canyons" are found along the north coast. The one in Prairie Creek Redwoods State Park is particularly awe-inspiring. Bracken, five-finger, lady, sword, and chain ferns smother the precipitous walls of the canyon. Lucky hikers might catch a glimpse of the herd of Roosevelt elk that roam the state park. These graceful animals look like a cross between a South American llama and a deer, and may even convince (if any convincing be necessary) walkers that they have indeed entered an enchanted land.

The namesake redwoods are obviously the draw to this (rather lightly visited) national park, but often, it is the region's spectacular coast that prompts a return visit. Dramatic bluffs, hidden coves, tide pools, and wilderness beaches are linked by a 40-mile length of the California Coastal Trail.

One of to the best times to visit the redwoods is in late spring when the rains (usually) stop. June, in the form of rhododendrons, is busting out all over, pink and conspicuous beneath the tall trees. While contemplating the tall trees, notice the shade-loving undergrowth of the redwood forest. Poison oak climbs 150 feet up some of the tall giants. California huckleberry, azalea, mosses, lichen, and five-fingered ferns are everywhere—springing out of logs and stumps in a wild and dazzling profusion that you might associate with the Amazon.

Coast Hwy. 1 is a beauty, if you're willing to put some serious hours in behind the wheel. You could visit Mendocino and environs in 1 day and the redwoods in

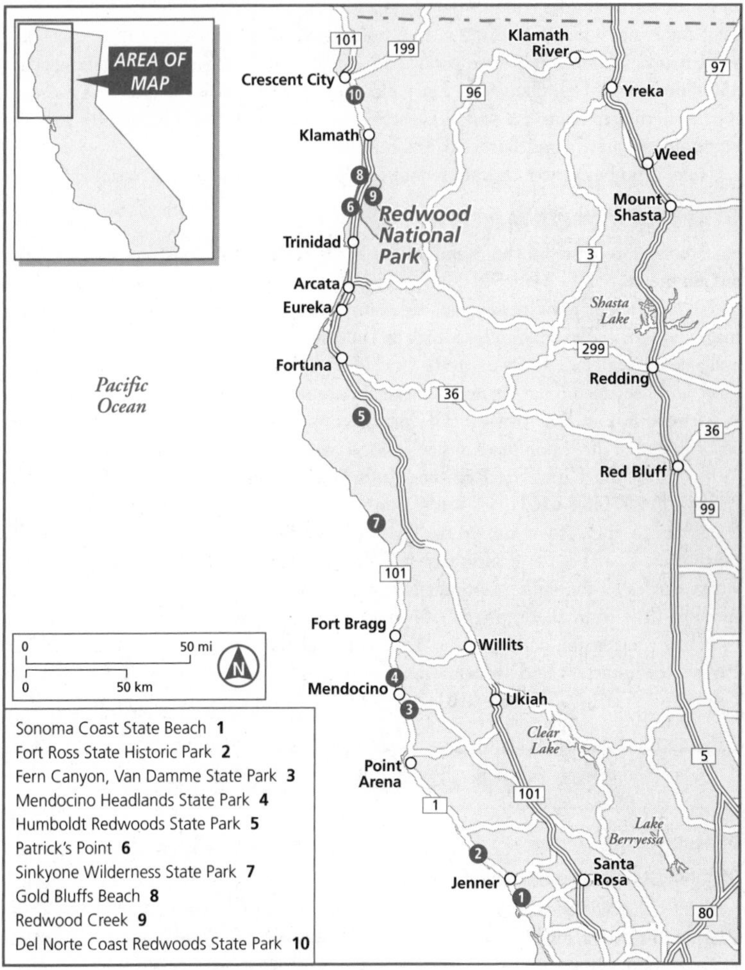

one more. But to really experience this magnificent coast, allow at least 4 days for a more leisurely drive and sufficient hiking time.

ESSENTIALS

GETTING THERE

By Car

The fastest route from San Francisco to Mendocino (about 166 miles) is via U.S. 101 north to Cloverdale. Then, take Hwy. 128 west to Hwy. 1, and then go north along the coast. It's about a 4-hour drive. (You could also take U.S. 101 all the way to Ukiah or Willits, and cut over to the west from there.) The most scenic route, if you have the time and your stomach doesn't mind the twists and turns, is to take Hwy. 1 north along the coast the entire way; it's at least a 5- to 6-hour drive.

Redwood National and State parks are located about 40 miles north of Eureka and 336 miles north of San Francisco. The park's southern gateway is the town of Orick, and the northern gateway to the park is Crescent City near the Oregon border. It's your best bet for cheap motels, gas, fast food, and outdoor supplies.

There is no bus service or train service to Mendocino or Redwood National Park.

VISITOR INFORMATION

Stock up on lots of free brochures and maps at the **Fort Bragg/Mendocino Coast Chamber of Commerce**, 332 N. Main St. (P.O. Box 1141), Fort Bragg, CA 95437 (✆ **800/726-2780** or 707/961-6300; www.mendocinocoast.com). Pick up a copy of the center's monthly magazine, *Arts and Entertainment,* which lists upcoming events throughout Mendocino. It's available at numerous stores and cafes, including the Mendocino Bakery, Gallery Bookshop, and Mendocino Art Center. You can also do some pre-trip research on Mendocino at **MendocinoFun.com** (www.mendocinofun.com), a nifty online events and activities website/blog to the region that's hosted by local outdoor enthusiasts, artists, and writers.

In Orick, you'll find the **Redwood Information Center,** P.O. Box 7, Orick, CA 95555 (✆ **707/464-6101,** ext. 5265). Stop here and pick up a free map; it's open daily from 9am to 5pm. If you missed the Orick center, don't worry: About 10 miles farther north on U.S. 101 is the **Prairie Creek Visitor Center** (✆ **707/464-6101,** ext. 5300), which carries all the same maps and information. It's open daily from 9am to 5pm in summer, daily from 10am to 4pm (sometimes later) in winter.

Before touring the park, pick up a free guide at the **Redwood National and State Parks Headquarters and Information Center,** 1111 Second St. (at K St.), Crescent City, CA 95531 (✆ **707/464-6101,** ext. 5064). It's open daily from 9am to 5pm.

SONOMA COAST STATE BEACH

Difficulty rating: Moderate

Distance: 7.6 miles round-trip from Wright's Beach to Goat Rock

Estimated time: 3½ hr.

Elevation gain: 200 ft.

Costs/permits: $6 state park day use fee

Best time to go: Year round

Website: www.parks.ca.gov

Recommended map: California State Parks Sonoma Coast State Beach

Trail head GPS: N 38 24.079, W 123 05.654

Trail head directions: Sonoma Coast State Beach's Wright's Beach Campground/Day Use Area is located off Hwy. 1, about 5 miles north of Bodega Bay. Park in the day-use lot and make your way to the trail head near the Camp Host at campsite #18.

The names alone are intriguing: Blind Beach and Schoolhouse Beach, Arched Rock and Goat Rock, Penny Island and Bodega Head. These colorfully named locales are some of the highlights of 16-mile-long Sonoma Coast State Beach. You could easily overlook these beaches because most are tucked away in rocky coves or hidden by tall bluffs and aren't visible from Hwy. 1. Kortum Trail is a pretty bluff-top route that connects some of these secret beaches.

From Wright's Beach Campground, hike north on signed Kortum Trail, named for conservationist Bill Kortum, whose efforts to establish and preserve public access to the coast contributed to the creation of the California Coastal Commission. The veterinarian also was a leader in the epic battles to stop construction of a nuclear power plant in nearby Bodega Bay and served in the 1970s on the Sonoma County Board of Supervisors.

The first part of the trail provides a sampling of things to come: offshore rocks, a coastal prairie, and a well-designed path that can be inspiring on clear days when dramatic coastal vistas unfold. During spring, wildflowers brighten the bluff: blue lupine, Indian paintbrush, and sea fig.

The trail switchbacks into Furlong Gulch, then rises steeply out of it and continues to the mouth of Pomo Canyon and Shell Beach. A short trail descends the bluffs to Shell Beach.

❶ Shell Beach Shell Beach is a popular field trip site for school children studying tide-pool life, and for high school and college students studying geology. The sheltered cove boasts a wide variety of exposed rocks and formations.

A quarter mile past Shell Beach, the level path crosses a ravine on a narrow footbridge and joins a length of boardwalk that traverses ground that can be mighty muddy in the rainy season and beyond.

❷ Peaked Hill The trail climbs to a saddle on the shoulder of Peaked Hill (376 ft.).

On fog-free days, enjoy northern vistas of the coastal mountains above the Russian River and down-coast views of Bodega Head and Point Reyes. Anchoring the south end of Sonoma Coast State Beach is the massive granite monolith of Bodega Rock. Geologists speculate that the inexorable creep of the Pacific Plate along the fault line carried the rock to this location from the Tehachapi Mountains, more than 300 miles away to the southeast.

❸ Goat Rock Kortum Trail comes to an end at the parking area for Blind Beach, located just south of Goat Rock. Goat Rock is connected to the mainland by a causeway. During the 1920s, Goat Rock was quarried and used to build a jetty at the mouth of the Russian River.

You won't find any goats at Goat Rock, but you might spot some boisterous harbor seals. (Stay at least 50 yd. from the seals, particularly during the Mar–Aug pupping season.)

Consider visiting the mouth of the Russian River, located a half-mile north of Goat Rock. The 110-mile-long river is one of the largest on the North Coast. At the river mouth, you can observe ospreys nesting in the treetops. The California brown pelican is one of several species of birds that breed and nest on Penny Island, located in the river mouth.

Fun Fact Hitchcock Haunt

Alfred Hitchcock fans will want to make the pilgrimage to Bodega, located off Highway 1 a few miles southeast of Bodega Bay. Drive past the roadside shops, turn the corner, look right, and voilà: a bird's-eye view of the hauntingly familiar Potter School House and St. Teresa's Church, both immortalized in Hitchcock's *The Birds,* filmed here in 1961.

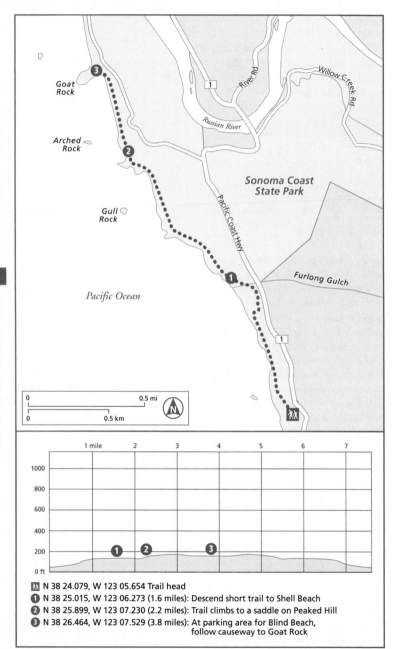

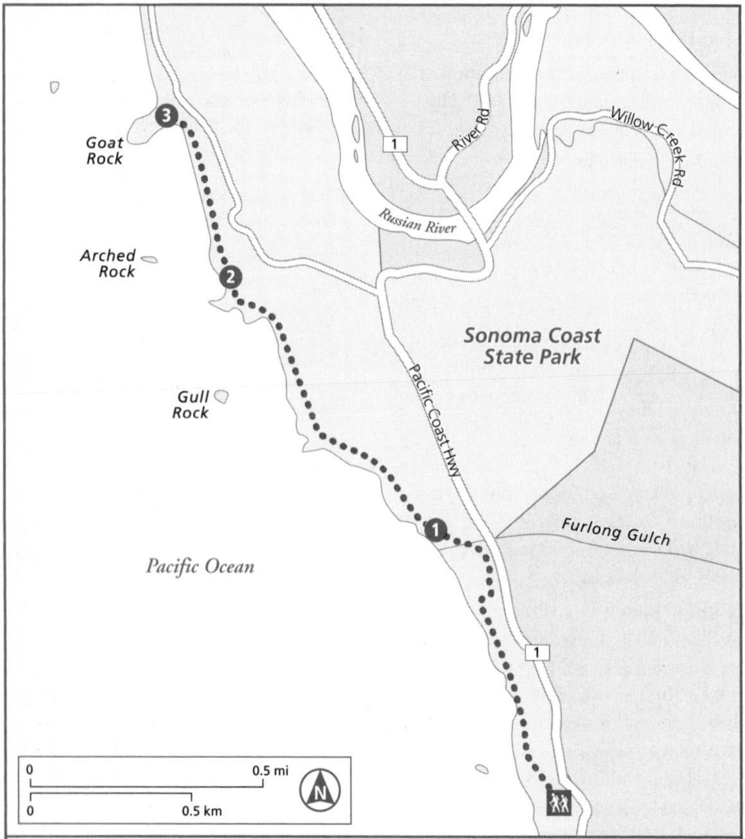

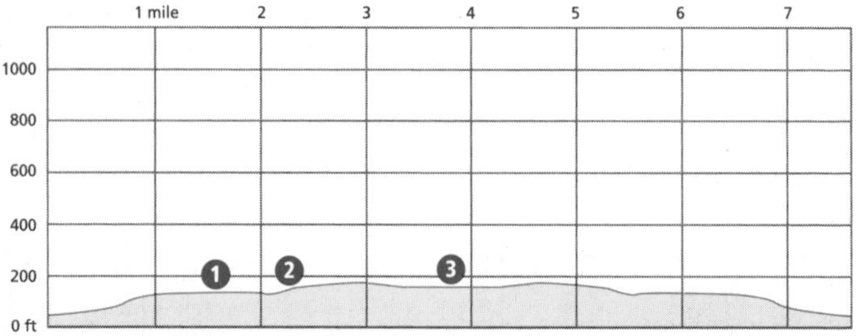

N 38 24.079, W 123 05.654 Trail head
1 N 38 25.015, W 123 06.273 (1.6 miles): Descend short trail to Shell Beach
2 N 38 25.899, W 123 07.230 (2.2 miles): Trail climbs to a saddle on Peaked Hill
3 N 38 26.464, W 123 07.529 (3.8 miles): At parking area for Blind Beach, follow causeway to Goat Rock

FORT ROSS STATE HISTORIC PARK ★ Kids

Difficulty rating: Easy

Distance: 0.5 mile round-trip to Fort Ross Cove; 4 miles round-trip to Reef Campground & Day Use Area

Estimated time: 2 hr.

Elevation gain: 220 ft.

Costs/permits: $6 state park entry fee

Best time to go: Year round

Website: www.fortrossinterpretive.org; www.parks.ca.gov

Recommended map: California State Parks Fort Ross State Historic Park

Trail head GPS: N 38 30.825, W 123 14.733

Trail head directions: Fort Ross State Historic Park is located off of Hwy. 1, 12 miles north of the hamlet of Jenner

Fort Ross, the last remnant of Czarist Russia's foothold in California, is a hiker's delight. Visit a redwood stockade and Russian Orthodox chapel and, after you've completed your walk through history, hike out on the lonely, beautiful headlands. North- or south-bound hikers will come across grand views of the fort and up-close looks at the result of earthquake action along the San Andreas Fault.

Napoleon was beginning his 1812 invasion of Russia when Fort Ross—named for Rossiya, itself—was built. The fort's location ideally suited the purposes of the colony. The site was easily defensible. Tall trees, necessary for the fort's construction and the shipbuilding that would take place in the nearby cove, covered the coastal slopes. The waters were full of sea otters—an attraction for the Russian American Fur Company, which would soon hunt the animals to near-extinction. Wheat, potatoes, and vegetables were grown on the coastal terrace and shipped to Russian settlements in Alaska. All in all, the fort was nearly self-sufficient.

Thanks to the state's replication and restoration efforts, the fort's building brings back the flavor of the Russians' foray into North America. The high stockade, built entirely of hand-hewn redwood timber, looks particularly formidable.

Also of interest are the seven-sided blockhouse, with its interpretive exhibits, and the small, wooden Orthodox chapel. Be sure to stop at the Fort Ross Visitor Center, which has Russian, Pomo, and natural history exhibits.

In 1990, the state park tripled in size; the addition was the former Call Ranch, more than 2,000 acres of wooded canyons and dramatic coastline.

From the old fort, you can walk 2 miles north along the coast via old logging roads dipping into Kolmer Gulch, where there's a picnic area, and continuing on to a stand of redwood and Douglas fir.

Exit the fort's main gate, follow the stockade walls to the left, and join the downhill path.

❶ Fort Ross Cove It's a short walk to secluded Fort Ross Cove, one of California's first shipyards. You'll find an interpretive display and picnic tables here.

❷ Creek Crossing Cross Fort Ross Creek on a small footbridge. Earthquake action along the mighty San Andreas Fault has altered the course of the creek by more than a half-mile here. Follow the path inland along the creek, which is lined with bay laurel, willow, alder, and Douglas iris. After a hundred yards of travel, look to your right for the path leading south.

The trail travels onto an open coastal terrace. You might see some sheep eating the pastoral vegetation. Cliff swallows,

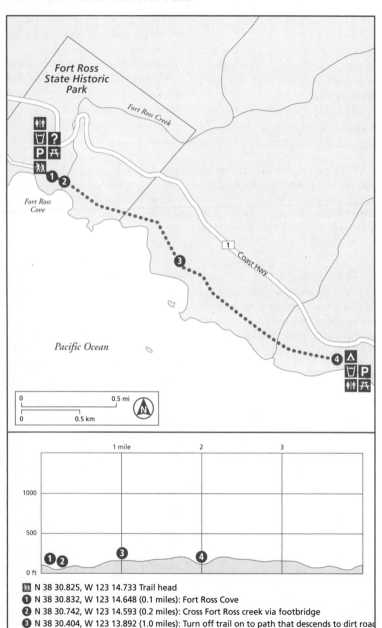

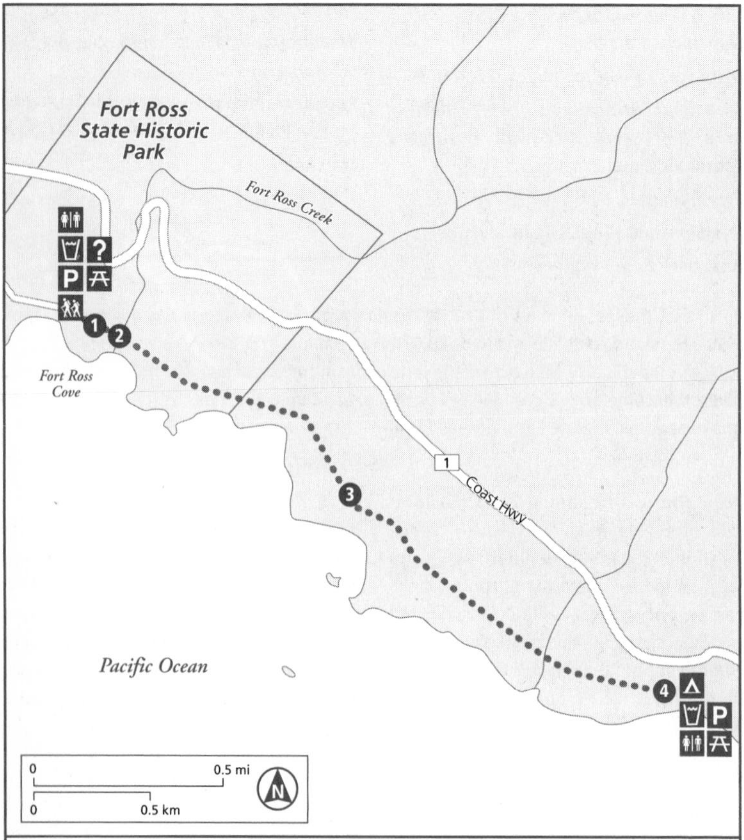

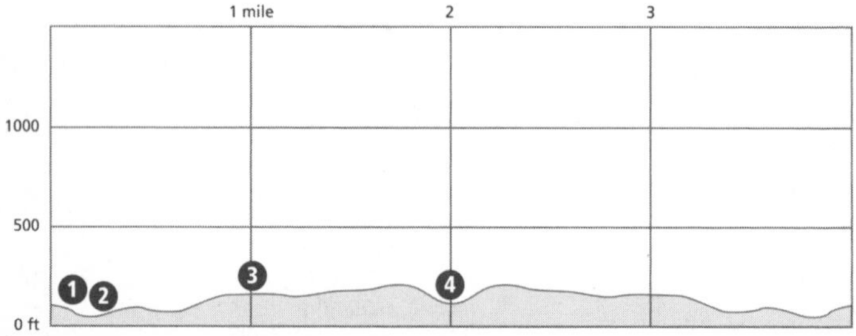

N 38 30.825, W 123 14.733 Trail head

1. N 38 30.832, W 123 14.648 (0.1 miles): Fort Ross Cove
2. N 38 30.742, W 123 14.593 (0.2 miles): Cross Fort Ross creek via footbridge
3. N 38 30.404, W 123 13.892 (1.0 miles): Turn off trail on to path that descends to dirt roa
4. N 38 29.980, W 123 12.940 (2.0 miles): Reef Campground

ospreys, finches, scrub jays, and California quail are among the abundant birdlife often sighted along the Fort Ross coast.

3 Join dirt road Follow the undulations of the rye-grass- and barley-covered headland, and meander first southeast, then southwest. Continue down-coast until you spot a path descending to a dirt road. (Don't try to climb the sheep fence; use the stile located where the road dead-ends.)

The native Kashaya Pomo used the reef area, located 2 miles down-coast from Fort Ross, for gathering a variety of seafood, including abalone, octopus, and shellfish. They caught fish with hooks and lines.

4 Reef Campground & Day Use Area Descend the dirt road to Reef Campground & Day Use Area, formerly a private campground and now a state park facility. It's a good place for a picnic.

Divers, anglers, surfers, bird-watchers, whale-watchers, tide-pool explorers, and hikers are all drawn to the reef area, but not in any great numbers, because this coast remains very lightly visited.

Down-coast from Reef Point, more adventure beckons the coastal hiker: Sonoma County's "lost coast," so named because high cliffs and high tides keep these 7 miles of beach remote from most hikers.

FERN CANYON, VAN DAMME STATE PARK

Difficulty rating: Moderate

Distance: 8 miles round-trip to Pygmy Forest

Estimated time: 3½–4½ hr.

Elevation gain: 400 ft.

Costs/permits: $6 state use entry fee

Best time to go: April to October

Website: www.parks.ca.gov

Recommended map: California State Parks Van Damme State Park

Trail head GPS: N 39 16.612, W 123 47.056

Trail head directions: Van Damme State Park is located off Hwy. 1, 3 miles south of Mendocino. Turn inland on the main park road and follow it through the canyon to a parking area at the beginning of signed Fern Canyon Trail.

Five-finger and bird's-foot, lady and licorice, stamp, sword, and deer—these are some of the colorful names of the ferns growing in well-named Fern Canyon. Little River meanders through the canyon, as does a lovely trail that crosses the river nine times. After Fern Canyon, a second special environment awaits the hiker: Pygmy Forest. You've got to see this truly Lilliputian forest to believe it.

At the trail head, pick up an interpretive brochure, which is keyed to a series of trailside metal fish markers.

In recent years, Fern Canyon—particularly the river that runs through it—has undergone a good deal of eco-rehab. Little River is crucial spawning habitat for steelhead and Coho salmon.

The first and second crossings of Little River give you an inkling of what lies ahead. During summer, the river is easily forded; in winter, expect to get your feet wet. The wide path brings you close to elderberry, salmonberry, wild cucumber, and a multitude of ferns. This lush canyon is also rich with young redwoods, red alder, big leaf maple, and Douglas fir.

Fern Canyon Trail, paved along its lower stretch, follows the route of an old logging skid road. For 3 decades, beginning in

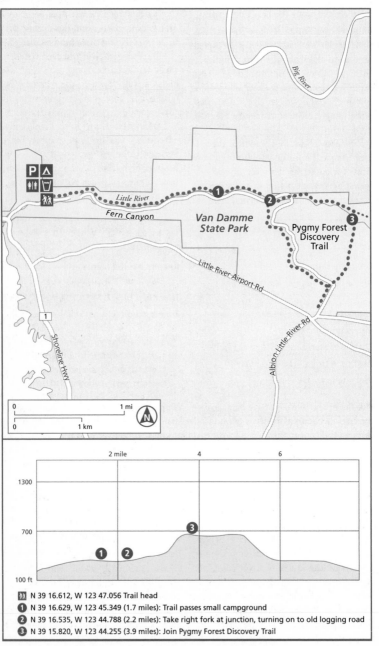

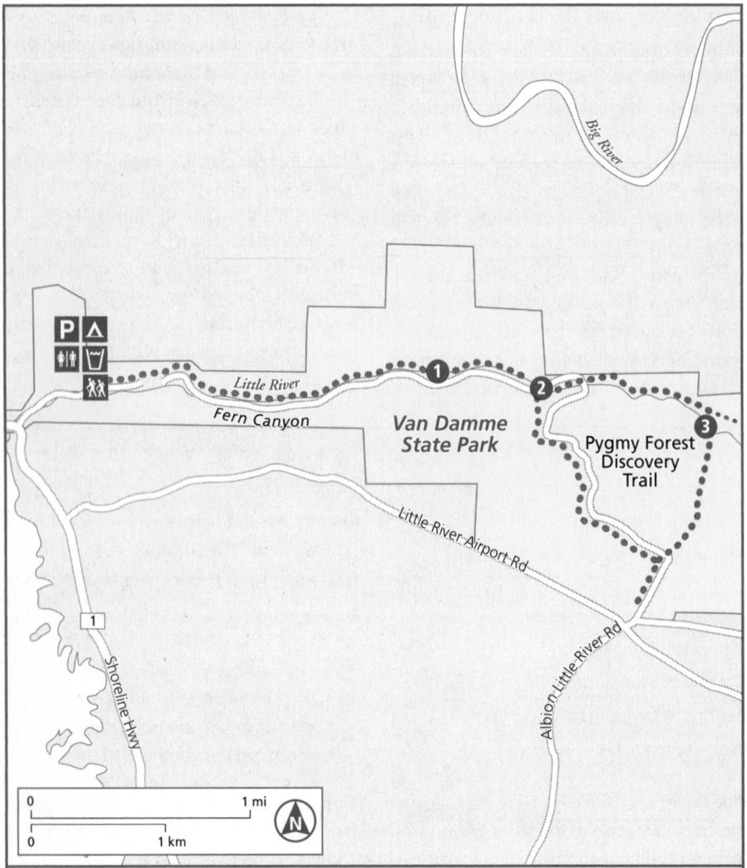

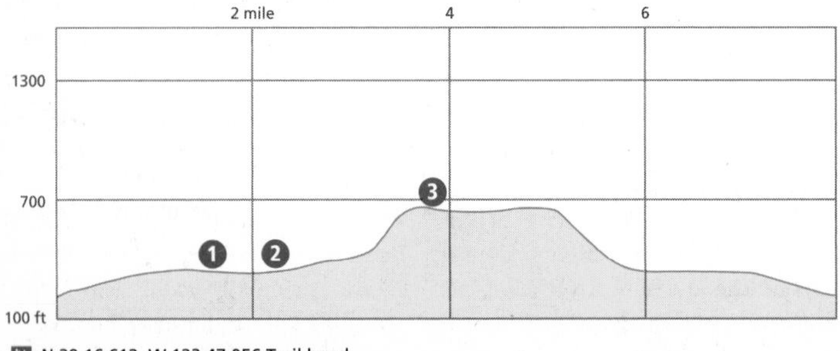

N 39 16.612, W 123 47.056 Trail head

1 N 39 16.629, W 123 45.349 (1.7 miles): Trail passes small campground

2 N 39 16.535, W 123 44.788 (2.2 miles): Take right fork at junction, turning on to old logging road

3 N 39 15.820, W 123 44.255 (3.9 miles): Join Pygmy Forest Discovery Trail

1864, ox teams hauled timber through the canyon. The road was improved and bridges constructed by the Civilian Conservation Corps during the 1930s.

A lumber mill once stood at the mouth of Little River. During the late 19th century, schooners used for shipping logs and lumber were constructed at a boat-works located at the river mouth. Lumberman/San Francisco businessman Charles F. Van Damme was born in the hamlet of Little River. He purchased land on the site of the former sawmill and bequeathed the river mouth and canyon to the state park system.

❶ Environmental Campsites About 2 miles out, the trail meanders past ten environmental (walk-in) campsites and continues another half-mile beyond the campsites to a trail fork. Take either fork, it matters not, for the two branches reunite in a quarter mile at another fork.

❷ Junction with Old Logging Road Take the right fork (an old logging road), which crosses Little River and ascends amidst second-growth redwoods and Douglas fir 1$^1/_3$ miles to a junction with the Pygmy Forest Discovery Trail.

❸ Pygmy Forest Discovery Trail A self-guided $^1/_3$-mile-long nature trail, built upon an elevated wooden walkway, loops through the Pygmy Forest. A nutrient-poor, highly acidic topsoil, combined with a dense hardpan located beneath the surface that resists root penetration, has severely restricted the growth of trees in certain areas of the coastal shelf in Mendocino County.

Sixty-year-old cypress trees are only a few feet tall and measure but a half-inch in diameter. Shrubs such as rhododendron, manzanita, and huckleberry are also dwarf-sized.

MENDOCINO HEADLANDS STATE PARK ★ Kids

Difficulty rating: Easy

Distance: 2.5 miles round-trip

Estimated time: 1$^1/_2$ hr.

Elevation gain: Minimal

Costs/permits: None

Best time to go: Year round

Website: www.parks.ca.gov

Recommended map: California State Parks Mendocino Headlands State Park

Trail head GPS: N 39 18.255, W 123 48.258

Trail head directions: From "downtown" Mendocino, follow Main St. up-coast past the Mendocino Hotel to Heeser Dr. Park wherever you can find a space. From the corner of Main St. and Heeser Dr., the trail leads southwest and soon forks; take the route down-coast toward Big River Beach.

Few coastal locales are as photographed as the town of Mendocino and its bold headlands. The town itself, which lies just north of the mouth of Big River, resembles a New England village, no doubt by design of its Yankee founders. Now protected by a state park, the headlands are laced with paths that offer postcard views of wave tunnels and tide pools, beaches, and blowholes.

With its Maine-village look, the cosmopolitan little port of Mendocino is a picturesque gem. Much heritage can be found here. Its citizenry not only preserved the town in a historical district, but succeeded in placing a portion of the majestic bluffs, threatened with a modern subdivision, under the protection of Mendocino Headlands State Park in 1972.

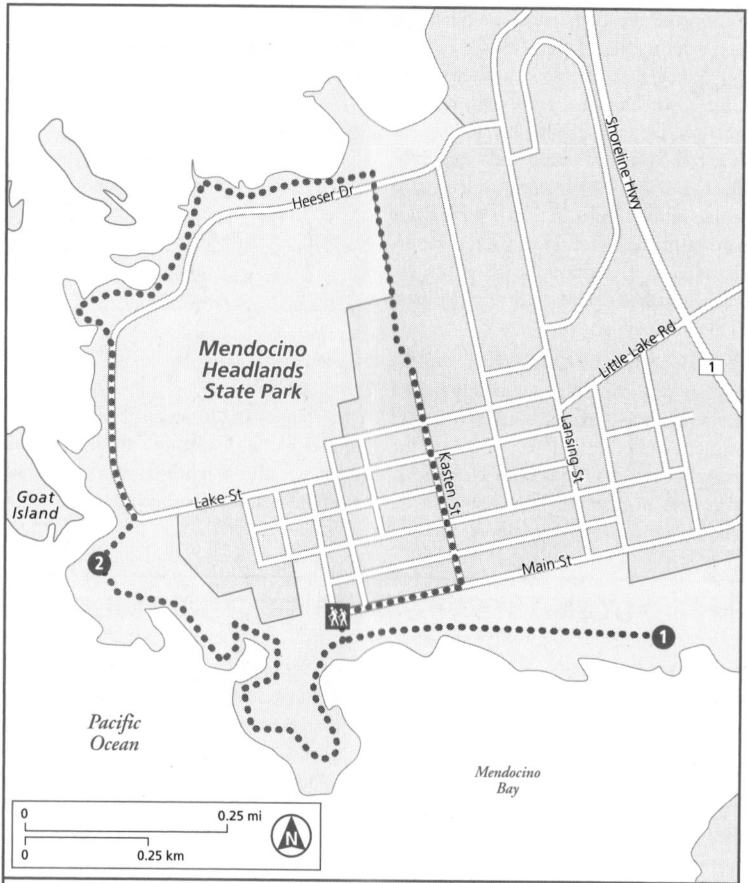

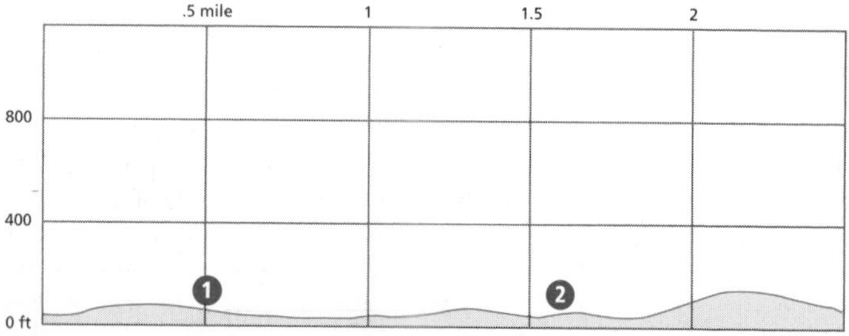

N 39 18.255, W 123 48.258 Trail head

1 N 39 18.227, W 123 47.780 (0.5 miles): Path descends to beach at mouth of Big River

2 N 39 18.304, W 123 48.610 (1.6 miles): Peace monument

A summer or weekend walk onto the headlands allows you to escape the crowds, while a winter walk, perhaps when a storm is brewing offshore, is a special experience, indeed.

Heading east, the trail delivers you to some bluff-top benches and a coastal access\way leading down to Portuguese Beach, known as Point Beach by locals. Wooden steps cross a gully, and the trail soon forks again—offering both a route along the edge of the bluffs and another heading on a straighter course toward Big River.

Like the town, the headlands have a storied past. *Booldam* ("Big River") is what the native Pomo called their village here. Wave tunnels, one measuring more than 700 feet long, penetrate the Mendocino Bay bluffs. By some fanciful accounts, they've been the death of ships, particularly during the days of sail, when a number of vessels were reportedly blown into the tunnels and never seen again.

Despite rough surf conditions, one of California's first "dog-hole ports" was located here. A railway, built in 1853, carried redwood lumber from a nearby mill to a chute located on the point. It was a tricky loading operation, to say the least.

Notice the cross-ties, remains of the old oxen-powered railway that hauled lumber to the bluff edge, where it was then sent by chute to waiting ships.

Wildflowers seasonally brightening the grassy headlands include lupine and Mendocino Coast paintbrush. More noticeable are non-native species gone wild—nasturtiums, calla lilies, hedge rose—as well as Scotch broom, an unwelcome pest that thrives along the north coast.

❶ Big River Beach After meandering past some Bishop pine, the path descends moderately to steeply to the beach where Big River empties into Mendocino Bay. The quarter-mile-long beach is also part of Mendocino Headlands State Park. Upriver is a marsh, Big River Estuary, that's a winter stopover for ducks and geese. Salmon and steelhead spawn upriver.

Backtrack the way you came, hiking west to the first junction from the trail head. The coastal trail leads to the blowhole. While no aqueous Vesuvius, the blowhole can at times be a frothy and picturesque cauldron.

The path continues northwest along the edge of the headlands for another half mile.

❷ Mendocino You'll pass a monument dedicated by the sister cities of Mendocino and Miasa, Japan "to the peaceful pursuit of the peoples of the Pacific and to the protection of the environment that all living things therein may exist in perpetual harmony."

From here, the coastal path parallels Heeser Drive, first north, then east, to meet Kasten Street. Follow Kasten Street south back down to Main Street. Turn right and return to the trail head.

Mendocino is a great town for the walker to explore. Grand Victorian houses and simple New England saltboxes mingle with a downtown that includes several fascinating 19th-century buildings. Among the architectural gems are the Masonic Hall, built in 1866 and topped with a redwood sculpture of Father Time, the Mendocino Hotel, with its antique decor, and the Presbyterian Church, constructed in 1867 and now a state historical landmark. Be sure to check out the historic Ford House perched above the bay on the south side of town. Inside the house are exhibits interpreting the human and natural history of the Mendocino coast, as well as the state park visitor center.

A Train Ride Through the Redwoods

Built as a logging railroad in 1885, the North Coast's vintage Skunk Train line was originally used for moving massive redwood logs from the rugged back-country to the Mendocino Coast sawmills. Today it's one of the North Coast's largest tourist attractions, taking visitors on a scenic route through the red-wood forest, crossing 31 bridges and trestles, cutting through two deep tun-nels, and chugging past giant trees that are more than 1,000 years old, before reaching a secluded, forested glen accessible only by train.

The trains run daily from the Fort Bragg Depot at the foot of Laurel Avenue from March 1 to November 30, and on Saturdays December through February. Schedules vary, particulary during holidays; call for details. In the summer, it's a good idea to make reservations. Tickets cost from $47 to $75 for adults and $22 to $40 children ages 3 to 11, depending on the day, time, and train. The 4½-hour Sunset Dinner Barbeque ride includes an elaborate barbeque dinner with huge baskets and trays of homemade brea, barbequed chicken and ribs, baked beans, garden salads, and a "surprise" dessert. For more information call ✆ **800/866-1690** or 707/459-1060, or see **www.skunktrain.com**.

HUMBOLDT REDWOODS STATE PARK ★★

Difficulty rating: Moderate

Distance: 9-mile loop

Estimated time: 4½–5½ hr.

Elevation gain: 100 ft.

Costs/permits: $5 state park day use fee

Best time to go: June to October; a sea-sonally installed footbridge over Bull Creek makes the loop trip easiest in summer

Website: www.humboldtredwoods.org; www.parks.ca.gov

Recommended map: California State Parks Humboldt Redwoods State Park

Trail head GPS: N 40 20.526, W 123 56.466

Trail head directions: From the north-central part of the Avenue of the Giants, 4 miles north of the park visitor center and just south of the hamlet of Red-crest, turn west on Mattole Rd. and drive 1½ miles to the parking area for the Rockefeller Forest Loop Trail. (If you want to make this a one-way hike and make car shuttle arrangements, a sec-ond trail head is located at the Big Trees Parking Area, another 3 miles west on Mattole Rd.)

Thriving along Bull Creek in the heart of Humboldt Redwoods State Park is more than a redwood grove; it's truly a forest. The Rockefeller Forest is the most impressive stand of redwoods found anywhere in the world. My favorite hike is the route along Bull Creek itself. This path offers curiosities (Flatiron Tree, Giant Tree, and more), as well as swim-ming in and sunning beside Bull Creek. And, of course, there are those spectacular red-woods, explored by a trail that not only stretches the legs, but the imagination, as well.

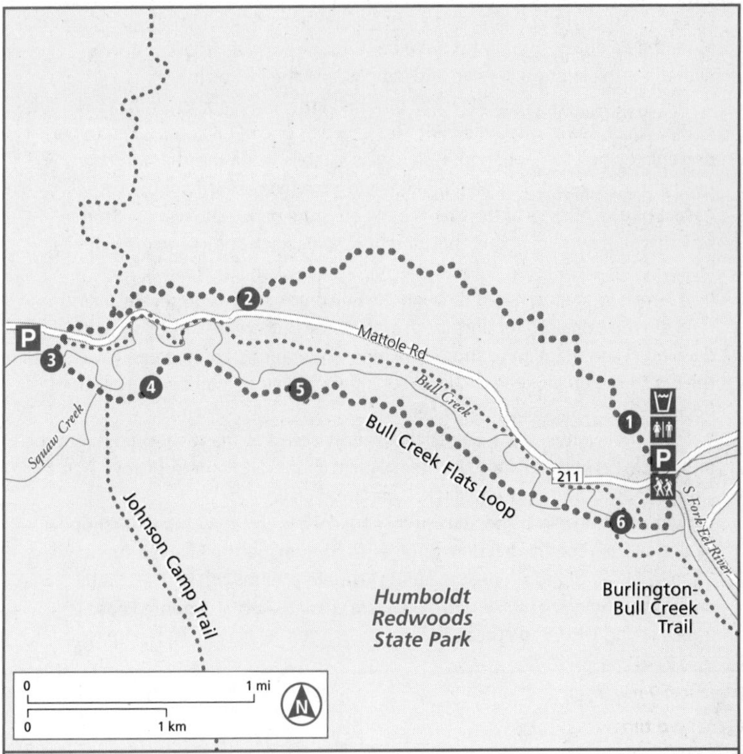

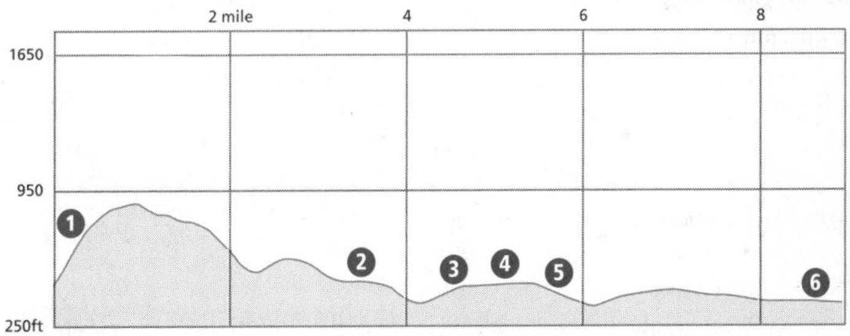

- N 40 20.526, W 123 56.466 Trail head
- ❶ N 40 20.759, W 123 56.633 (0.3 miles): Turn right at junction with Bull Creek Flats Loop Trail
- ❷ N 40 20.759, W 123 56.633 (3.5 miles): Path rises to run parallel to Mattole Road
- ❸ N 40 20.984, W 123 59.566 (4.5 miles): At parking area, cross footbridge over Bull Creek
- ❹ N 40 20.890, W 123 59.044 (5.1 miles): Stay on trail past junction with Johnson Camp Trail on the right
- ❺ N 40 20.857, W 123 58.287 (5.8 miles): Walk through hollowed-out log
- ❻ N 40 20.400, W 123 56.641 (8.7 miles): Cross Bull Creek on log and reconnect with Rockefeller Loop Trail

Avenue of the Giants

Famed Avenue of the Giants offers a good look at Humboldt County's redwoods. More than a dozen short paths meander through Avenue-adjacent groves named for the famous, the rich and famous, and the just plain rich.

The 32-mile parkway, the parallel scenic alternate to Hwy. 101, runs the length of Humboldt Redwoods State Park. This park was one of California's first to be preserved when the state park system was established in the 1920s. Today, it protects about one-eighth of all remaining old-growth coast redwoods.

Just off the Avenue of the Giants in Weott is the park visitor center. Stop to pick up maps, inquire about trail conditions and check out the nature exhibits, including an excellent one about the importance of ancient forests.

A 5-mile-long road winds through the Bull Creek area, as do several hiking trails. If you're pressed for time, both ends of the Bull Creek Flats Loop Trail detailed in this guide have shorter, inviting explorations. You can easily walk from the Big Trees parking area to Giant Tree, then stroll along Bull Creek. The short Rockefeller Forest Loop Trail is a gem.

From the Avenue of the Giants, there's easy access to many short trails into the redwoods. Favorites include Children's Forest Loop Trail, Founders Grove Trail, Drury–Chaney Trail, and Franklin K. Lane Grove Trail.

If you want to climb above the redwoods for a grand view, take Grasshopper Peak Trail from the Garden Club of America parking lot. The hike is a strenuous 12-mile round-trip to a lookout; grand views are your reward for the climb.

Also beginning at the superb 5,000-acre Garden Club of America Grove is 2-mile round-trip Canoe Creek Trail.

Begin the hike on the right branch of the Rockefeller Loop (a very pleasant family hike in its own right) and follow it for a short quarter-mile or so to a junction, bearing right onto Bull Creek Flats Loop Trail.

1 Junction with Bull Creek Flats Loop Trail The path heads up-creek, along a path crowded in places by rushes and horsetail. A mile out, the trail breaks into a clearing, a half-mile farther crosses a tributary creek on a bridge; another mile more, a log bench beckons you to take a break.

2 Mattole Road About a mile from the Big Trees Parking Area, the path climbs to closely parallel Mattole Road. After crossing a couple side creeks on wooden bridges, you arrive at the parking lot.

3 Big Trees Parking Area From here, cross the (summer-only) footbridge over Bull Creek; at other times, if the water level is low, carefully wade across the Eel River. Follow the signs to the oddly shaped Flatiron Tree and to Giant Tree. The Giant is not the world's tallest redwood, but it is the biggest—the champion by virtue of its combined height, diameter, and crown size.

4 Johnson Camp Trail Junction Leaving behind the Giant Tree, the path travels through a fern-filled forest, crosses Squaw Creek on a bridge, and soon passes a junction with the right-forking Johnson Camp Trail. Not only do the ancient trees towering above make you feel small, their fallen cousins, which require a 75-yard zig and a 75-yard zag by trail to get around, are also humbling to the hiker.

The matchless old-growth forest along Bull Creek was a cause célèbre with early California conservationists, who struggled to save the redwoods from the mill. Out of this struggle to save Humboldt County's tall trees came the formation of the Save-the-Redwoods League in 1918.

Thanks to John D. Rockefeller, Jr., quietly funneling $2 million to the League, matching state funds, conservationists were able to purchase some 10,000 acres along Bull Creek from the Pacific Lumber Company in 1930.

5 Hike-through Hollow Log The trail enters and exits a hollow, hike-through log, then meanders a bit, north and south, with Bull Creek. A mile and a half from the Big Trees area, the path plunges into the fern-filled canyon of Connick Creek, emerging to travel past awesome redwoods, including the so-called Giant Braid, a trio of redwoods twisted together, located 2 miles from the Big Trees Parking Area.

For the most part, as you hike along, you'll hear but not see Bull Creek; that is, until a half-mile or so from the Rockefeller Loop, when the path drops close to the creek. The trail explores some more magnificent redwoods on the flats above the creek.

6 Rockefeller Loop Trail Your redwood journey ends when you cross Bull Creek on a redwood log that spans the creek and reconnect with Rockefeller Loop Trail for the short walk back to the parking area.

PATRICK'S POINT ★

Difficulty rating: Easy

Distance: 4 miles round-trip from Palmer's Point to Agate Beach Campground

Estimated time: 1½–2½ hr.

Elevation gain: 100 ft.

Costs/permits: $6 state park day use fee

Best time to go: April to November

Website: www.parks.ca.gov

Recommended map: California State Parks Patrick's Point State Park

Trail head GPS: N 41 07.768, W 124 09.820

Trail head directions: Patrick's Point State Park is located 30 miles north of Eureka and 5 miles north of Trinidad. Exit Hwy. 101 on Patrick's Point Dr. and follow this road to the park. Once past the park entrance station, follow the signs to Palmer Point.

Though Patrick's Point State Park is positioned in the heart of the redwoods, other trees—Sitka spruce, Douglas fir, and red alder—predominate on the park's rocky promontories. The scolding *krrrack-krrrack* of the Steller jay is the only note of dissent heard along the trail.

Rim Trail follows an old Indian pathway over the park's bluffs. Spur trails lead to rocky points that jut into the Pacific and offer commanding views of Trinidad Head to the south and Big Lagoon to the north. The trail plunges into a lush community of ferns, salmonberry, and salal.

1 Abalone Point At a half-mile out, you'll pass a side trail leading to the park campground. The path skirts Abalone Campground and, at the ¾-mile mark, reaches Abalone Point.

Abalone Point is the first of a half-dozen short spur trails that lead from Rim Trail to Rocky Point, Patrick's Point, Wedding Rock, Mussel Rocks, and Agate Beach. Take any or all of them. These side trails can sometimes be confused with Rim Trail; generally speaking, the spurs are much more steep than those on Rim

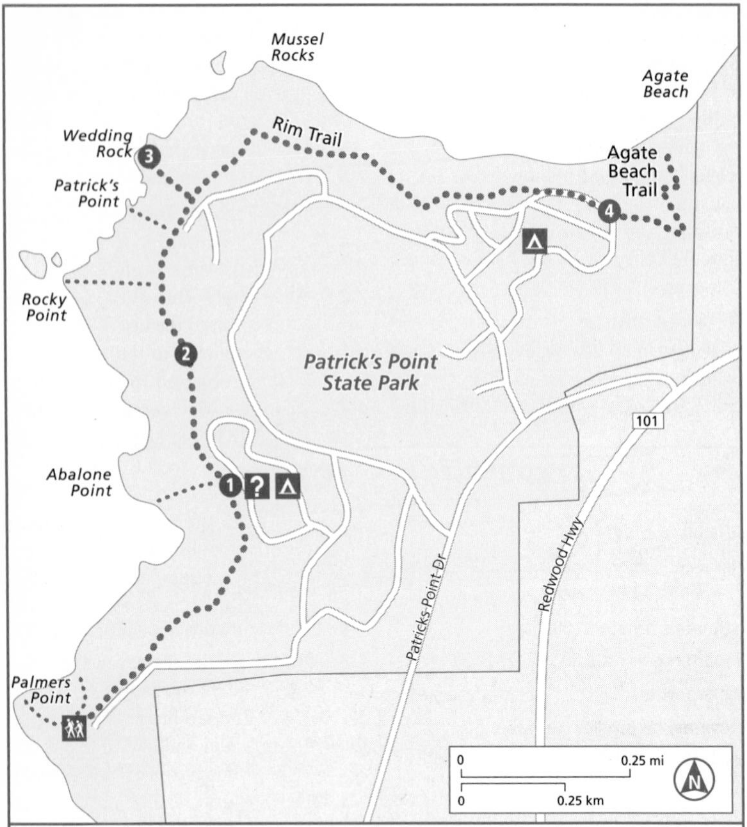

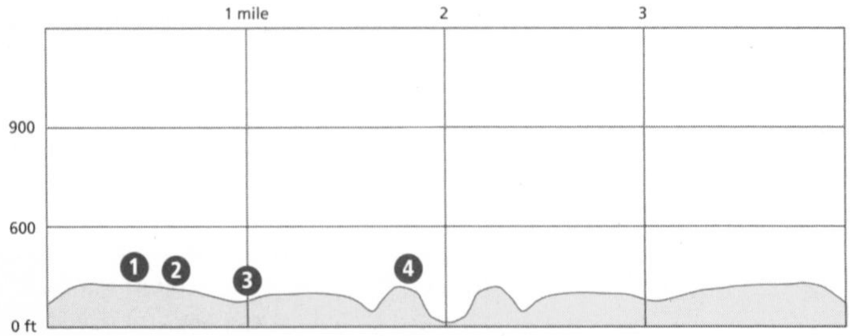

N 41 07.768, W 124 09.819: Trail head

1. N 41 08.056, W 124 09.563 (0.5 miles): Abalone Point
2. N 41 08.216, W 124 09.629 (0.7 miles): Patrick's Point
3. N 41 08.450, W 124 09.679 (1.0 miles): Wedding Rock
4. N 41 08.380, W 124 08.922 (1.8 miles): Continue on Agate Beach Campground road to Agate Beach Trail

Trail, which contours along without much elevation change.

For hundreds of years, the Yurok spent their summers in the Abalone Point area of the headlands. The Yurok gathered shellfish and hunted sea lions. Game and a multitude of berries were plentiful in the surrounding forest.

The area now called Patrick's Point also had some spiritual significance to the native people. According to the Yurok, Sumig, spirit of the porpoises, retired to Patrick's Point when humans began populating the world.

Another 1/3-mile of trail leads to a 1/4-mile-long spur trail extending to Rocky Point. Continuing northward, the trail arrives at the short side trail leading to park namesake Patrick's Point.

2 Patrick's Point Point and State Park take their names from Patrick Beegan, who homesteaded this dramatic, densely forested headland in 1851.

> From Patrick's Point, admire the precipitous cliffs and rock-walled inlets. Gaze offshore at the sea stacks, a line of soldiers battered by the surging sea. Seals and sea lions haul out on the offshore rocks, which also double as rookeries for gulls, cormorants, and pigeon guillemots.

3 Wedding Rock Next en route, Wedding Rock, is reached by a 1/4-mile spur trail. The romantically named rock is not an island, but a dramatic protrusion into the Pacific, fastened to the mainland by a narrow neck of land. The path uses this land bridge and steps to ascend to an overlook.

Rim Trail meanders through a tapestry of trillium and moss, rhododendron and azalea. Sword ferns point the way to a grove of red alder.

Rim Trail ends at the north loop of the Agate Beach Campground road.

4 Agate Beach Trail To explore Agate Beach, continue a short distance along the road to the signed trail head for Agate Beach Trail. This short, steep trail switchbacks down to the beach.

In marked contrast to the park's rocky shore that you observed from Rim Trail, Agate Beach is a wide swath of dark sand stretching north to Big Lagoon.

Beachcombers prospect for agates in the gravel bars and right at the surf line. The agates found here are a nearly transparent variety of quartz, polished by sand and the restless sea. Jade, jasper, and other semi-precious stones are sometimes found here. One more noteworthy sight is the huge quantity and unique sea-sculpted quality of the driftwood on this beach.

Return up Agate Beach Trail to the bluff tops and Rim Trail. While it's possible to make a loop trip of this hike by following the park's inland paths to the visitor center and back to Palmer's Point, I prefer returning via Rim Trail. When it comes to a terrific coastal trail, you really can't have too much of a good thing. Nevertheless, the park visitor center is well worth a visit, as is Sumeg Village, a re-creation of a Native Yurok community.

SINKYONE WILDERNESS STATE PARK (Kids)

Difficulty rating: Easy

Distance: 4.5 miles round-trip to Whale Gulch

Estimated time: 2 1/2 hr.

Elevation gain: Minimal

Costs/permits: $5 state park day use fee

Best time to go: May to November

Website: www.parks.ca.gov

Recommended map: Wilderness Press California's Lost Coast

Trail head GPS: N 39 56.559, W 123 57.889

Trail head directions: From Hwy. 101, take either the Garberville or Redway exit and proceed to "downtown" Redway, located 3 miles north of Garberville on Business 101. Turn west on Briceland Rd. After 12 miles of travel, fork left to Whitethorn. A mile or so past the hamlet of Whitethorn, the pavement ends, and you continue on a potholed dirt/mud road for 3½ miles to a junction called Four Corners. Proceed straight ahead 3½ miles to the Sinkyone Wilderness State Park Visitors Center. The park road is steep, winding, and only one lane wide.

Sinkyone Wilderness State Park rewards the hardy explorer with magnificent vistas and varied terrain—dense forests, prairies, coastal bluffs, and beaches. Lost Coast Trail, as it travels the northernmost part of the state park, provides a relatively easy introduction to a challenging trail. The land we now call Sinkyone Wilderness State Park, located about 225 miles north of San Francisco, has long been recognized as something special. During the late 1960s, the great Catholic theologian, Thomas Merton, felt that the Needle Rock area would be an ideal place for a life of prayer and contemplation, and talked of establishing a monastic community there.

Usal Road meanders along the northern boundary of Sinkyone Wilderness State Park. The road, lined with heavy brush and trees, has changed little since Jack London and his wife drove it in a horse-drawn carriage on a trip from San Francisco to Eureka in 1911.

The sea is an overwhelming presence here, and its rhythmic sounds provide a thunderous background for a walk along land's end. The sky is filled with gulls and pelicans, sea lions and harbor seals gather at Little Jackass Cove, and the California gray whale migration passes near shore during winter and early spring.

A herd of Roosevelt elk roams the park. These magnificent creatures were once common here and in the King Range, but were exterminated in the last century. The Roosevelt elk that lucky visitors see today are "extras" relocated from Prairie Creek State Park.

Lost Coast Trail travels the length of Sinkyone Wilderness State Park north through King Range National Conservation Area. The 60-mile trail offers a terrific week-long backpacking adventure.

Roosevelt Elk

Gold Bluffs Beach (both bluffs and beach) is prime Roosevelt elk territory. Roosevelt elk are enchanted-looking creatures with chocolate-brown faces and necks, tan bodies, and dark legs. And they're big: a bull can tip the scales at 1,000 pounds.

While nearby elk-viewing opportunities abound—particularly along more southerly stretches of Gold Bluffs Beach, and on namesake Elk Prairie up by Hwy. 101 and the Prairie Creek visitor center—the Roosevelts seem all the more majestic in a wilderness setting.

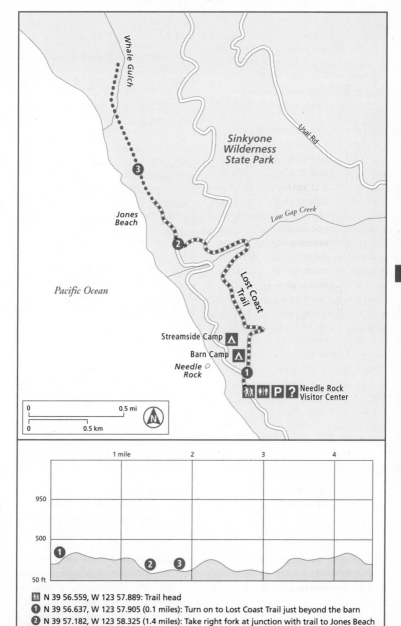

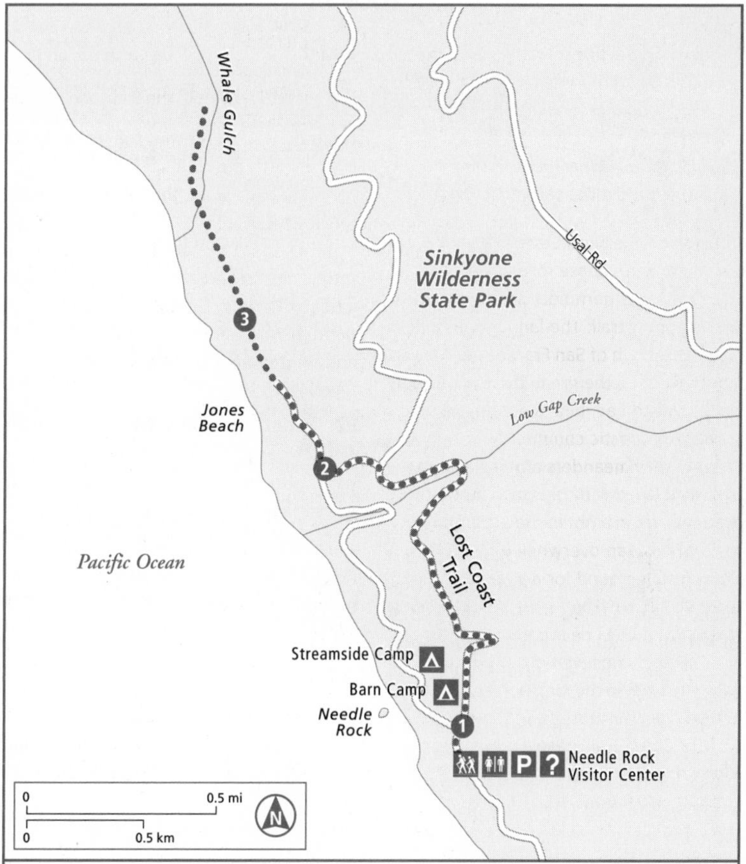

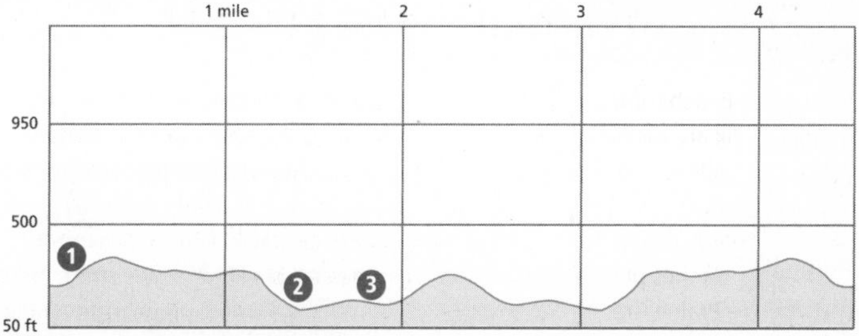

N 39 56.559, W 123 57.889: Trail head

1 N 39 56.637, W 123 57.905 (0.1 miles): Turn on to Lost Coast Trail just beyond the barn

2 N 39 57.182, W 123 58.325 (1.4 miles): Take right fork at junction with trail to Jones Beach

3 N 39 57.478, W 123 58.551 (1.8 miles): Join the rough path to Whale Gulch

This state park, along with King Range National Conservation Area to the north, comprise California's Lost Coast, 60 miles of the state's wildest shoreline. One reason the coast is "lost" is because no highways cross it. So rugged is this country, highway engineers were forced to route Hwy. 1 many miles inland from this coast—and the region has remained sparsely settled and unspoiled.

Begin at the Needle Rock Visitor Center, where maps and information are available. During the 1920s, a small settlement and shipping point were established at Needle Rock. The Calvin Cooper Stewart family were the main residents of Needle Rock, and today, their ranch house serves as the park visitor center.

From the park visitor center, walk up the park road toward the old barn, now a rustic overnight retreat for "indoor" camping.

❶ Join Lost Coast Trail Signed Lost Coast Trail leads behind the barn and dips in and out of a gully. Observe the restless Pacific surge through famed Needle Rock, located just offshore from a dark sand beach.

The trail leads past Barn Camp and Streamside Camp, two the park's primitive but superb camps. After a traverse of lovely bluffs to Low Gap Creek, the path heads inland briefly and crosses a bridge over a creek.

❷ Junction with Trail to Jones Beach Reaching a stand of eucalyptus, which shelters the Jones Beach campsites, the trail forks. The left fork leads 1/4 mile to Jones Beach. This spur trail to the beach is well worth the effort. If it's low tide, you can walk back along the black sand beach to the trail head.

Lost Coast Trail (the right fork) descends into a canyon and crosses marshy ground. The path traces the edge of a cattail-lined pond before climbing to higher ground and serving up a bird's-eye view of Whale Gulch.

❸ Junction with Trail to Whale Gulch Join the rough, unmaintained path, which descends to Whale Gulch, where there is a small lagoon and piles of driftwood logs. Return to the trail head the way you came.

For a short extension of your hike, continue north on the Lost Coast Trail as it travels inland, descends the south wall of Whale Gulch, then crosses a creek to ascend to the north side of the gulch. Beyond the gulch, the trail ascends out of the park up Chemise Mountain and into the King Range National Conservation Area.

GOLD BLUFFS BEACH ★★

Difficulty rating: Moderate

Distance: 6 miles round-trip to Ossagon Rocks

Estimated time: 4 hr.

Elevation gain: Minimal

Costs/permits: $6 state park entry fee

Best time to go: May to October

Website: www.nps.gov/redw

Recommended map: National Park Service Redwood National Park

Trail head GPS: N 41 24.194, W 124 03.867

Trail head directions: From Hwy. 101 in Orick, drive 2 miles north to Davison Rd. Turn left (west) and proceed 7 miles to road's end at the Prairie Creek Redwoods State Park Fern Canyon trail head. Coastal Trail shares the same trail head as the Fern Creek Trail (see the box on p. 122). It begins on the north side of Home Creek, which is an easy fjord in summer but may present a challenge during the rainy season.

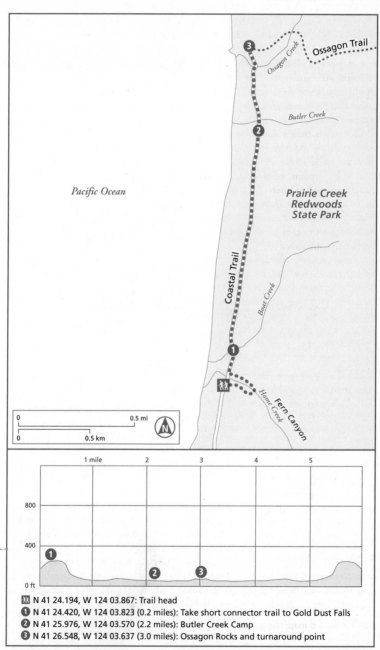

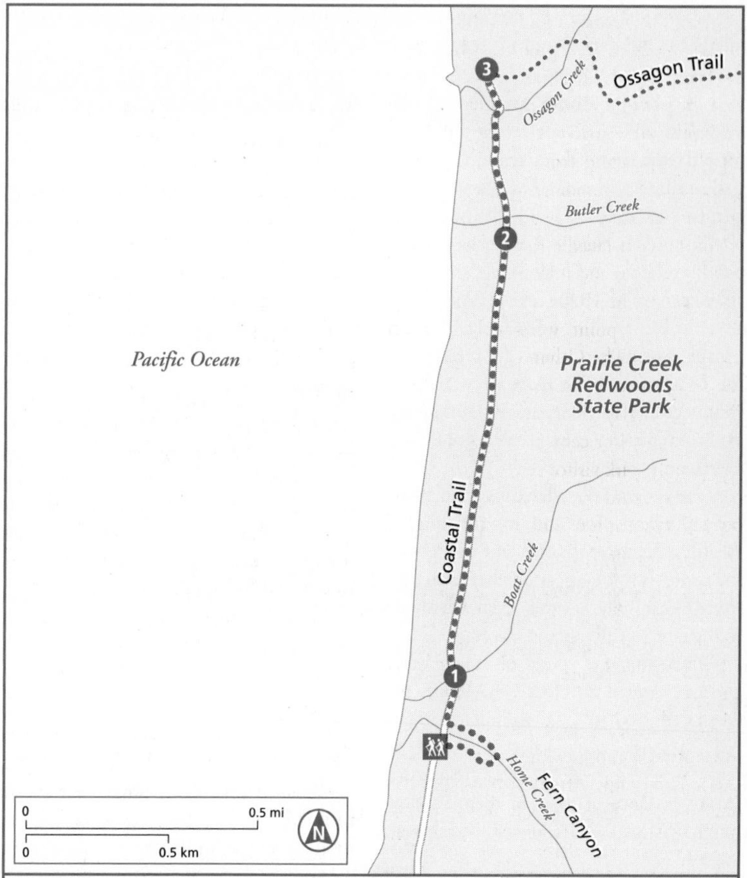

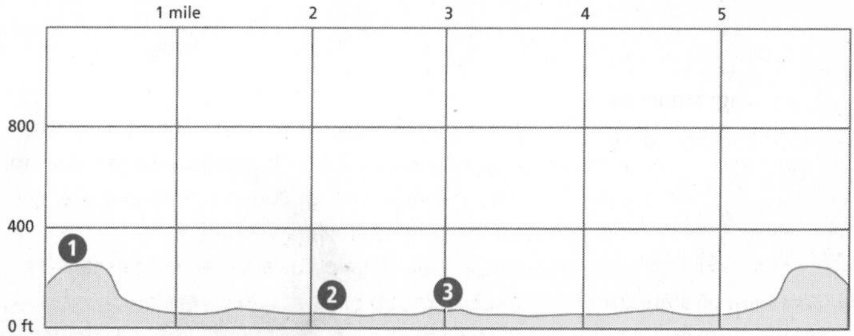

N 41 24.194, W 124 03.867: Trail head
1 N 41 24.420, W 124 03.823 (0.2 miles): Take short connector trail to Gold Dust Falls
2 N 41 25.976, W 124 03.570 (2.2 miles): Butler Creek Camp
3 N 41 26.548, W 124 03.637 (3.0 miles): Ossagon Rocks and turnaround point

Wildlife-watching, waterfalls, and a wilderness beach are just a few of the highlights of a hike along the northern reaches of Gold Bluffs Beach. While even one of these en route attractions makes for a compelling hike, the mere prospect of so many engaging environments can put a hiker into sensory overload before reaching the trail head.

Join the path for a brief meander through the forest and then out across the grass-topped dunes on the northern part of Gold Bluffs Beach. The beach is a beauty—11 miles of wild, driftwood-littered shore, backed by extensive dunes. Sand verbena, bush lupine, and wild strawberry splash color on the sand.

Gold Bluffs was named in 1850 when prospectors found some gold flakes in the beach sand. The discovery caused a minor gold rush. A tent city sprang up on the beach, but little gold was extracted.

Coastal Trail is bordered by high bluffs on its inland side and by the mighty Pacific. The hiker is often out of sight of the surf, but never altogether removed from its thunderous roll, even when the trail strays 1/4-mile inland.

A mile out, the sound of falling water and an unsigned path forking right into the forest calls you to Coastal Trail's first cascade, a long, wispy waterfall framed by ferns. Waterfalls near the coast are a rarity, so the presence of three of them in close proximity to Coastal Trail is a special treat, indeed.

❶ Gold Dust Falls Another 1/4 mile along the main path brings you to the short connector trail leading to Gold Dust Falls, a long, slender tumbler spilling some 80 feet to the forest floor. A well-placed bench offers repose and a place to contemplate the inspiring cataract.

A minute or so more down the main trail brings you to another brief spur trail and the third of Coastal Trail's cascades.

❷ Butler Creek Camp Coastal Trail edges from prairie to forest and reaches Butler Creek Camp, a hike-in retreat at 2 1/4 miles. The small camp is located at a convergence of environments—creek-side alder woodland, a prairie matted with head-high native grasses, and the creek mouth and beach beyond.

Cross Butler Creek and travel the grassy sand verbena-topped prairie for a final 1/2 mile to cross Ossagon Creek and junction with Ossagon Trail. Continue on Coastal Trail a bit farther north, then bid adieu to the path and head ocean-ward to Ossagon Rocks.

❸ Ossagon Rocks While, in the case of this hike, the journey overshadows the destination, the odd Ossagon Rocks are

Fern Canyon

A couple beautiful "fern canyons" are found along the northern California Coast, but the Fern Canyon in Prairie Creek Redwoods State Park is undoubtedly the most awe-inspiring. Five-finger, deer, lady, sword, and chain ferns smother the precipitous walls of the canyon. Bright yellow monkeyflowers abound, as well as fairy lanterns, those creamy white, or greenish, bell-shaped flowers that hang in clusters.

Ferns are descendants of an ancient group of plants that were much more numerous 200 million years ago. Ferns have roots and stems similar to flowering plants, but are considered to be a primitive form of plant life because they reproduce by spores, not seeds.

Don't miss taking this hike, even if it means cutting one of your other adventures short to squeeze it into your itinerary.

intriguing in their own way. The rocks resemble sea stacks, though they're positioned right at land's end, not in their usual offshore location.

Truly, this is a trail worth repeating, so you won't mind retracing your steps back to the trail head. However, if you want to extend the adventure (by 1.5 miles for a total roundtrip hike of 7.5 miles), you can loop back from Butler Creek Camp onto the state park's bluffs and return via West Ridge, Friendship Ridge, and James Irvine trails.

Back at the trail head, check out the 1-mile loop trail that leads along the pebbled floor of Fern Canyon. In the wettest places, the route follows wooden planks across Home Creek. With ferns pointing the way, you pass through marshy areas covered with wetlands grass and dotted with a bit of skunk cabbage. Lurking about are Pacific giant salamanders.

REDWOOD CREEK ★

Difficulty rating: Strenuous

Distance: 16.4 miles round-trip to Tall Trees Grove

Estimated time: 8–10 hr.

Elevation gain: 350 ft.

Costs/permits: None

Best time to go: Summer, when footbridges are in place

Website: www.nps.gov/redw

Recommended map: National Park Service Redwood National Park

Trail head GPS: N 41 18.061, W 124 02.370

Trail head directions: From Hwy. 101, about 3 miles north of Redwood Information Center and 2 miles from the town of Orick, turn east on Bald Hills Rd. Take the first right to the Redwood Creek trail head. A free permit is necessary for overnight camping along this trail and can be obtained at Redwood Information Center.

Redwood Creek Trail passes through regenerating forest of red alder as well as old-growth Sitka spruce and redwood. Lovely meadows flank Redwood Creek. The three bridges that cross Redwood Creek are in place only during the summer. Check trail conditions at the visitor center before attempting this hike during the wetter seasons.

Redwood Creek Trail travels through the heart of Redwood National Park to Tall Trees Grove, site of what was once considered the world's tallest measured tree.

After one of the 1960's classic conservation battles, a narrow corridor of land along Redwood Creek was acquired to protect the world's highest trees. Taller trees have been discovered in other locales in Redwood National and State parks, but the whereabouts of these giant redwoods has not been disclosed, and the Howard Libbey Tree in Tall Trees Grove is the tallest redwood accessible to the public.

A visit to the majestic colonnades of redwoods that form the heart of the national park is apt to be a humbling experience. Voices hush, children shush, eyes look skyward in reverence. It's little wonder that some hikers feel they've entered a natural cathedral and regard their time with the Tall Trees as a kind of spiritual experience.

❶ First Bridge About 1½ miles from the trail head, the path reaches the first bridge crossing of Redwood Creek.

Continue your southern progress, pausing at occasional clearings to get the "big

Tall Trees Grove an Easier Way

While the epic 16.4-mile round-trip adventure along Redwood Creek to the Tall Trees is a marvelous all-day hike (or backpacking trip), Tall Trees Grove Trail (4.2 miles round-trip with 500-ft. elevation gain) is by far the most-traveled route to the tall trees and, of course, a far easier way to go.

A (free) permit is required to drive to the trail head. Obtain one of the limited number of permits from the park information center. (Usually, even during the summer months, there are sufficient permits for all who want to make the drive and hike to the grove.) With the permit comes a combination (changed regularly) to a lock on a gate across Tall Trees Grove Access Road.

From the Redwood Information Center, travel 3 miles north on Hwy. 101 to Bald Hills Road. Turn right and drive east 6½ miles to Tall Trees Grove Access Road and turn right. Use the combination given you to unlock the gate, close the gate behind you, and head 5½ miles to the end of the gravel road and parking.

A pavilion stands at road's end where there's a sign-in book for hikers. Pick up an interpretive pamphlet, with descriptions corresponding to numbered posts along the trail, from a box at the trail head.

From the parking area, the trail descends to reach a junction with Emerald Ridge Trail in ¼ mile. Continue with Tall Trees Trail, which drops rapidly and enters old-growth redwoods accompanied by ferns and tangles of huckleberry. Showy rhododendron color the dark forest.

The path hits bottom, so to speak, at a grouping of redwood giants. This collection and the handsome one near the junction of the Tall Trees Loop Trail and Redwood Creek Trail are among the standouts of Tall Trees Grove.

Other loop trail highlights include what was the tallest measured redwood. En route gaze at what were once considered the third-largest and sixth-largest sempervirens. After completing the loop, retrace your steps to the trail head.

picture" of Redwood Creek. The 9-mile stretch along Redwood Creek known as "the worm" was downslope from private timberlands, where there was extensive and insensitive clear-cut logging. Resulting slope erosion and stream sediments threatened the big trees, so to protect this watershed, the National Park Service purchased an additional 48,000 acres, mostly in Redwood Creek basin. For decades, the park service has been rehabilitating the scarred slopes high above Redwood Creek.

As the trail meanders with the creek, three distinct communities of flora can be discerned. Extensive grass prairie, emerald green during the wet season, and golden brown during the drier months, dominates the eastern slopes above Redwood Creek. Downslope of the grassland are vast clear cuts, slowly recovering as new-growth red alder forest. Near the creek are the groves of old-growth redwoods and a lush understory of salmonberry, oxalis, and sword fern.

During the summer months, the hiker may descend to Redwood Creek and travel the creek's gravel bars nearly to Tall Trees Grove. The river bars are fine pathways and also serve as campsites for backpackers.

❷ Meeting Tributary Creeks About halfway along, you'll observe a series of creeks flowing into Redwood Creek, including Bond Creek at about the 5½-mile mark

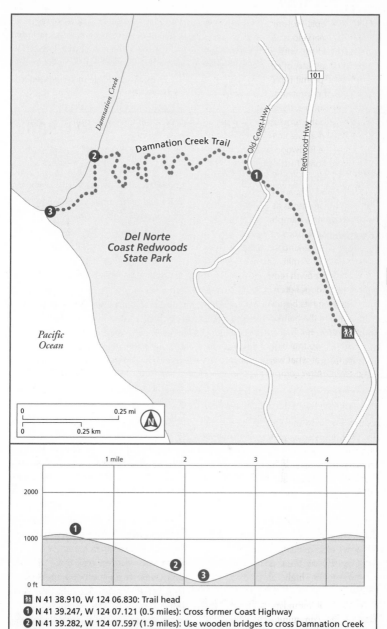

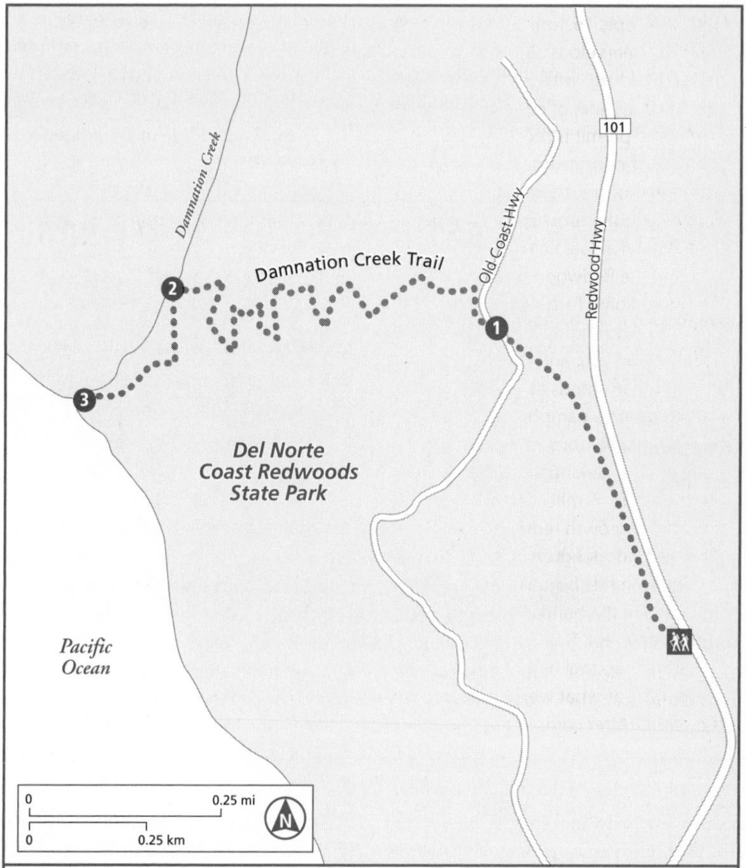

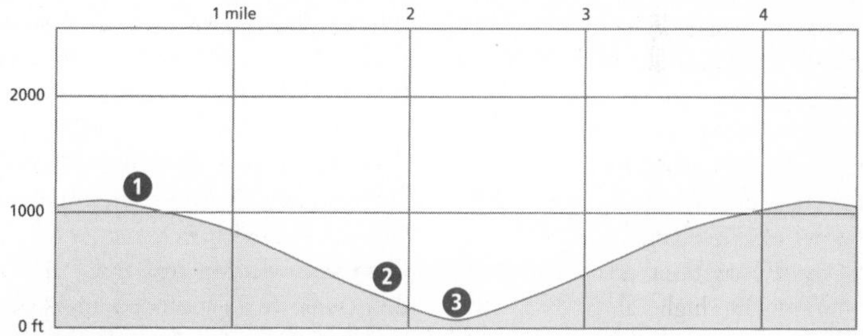

N 41 38.910, W 124 06.830: Trail head

❶ N 41 39.247, W 124 07.121 (0.5 miles): Cross former Coast Highway

❷ N 41 39.282, W 124 07.597 (1.9 miles): Use wooden bridges to cross Damnation Creek

❸ N 41 39.149, W 124 07.744 (2.2 miles): The beach at Damnation Cove

and Forty-Four Creek at 6½ miles. The redwoods congregate in especially large families on the alluvial flats along Redwood Creek.

Nearly 8 miles along, the path crosses Redwood Creek on the last (summer-only) footbridge and meets Tall Trees Grove Trail.

❸ Junction Tall Trees Grove Trail A left on this 1¼-mile-long loop trail takes you to Howard Libbey, tallest in the grove. If you have a ride waiting at the upper parking lot at the end of Tall Trees Grove Access Road, follow Tall Trees Grove Trail 1½ miles (with 500-ft. elevation gain) to the road head.

DEL NORTE COAST REDWOODS STATE PARK

Difficulty rating: Moderate

Distance: 4.5 miles round-trip from Hwy. 101 to Damnation Cove

Estimated time: 2½–3 hr.

Elevation gain: 1,000 ft.

Costs/permits: None

Best time to go: May to October

Website: www.nps.gov/redw

Recommended map: National Park Service Redwood National Park

Trail head GPS: N 41 38.910, W 124 06.830

Trail head directions: From Hwy. 101 in Crescent City, head 8 miles south to the signed turnout on the coast side of the highway at mile-marker 16.

Del Norte Coast Redwoods State Park delivers the scenery in its name: an impressive coastline fronts magnificent old-growth redwoods. Steep Damnation Creek Trail plunges through a virgin redwood forest to a hidden rocky beach. Giant ferns, and the pink and purple rhododendron blossoms climbing 30 feet overhead, contribute to the impression that one has strayed into a tropical rainforest. The combination of redwoods—and a mixed forest of Sitka spruce, Douglas fir, and red alder—and the coast adds up to some terrific hiking.

The trail soon leaves the sights and sounds of the highway behind as it climbs through redwood forest for ¼ mile, crests a ridge, and begins its ocean-ward descent. Joining the redwoods on the wet and wild coastal slope are other big trees—Sitka spruce and Douglas fir—as well as a carpet of oxalis.

As you descend, you'll walk in the footsteps of the native Yurok, who used this trail to reach the beach, where they gathered seaweed and shellfish.

The Damnation Creek name, as the story goes, was proffered by early settlers who had a devil of a time making their way through the thick forest near the creek banks. Even trailblazer Jedediah Smith, whose expedition camped alongside Damnation Creek in June of 1828, found it very rough going.

❶ Junction with Coastal Trail At ½ mile, you'll junction a stretch of pavement—a retired length of the old Coast Highway, now part of Coastal Trail that connects the redwood parks. The old Redwood Highway (Hwy. 101) was abandoned in 1935 for its present route. Make a note to return to hike the highway/trail that traverses the coastal slopes of Del Norte Redwoods State Park and extends north to Enderts Beach.

❷ Cross wooden bridges Damnation Creek Trail's steep switchbacks carry you ever downward. About halfway to the beach, you'll be treated to tree-framed views of the Pacific as the trail angles along with Damnation Creek. Wooden bridges facilitate the crossing of two branches of Damnation Creek.

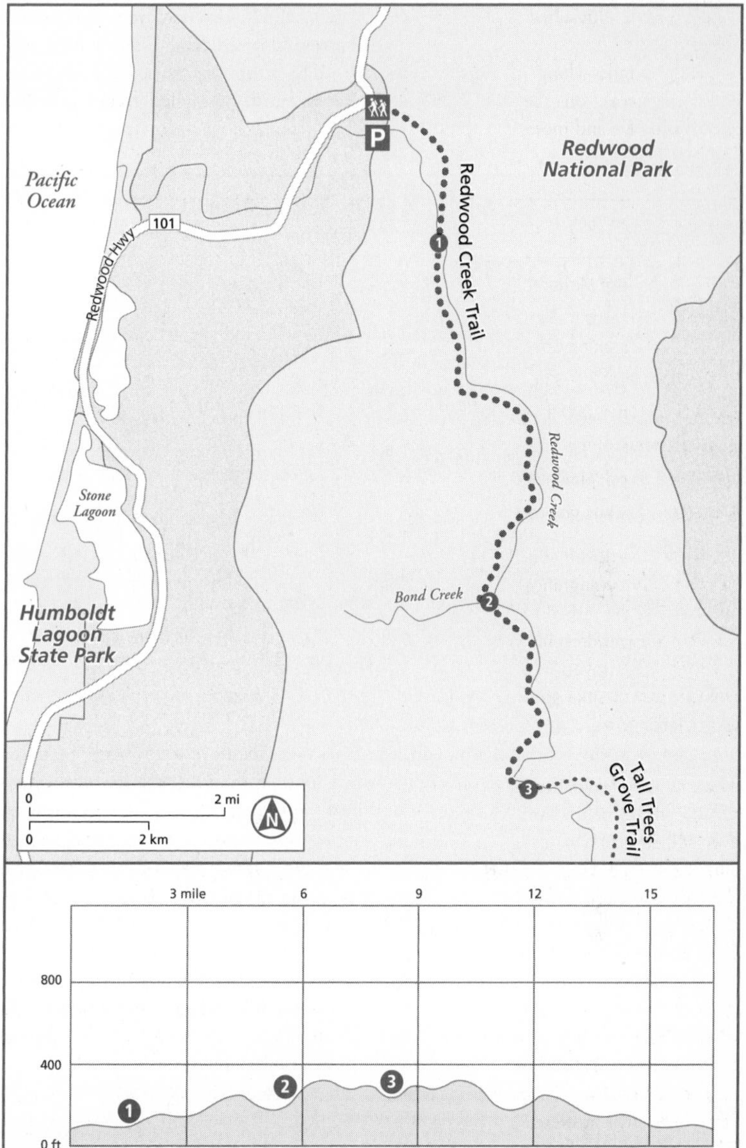

N 41 18.061, W 124 02.370: Trail head

1 N 41 16.916, W 124 01.798 (1.6 miles): First bridge crossing of Redwood Creek

2 N 41 14.074, W 124 01.297 (5.7 miles): Bond Creek flows into Redwood Creek

3 N 41 12.391, W 124 00.688 (8.2 miles): Join Tall Trees Grove loop trail

Near trail's end, you'll reach a cliff-top perch above the mouth of Damnation Creek. It's an inspiring view: the creek flowing into the surging Pacific, sea stacks, and rocky Damnation Cove.

❸ **Damnation Cove** A last bit of somewhat sketchy trail delivers you to the beach. If it's low tide, you can explore north and south along Damnation Cove. If it's high tide, stay back from the rough surf and relax on higher ground.

SLEEPING & EATING

ACCOMMODATIONS

Mendocino

★ **Agate Cove Inn** An unobstructed view of the wild and rugged coast characterizes every aspect of this extraordinary location. The perfect hideaway for hikers who want to soak up the natural setting, even when away from the trail. Ten lovely rooms come well-appointed, private, and spacious. Memorable breakfasts are served on the porch with a view.

11201 N. Lansing St., Mendocino, CA 95460. ✆ **800/527-3111** or 707/937-0551. www.agatecove.com. 10 units. $149–$309 double. Rates include full breakfast. MC, V. **Close to:** Mendocino Headlands State Park.

★ **Beachcomber Motel** Mendocino style at affordable prices. The hiking at nearby MacKerricher State Park will keep you busy for days, and the inviting back deck will help you rest and relax. Accommodations range from no-frills, yet comfortable, rooms to a deluxe king-size suite with extravagant views; some rooms have kitchenettes.

1111 N. Main St., Fort Bragg, CA 95437. ✆ **800/400-7873** or 707/964-2402. www.thebeachcombermotel.com. 75 units. $79–$250 double. Rates include continental breakfast. AE, DC, DISC, MC, V. **Close to:** Mendocino Headlands State Park.

★★ **Little River Inn** Rooms, suites, and cottages with Jacuzzis and fireplaces, and furnished in rustic country charm, enhance this eco-conscious retreat. Llamas roam the scenic gardens of this pet-friendly family-owned spot. At the inn's standout restaurant, you can sample the finest in local seafood, grilled meats, and fresh produce while taking in a spectacular view.

Coast Hwy. 1, Little River, CA 95456. ✆ **888/488-5683** or 707/937-5942. www.littleriverinn.com. 64 units. $130–$190 double; $225–$330 cottage. **Close to:** Mendocino Headlands State Park.

Redwoods

★★ **Benbow Inn** Long ago and faraway. That's the feeling imparted by this elegant National Historic Landmark, all elegance and history, located just steps from the state park. The onetime set for Hollywood films, you'll feel like a star in these fine accommodations and amenities, once enjoyed by luminaries like Clark Gable and Spencer Tracy.

445 Lake Benbow Dr., near Avenue of the Giants, Garberville, CA 95542. ✆ **800/355-3301** or 707/923-2124. www.benbowinn.com. 55 units. $90–$450 double; $395–$595 cottage. AE, DISC, MC, V. **Close to:** Humbolt Redlands State Park.

Curly Redwood Lodge All natural and nostalgia, this clean and comfortable no-frills spot feels familiar—with its redwood trim and quiet location—even though it's on the highway. The nothing fancy is part of its charm in a world given over to luxury and excess. You'll get a good night's sleep at low cost—a bit of a rarity in these parts.

701 Redwood Hwy., S U.S. 101, Crescent City, CA 95531. ✆ **707/464-2137.** www.curlyredwoodlodge.com. 36 units. Summer $62–$87 double; winter $48–$78 double. AE, DC, MC, V. **Close to:** Del Norte Coast Redwoods State Park.

Crescent Beach Motel Modestly priced, clean, and comfortable. The only motel located on the bay, this newly remodeled one offers affordable simplicity. Just a mile from town, some rooms feature decks and a view of the bay.

1455 Redwood Hwy., S U.S. 101, Crescent City, CA 95531. ✆ **707/464-5436.** www.crescentbeachmotel.com. 27 units. Summer $118 double, $125 3-person room, $135 4-person room; winter double from $81. AE, DISC, MC, V. **Close to:** Del Norte Coast Redwoods State Park.

RESTAURANTS

Mendocino

★ **Bay View Café** AMERICAN With food that makes you say, "Yum," views that go on forever, and a fern-filled dining room, you'll feel like you've entered a very special place, indeed. One of Mendocino's most popular eateries, this cafe serves savory breakfasts, sandwiches, seafood, and memorable Southwestern specialties, all at moderate prices.

45040 Main St., Mendocino, CA 95460. ✆ **707/937-4197.** Main courses $6–$15. No credit cards. Summer daily 8am–9pm; winter Mon–Thurs 8am–3pm, Fri–Sun 8am–9pm. **Close to:** Mendocino Headlands State Park.

★★★ **North Coast Brewing Company** AMERICAN A wonderful, historic building houses this fun-filled, award-winning brewpub that offers really great beers, and then some. A free brewery tour and shopping opportunities are part of the menu—in addition to basic pub grub and upscale specialties. Try the sumptuous glazed roast Cornish game hen for a memorable treat.

455 N. Main St., Fort Bragg, CA 95437. ✆ **707/964-3400.** www.northcoastbrewing.com. Main courses $7–$22. DISC, MC, V. Wed-Sun 2–9:30pm; bar menu 2–5pm, dinner menu 5–9:30pm. **Close to:** Mendocino Headlands State Park.

The Restaurant PACIFIC NORTHWEST For more than 30 years, this family-run restaurant has got it right. Drawing on international influences seasoned with local ingredients and a fresh flair, the kitchen creates a wide-ranging menu guaranteed to please. Vegetarian specialties, Asian noodles, seafood, steaks, and even a kid's menu highlight the main course menu selections.

418 N. Main St., Fort Bragg, CA 95437. ✆ **707/964-9800.** www.therestaurantfortbragg.com. Main courses $20–$30 (includes soup or salad); a la carte items $10–$15. AE, DISC, MC, V. Thur–Mon, from 5pm. **Close to:** Mendocino Headlands State Park.

Redwoods

★★ **Beachcomber** SEAFOOD Ahoy, matey; it's a sailor's delight, a landlubber's treat. Decor is all nautical and nice; the menu is a simple pleasure for seafood lovers who appreciate their gifts from the sea unfettered and unadorned. Grills fired with wood impart distinctive local flavor to local fish, shellfish, and if you must, juicy steaks.

1400 U.S. 101, Crescent City, CA 95531. ✆ **707/464-2205.** Main courses $6–$15. AE, DISC, MC, V. Fri–Tues 5–9pm. Closed Dec–Jan and part of Feb. **Close to:** Del Norte Coast Redwoods State Park.

Plaza Grill AMERICAN Everything a place called a grill should be: it nicely offers all the basics—burgers and fries, chicken, fish, and steaks, as well as healthy salads and a fine children's menu. Located upstairs from a chi-chi landmark *ristorante,* this comfortable American-food hangout offers affordable ambience and tasty meals.

791 8th St., Jacoby's Storehouse (at the corner of 8th and H sts.), Arcata, CA 95519. ✆ **707/826-0860.** Main courses $7–$17. AE, DISC, MC, V. Sun–Thurs 5–8:30pm; Fri 5–11pm; Sat 5–10pm. **Close to:** Humbolt Redlands State Park.

★ **Samoa Cookhouse** AMERICAN A historic cookhouse that once served the hungry lumberjacks who toiled in nearby forests. Bring your appetite and leave your finicky health-food concerns at home. Heavy-duty breakfasts, lunches, and dinners stick to the ribs—if not the hips. Red-checked tablecloths and memorabilia on the walls complete the picture of this relic from days gone by.

Cookhouse Rd., Samoa, CA 95564. ✆ **707/442-1659.** www.samoacookhouse.net. Main courses $7.45–$12. AE, DISC, MC, V. Mon–Sat 7am–3:30pm and 5–10pm; Sun 7am–10pm (closes 1 hr. earlier in winter). From U.S. 101, take Samoa Bridge to the end and turn left on Samoa Rd., then take the first left. **Close to:** Humbolt Redlands State Park.

Wine Country & Gold Country

The environment that contributes to the making of fine wine—rolling hills, fertile valleys, warm days, and cool nights—also adds up to some beautiful countryside. California's Wine Country—Napa Valley, Sonoma Valley, and parts of other adjacent counties—has swelled from about 25 wineries in 1975 to more than 400 today. While most visitors drive directly from tasting room to tasting room, the traveler seeking to really get to know the Wine Country will experience its natural beauty by sojourning afoot.

The Wine Country not only boasts a distinct cuisine and culture, but a distinct geology and ecology, as well. Those hills not planted in grapes are rolling grassland dotted with coastal live oaks and valley oaks. Trails lead through swaths of chaparral on lower slopes and amidst Douglas fir, California buckeye, and madrone at higher elevations.

Nearby parks are great places to unwind and uncork—and also to take a hike. Nestled in the land of grape are several inviting state parks, including Bothe-Napa Valley and Sugarloaf Ridge. These parks are laced with hiking trails and offer grand views of the valleys and vineyards below.

Famed for its mineral deposits and gold mines, California's Gold Country attracted waves of fortune seekers from around the world. Most of the gold was mined long ago, but the wonderful scenery in the High Sierra foothills remains, a favorite of hikers and history buffs. Hwy. 49 pays tribute to the Gold Rush and links a wonderful collection of restored mining towns and parks that preserve the heritage of that colorful era. Marshall Gold Discovery State Historic Park, Empire Mine State Historic Park, and other Gold Country parks preserve tunnels, trails, mines, and mountains made famous by the 49ers.

Also on the western slope of the Sierra Nevada are the famed giant sequoia groves of Calaveras Big Trees State Park. The "Big" in the park name is no exaggeration; sequoias are the largest living things on Earth.

If you're strictly on a wine-tasting mission, Napa Valley is the place, with its highly organized tours, tastings, and large scale wineries. For the hiker, the Sonoma Valley, on the other side of the Mayacamas Mountains from Napa, may have more appeal. Sonoma has a lower density of wineries (and they tend to be smaller and family-owned concerns), fewer restaurants and lodging, and more pastoral countryside to explore.

For your Wine Country visit, take a morning hike through the countryside and enjoy a sumptuous picnic at midday. Forget the power bars and trail mix, and plan a meal with some fine cheese, sourdough bread, fresh fruit, and yes, a glass of wine. Later in the afternoon, take a shorter walk and stop at a winery or two.

Both the Wine Country and Gold Country are splendid destinations in autumn. In the Wine Country, it's harvest time, and the wineries are in full scale operation. Autumn colors the trees in the Sierra foothills with gold and other fall hues.

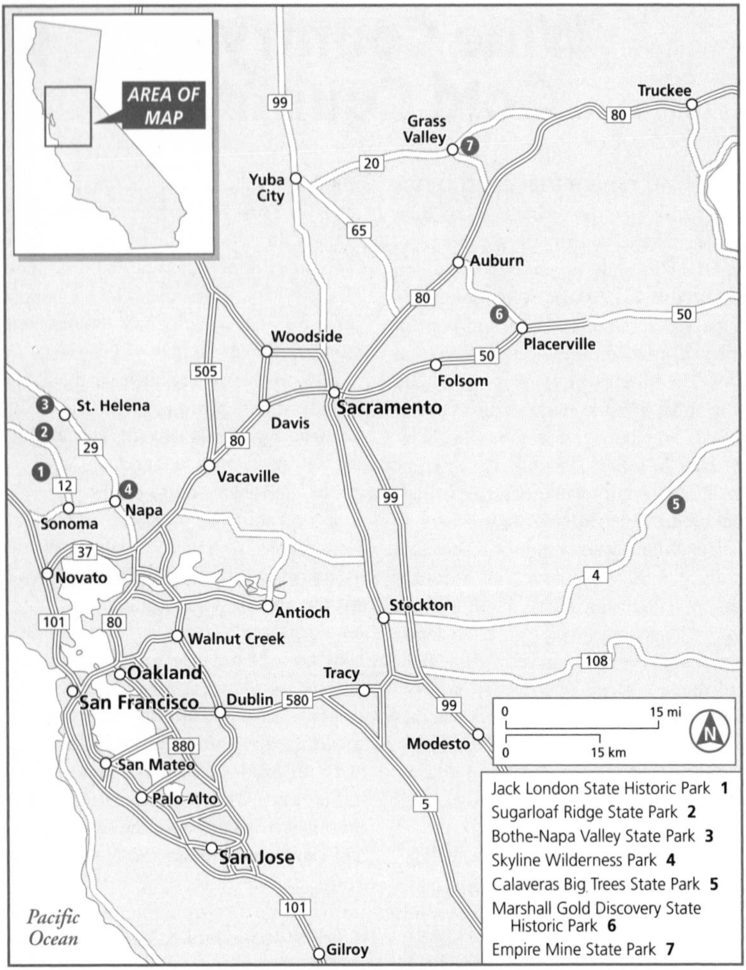

Hwy. 49 winds its way for about 350 miles through the Gold Country, a region that requires two to three packed days to explore. I suggest making a base camp in a B&B in Grass Valley or Nevada City, then venturing out to explore the marquee Gold Country state parks—Empire Mine and Marshall Gold Discovery.

Calaveras Big Trees State Park is well worth an entire day on its own, or try to arrange a side trip to see the big trees if you're on your way to and from Yosemite.

ESSENTIALS

GETTING THERE

By Air

California's Wine Country is easily accessed by the Bay Area's two major airports: San Francisco International (SFO) and Oakland International (OAK) across the Bay Bridge. San Francisco International Airport (✆ **650/821-8211;** www.flysfo.com) is a 2-hour drive to the Wine Country. Oakland International Airport (✆ **510/577-4000;** www.oaklandairport.com) is less crowded than SFO and more accessible, but offers fewer carriers. It's a bit more than a 1-hour drive from downtown Napa.

The closest runway to Gold Country is Sacramento International Airport (✆ **916/929-5411**), 12 miles northwest of downtown Sacramento.

By Car

To get to Sonoma Valley from San Francisco, cross the Golden Gate Bridge and head north on U.S. 101. Exit at Hwy. 37; after 10 miles, turn north onto Hwy. 121. After another 10 miles, turn north onto Hwy. 12 (Broadway), which will take you directly into the town of Sonoma. To get to Napa from San Francisco, cross the Golden Gate Bridge and head north on U.S. 101. Turn east on Hwy. 37 (toward Vallejo), then north on Hwy. 29, the main road through Napa Valley. Or take the scenic route: On Hwy. 121/12, follow the signs toward Napa and turn left onto Hwy. 29.

About 60 miles northeast of Sacramento, Nevada City and Grass Valley are far and away the top visitor destinations of the Gold Country. From I-80 in Auburn, take Hwy. 49 north to the two towns.

VISITOR INFORMATION

While you're in Sonoma, stop by the **Sonoma Valley Visitors Bureau,** 453 1st St. E. (✆ **866/996-1090** or 707/996-1090; www.sonomavalley.com). It's open Monday through Saturday from 9am to 5pm (to 6pm in the summer) and Sunday 10am to 5pm. If you prefer advance information from the bureau, contact them to order the free *Sonoma Valley Visitors Guide,* which lists almost every lodge, winery, and restaurant in the valley. An additional **Visitors Bureau** is a few miles south of the square at Cornerstone Festival of Gardens at 23570 Arnold Dr. (Hwy. 121; ✆ **866/996-1090**); it's open daily from 9am to 4pm (to 5pm during summer).

Once in Napa Valley, stop first at the **Napa Valley Conference & Visitors Bureau,** 1310 Town Center Mall, Napa, CA 94559 (✆ **707/226-7459**), and pick up the *Napa Valley Guide.* You can call or write in for the *Napa Valley Guidebook,* which includes information on lodging, restaurants, wineries, and other things to do, along with a winery map; the bureau charges a $5 postage fee. If you don't want to pay for the official publication, point your browser to www.napavalley.org, the NVCVB's official site, which has lots of the same information for free.

Another good source is WineCountry.com (www.winecountry.com).

For info on The Gold Country, visit **Grass Valley & Nevada County Chamber of Commerce,** 248 Mill St., Grass Valley (✆ **800/655-4667** in California or 530/273-4667; www.grassvalleychamber.com) or the **Nevada City Chamber of Commerce,** 132 Main St., Nevada City (✆ **800/655-6569** or 530/265-2692; www.nevadacitychamber.com).

JACK LONDON STATE HISTORIC PARK ★★

Difficulty rating: Easy to lake; moderate to Sonoma Peak

Distance: 2 miles round-trip to the lake; 8.25 miles round-trip to the top of Sonoma Mountain

Estimated time: 1½ hr. leisurely stroll around Beauty Ranch; 4 hr. for the hike up Sonoma Mountain

Elevation gain: 1,800 ft.

Costs and permits: $5 state park entry fee

Best time to go: Year round

Website: www.jacklondonpark.com; www.parks.ca.gov

Recommended map: California State Parks Jack London State Historic Park

Trail head GPS: N 38 21.379, W 122 32.701

Trail head directions: From Santa Rosa, head east; from Sonoma, head north on Hwy. 12. Take the signed turnoff (Arnold Dr.) a mile to the hamlet of Glen Ellen. Turn right on Jack London Ranch Rd. and proceed 1¼ miles to the state park. To visit the museum, turn left; for trail head parking, angle right.

This excursion is a meander through the main part of what Jack London called his "Beauty Ranch," including a trek to a small lake, and the chance to tackle Sonoma Mountain, which offers grand Wine Country views. Visit the park museum, walk the trails past his home and haunts, and gain a deeper appreciation of London the man and his contribution to American literature.

From the parking area, the path ascends 100 yards southwest through a eucalyptus grove to a trail map and picnic area. Proceed straight ahead, past an old barn to a dirt road, where you go right.

❶ London's Cottage A side trail leads to the cottage where London worked in his final years. The dirt road then forks. Head right along a vineyard, meandering past "Pig Palace," London's hog pen deluxe, as well as assorted silos.

About a half-mile from the trail head, you'll crest a hill and get your first great view of the Valley of the Moon. The trail soon splits: equestrians go left, hikers go right on a narrow footpath through a forest of Douglas fir, bay laurel, and madrone that ascends past some good-sized redwoods.

❷ Lake Trail Lake Trail loops around the London's little lake, where the couple swam and enjoyed entertaining friends. This is a good turnaround point for families with young children.

❸ Mountain Trail Sonoma Mountain–bound hikers will take the Mountain Trail, a dirt road which curves east to Mays Clearing, another fine vista point offering Valley of the Moon panoramas.

❹ London hunting camp Mountain Trail climbs steadily, crosses two forks of fern-lined Graham Creek, and ascends to what was once Jack London's hunting camp (Deer Camp), tucked in a grove of redwoods. It's marked "Rest Area" on the park map.

Mountain Trail resumes climbing, steeper now, beneath big black oaks, for another mile, ascending to the headwaters of Middle Graham Creek and up to the park boundary. The park map shows the path ending here; actually, though, it continues another quarter-mile to the crest of Sonoma Mountain's east ridge.

Fun Facts Jack London

There have been few more colorful, individualistic, and ultimately, more tragic figures in American literature than Jack London. Born in San Francisco in 1876, London struggled to release himself from the stifling burdens of illegitimacy and poverty.

His quest led him on a succession of rugged adventures in far-flung locales. He was an oyster pirate in San Francisco Bay, a gold prospector in the frozen Klondike, and a sailor in the South Seas. He drew largely on his rough-and-tumble experiences throughout his prolific career as a writer of novels, short stories, and magazine articles.

London, who by most accounts was the most successful writer of his time—in terms of financial earnings, fame, and popularity—is today best-known for his outdoor adventure stories. *White Fang, The Call of the Wild,* and *To Build a Fire,* his most popular works, have stereotyped the writer as one who depicts the theme of the individual's struggle to survive, using nature's harshness as a backdrop. But London's message was more complex than that, yet through time it's been largely ignored.

A passionate humanist, London was deeply committed to the cause of socialism. In his day, before the Russian Revolution skewed the promise of utopian socialism, London viewed socialism as the way to restore human dignity and respect for the individual. He raged against the oppressive social conditions of the Industrial Age in *The People of the Abyss, Martin Eden,* and *The Iron Heel.*

London's life was a mass of contradictions. He was a wealthy socialist, a he-man who was plagued with ill health, an imaginative writer who feared he would one day run out of ideas. He and his wife Charmian lived in the bucolic setting of Glen Ellen, far from the crowded city conditions he decried.

London first purchased land in the Sonoma Valley in 1905, and continued to add to his holdings until he owned 1,350 acres. As he described the setting: " . . . there are great redwoods on it . . . also there are great firs, tanbark oaks, live oaks, white oaks, black oaks, madrone, and manzanita galore. There are canyons, several streams of water, many springs . . . I have been riding all over these hills, looking for just such a place, and I must say that I have never seen anything like it."

The Jack London Ranch is now the site of Jack London State Historic Park, established in 1960 in accordance with the wishes of his wife.

Among the attractions to be found in the park are the House of Happy Walls Museum, built by Charmian London as a memorial to her husband's life and work, and the remains of the Wolf House mansion, suspiciously burned to the ground shortly before the Londons were scheduled to move in. Devotees of the author should make the 1½-mile pilgrimage to Jack London's gravesite and to the Wolf House ruins.

5 Sonoma Mountain Stop and take in some superb Wine Country views from Sonoma Mountain, the park's summit. The actual mountaintop, 80 feet higher in elevation than the east summit, is located another ¼ mile to the west.

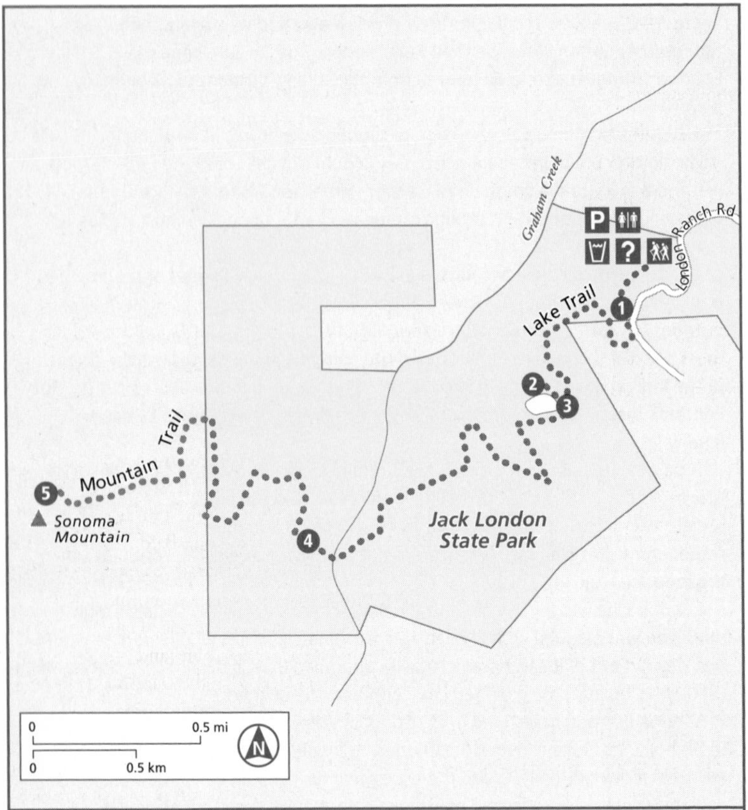

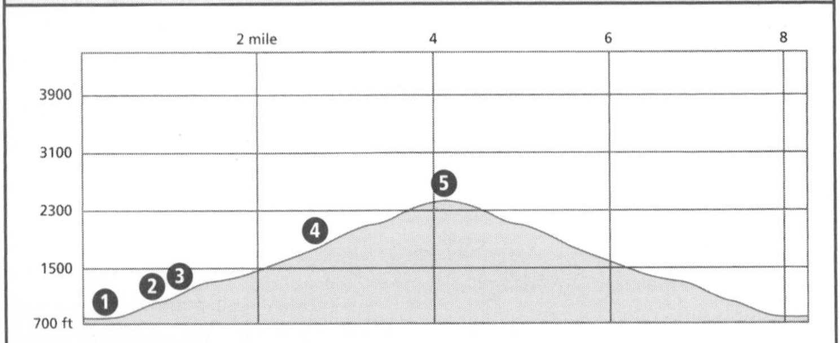

N 38 21.379, W 122 32.701 Trail head
❶ N 38 21.225, W 122 32.816 (0.3 miles): Jack London's cottage
❷ N 38 21.043, W 122 33.090 (1.0 miles): Join Lake Trail
❸ N 38 21.997, W 122 33.081 (1.1 miles): Join Mountain Trail
❹ N 38 20.673, W 122 33.888 (2.6 miles): Deer Camp, Jack London's former hunting camp
❺ N 38 20.794, W 122 34.726 (4.1 miles): Sonoma Mountain summit

SUGARLOAF RIDGE STATE PARK

Difficulty rating: Moderate

Distance: 6-mile loop through park

Estimated time: 3–4 hr.

Elevation gain: 1,400 ft.

Costs/permits: $5 state park entry fee

Best time to go: Spring and autumn

Website: www.parks.ca.gov

Recommended map: California State Parks Sugarloaf Ridge State Park

Trail head GPS: N 38 26.274, W 122 30.881

Trail head directions: From Hwy. 101 in Santa Rosa, exit on Hwy. 12 and travel east 11 miles to Adobe Canyon Rd. Turn left and follow it 4 miles to the hikers' parking lot a bit before road's end.

The state park is laced with lovely trails leading through three distinct ecosystems: chaparral, grassland, and woodland. In the canyons watered by Sonoma Creek and its tributaries grow Douglas fir, oak, big-leaf maple, and even a grove of redwood. Your reward for climbing Bald Mountain is a terrific view stretching from the Napa Valley vineyards to the snowy peaks of the Sierra Nevada.

From the east end of the parking lot, hit the trail, which leads into a meadow and soon splits. Here, you'll join Lower Bald Mountain Trail, which crosses a meadow. The park's grassy meadows are bedecked in spring with a multitude of colorful wildflowers, from Indian pinks to blue dicks. Also look for lupine, California poppy, cream cups, buttercups, and Mariposa lily. Bordering the meadow is quite a mixture of trees: maples, black oaks, alder, and bay.

The trail ascends through an oak and madrone woodland. After a mile's brisk climb, the path intersects paved Bald Mountain Trail. A strategically placed bench allows you to catch your breath and to gaze out over the park.

❶ Bald Mountain Trail Proceed right on the road, which ascends steeply 1/4 mile to signed Vista Trail.

Those forsaking the climb up Bald Mountain or desiring a shorter hike can join Vista Trail, which drops into a couple of ravines watered by seasonal Sonoma Creek tributaries. Vista Trail serves up promised vistas of Sugarloaf Ridge, then descends through Columbine Meadow. Cross Sonoma Creek, join Gray Pine Trail, and cross a meadow.

At a signed trail junction, you can select Meadow Trail, which crosses a meadow and returns you to the trail head.

For those pursuing Bald Mountain, the Bald Mountain Trail ascends into the chaparral—chamise, ceanothus, and coyote bush. In the spring, California poppies, along with blue and white lupine, blossom alongside the trail. My favorite is the showy purple bush lupine.

At the 1 3/4-mile mark, ignore the trail leading to Red Mountain, a 2,548-foot peak that hosts an array of communications equipment. Continue another 1/4 mile, accompanied by oaks, big-leaf maple, and bay, to a junction. The paved road curves toward Red Mountain. Turn right on Bald Mountain Trail, which continues as a dirt fire road.

As you ascend, you'll note that chaparral blankets the highest ridges, except in the vicinity of aptly named Bald Mountain; the park's high point is instead surfaced with grass and a bluish rock (serpentine). At the 2 1/2-mile mark, you'll reach a junction with Gray Pine Trail and be within steps of the summit.

❷ Junction with Gray Pine Trail and Summit of Bald Mountain From the top of 2,729-foot Bald Mountain, a

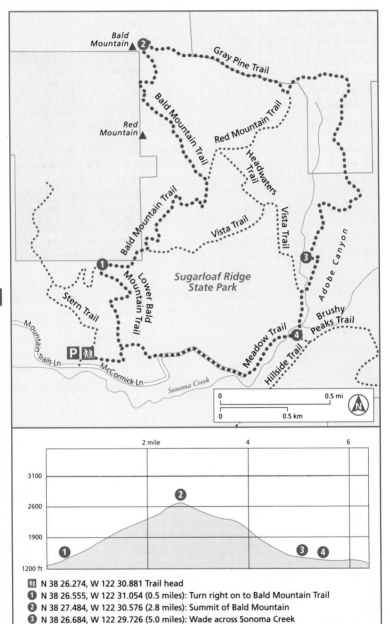

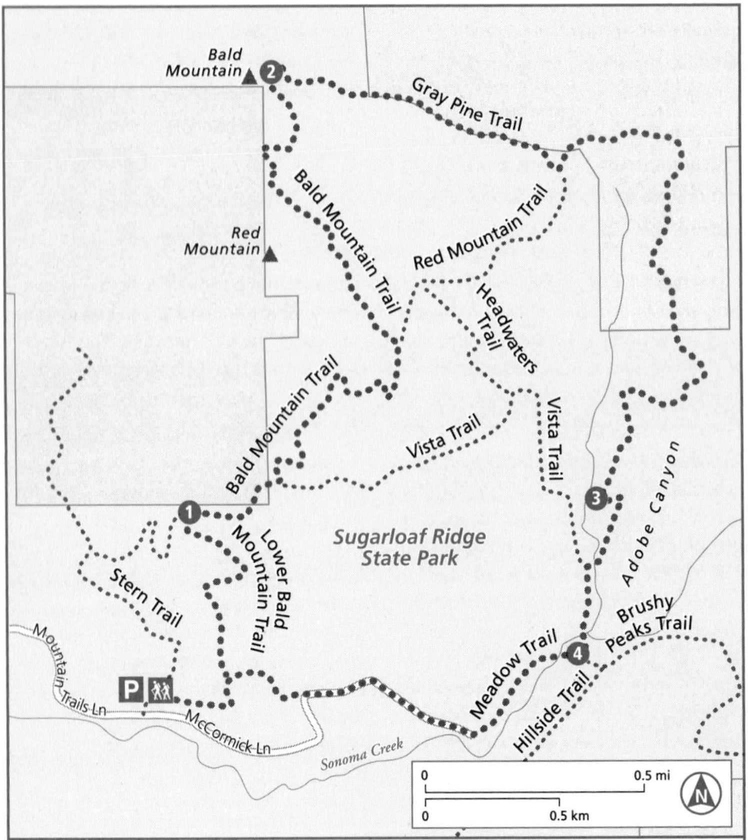

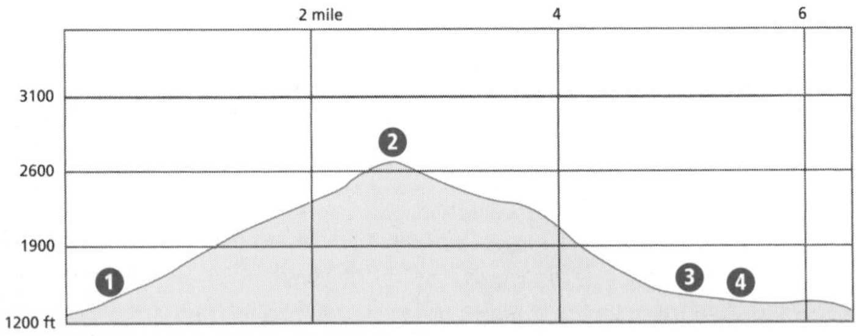

N 38 26.274, W 122 30.881 Trail head

1. N 38 26.555, W 122 31.054 (0.5 miles): Turn right on to Bald Mountain Trail
2. N 38 27.484, W 122 30.576 (2.8 miles): Summit of Bald Mountain
3. N 38 26.684, W 122 29.726 (5.0 miles): Wade across Sonoma Creek
4. N 38 26.381, W 122 29.823 (5.3 miles): Join Meadow Trail at junction

Fun Facts The Sweet Scenery Known as Sugarloaf

Today, we buy granulated sugar in sacks or boxes, but grocers of the 19th century sold crystallized sugar in a sugarloaf—a conical shape that resembled an upside-down ice cream cone. "Sugarloaf" names several promontories in California, including Sugarloaf Mountain in the Santa Monica Mountains—reportedly inspiration for the Paramount Pictures logo.

In Northern California, a distinguished sugarloaf rising above the Wine Country is the highlight of Sugarloaf Ridge State Park. The ridge is part of a length of Coastal Range called the Mayacamas Mountains, which border Sonoma and Napa valleys. The distinct ridge, volcanic in origin, is impressive—and just a little bit spooky when wrapped in mist or when turkey vultures circle it.

stunning view of the Napa Valley below, with Mount Saint Helena above, unfolds. Look to the southwest for Mount Tamalpais and the Golden Gate Bridge; 50 miles to the southeast, you can see the mighty Mount Diablo. On especially clear days, the panorama includes the High Sierra, Point Reyes, and San Francisco Bay.

A bench on the summit is as splendid a place for lunch as the hiker will find.

After savoring the view, descend eastward on Gray Pine Trail, a fire road. "And the gray pines are where?" you wonder as you hike down the mountain. Might this trail instead have been better named for other trees (Douglas fir or oak) or bushes (manzanita or scrub oak)?

After a mile or so, the tall, single-needled gray pines do show up alongside the trail. The trail then leaves the pines behind and drops to a branch of Sonoma Creek, following its banks on a more mellow descent.

3 Creek crossing You'll cross the creek (easy to wade except in times of high winter/early spring run-off). You'll pass a trail intersection with Vista Trail and soon thereafter need to cross Sonoma Creek again. Bridges have been planned for years, but apparently have not been very high on the park priority list.

4 Meadow Trail Five miles into your hike, Gray Pine Trail ends at an intersection with Meadow Trail. Join Meadow Trail for a traverse of the meadow. You'll cross a parking lot, pass Ferguson Observatory (a small facility with a classroom and a reputation for fine astronomy instruction), then continue on Meadow Trail to a junction with Lower Bald Mountain Trail. Retrace your steps a quarter mile to the trail head.

BOTHE-NAPA VALLEY STATE PARK ★

Difficulty rating: Moderate

Distance: 4.5 miles round-trip

Estimated time: 2–3 hr.

Elevation gain: 900 ft.

Costs/permits: $5 state park entry fee

Best time to go: Spring and autumn

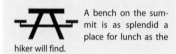

Website: www.parks.ca.gov

Recommended map: Bothe-Napa Valley State Park map

Trail head GPS: N 38 33.150, W 122 31.306

Trail head directions: Bothe-Napa Valley State Park is located on the side of Hwy. 29 in the Napa Valley, 5 miles north of St. Helena, 4 miles south of Calistoga. Follow the park road 1/4 mile past the entry kiosk to parking and Ritchey Canyon trail head.

It's a great place to unwind and uncork. At least, that's what most visitors discover when they picnic at Bothe-Napa Valley State Park, in the heart of the Wine Country. But if it's the park's proximity to wineries (just down the road are Beringer Vineyards, Charles Krug Winery, and a dozen more) that first lures travelers, it's the park's beauty that brings them back: year-round Ritchey Creek, shaded by redwoods and Douglas fir, plus inspiring Wine Country views from Coyote Peak, are just a few spectacular spots.

You'll begin your hike on Ritchey Canyon Trail, which travels west beneath big-leaf maple, madrone, and oaks, soon crosses a paved road and begins paralleling the road to the campground, as well as Ritchey Creek.

During the 1800s, this land belonged to Dr. Charles M. Hitchcock of San Francisco, who built a second home called "Lonely" in 1872.

Life in the country seemed to have resulted in the fierce independence of Hitchcock's daughter, Lillie. An early feminist, she scandalized her social set by riding horseback astride, forcing her way into an exclusive men's club, and winning poker games.

As a child, Lillie Hitchcock was rescued from a fire that killed two of her playmates. As an adult, she was an enthusiastic booster of San Francisco's firemen. When she died in 1929, Lillie Hitchcock Coit left the city of San Francisco the money to build Coit Tower, a memorial to the city's firemen.

Reinhold Bothe acquired part of the Hitchcock/Coit estate and developed a resort, Paradise Park, with cabins and a swimming pool. The resort was popular during the 1930s, much less so after World War II. The state park system purchased Paradise Park from Bothe in 1960.

Beneath the tall Douglas fir and redwoods grows a tangle of ferns, bay laurel, and wild grape. After 1/2 mile, you'll pass a junction with Redwood Trail and, at the 1-mile mark, a path that veers northeast back to the campground.

❶ Ritchey Canyon Continue through mixed forest past a junction with Vineyard Trail, 1 1/2 miles from the trail head. Stay with Ritchey Canyon Trail for another half mile and continue your exploration of the 3-mile-long, fern-lined, redwood-shaded canyon. The redwoods sprouted from the roots of trees felled in the 1850s during the settlement of Napa Valley. The second-generation trees are thriving. Adding a magical touch to the forest scene are redwood orchids and trillium growing at the base of the redwoods.

❷ Bridge at Ritchey Creek Bid farewell to Ritchey Canyon Trail when you reach a concrete bridge. Cross the little bridge, note east-west-trending Redwood Trail, and join South Fork Trail, heading south along the south fork of Ritchey Creek. Follow the fern-lined footpath amidst redwoods 1/2 mile to a junction. South Fork Trail curves west, but you'll bear left with Coyote Peak Trail.

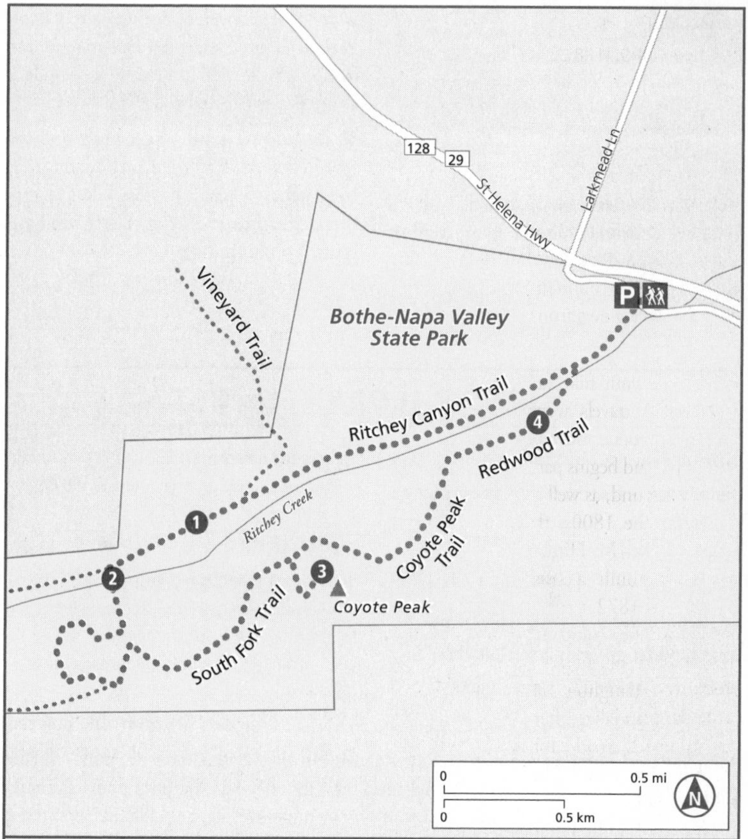

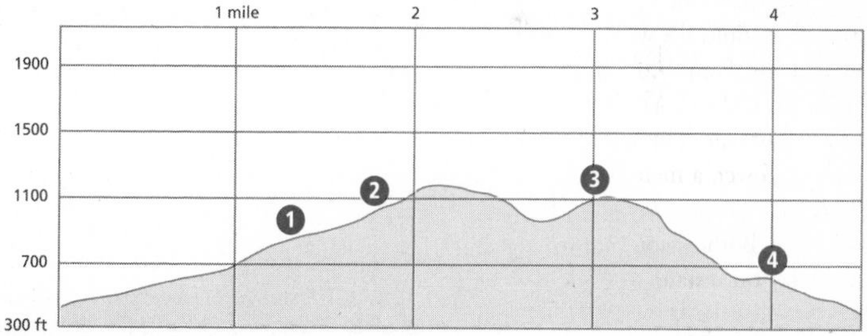

N 38 33.150, W 122 31.306 Trail head

❶ N 38 32.630, W 122 32.560 (1.3 miles): Pass junction with Ritchey Canyon

❷ N 38 32.533, W 122 32.832 (1.6 miles): Cross concrete bridge and join South Fork Trail

❸ N 38 32.556, W 122 32.248 (3.0 miles): Turn right on to short trail to summit of Coyote Peak

❹ N 38 32.860, W 122 31.622 (4.0 miles): Turn right on to Redwood Trail

The Coyote Peak Trail rises through and above the redwoods and Ritchey Canyon onto the chaparral-cloaked slopes of Coyote Peak. From this high and dry terrain, you'll get fine vistas of the Wine Country and mighty Mount St. Helena.

At the 2¾-mile mark, you'll reach a junction with the ¼-mile-long summit trail to Coyote Peak on your right.

❸ Coyote Peak Scramble up the steep, rocky summit path, making sure you savor the view south over the Napa Valley. Best views are short of the summit, which is tree-covered. Backtrack to Coyote Peak Trail and descend a half mile amidst oak, madrone, and eventually redwoods to a junction with Redwood Trail.

❹ Redwood Trail Turn right and follow Redwood Trail on a mellow meander by Ritchey Creek. At the hike's 4-mile mark, you'll meet Ritchey Creek Trail and return to the trail head.

SKYLINE WILDERNESS PARK

Difficulty rating: Moderate

Distance: 6 miles round-trip to Lake Marie with return via Skyline Trail

Estimated time: 2–3 hr.

Elevation gain: 850 ft.

Costs/permits: $4 parking fee

Best time to go: Spring and autumn

Website: www.ncfaa.com/skyline/skyline_park.htm

Recommended map: Park map available at entry station or as a download from website

Trail head GPS: N 38 16.769, W 122 14.891

Trail head directions: From Hwy. 29 in Napa, take the Hwy. 121/Imola Rd. exit and drive east on Imola Rd. to the entrance for Skyline Wilderness Park.

Napa Valley is home to more than 200 wineries but only one wilderness park—Skyline Wilderness Park, located on the outskirts of the city of Napa. The park offers the most hiking in Napa County, with trails that tour grassy meadows, oak woodlands, and alder-shaded creeks. Deer, wild turkeys, and feral pigs are among the wildlife commonly sighted in the park. As the park is very near the city center, you won't have to go far for post-hike refreshment.

The Skyline Trail leads past all manner of warning signs (from wild pigs to poison oak), an RV campground, and a California native plant garden, then skirts a picnic ground and soon reaches a junction with Lake Marie Trail, a dirt road. Note Skyline Trail on your right; this will be your return route from Lake Marie. Skyline Trail is part of the Bay Area Ridge Trail, a long-distance path that follows the hills and coastal mountains around San Francisco and its adjacent cities and counties.

The wide path leads past remnants of Napa State Hospital's old orchards (olive, walnut, and fig trees), once cultivated by patients, and ascends to a park viewpoint at ½-mile.

❶ Fig Tree The trail rolls along, likely bringing encounters with the park's many coveys of California quail and sightings of red-winged blackbirds. It then descends to a junction with Bayleaf Trail. Here, you can't miss the enormous fenced-off Fig Tree, believed to be more than 100 years

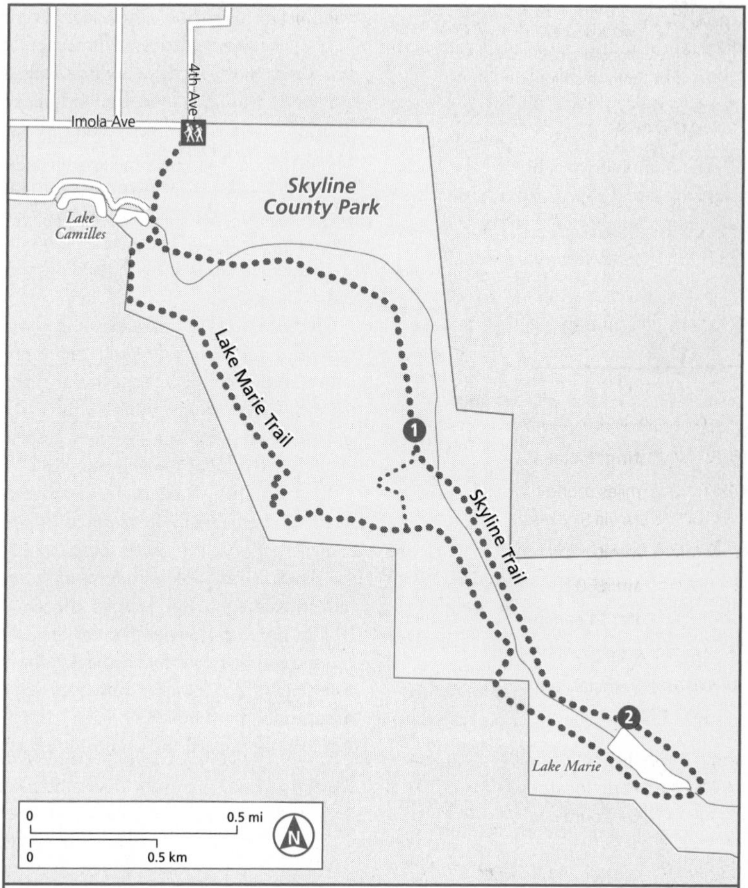

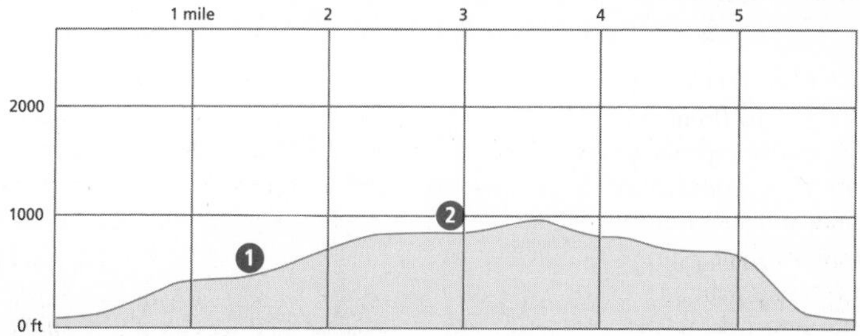

N 38 16.769, W 122 14.891 Trail head

❶ N 38 16.161, W 122 14.319 (1.4 miles): Fig tree at junction with Bayleaf Trail

❷ N 38 15.598, W 122 13.724 (2.9 miles): Reach Lake Marie

old. Bayleaf and Buckeye trails invite the hiker to jaunts on the other side of Marie Creek, but stick with Lake Marie Road, where you'll soon drop into a shady environment of oak and bay laurel.

❷ **Lake Marie** Just 1/4 mile short of Lake Marie, you'll pass a connector with Skyline Trail and soon reach Lake Marie. Contemplate the lake from a bench or from atop the lake's earthen dam. You can circle the lake by trail.

For a longer, but scenic return, double-back to Skyline Trail, which parallels Lake Marie Road for a mile or so. Two moderate ascents deliver hilltop vistas of Marie Creek Canyon and rolling oak-dotted hills, as well as the Wine Country and San Pablo Bay.

What is now parkland was once the grounds of a state mental hospital. When the Napa Asylum for the Insane was constructed in 1875, it was universally regarded as the most outstanding public building in all of California. Picture a gigantic Gothic-style farmhouse, five stories high, 1-mile in circumference.

Later generations were more critical of the building, designed in a style called "Domestic Gothic" by its architect, who topped it with towers and decorated it with gargoyles. To critics, it all looked medieval creepy, the setting for a Hollywood horror film.

The diagnosis and treatment of mental illness was not exactly a well-developed science in the 19th century, and many folks who were simply poor, homeless, or unlucky in love and business ended up housed with the truly insane. Funds for the facility were limited, so patients were put to work tending vegetable gardens, orchards, and vineyards, or feeding pigs and milking cows.

The farm work, as well as spending leisure time in a tranquil, beautifully landscaped setting, had therapeutic benefits for many patients. Wine Country tourists of the 1920s and 1930s drove through the lovely hospital grounds and stopped to swim and picnic.

By the 1940s, modern medical treatment of the mentally ill required indoor clinical facilities. Napa State Hospital, as it was later called, was adjudged unfit for human habitation and demolished.

The property (owned by the State of California) lingered for decades, slowly reverting back to nature. Conservationists, spearheaded by the Skyline Park Citizens Association, rescued the land from private developers and created an 850-acre park in 1983; the association manages the park today for the county of Napa.

CALAVERAS BIG TREES STATE PARK ★★

Difficulty rating: Easy to moderate

Distance: 5 miles round-trip on South Grove Trail

Estimated time: 2 1/2–3 hr.

Elevation gain: 400 ft.

Costs/permits: $5 state park entry fee

Best time to go: May to October

Website: www.parks.ca.gov; www.bigtrees.org

Recommended map: Calaveras Big Trees State Park map

Trail head GPS: N 38 15.316, W 120 15.662

Trail head directions: The park is located off Hwy. 4, 4 miles northeast of Arnold, and 21 miles from Angels Camp and the junction with Hwy. 49. Once in the park, continue 9 miles along the scenic park road (Walter W. Smith Memorial Pkwy) to South Grove trail head. Snow closes the road to South Grove; call the park for latest road and weather conditions.

The "Big Trees" in the park name is a tip-off: Two groves of giant Sequoia redwoods are the highlights of Calaveras Big Trees State Park. Most visitors tour the easy-to-access North Grove, while hikers in the know head for the park's more remote South Grove, which has ten times the number of big trees and is far less visited than North Grove. North Grove is protected in a "Natural Preserve," the highest category of environmental protection offered by the state park system.

As you set off on South Grove Trail, you'll soon cross Beaver Creek on a footbridge and reach the junction with Bradley Trail. This 2½-mile-long path loops through land logged in the early 1950s. After the loggers left, park caretaker Owen Bradley planted sequoia seedlings, and today, about 150 young Sierra redwoods thrive in Bradley Grove, a testament to forest regeneration and to the future.

You'll likely have some—but not too much—company in remote South Grove, which offers an opportunity for solitude among the giants rarely possible in popular and easier-to-access North Grove.

Interpretive pamphlets for South Grove (and North Grove) trails are available for a small donation at their respective trail heads or at the park's museum and visitor center.

The biggest trees in the park are truly big—250 to 300 feet high and 25 to 30 feet across. And they're ancient—2,000 to 3,000 years old. The trees are relics from a warmer and wetter clime and time—the Mesozoic Era, some 180 million years ago, when dinosaurs roamed the Earth. Once much more numerous, the big trees survive now only in 75 groves on the western slope of the High Sierra.

South Grove Trail then climbs moderately through tall sugar and ponderosa pines, and rises out of the Beaver Creek drainage. After crossing a fire road, the path meanders upstream alongside Big Trees Creek.

❶ Loop Trail Begins At the 1⅓-mile mark, begin the loop trail segment of the hike. Bear right at the trail junction and tramp amongst the Sierra redwoods, incense cedar, and occasional big-leaf maple.

"A flowering glade in the very heart of the woods, forming a fine center for the student, and a delicious resting place for the weary," is how the great naturalist John Muir described the forest of giant sequoia, ponderosa pine, and incense cedar now protected by Calaveras Big Trees State Park.

Just past a large hollow redwood lying across the creek, the path angles left and crosses Big Trees Creek on a footbridge.

❷ Trail to Agassiz Tree About 2¼ miles from the trail head, you'll reach another junction. You can bear left to complete the loop trail, but better yet, head right to visit Agassiz Tree, largest in the park. One of the more curious Sierra redwoods encountered en route is aptly-named Chimney Tree; its insides were long ago consumed by fire, forming a "chimney" in a still-living tree.

Agassiz Tree, one of the "Top Ten" Sierra Redwoods in size, honors 19th-century naturalist Louis Agassiz, last of the scientific creationists and a pioneer in Ice Age theory, and plant and animal classification.

Though the trail ends here at this biggest of the big trees, the adventurous can continue another mile along Big Trees Creek and get up-close looks at other magnificent South Grove specimens: The Moody Group, named for a 19th-century evangelist; storied Old Goliath, felled by a windstorm in 1861; and three mammoth trees called The Portals.

❸ Back to the Loop Trail Retrace your steps back to Loop Trail junction, this time branching right and descending back to the trail head.

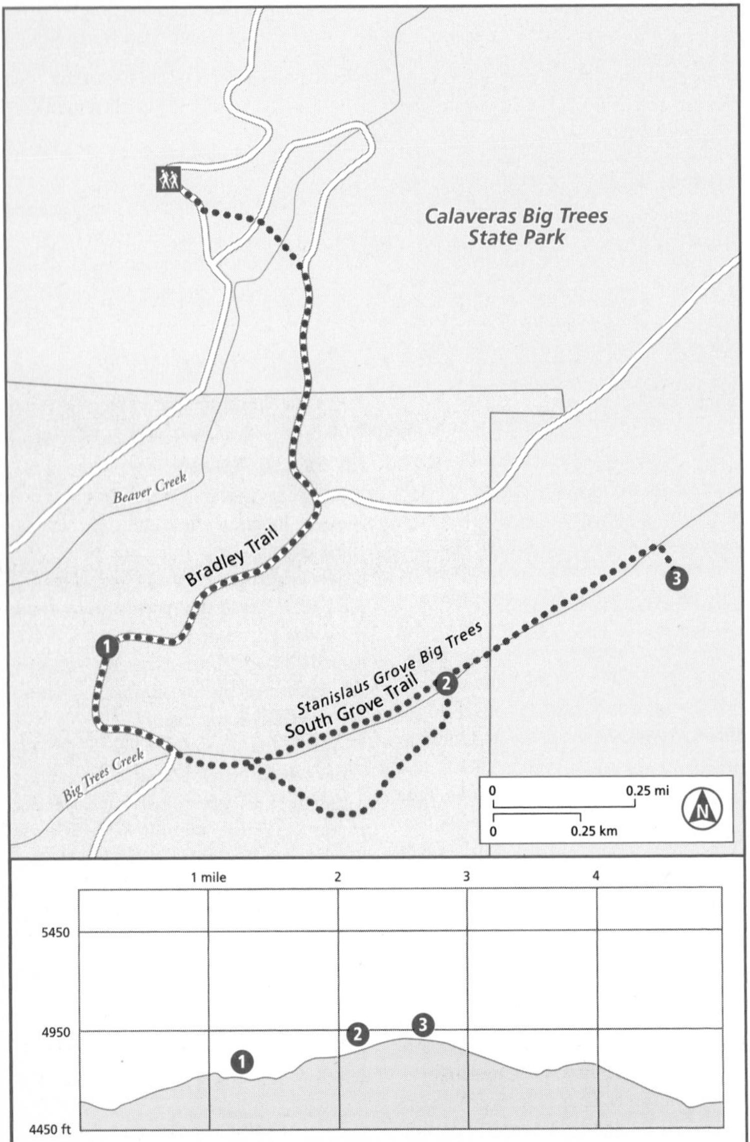

N 38 15.316, W 120 15.662 Trail head

1. N 38 14.631, W 120 15.793 (1.3 miles): Turn right at junction and join loop trail
2. N 38 14.564, W 120 15.126 (2.3 miles): Turn right at junction to visit Agassiz Tree
3. N 38 14.719, W 120 14.688 (2.8 miles): Turn right to rejoin South Grove trail and return to trail head

About the Big Trees

The big trees of Calaveras County became world famous in the 1850s, thanks in part to some circus-style promoters, who chopped down "Discovery Tree" and took it on tour. Another set of profiteers stripped the bark off the "Mother of the Forest" and exhibited the "reassembled" tree in New York and in England's famed Crystal Palace.

Fortunately—for the trees, anyway—most of the truly curious came to visit the Sierra redwoods, rather than expecting the trees to "visit" them. Scientists, celebrities, and thousands of just plain fascinated folks made their way to Calaveras County, often staying in the Mammoth Grove Hotel built close to the big trees.

For a time, scientists believed the giant sequoias in North Grove were the only ones on Earth. With the discovery of other, greater groves in the Yosemite–Sequoia National Park areas, the Calaveras Big Trees, as a tourist attraction, declined somewhat in importance.

The park has some great campgrounds and picnic areas, as well as an opportunity for trout fishing and a dip in the Stanislaus River. Most visitors, however, come to see the big trees, particularly those found in North Grove. A gentle 1-mile trail meanders through the grove, leading to such grand sequoia specimens as Abraham Lincoln, Siamese Twins, Empire State, and Father of the Forest.

MARSHALL GOLD DISCOVERY STATE HISTORIC PARK (Kids)

Difficulty rating: Easy

Distance: 4-mile loop

Estimated time: 2 hr.

Elevation gain: 450 feet

Costs/permits: $5 state park entry fee

Best time to go: May to October

Website: www.parks.ca.gov

Recommended map: Marshall Gold Discovery State Historic Park map

Trail head GPS: N 38 48.244, W 120 53.624

Trail head directions: Marshall Gold Discovery State Historic Park is located on Hwy. 49 in the town of Coloma, some 6½ miles north of Placerville. Drive north through the state park to the North Beach parking area. Cross Hwy. 49 to a meadow and signed Monroe Ridge Trail. You'll soon pass Monroe Orchard on the right.

Monroe Ridge Trail is a fine Gold Country ramble that offers great views, both panoramic and close-up, of what is likely the single most important locale in California history. This hike visits James Marshall Monument, where a bigger-than-life figure holds a bigger-than-life gold nugget and points to the spot where he made the discovery that put California on the world map.

Monroe Ridge Trail's name honors a pioneering African-American family who first settled here during the Gold Rush era. Family matriarch Nancy Gooch was brought to California as a slave but was soon freed when California entered the

Marshall Gold Discovery State Historic Park

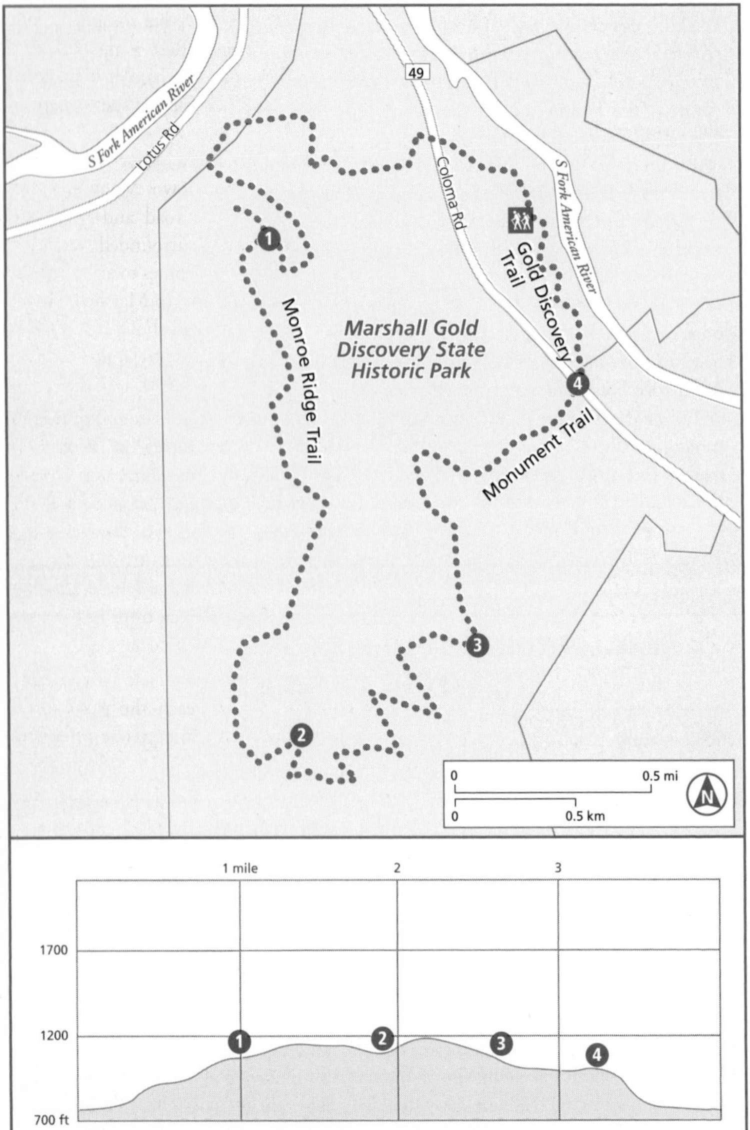

N 38 48.244, W 120 53.624 Trail head
❶ N 38 48.219, W 120 53.976 (1 miles): Walk past brass plaque to vista point
❷ N 38 47.704, W 120 53.908 (1.9 miles): High point of Monroe Ridge
❸ N 38 47.799, W 120 53.671 (2.6 miles): James Marshall monument
❹ N 38 48.063, W 120 53.527 (3.2 miles): Cross Highway 49 to reach Gold Discovery Trail

Union as a free state. She earned her living by doing laundry and domestic chores for miners, and earned enough to purchase the freedom of her son Andrew Monroe and his wife Sara Ellen, who were still enslaved in Missouri.

The Monroes had a successful fruit orchard, prospered, and began buying land. Some of the family holdings included the famed gold discovery site, which the parks department purchased from the Monroe family in the 1940s.

1 North Vista Point The path ascends past a brass plaque recognizing the Monroe family homesite and into oak woodland. The trees and tangles of blackberries frame views of the American River. Switchbacks lead to the crest of the ridge, populated by masses of manzanita and some pines.

A mile out, you'll reach a vista point with a picnic table. Stop here for a break and take in the great views of the river. The path travels south along Monroe Ridge and passes a short side trail to an old mine shaft (stay away!).

2 South Vista Point Switchbacks lead to Monroe Ridge's high point and a second picnic table and viewpoint located 3/4 mile past the first one. Rest a moment and admire the vista—the hamlet of Coloma and the South Fork of the American River.

More switchbacks, these taking you somewhat steeply down Monroe Ridge, lead to an old dirt road and to an old springhouse, now surrounded by ferns. Monroe Ridge Trail comes to an end at the paved road extending to Marshall Monument. Ascend the road about 100 yards to the top of a hill and to James Marshall Monument, built in 1890.

3 Monument Trail From the monument, join wide Monument Trail, bordered by a split rail fence, on a steep descent to the heart of the park and the American River. Nearing a picnic area and Hwy. 49, you'll pass a bedrock mortar, grinding holes left behind by the native Miwok who were driven from their ancestral lands by the Gold Rush.

4 Gold Discovery Trail Carefully cross Hwy. 49 to reach the park's Gold Discovery Trail, an interpretive path. You

Coloma

Coloma, birthplace of the Gold Rush, is a tiny village within the boundaries of Marshall Gold Discovery State Historic Park. Several historic buildings line Hwy. 49, as well as narrow back streets.

Park highlights include an operating replica of Sutter's Mill and the Gold Discovery Museum, with its mining exhibits and videos telling the story of Marshall's discovery.

A walking tour takes in a number of 49er-era buildings, as well as structures dating from later in the 19th century. Step into the Wah Hop Store, a Chinese general store. Visit Marshall Cabin, where Marshall, who benefited little from his great discovery, died bitter and penniless.

Other walks into history include a stroll down Main Street Coloma and a visit to the Pioneer Cemetery and Coloma Winery.

can visit a replica of the Sutter Sawmill just to the south. Follow the riverside pathway to the actual site of Sutter's Mill on the American River, stop at the actual Gold Discovery site.

It was here in 1848 James Marshall discovered gold; a year later, the world discovered California. Marshall, a carpenter, was constructing a sawmill in partnership with John Sutter when he spotted some golden flecks in the American River. He went to Sutter's Fort to share his news with his employer. The two tried to keep the gold news secret but word leaked out and the world rushed in.

The population of the hamlet of Coloma swelled to 10,000 in 1849. Two years later, the gold gave out, and most of the miners left.

After your gold discovery site-seeing tour, return to the North Beach parking area and the trail head.

EMPIRE MINE STATE HISTORIC PARK ★

Difficulty rating: Easy

Distance: 2.4 miles round-trip

Estimated time: 1½ hr.

Elevation gain: 100 feet

Costs/permits: $5 state park day-use fee

Best time to go: May to October

Website: www.parks.ca.gov; www.empiremine.org

Recommended map: California State Parks Empire Mine State Historic Park map

Trail head GPS: N 39 12.399, W 121 02.791

Trail head directions: Empire Mine State Historic Park is located in Grass Valley, 2 miles east of Hwy. 49 on East Empire St. The trail head is close to the Visitor Center.

Ramble through some pretty Gold Country and visit a tremendously successful and highly industrialized gold mining operation. Hardrock Trail visits mines, machinery, a stamp mill, and much more. Learn all the details of the complexities of hard-rock mining or just enjoy a short hike through history amidst ponderosa pine, sugar pine, and big-leaf maple.

Step past an impressive mining equipment exhibit at the beginning of this trail, filled with massive rusting mine machinery. One highlight is the huge headframe that supported the track which carried men, equipment, and rock to and from the mine. The Stamp Mill building must have been something: 80 1,750-pound stamps working 24/7, smashing tons of ore into fine sand. Just imagine the noise!

Empire Mine, one of California's richest, produced more than 6 million ounces of gold during its 100 years of operation. The gold mine, along with 784 acres of Gold Country, is preserved in Empire Mine State Historic Park.

Shortly after the great gold rush of 1849, logger George Roberts discovered an outcropping of gold-bearing quartz about where today's visitors park their cars. Miners swarmed these hills to lay claim to the riches below. Trouble was, the gold was way below the surface, which pretty well thwarted most of the low-tech, low-budget prospectors. The miners dug 20- to 40-foot "coyote holes," tunneled and blasted, only to see their efforts fall victim to cave-ins or floods.

Around 1851, George Roberts and his fellow gold-seekers sold their claims to a consortium that consolidated them and dubbed the operation the Empire Mine. San Francisco businessman William Bourn and his son William, Jr., took over in 1870 and, after investing more money and digging deeper than many thought possible, eventually turned a profit in the 1880s and beyond.

Empire Mine

Much of the Empire's success can be attributed to the experienced hard-rock miners from Cornwall, England, who came here. By some accounts, the 1890 population of Grass Valley was 85% Cornish. Cornish miners brought with them what we now call the Cornish pasty, a meat & potato pie, available today in nearby Grass Valley restaurants.

Park visitors can get a look at the main mine shaft from an observation platform. At the visitor center are interpretive exhibits and gold samples displayed in an open vault.

The advantages of owning a gold mine are evident when one takes a look at the Empire Cottage, an English manor-style home designed by famed San Francisco architect Willis Polk for William Bourn, Jr., in 1898. Quite a "cottage!"

Join one of the park's scheduled tours of the Empire Cottage and/or Empire Mine. Or take a walking tour on your own past structures, building foundations, and mining machinery.

After your walk through history, hit the trail. The park has 10 miles of pathways—above ground, that is. Below you, the earth is honeycombed with some 367 miles of tunnels, some nearly a mile deep.

Hardrock Trail heads south and soon junctions Union Hill Trail.

❶ Junction with Union Hill Trail Union Hill Trail leads to the fringe of the fast-growing community of Grass Valley. The Union Hill section of the park is wooded (sugar pine, ponderosa pine, incense cedar, and Douglas fir), along with some oaks and big-leaf maple. A few fruit trees—apple, pear, and cherry—are reminders of early settlers in the area.

Branching off Union Hill Trail are two others that explore Union Hill. Along Pipeline Trail are remains of a water pipe that carried water from a reservoir to the north and generated power to operate mining machinery. Indian Ridge Trail is a historic pathway used by the Nisenan tribe of Maidu.

Continue on Hardrock Trail to a crossing of seasonal Little Wolf Creek and a junction with Osborn Hill Loop Trail.

❷ Junction with Osborn Hill Loop Trail Mile-long Osborn Hill Loop Trail ascends to a couple more mine sites and offers a great view of the Sacramento Valley.

Hardrock Trail curves west, traveling amidst a black oak woodland and paralleling Little Wolf Creek. The path turns north and traverses Sand Dam, a dirt berm, to a junction with WYOD (Work Your Own Diggings) Trail.

❸ Junction with WYOD Trail The 1/2-mile Work Your Own Diggings loop leads past some rather unsuccessful independent mining operations to the crest of the park's tallest tailings pile.

Hardrock Trail continues north through pine forest, passes the second and northern leg of WYOD Trail, and reaches the site of the Pennsylvania Mine and a parking area off Empire Street.

❹ Pennsylvania Mine The Pennsylvania was one of many mines taken over by the mining-empire building owners of the Empire Mine. Hardrock Trail (or Empire Street Trail, if you prefer) heads east, paralleling East Empire Street, back to the visitor center and heart of the park.

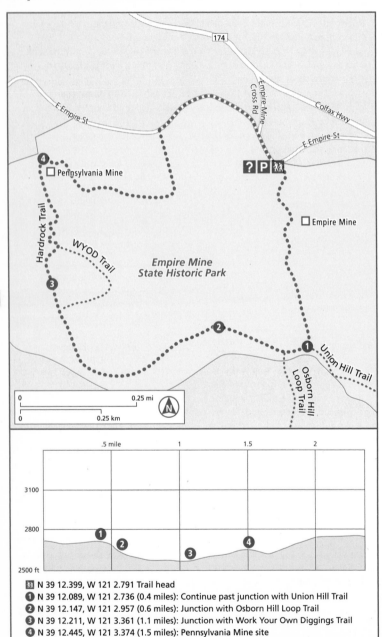

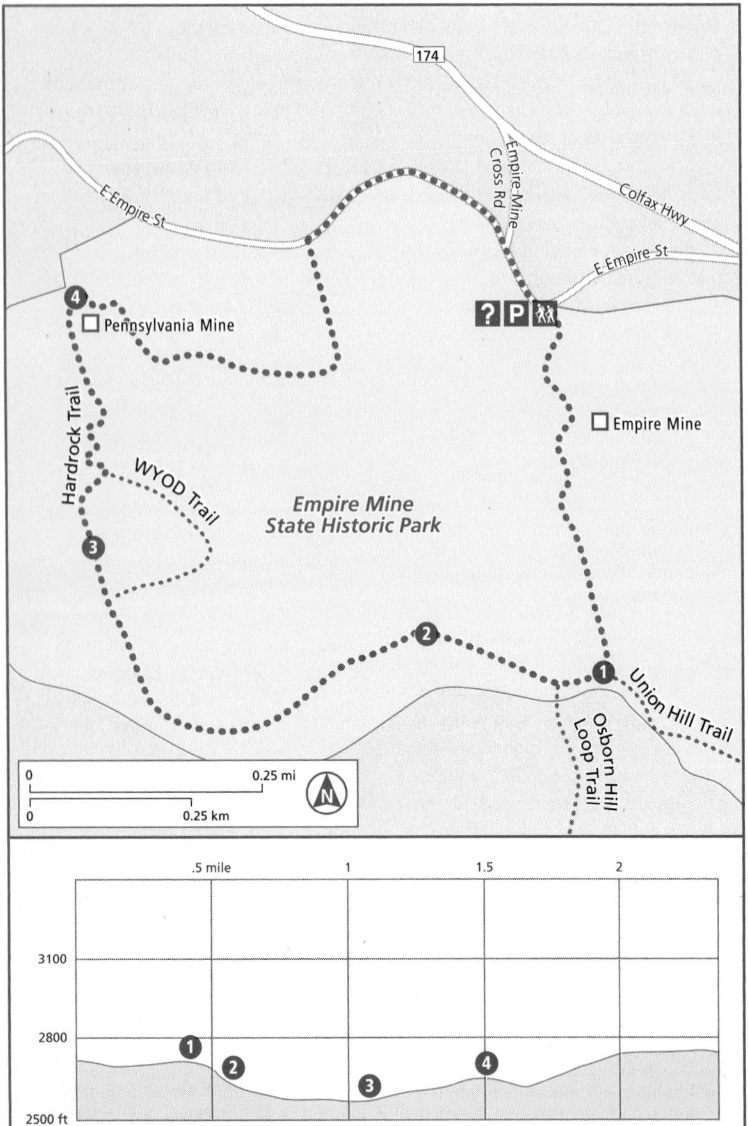

N 39 12.399, W 121 2.791 Trail head

1. N 39 12.089, W 121 2.736 (0.4 miles): Continue past junction with Union Hill Trail
2. N 39 12.147, W 121 2.957 (0.6 miles): Junction with Osborn Hill Loop Trail
3. N 39 12.211, W 121 3.361 (1.1 miles): Junction with Work Your Own Diggings Trail
4. N 39 12.445, W 121 3.374 (1.5 miles): Pennsylvania Mine site

ACCOMMODATIONS

Wine Country

Best Western Sonoma Valley Inn It's a family affair at this lovely spot, just steps away from the historic Sonoma plaza. Rooms include HBO, a complimentary bottle of local wine, and continental breakfast; most feature a private deck or balcony. Enjoy laps in the saltwater pool or arrange a post-hike massage.

550 2nd St. W., 1 block from the plaza, Sonoma, CA 95476. ✆ **800/334-5784** or 707/938-9200. www.sonomavalleyinn.com. 80 units. $114–$361 double. Rates include continental breakfast. AE, DC, DISC, MC, V. **Close to:** Jack London State Historic Park.

★ **Calistoga Spa Hot Springs** The entire family will be welcome here at this simple, comfortable, and centrally located spot, with shopping and dining just a short walk away. Little kids can frolic in the wading pool, while the rest of the family can enjoy the (heated) pools, spa, and exercise facilities, as well as the convenient barbecues.

1006 Washington St., at Gerrard St., Calistoga, CA 94515. ✆ **866/822-5772** or 707/942-6269. www.calistogaspa.com. 57 units. Nov–Feb $115–$175 double; Mar–Oct $136–$196 double. MC, V. **Close to:** Bothe-Napa Valley State Park.

★★★ **Fairmont Sonoma Mission Inn & Spa** Truly a glittering diamond in the rough. First-class luxury with historical appeal, modern amenities (including naturally heated artesian mineral water pools), full concierge services, restaurants, and complimentary afternoon wine-tasting. The world-class spa attracts the rich and famous from around the world, who soak away their cares in this elegant retreat away from it all.

101 Boyes Blvd., at the corner of Boyes Blvd. and CA 12, Sonoma, CA 95476. ✆ **800/441-1414** or 707/938-9000. www.fairmont.com/sonoma. 226 units. $259–$1,259 double. AE, DC, MC, V. From central Sonoma, drive 3 miles north on Hwy. 12 and turn left on Boyes Blvd. **Close to:** Jack London State Historic Park.

Gold Country

★★ **Deer Creek Inn Bed & Breakfast** Comfortable elegance reigns in this 1860s three-story Victorian inn located close to town. Nicely appointed, private rooms are warmly furnished with antiques, but not too fussy. You can get tasty gourmet breakfasts in the morning and local wine tasting in the afternoon. A great place to relax and enjoy the moment.

116 Nevada St., Nevada City, CA 95959. ✆ **800/655-0363** or 530/265-0363. www.deercreekinn.com. 6 units. $160–$225 double. Rates include breakfast. MC, V. **Close to:** Marshall Gold Discovery State Historic Park.

Holbrooke Hotel Mark Twain slept here; so did several presidents. This distinctive hotel, the oldest one in town, is a cherished landmark. History buffs will appreciate the elegant remnants of the Gold-Rush days that furnish the rooms. Rooms are in the main building—a one-time saloon—or the next-door annex.

212 W. Main St., Grass Valley, CA 95945. ✆ **800/933-7077** or 530/273-1353. www.holbrooke.com. 28 units. $115–$225 double. Rates include continental breakfast. AE, DC, DISC, MC, V. **Close to:** Empire Mine State Park.

Nevada City Inn The location is near the historic district, and the accommodations recall a simpler time and place. A 1940s motor court, refurbished and well maintained, is a step into yesterday, the perfect retreat for the hiking traveler. Standard motel rooms and larger cottages—fully furnished with kitchens—are available.

760 Zion St., Nevada City, CA 95959. ✆ **800/977-8884** or 530/265-2253. www.nevadacityinn.net. 20 units, 7 cottages. $69–$109 double; $115–$189 cottage. Rates include continental breakfast. AE, DC, DISC, MC, V. **Close to:** Marshall Gold Discovery State Historic Park.

RESTAURANTS

Wine Country

★ **Black Bear Diner** DINER Everything a diner should be: low-priced, big portions of tasty and traditional favorites, service with a smile, a good-old-fashioned jukebox, discounts for seniors, and kids are welcome. You won't leave here hungry, whether you're here for breakfast, lunch, or dinner. This is the place for comfort food, all-American nostalgia, and lots of fun for all.

201 W. Napa St., Sonoma, CA 95476. ✆ **707/935-6800.** www.blackbeardiner.com. Main courses breakfast $5–$8.50, lunch and dinner $5.50–$17. AE, DISC, MC, V. Daily 6am–9:30pm (closing varies on weekends). **Close to:** Jack London State Historic Park.

★★★ **Oakville Grocery Co.** PICNIC California's Wine Country is known for its appeal to foodies; they all end up here. This is *the* place to select supplies for a special breakfast or a picnic on the trail. The dazzling and tempting array includes home-baked pastries and fresh breads, a range of meats, fish, and prepared foods. It also has an espresso bar.

7856 St. Helena Hwy., at Oakville Cross Rd., Oakville, CA 94562. ✆ **707/944-8802.** Mon–Fri 7am–6pm; Sat–Sun 8am–6pm. AE, DC, DISC, MC, V. **Close to:** Skyline Wilderness Park.

★★ **Wolf House** ECLECTIC Elegance in dining with a clubby atmosphere, memorable meals, and a location par excellence, right on the shaded shores of Sonoma Creek. Local gourmet touches to traditional lunch favorites (the burger with blue cheese from Point Reyes is great!); dinnertime specialties topped off with your choice of fine local wines.

13740 Arnold Dr., at London Ranch Rd., Glen Ellen, CA 95442. ✆ **707/996-4401.** www.jacklondonlodge.com/rest.html. Main courses brunch and lunch $8–$15, dinner $17–$32. AE, MC, V. Brunch Sat 11am–3pm and Sun 10am–3pm; lunch Tues–Fri 11am–3pm; dinner Tues–Sun 5:30–9:30pm. **Close to:** Jack London State Historic Park.

Gold Country

★ **Firewood** AMERICAN Hike a mile or two extra to justify the feast you'll enjoy at this notable cafe with unexpectedly delicious foods. You'll have a tough time choosing from among the specialties, including fish tacos, ribs, and gourmet pizzas at a great price. Try local wines and microbrews for a real treat.

420 Main St., Murphys, CA 95247. ✆ **209/728-3248.** Main courses $5–$10. MC, V. Wed–Sun 11am–9pm. **Close to:** Calaveras Big Trees State Park.

Mel and Faye's Diner AMERICAN This family-run classic diner hasn't changed much since 1955. Forget about fast food blandness marketed to the masses when you enter this authentic food palace. Go for the yummy burger, complete with special sauce and onions, chocolate shake, and fries; stay for the pie—and hike many miles tomorrow to justify it all.

205 Hwy. 49, at Main St., Jackson, CA 95642. ✆ **209/223-0853.** Menu items $4–$8. MC, V. Daily 4am–10pm. **Close to:** Empire Mine State Park.

★★ **Tofanelli's** INTERNATIONAL Well-known arounc
food—lots of it—at a good price. This mainstay among the loc
dining experience with its pleasant variety of dining spaces—incl
a dining room, and a lovely atrium. Choose from traditional pas
or an ever-changing variety of inspired specialties.

302 W. Main St., across from the Holbrooke Hotel, Grass Valley, CA 95945.
tofanellisgoldcountrybistro.com. Main courses $15–$21. AE, DISC, MC, V. Lu ... 30am–2:30pm, Sat–Sun 11am–2:30pm; dinner Mon–Thurs 5–8:30pm, Fri–Sat 5–9pm, ... 4–8pm. **Close to:** Empire Mine State Park.

Yosemite National Park

Known the world over for its great granite cliffs and domes, enormous waterfalls, and giant sequoias, Yosemite is everything a national park should be and more. Such well-known Yosemite Valley destinations as Vernal Fall, Nevada Fall, Yosemite Falls, and Half Dome are magnets for hikers. Equally attractive are many more sights outside the valley: Tuolomne Meadows, Cathedral Peak, Clouds Rest, the Mariposa Grove of Big Trees, and many more.

The park boasts a magnificent High Sierra backcountry, one that (by rather severe Sierra standards, anyway) is quite accessible. Well-marked trails lead to wildflower-festooned alpine meadows, lovely lakes, tarns, cross-country trails, and peaks.

John Muir is inextricably linked with Yosemite. The great naturalist's pioneering work in glacier theory and passionate efforts to make Yosemite a park have long been admired.

Beginning in the 1950s, Yosemite (most particularly Yosemite Valley) suffered from overcrowding: the cafes and cafeterias, the campgrounds, the creaky little Curry cabins, the ranger talks, and campfire circles. Park visitation increased from about a million visitors a year in the 1950s, to two million a year in the 1960s, to four million a year in the 1990s. Then, and now, such heavy visitation sometimes results in summer traffic jams in Yosemite Valley, and crowding at overlooks, concessions, Yosemite Village, and on the shuttle bus system. The good news is that efforts to reduce auto traffic in the valley by extensive use of buses have been at least partially successful. When the Park Service implements other programs to ease traffic and reduce commercial facilities, the pay-off will be an even richer park experience for hikers and visitors of all kinds.

Unlike the motorist, diner, or souvenir shopper, the hiker feels fewer effects of Yosemite's crowds. With the exception of the heavily trafficked "waterfall trails" and a couple other valley footpaths, the hiker is far less likely to feel the impact of such crowding and may even be surprised at achieving a measure of solitude.

Some Yosemite Valley trails are accessible all year. While the park has glaciated peaks that rise to more than 13,000 feet in elevation, Yosemite Valley is less than a mile high, and some park areas are even below 3,000 feet. In spring, Yosemite's waterfalls are at their most majestic. In summer, alpine slopes burst into bloom. Autumn is a favorite time for a walk. The "Range of Light" is particularly dramatic, and the aspens glow like fire in the wind.

My selection of hikes was a difficult task, indeed, because I had to choose among two or three dozen favorites—each a wonderful hike in its own right. Those hikes detailed here represent a range of difficulty levels and a variety of locations—from Yosemite Valley to Glacier Point to Tuolumne Meadows.

Yosemite's trails are, for the most part, well-engineered, well-maintained, and well-signed. Opportunities for summer solitude may be few on the major trails, but the farther away from a road one hikes, the greater the opportunity for tranquility. The journey on these pathways is often as pleasurable as the famed destinations they reach.

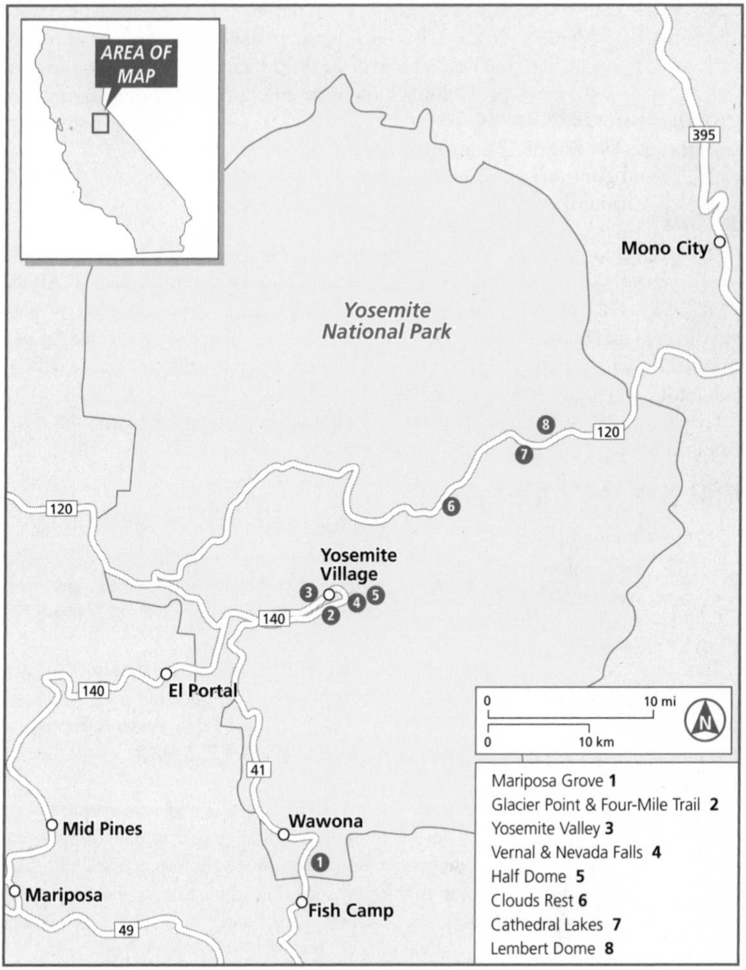

ESSENTIALS

GETTING THERE

By Air

Fresno–Yosemite International Airport (© **559/621-4500**), located 90 miles from the south entrance at Wawona, is the nearest major airport, serving over 25 cities with more than 100 flights daily. Airlines include Alaska, Allegiant Air, American/American Eagle, Continental, Delta, Express-Jet, Frontier, Hawaiian, Horizon, Mexicana, Northwest, United, and US Airways.

By Car

Yosemite is a 3½-hour drive from San Francisco and a 6-hour drive from Los Angeles. Many roads lead to Yosemite's four entrances. From the west, the Big Oak Flat Entrance is 88 miles from Manteca via CA 120, which passes through the towns of Groveland, Buck Meadows, and Big Oak Flat. The Arch Rock Entrance is 75 miles northeast of Merced via CA 140, which passes through Mariposa and El Portal. The South Entrance is 64 miles north of Fresno and passes through Oakhurst, Bass Lake, and Fish Camp. From the east, the Tioga Pass Entrance is the only option. It is 10 miles west of Lee Vining via CA 120, usually open only in the summer.

By Bus

Daily bus transportation into the park from Merced, Mariposa, and other communities is provided by the **Yosemite Area Regional Transportation System (YARTS; ✆ 877/989-2787** or 209/388-9589; www.yarts.com). Buses are not subject to park entry fees. From Merced, several YARTS buses depart daily from the airport, the Amtrak train station, and the Greyhound bus terminal. Round-trip fare is $25 for adults; $18 for children 12 and under, and seniors 62 and older.

Greyhound (**✆ 800/231-2222;** www.greyhound.com) also links Merced with other California cities.

VISITOR INFORMATION

If you're planning a visit to Yosemite National Park, you can get general information on accommodations, weather, and permits from the park's touchtone phone menu at **✆ 209/372-0200** or online at www.nps.gov/yose. The hearing-impaired can get information by calling **✆ 209/372-4726.** For camping reservations, call **✆ 877/444-6777** or visit www.recreation.gov.

You can buy books and maps from the nonprofit **Yosemite Association,** P.O. Box 230, El Portal, CA 95318 (**✆ 209/379-2646;** www.yosemite.org). For information on much of the lodging within Yosemite National Park, contact **DNC Parks & Resorts at Yosemite,** 6771 N Palm Ave., Fresno CA, 93704 (**✆ 559/252-4848;** www.yosemitepark.com).

In the park, the biggest visitor center is the **Valley Visitor Center** in Yosemite Village (**✆ 209/372-0200**), which provides all sorts of information, offers daily ranger programs, and is conveniently located near restaurants and shopping. You can talk with park rangers about your plans for exploring the park, and check bulletins for information on current road conditions and campsite availability; the boards also serve as a message board for visitors. There are several exhibits on the park, its geologic history, and the history of the valley. This center provides information on bears and also has information on the impact that humans have on the park.

A shop sells maps, books, videos, postcards, posters, and the like. Nearby is the **Yosemite Valley Wilderness Center,** with high-country maps, information on necessary hiking and camping equipment, trail information, and a ranger on hand to answer questions, issue permits, and offer advice about the high country.

Information on lodging and activities outside the park is available from the visitor centers and chambers of commerce in the park's surrounding cities. If you're coming from the west on CA 120, contact the **Tuolumne County Visitor Center** in Sonora (**✆ 800/446-1333** or 209/533-4420; www.thegreatunfenced.com) or the **Yosemite Chamber of Commerce** in Groveland (**✆ 800/449-9120** or 209/962-0429; www.groveland.org). On CA 140, contact the **Mariposa County Visitors Bureau** (**✆ 866/**

Southern Yosemite Mountain Guides

Of the dozens of outdoor recreation companies that offer guided hiking and backpacking trips throughout the Yosemite region, the best is **Southern Yosemite Mountain Guides.** For nearly 2 decades, the professional guides from SYMG have been leading visitors to the most spectacular wilderness regions throughout Yosemite National Park and the High Sierra. SYMG founder and president Ian Elman and his staff are among the top outdoor guides in the nation and are masters at providing a fun, thrilling, and safe experience for all their clients, whether it's a casual naturalist-led day hike through the Giant Sequoias or a 7-day backpacking odyssey through Southern Yosemite's Ansel Adams Wilderness (one of the best kept secrets of the region). SYMG also offers guided fly fishing and mountaineering trips, as well as half-day and 1-day clinics on fly fishing and rock climbing. Check out the wide variety of trips they offer on their website at **www.symg.com**, and then give Ian a call at ✆ **800/231-4575**.

425-3366 or 209/966-7081; www.homeofyosemite.com). On CA 41, south of the park, call the **Yosemite Sierra Visitors Bureau** in Oakhurst (✆ **559/683-4636;** www.yosemitethisyear.com). From Lee Vining on the park's eastern boundary, contact the **Lee Vining Chamber of Commerce** (✆ **760/647-6629;** www.leevining.com). There's a **California Welcome Center** at 710 W. 16th St. in Merced (✆ **800/446-5353** or 209/384-7092; www.yosemite-gateway.org).

GETTING AROUND

There are four entrances to Yosemite: the Big Oak Flat Entrance and the Arch Rock Entrance from the west; the South Entrance; and the Tioga Pass Entrance from the east. Make sure to get a copy of the bi-weekly *Yosemite Today* when you visit for up-to-date information on ranger programs and other park events and activities.

ORIENTATION

All four main entrances to the park meet in Yosemite Valley, the most popular of the park's three destination points (the other two being Tuolumne Meadows and Wawona). It's relatively easy to find your way around Yosemite. All road signs are clear and visible. At first, Yosemite Valley might seem to be a confusing series of roadways, but you'll soon realize that all roads lead to a one-way loop that hugs the valley's perimeter, It is easy to find yourself heading in the wrong direction, so be alert whenever you merge and just follow the signs.

I highly recommend visitors use the year-around shuttle bus service in Yosemite Valley. Wawona and Tuolumne Meadows offer a similar service during the summer months only. Driving in any of these places during peak season—or even off-season in the valley—is not enjoyable, so use the shuttles as much as possible.

MARIPOSA GROVE ★

Difficulty rating: Easy to moderate

Distance: 1.6 miles round trip to Grizzly Giant; 6.2 miles including loop trail

Estimated time: 1–2½ hr.

Elevation gain: 100 ft. to Grizzly Giant; 1,000 ft. on loop trail

Costs/permits: $20 entry fee

Best time to go: May to October

Website: www.nps.gov/yose

Recommended map: Yosemite National Park map

Trail head GPS: N 37 30.088, W 119 36.639

Trail head directions: From Hwy. 41 at Yosemite's South Entrance Station, drive east 2 miles to Mariposa Grove. The huge parking lot can fill up by 10am on a busy summer morning. When the lot is full, NPS stops vehicle entries and provides free shuttle service from Hwy. 41.

Mariposa is by far the largest of Yosemite's three groves of giant sequoias and the one that inspired the creation of the national park. See the Grizzly Giant, the Three Graces, the California Tunnel Tree, and many more outstanding big trees.

At the trail head, accept that you will have lots of company on your walk among the world's largest living things. The enormous trees—combined with easy access, close proximity to the park's south entrance, a gift/snack shop, and a narrated open-air tram tour, no less—really draw a crowd.

❶ Mariposa Grove The magnificent sequoias of Mariposa Grove, along with the wondrous Yosemite Valley, prompted President Abraham Lincoln to set aside Yosemite as a reserve and grant it (temporarily) to the state of California for its protection.

Thus, it's not exaggeration to say that this grove of giant sequoias inspired the first steps toward the establishment of our entire system of national parks.

The Spanish named this region Mariposa for the many fluttering butterflies in these hills; the grove was named for the county of Mariposa. During the 19th century and well into the 20th, Mariposa Grove rivaled Calaveras Grove and the groves of big trees in Sequoia National Park in popularity.

At the start of the trail, pick up a copy of the park service's *Mariposa Grove of Giant Sequoias* pamphlet (available in several different languages) from the dispenser and begin walking the gentle path.

You'll soon arrive at the Fallen Monarch, which came to the nation's attention in 1899 via a widely circulated photo of U.S. Calvary officers (with their horses!) posed atop the horizontal tree. Fallen Monarch offers a close-up view of the wide but shallow root structure of a great sequoia. The roots usually sink no deeper in the ground than 6 feet, though they can spread out more than 150 feet.

Cross the road, ascend some steps, and cross the road again. You'll spot a number of sequoias with blackened bark. In years past, the park service resolutely suppressed all wildfires. However, with the realization in the 1970s that sequoia reproduction depends on fire, the occasional lightning-caused blaze has been allowed to burn, and controlled burns have been proscribed in order to simulate natural conditions.

❷ Three Graces The path leads to Three Graces, with roots so intertwined that it's believed should one tree fall, the other two would topple, as well. Apart from the three is a more solitary sequoia dubbed The Bachelor.

❸ Grizzly Giant Old Grizzly, grove patriarch, blackened and scarred, is estimated to have sprouted some 2,700 years ago; it's lived through most of the march of Western Civilization and believed to be the oldest sequoia in Mariposa Grove.

> At a signed junction, take the fork toward Grizzly Giant and ascend the path to meet the 200-foot-tall behemoth that measures 30 feet in diameter. One of its limbs is larger than the trunks of most other species of trees.

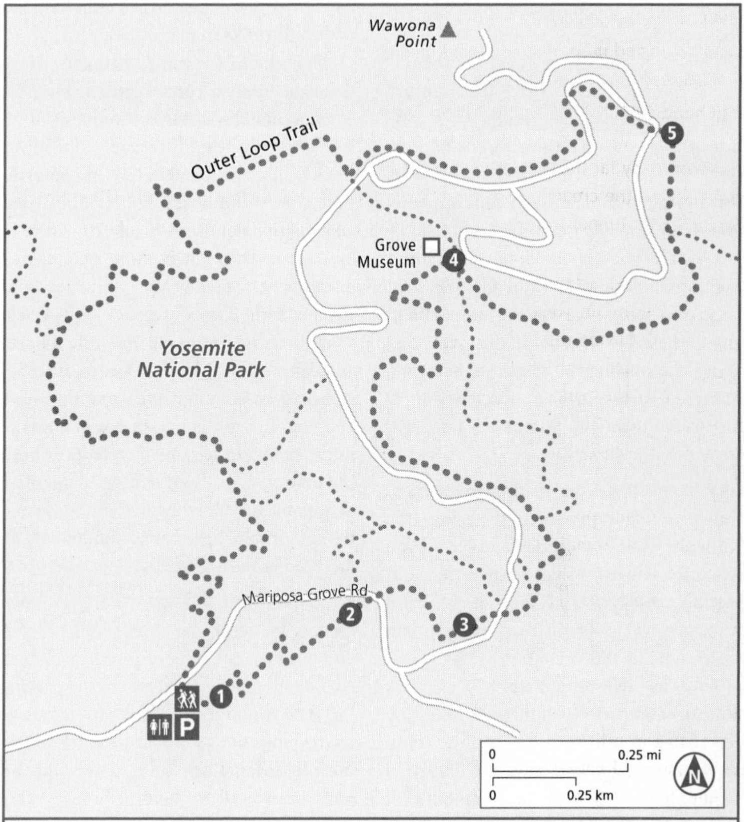

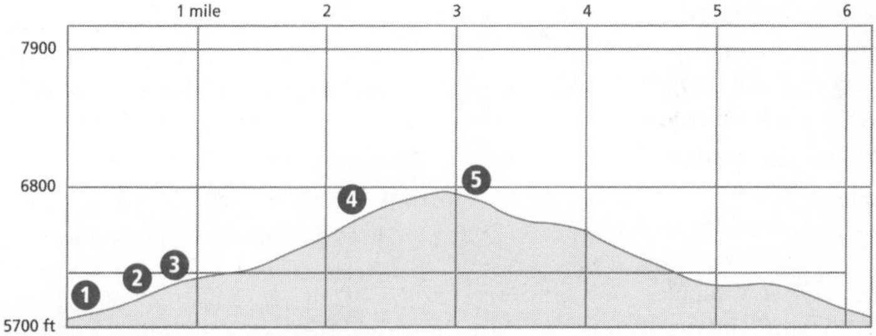

N 37 30.088, W 119 36.639 Trail head

❶ N 37 30.064, W 119 36.577 (0.1 miles): Fallen Monarch tree

❷ N 37 30.228, W 119 36.294 (0.6 miles): The Three Graces trees

❸ N 37 30.193, W 119 36.064 (0.8 miles): Old Grizzly tree

❹ N 37 30.766, W 119 36.088 (2.2 miles): Follow Museum Trail to Grove Museum

❺ N 37 30.951, W 119 35.680 (3.1 miles): Junction with Outer Loop Trail

For most visitors, the famed tree is the unofficial "tourist turnaround;" from here to the Upper Grove, you'll proceed with less company.

Not far from Grizzly Giant is the California Tunnel Tree. No late-19th-century visit was complete without a stage ride through a tree with a tunnel in its midsection. The sequoia still stands, though its drive-through days are over. You can, however, walk through the tunnel.

Onward you go on Upper (or Outer) Loop Trail to the Faithful Couple, two large trees fused together for 50 feet or so along their lower trunks, but separated above. Generations of wildfire have nearly bisected Clothespin Tree, which definitely has drive-through potential, but was spared that indignity.

4 Museum After visiting this curiosity, meet the tram road, then join the Museum Trail, which descends to Grove Museum, where you can learn more about sequoia ecology and history. The museum is located on the site of Yosemite guardian Galen Clark's 1864 cabin.

Curious Telescope Tree has a trunk almost completely hollowed out by repeated fires. One can look up the trunk to see the stars and sky. Obviously, a sequoia needs only a small amount of trunk to survive, though the survivability of such trunk-compromised trees such as the Telescope Tree and Clothespin Tree in a windstorm will be lots less than sequoias with full trunks in place.

Thousands of wagons, then cars, drove through Wawona Tunnel Tree, from 1881, when a tunnel was bored through it, until 1967, when it fell. Historians point to the tree's falling as a marker event in conservation history and note a societal shift from viewing the sequoias as freaks of nature to looking at them in a more enlightened ecosystem-oriented way.

The path curves west to visit Galen Clark Tree, honoring the Yosemite pioneer and discoverer of Mariposa Grove. In 1857, doctors gave Clark but a few months to live and sent him to the mountains in hopes of miracle cure. In testament to nature's healing powers, Clark lived to serve as guardian of Yosemite's giant sequoias for 50 years and to author his first book, *Indians of the Yosemite,* at the age of 90.

5 Outer Loop Trail You have two choices for returning to the trail head. If you want to stay in the sequoias, backtrack to the museum and descend to the parking lot. The Outer Loop Trail travels out of the sequoias into a lovely mixed forest of incense cedar, sugar pine, and white fir, and circles back to the trail head parking lot.

GLACIER POINT & FOUR-MILE TRAIL ★★

Difficulty rating: Moderate

Distance: 9.2 miles round trip to Glacier Point

Estimated time: 5–6 hr.

Elevation gain: 3,200 ft.

Costs/permits: $20 national park entry fee

Best time to go: May to October

Website: www.nps.gov/yose

Recommended map: Yosemite National Park map; Tom Harrison map of Yosemite Valley

Trail head GPS: N 37 44.038, W 119 36.110

Trail head directions: The signed trail head and pullouts for parking are located along Southside Dr. in Yosemite Valley, 1¼ miles west of Yosemite Village. To reach Glacier Point, head out of the valley about 9 miles south on Hwy. 41, then follow Glacier Point Rd. 16 miles east to the parking lot and trail head.

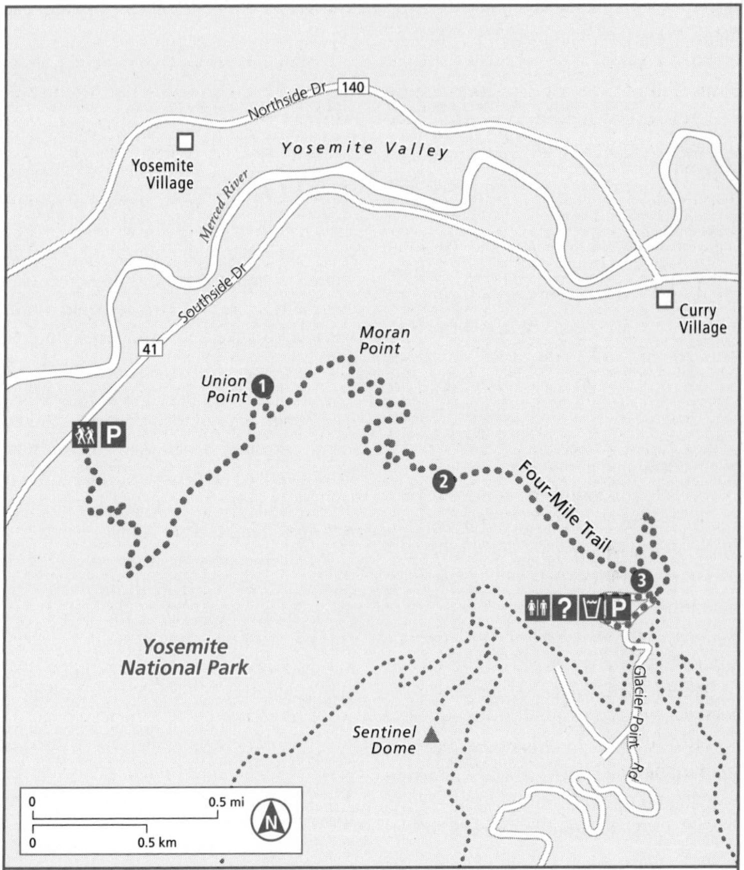

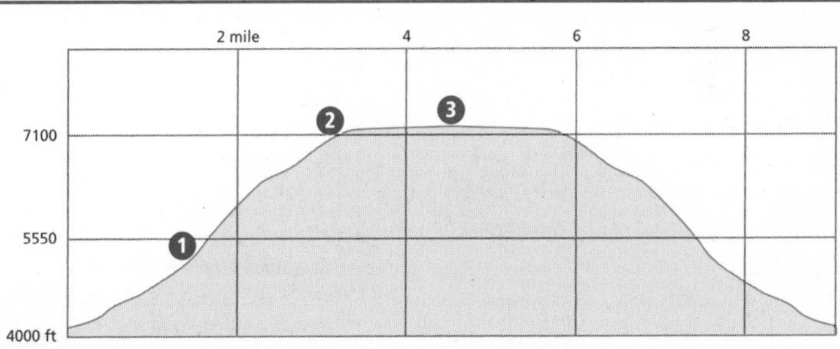

N 37 44.038, W 119 36.110 Trail head

1. N 37 44.140, W 119 35.549 (1.4 miles): Grade increases as you enter oak woodland
2. N 37 43.934, W 119 35.026 (3.3 miles): Pass through Trail Gate
3. N 37 43.687, W 119 34.403 (4.4 miles): Glacier Point

Four-Mile Trail is a Yosemite classic, the original route to Glacier Point. As you climb, you'll get panoramic views (quite a different perspective from the usual postcard ones), beginning with the meandering Merced River, then Upper Yosemite Falls, El Capitan, Half Dome, Vernal Fall, and much, much more.

As if to disguise its charms, the first 25% of Four-Mile Trail is simply a mellow meander across the valley floor followed by a moderate ascent among oak and manzanita.

Hotelier James McCauley hired John Conway to construct a trail from Yosemite Valley to Glacier Point. Hikers paid a $1 toll to trek the trail. When first constructed in 1872, the path extended 4 miles, but after an overhaul in the 1920s and the addition of some switchbacks, it now measures 4.6 miles. No matter, the original trail name is still with us.

For us impatient hikers, it seems to take a long time to leave traffic noises behind. More patient sojourners will admire the mossy rocks and splashes of wildflowers in the spring.

In my very early (Boy Scout) days of hiking Yosemite, Four-Mile Trail seemed far longer than its name suggested. We scouts were more than a little surprised—to put it mildly—to struggle up the trail and find hordes of tourists who had driven to the point.

You mean we could've driven up to Glacier Point?

Walking up to it means you'll appreciate the view more, our scoutmaster assured us. Took me a long time—decades, in fact—before I really appreciated our scoutmaster's wisdom. Indeed, the Yosemite Valley panorama does seem more satisfying after a hike with a 3,200-foot elevation gain. Hold on to that thought.

❶ The Real Climb Begins About $1\frac{1}{2}$ miles out, the real climb begins—first through more oak woodland, then among incense cedar and white fir. It's about $2\frac{1}{3}$ miles of very steep ascent, rewarded by ever-more expansive vistas of Yosemite Valley and ever-more lofty views of Yosemite Falls, until you reach a point where you're actually looking down at the famed falls.

❷ Trail Gate Trail Gate, a bit more than 3 miles from the trail head, is just that: a gate across the trail that's closed in winter to stop hikers from hiking to Glacier Point. Even sans gate, it would not be sensible to hike snow-slippery slopes in winter.

The trail passes under Sentinel Rock, a 8,122-foot promontory that some hikers claim provides better views than those from Glacier Point. Certainly, it's a whole lot less crowded on Sentinel Rock's summit than along Glacier Point's guardrail.

From Four-Mile Trail, Yosemite Falls is revealed to the hiker in all its glory. Elsewhere in Yosemite Valley, the view of the falls is just a bit impeded by trees or rocks, but from the path, you'll enjoy full frontal exposure to the cascade. Yosemite Falls is at its most awesome in spring, when Sierra snowmelt stokes the mighty cascade.

❸ Glacier Point Finally, you finish all those switchbacks, and the last mile is a cooler, calmer climb and contour amidst sugar pine and white fir to Glacier Point.

> Glacier Point offers restrooms, a snack bar, the old Geology Hut, a new amphitheater, and a $\frac{1}{4}$-mile paved pathway. And, of course, the same stunning view that has wowed generations of Yosemite visitors still remains.

Get an early start; portions of the path travel through clusters of manzanita and chinquapin and can be quite hot on a summer afternoon.

The Glacier Point Road, which provides the only access by car to the point and upper trail head for the Four-Mile Trail, usually opens around late May or early June, and closes in late October or early November, depending on conditions.

A tour bus bound for Glacier Point departs three times daily (8:30am, 10am, and 1:30pm) from Yosemite Lodge at the Falls. This tour operates from late spring to early fall, conditions permitting. Hikers wishing to catch a ride up and hike down to Yosemite Valley can purchase one-way tickets to Glacier Point. An adult round-trip ticket costs $33, a one-way ride $20; seniors cost $26/$18, and children cost $26/$12.

YOSEMITE VALLEY ★

Difficulty rating: Moderate

Distance: 5.5-mile loop

Estimated time: 3–4 hr.

Elevation gain: 100 ft.

Costs/permits: $20 national park entry fee

Best time to go: April to October

Website: www.nps.gov/yose

Recommended map: Tom Harrison map of Yosemite Valley

Trail head GPS: N 37 44.506, W 119 36.064

Trail head directions: Day-use parking is available at Yosemite Lodge at the Falls. Or take the Valley Shuttle bus to stop #8, right in front of the lodge. Walk to the eastern end of the lodge complex and parking area, and curve up to Northside Drive.

The tram tour of Yosemite Valley is fine, but to really appreciate the valley, hit the trail. On this heart of the valley walkabout, you'll enjoy vistas of many of its most famed attractions.

Cross Northside Drive to meet the east-west-trending footpath near its junction with Lower Yosemite Fall Trail and hike west (left) on the path. The wide path soon leads to the major Yosemite Falls trail head and the wide asphalt paths that lead to the falls. Enjoy vistas of the three-tiered wonder as you continue southwest to the busy parking lot of Camp 4.

❶ Camp 4 Camp 4, by far the least expensive place to sleep in the park ($5 per night per person), attracts at least four kinds of visitors: Europeans (mostly young), Americans (mostly young), budget travelers of all ages, and rock climbers.

Some of the best rock climbers in the world came to the valley to challenge Yosemite's walls in the years after World War II. They gathered at Camp 4 to share their ideas about routes and gear. One superb climber, Yvon Chouinard, developed technical climbing gear and sold it in the camp parking lot. This enterprise proved to be the roots of his highly successful Patagonia Company.

This campground was drive-in, not walk-in, until 1976. True, other valley campgrounds were noisy and crowded, but Sunnyside was particularly cacophonic.

In 2003, the camp was placed on the National Register of Historic Places for "its significant association with the growth and development of rock climbing in the Yosemite Valley during the 'golden years' of pioneer mountaineering." The name Sunnyside was dropped, and it was renamed Camp 4 in recognition of its historical roots.

Follow the path southwest through camp and the surrounding woodland to

Northside Drive. A crosswalk beckons you to cross the road and check out Leidig Meadow.

The meadow, named for hoteliers Isabella and George Leidig, who constructed an inn situated below Sentinel Rock in 1869, offers grand views of Half Dome, Cloud's Rest, and much more.

After admiring the meadow, double-back across Northside Drive and continue on the path a short distance to the actual crossing of the road and a trail sign indicating it's 2.3 miles to El Capitan and 5.9 miles to Bridalveil Fall.

The path meanders between Northside Road and the willow- and cottonwood-cloaked north bank of the Merced River.

> If you want to take a break in a place with all the facilities, cross Northside Road to El Capitan Picnic Area. Better yet, while sojourning along the Merced, pick your own favorite riverside spot for a rest.

This part of the valley floor has been in eco-rehab for a long time. The Merced River Restoration, which started in 1995 and continues today, aims to assist vegetation trampled by countless visitors and no longer growing. The Park Service makes use of controlled burns to reduce high brush, built up over the decades because fire, a natural element for a healthy forest, has long been suppressed in Yosemite Valley. Yosemite's classic valley trails, including this one, are also slated to be restored to their original grandeur.

While hikers can't help spending a lot of time looking up at the majestic walls of the 7-mile-long valley, the valley floor is worth a close look, as well. Yellow pine forest is the dominant environment, though tree-lovers will find other pines (including ponderosa, lodgepole, and sugar), as well as oaks, willows, and dogwood. The valley's large meadows are seasonally sprinkled with such wildflowers as Chinese Houses, California poppy, Western buttercup, Indian pink, and star flower.

❷ Devil's Elbow, Merced River Continue another 1/2 mile west along the Merced to Devil's Elbow, which doesn't sound named for fun, but actually is kind of Yosemite's Riviera—a sandy beach with plenty of flat rocks for sunbathing.

> The view of El Capitan from Devil's Elbow was one of the great photographer Ansel Adams' favorites, and some of his most famous photos of the mighty El Cap were taken here.

❸ El Capitan Bridge Cross the river via the road over El Capitan Bridge. The bridge is a great place from which to observe mighty El Capitan, towering 3,593 feet above the Merced River. Rock climbers can frequently be seen ascending the monolith, believed to be the largest block of exposed granite in the world.

From the bridge, pick up the signed bridle path ("Curry Village 4.1 miles") heading southeast. Admire the Cathedral Rocks and Cathedral Spires on the eastern side of the valley; some hikers think these rocks are as impressive as or more impressive than El Capitan. One of the most famous works of art inspired by Yosemite, *Cathedral Rocks, Yosemite Valley, Winter,* was created in 1872 by the renowned landscape painter Albert Bierstadt.

Cross Southside Drive, head briefly south, then east, on a 2-mile stretch of trail in the shadow of the valley's south wall. Savor magnificent views of the valley's north wall, including Upper and Lower Yosemite Falls.

Hiking this stretch of Yosemite Valley's floor delivers a view lost to most motorists.

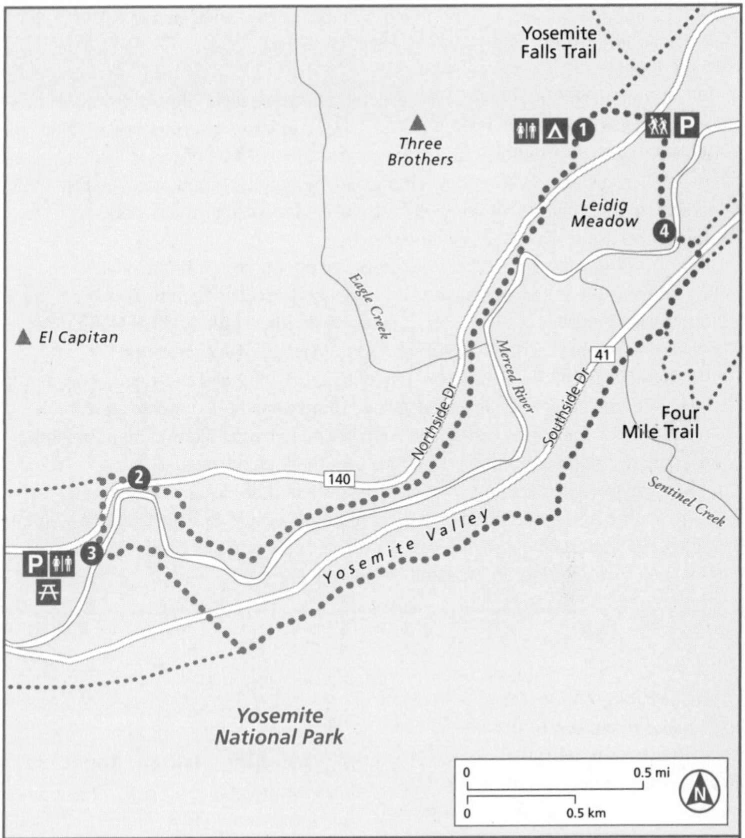

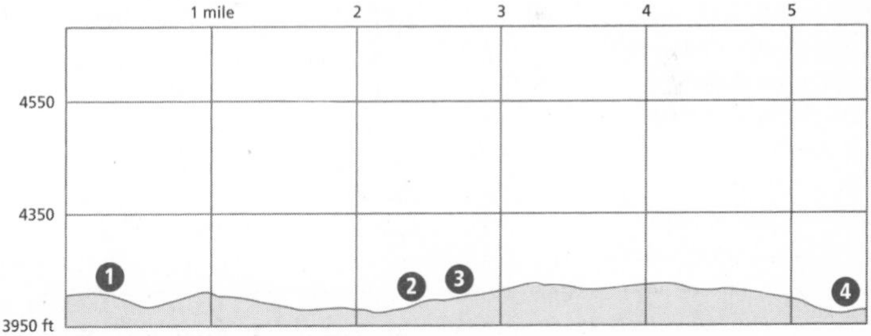

N 37 44.506, W 119 36.064 Trail head
❶ N 37 44.478, W 119 36.312 (0.3 miles): Camp 4
❷ N 37 43.612, W 119 37.746 (2.4 miles): Devil's Elbow beach
❸ N 37 43.437, W 119 37.893 (2.7 miles): Cross the river over El Capitan bridge
❹ N 37 44.218, W 119 36.036 (5.4 miles): Swinging Bridge picnic area

Hiking Yosemite Valley

Two generations of so-called hiking authorities have repeated two words of advice about the floor of Yosemite Valley: "Stay away."

I disagree.

Considering the crowds and congestion that often overwhelm Yosemite Village and its asphalt arteries, the valley's trail system offers a surprisingly, and refreshingly, natural experience. To be sure, Yosemite's heart-of-the-valley trails are very well used; however, they're not overwhelmed by hikers. And you just might find that traveling in company with hikers from across the nation and around the world is a unique experience, too.

For purposes of a quick hiker's geographical orientation, Yosemite Valley can be said to begin on the west, where Bridalveil Fall cascades from the valley's south wall. The valley extends east as far as Washington Column, that stone pillar positioned above where Tenaya Creek and the Merced River converge.

Veteran valley hikers all have their favorite loops, long and short. Some divide the hiking into east valley and west valley segments. Others characterize Yosemite Valley floor walking as the Village Loop or Lodge Loop. Hiking options are limited only by the finite number of bridges over the Merced River.

Note that you're following what is my favorite middle-distance Yosemite Valley jaunt. Lengthen the described loop by continuing west to Bridalveil Meadow and Bridalveil Fall, or by meandering east via the network of paths connecting the Ahwanee, Curry Village, and Yosemite Village.

When you get away from what John Muir termed "blunt-nosed mechanical beetles" and set out afoot, the scale and grandeur of all that stone meeting sky—Royal Arches, North Dome, Clouds Rest, Half Dome, and more—seems to increase exponentially.

Isn't it romantic?

Well, a lot of people think so. Yellow Pine Beach and Sentinel Beach along the Merced River are favorite sites for weddings. Cross Southside Drive to visit the fine facilities—picnic tables and restrooms—and check out the nuptials-friendly scene: a pretty part of the river, lovely meadows, and inspiring views of Yosemite Falls.

4 Swinging Bridge Picnic Area Back on the trail, your path crosses Sentinel Creek and, after another $^1/_4$ mile, passes a junction with famed Four-Mile Trail (see "Glacier Point & Four-Mile Trail," above) that ascends to Glacier Point. Continue another $^1/_4$ mile and cross Southside Drive to Swinging Bridge Picnic Area. Cross the bridge and return to Yosemite Lodge by joining the paved bike path that skirts Leidig Meadow.

VERNAL & NEVADA FALLS ★★

Difficulty rating: Moderate to strenuous

Distance: 3 miles round trip to Vernal Fall; 7 miles round trip to Nevada Fall; add another 1.5 miles without shuttle bus

Estimated time: 2–5 hr.

Elevation gain: 1,000 ft. to Vernal Fall; 2,000 ft. to Nevada Fall

Costs/permits: $20 national park entry fee

Best time to go: March to November

Website: www.nps.gov/yose

Recommended map: Half Dome Trail Map; Tom Harrison map of Yosemite Valley

Trail head GPS: N37 44.374, W 119 34.380

Trail head directions: Park in the Curry Village day-use lot and take the shuttle bus to the stop for Happy Isles. If you take this hike during the off-season, you'll have to walk a mile from Curry Village to the trail head.

Two famous falls and two famous footpaths are the highlights of this popular hike that many consider Yosemite's most scenic. Vernal and Nevada Falls are cascades of uncommon beauty, Merced River spills that plunge over bold granite cliffs. Mist billows from the crashing water, rainbows arch toward the heavens. Magnificent Mist Trail and John Muir Trail get you there and back.

You'll head out on a paved pathway, before crossing a bridge over the Merced River. The Park Service's latest reconstruction of the mile or so of trail between Happy Isles and the base of the Mist Trail stairs included the installation of a functioning drainage system. Thus, the 7-foot-wide path is considerably less slick these days, now that water is channeled off the trail.

Yosemite Valley visitors who are short of time should at least make the $1^{1}/_{2}$-mile round trip pilgrimage to Vernal Fall Bridge. En route, you'll get views of two more falls—Illilouette and Upper Yosemite.

❶ Vernal Fall Bridge Ascend amidst oak and bay, and reach Vernal Fall Bridge after $^{3}/_{4}$ mile. Here, you'll find the first of a trio of toilets, also to be found near Vernal Fall and Nevada Fall. There's probably something about the sight and sound of rushing water that has subliminal effects on our systems, so the facilities are most welcome.

❷ Mist Trail Climbing onward, you'll soon choose Mist Trail at a junction and ascend mist-slickened stairs carved into the rock. The more water in the Merced River, the more misty is Mist Trail—and the more magnificent the hike, some would claim. If the river is up, as it usually is in the spring, expect to get hosed by spray.

For a hike up Mist Trail, wear rain gear. On a warm summer day, however, you could just get wet, and dry out on the sunny rocks above the falls.

A guard rail adds a measure of security for hikers climbing the granite cliffs.

> As you emerge from the mist, you might be lucky enough to see a rainbow superimposed over the spectacular scene, like some special effect in a movie—only better because it's real. Tramp the balance of the trail to the top of the Vernal Fall and a viewpoint.

After admiring Vernal Fall, walk up river to Emerald Pool and Silver Apron, a beautiful, broad, river-washed rock formation that resembles a fan. Emerald Pool is sometimes a tranquil pool, sometimes a torrent, depending on rainfall and the season.

Heed the international NO SWIMMING signs. The polished granite bed of the river looks—and is—slippery. And the Merced River itself, perhaps in comparison to the thundering falls, looks more mellow than it really is. Fatal accidents have occurred here, the most recent in 2005, when a hiker waded into the deceptively powerful current to fill his water bottle, slipped, and was swept over Vernal Fall.

❸ Nevada Fall Cross a footbridge over the Merced, then curve briefly through the woods. The path, at first, isn't quite as steep as that to Vernal Fall, but it's

Vernal & Nevada Falls

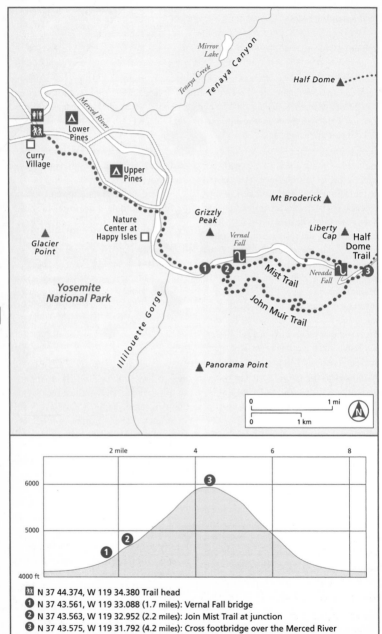

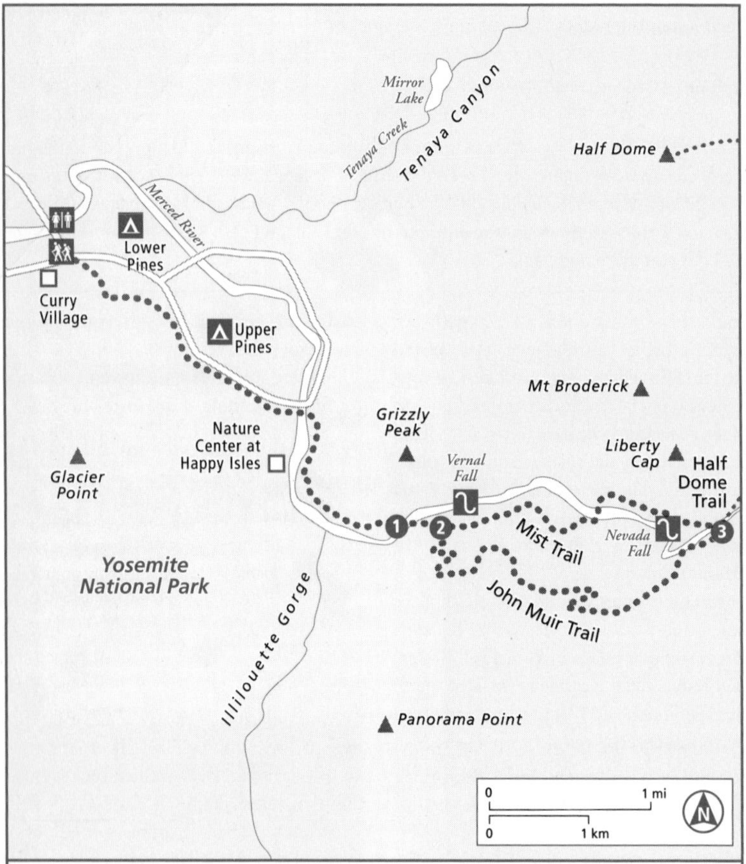

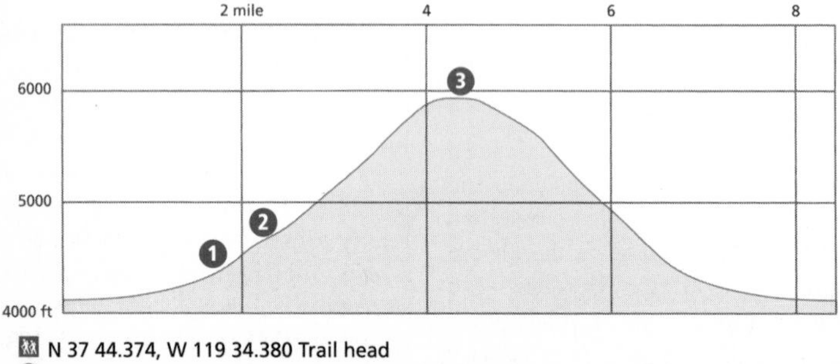

N 37 44.374, W 119 34.380 Trail head

❶ N 37 43.561, W 119 33.088 (1.7 miles): Vernal Fall bridge

❷ N 37 43.563, W 119 32.952 (2.2 miles): Join Mist Trail at junction

❸ N 37 43.575, W 119 31.792 (4.2 miles): Cross footbridge over the Merced River

Moments **White-Water Rafting Ad**

Zephyr Whitewater Expeditions (✆ **800/431**
zrafting.com) offers one of the most direct wa
ite—especially if you're not an experienced b
are ideal for white-water fans in the spring (w
most exciting) and for families later in the se
through the park, it's still an all-wilderness ac
never forget. Be sure to reserve a spot well i

plenty vertical, all right! When you ascend near the base of Nevada Fall, you'll note that it, too, is quite the mist generator, but it sprays down-canyon, not over the trail.

Tackle two dozen or so switchbacks, a task that seems to bring out the best in hikers, who can frequently be heard encouraging each other on the climb. Finally, you reach the top and a junction with the trail to Half Dome. (See "Half Dome," below.)

To visit the fall and to return to the valley via John Muir Trail, descend 1/4 mile to the top of Vernal Fall. Warm, sunny, and flat rocks suggest a scenic lunch stop. This is one of the better top-down looks at a waterfall because the rock lip of the overlook juts out, and Nevada Fall's cascade is not precisely vertical. More than one mountaineer has remarked upon the resemblance of the 594-foot falls to an avalanche of snow.

Cross the Merced on a bridge and begin your return to Happy Isles on the John Muir Trail, carefully negotiating some slippery switchbacks. The path travels below the well-named Panoramic Cliffs and serves up grand over-the-shoulder views back at Half Dome, Liberty Cap, and Nevada Fall. Nearing the Merced again, you'll meet a bridle trail, but stick with the footpath, bearing right to return to this hike's first junction with the Mist Trail. Bear left and retrace your steps to Vernal Fall Bridge and Happy Isles.

HALF DOME ★★★

Difficulty rating: Strenuous

Distance: 16.5 miles round trip from Happy Isles to Half Dome; 14.2 miles round trip via Mist Trail

Estimated time: 9–11 hr.

Elevation gain: 4,800 ft.

Costs/permits: $20 national park entry fee

Best time to go: Mid-May/early June to mid-October

Website: www.nps.gov/yose

Recommended map: Half Dome Trail Map; Tom Harrison map of Yosemite Valley

Trail head GPS: N 37 44.260, W 119 33.461

Trail head directions: Leave your car in the large lot at Curry Village. Take the shuttle bus to Happy Isles. If you're getting an early start (before shuttle service begins at 7am), you must hike up-valley about 3/4 mile from Curry Village day-use parking to Happy Isles along the shuttle bus route. This increases your already long hiking day to 18 miles round trip.

osemite's icon summit definitely makes it onto the once-in-a- see-before-you-die lists. You will long remember the final climb on o the summit and the fabulous views.

ach Vernal Fall, you'll have a tween Mist Trail and John Muir Mist Trail shaves almost a mile from distance but is a strenuous, stair-stepping oute. The right fork—the JMT—makes a more moderate ascent via well-engineered switchbacks. I strongly recommend the more energy-conserving, knee-sparing Muir Trail for travelers to Half Dome.

❶ Half Dome Trail Just above Nevada Fall, you'll reach a junction with the trail to Half Dome. The path heads up-river, now a much more mellow Merced, slower and deeper than the one you've seen on the way to Vernal and Nevada falls.

❷ Little Valley Yosemite Camp A mile out from Nevada Fall, the trail splits. A slightly shorter (and steeper) bypass route forks to the left, but I suggest sticking with the trail leading to Little Yosemite Valley Camp, site of the last toilet on the way to Half Dome.

Leaving the camp behind, you'll climb again, gaining 900 feet in elevation over the next $1^1/_2$ miles to reach a junction, 6 miles from the start of this hike.

❸ Half Dome Trail Bid adieu to the John Muir Trail, which heads east, and continue north on Half Dome Trail. In a half-mile, look eastward (right) for a short side trail to a spring, last water source en route.

Now, the granite grandeur unfolds: Half Dome on your left, Cloud's Rest on your right. Warning signs remind you not to proceed to Half Dome in bad weather or if bad weather threatens.

Half Dome Yesterday & Today

First to surmount Half Dome was George Anderson who, in 1875, doggedly drilled his way to the top, securing eyebolts every 5 feet or so, standing on the last bolt while drilling the next. John Muir followed fast on the heels—and eyebolts—of his fellow Scot. Today, Yosemite's icon summit is scaled by rock climbers using several different routes. And Half Dome can be conquered by the experienced hiker, too.

The very long day hike begins in Happy Isles, where the John Muir Trail begins. Past Vernal Fall and Nevada Fall you climb, then on through Little Yosemite Valley. The final assault on the summit requires climbing at an almost 45-degree angle up slick granite with the help of twin cables that hikers grip to haul themselves to the top.

Depending on weather conditions, the park service installs the cables in mid-May and removes them in early October. Bring gloves to wear for the cable part of the climb.

The acrophobic and out-of-shape should hike elsewhere. Even the most experienced hikers should remember that mid-afternoon summer thunderstorms in Yosemite are common. The last place you want to be in an electric storm is atop Half Dome, forced to make a hurried descent over slippery rock while holding on to wet metal cables. Get an early start on this trail. You want to top Half Dome and begin your descent by early afternoon, just in case a thunderstorm blows into the valley.

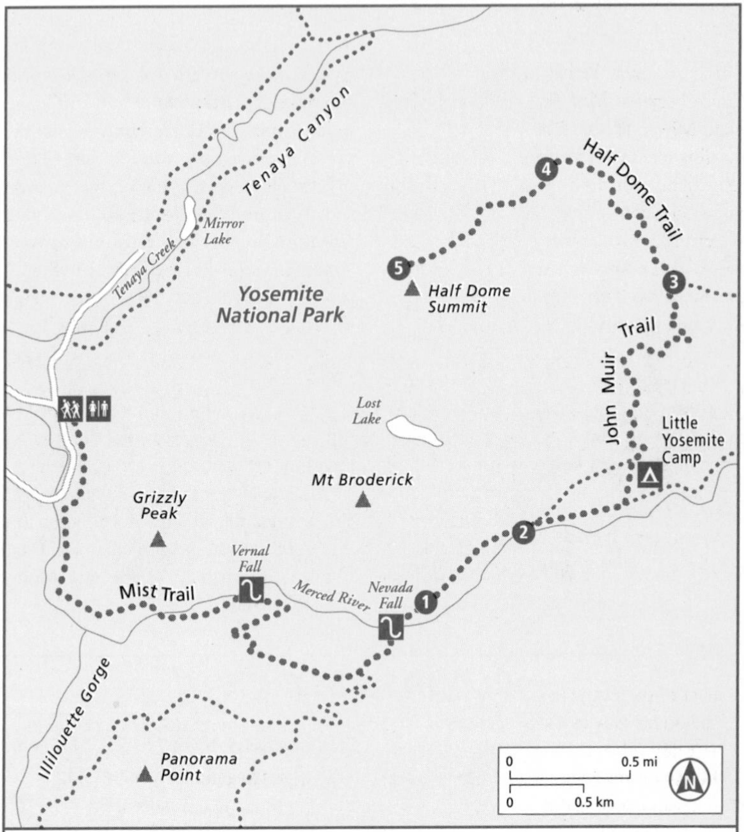

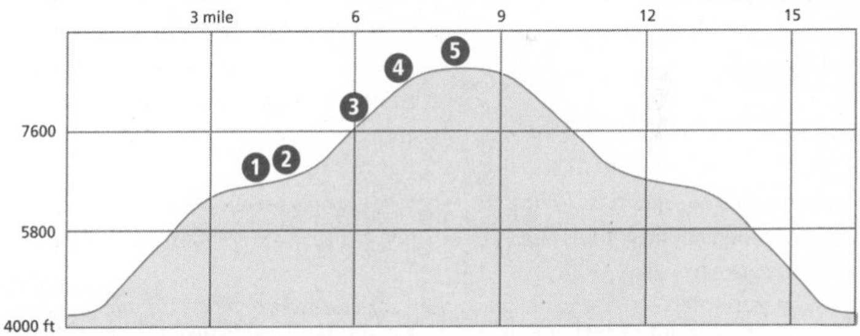

N 37 44.260, W 119 33.461 Trail head

1. N 37 43.542, W 119 31.829 (3.5 miles): Pass junction with Half Dome Trail just above Nevada Falls
2. N 37 43.836, W 119 31.387 (4.2 miles): Little Yosemite Valley Camp
3. N 37 44.707, W 119 30.718 (6.0 miles): Turn north on to Half Dome Trail
4. N 37 45.066, W 119 31.309 (7.1 miles): Final ascent begins at granite steps
5. N 37 44.761, W 119 31.911 (8.2 miles): Half Dome summit

To the non-climber of yesteryear, and even to modern hikers nearing the mighty mount, Half Dome seems impossible to ascend.

In his 1870 *Yosemite Guide-Book,* California's leading geologist, Josiah Whitney, pronounced Half Dome "perfectly inaccessible" and described it as "the only one of all the prominent points about the Yosemite which never has been and never will be trodden by the human foot."

❹ **Granite steps** About 3/4 mile from the top, you begin the final ascent, first climbing granite steps, then topping a minor dome before descending briefly to a saddle, where you find the cables. Thanks to those who've passed this way before you, there will be a pile of gloves at the base of the cableway. Put on a pair of gloves, get a grip on the cables (and yourself) and start climbing. You'll surmount a series of horizontal bars while gripping a pair of chains. The 400 feet of ascent feels like you're going straight up the smooth granite, but the pitch is probably more like a 45-degree angle.

❺ **Summit** Make your way carefully over to the dome's very highest point, located at the north end. Enjoy the view of every major feature in Yosemite Valley, as well as a panorama of Yosemite Wilderness peaks, but stay away from the cliff edge.

Up top, there's a lot of top—a very broad summit, indeed. Football fans will note there's room on top for seventeen granite gridirons. From the 8,842-foot dome, you get 360-degree vistas: up and down Yosemite Valley, Clouds Rest, and Cathedral Peak, the jagged Sierra crest.

Earlier generations of hikers camped on top so as to admire what are by all accounts the amazing sunrises, but in the 1990s, the National Park Service stopped the practice for reasons of sanitation (no dirt to bury waste) and salamanders (Half Dome is the habitat of the rare Mount Lyell salamander).

CLOUDS REST ★★

Difficulty rating: Strenuous

Distance: 14 miles round trip from Tenaya Lake to Clouds Rest

Estimated time: 7–8 hr.

Elevation gain: 1,900 ft.

Costs/permits: $20 national park entry fee

Best time to go: June to October

Website: www.nps.gov/yose

Recommended map: Trail map of the Yosemite High Country; Tom Harrison map of Yosemite Valley

Trail head GPS: N 37 49.543, W 119 28.209

Trail head directions: From Hwy. 120 (Tioga Pass Rd.), 9 miles west of the Tuolomne Meadows Visitor Center and some 16 miles east of White Wolf, proceed to the Sunrise Lakes Trailhead parking. You can also ride the Tuolumne Meadows shuttle bus to the stop by the parking area.

Climb to where the clouds rest, 9,926 feet high in the sky. Clouds Rest is higher than Half Dome, and is safer and easier to climb. In addition, Clouds Rest offers better views than the famed Yosemite icon (some hikers say the best in the national park). From atop Clouds Rest, Yosemite's largest granite face, savor a panorama of rounded domes and sharp ridges, as well as the pageantry of Yosemite Valley.

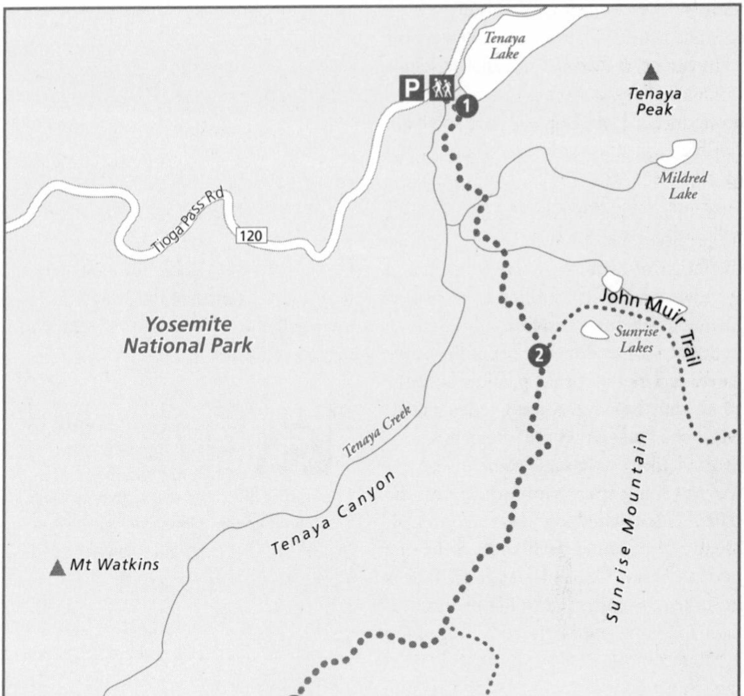

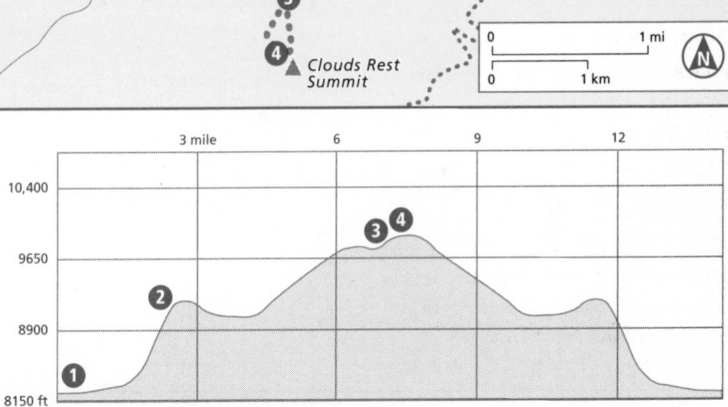

N 37 49.543, W 119 28.209 Trail head

1 N 37 49.578, W 119 28.062 (0.2 miles): Tenaya Lake

2 N 37 48.049, W 119 27.517 (2.4 miles): Continue straight past junctions with Sunrise Lakes, John Muir Trail

3 N 37 46.176, W 119 29.287 (6.8 miles): Turn on to Summit Trail

4 N 37 45.852, W 119 29.377 (7.0 miles): Summit of Clouds Rest

Follow the signs for Sunrise High Sierra Camp, where you'll soon cross Tenaya Creek (there's no bridge—you might have to wade across in spring), and make your way across meadowland and among stands of lodgepole pine.

❶ Tenaya Lake Tenaya Creek flows into Tenaya Lake, which makes everybody's Top Ten High Sierra Lakes list. Tucked in a basin of polished granite, the lake sparkles in the Sierra sun. No wonder they call this the Range of Light! (If you're in the mood for more hiking after this trek, be sure to saunter along Tenaya's shores. Most visitors to the lake named for the chief of the native Awahneeche head for the picnic area or the white-sand strand and seem pretty oblivious that a trail follows the lakeshore.)

You'll likely have some company on the way to Clouds Rest, but nowhere near the traffic encountered on the trail to Half Dome. While an easier hike than the one up Half Dome, the path to Clouds Rest is far from easy. After $1\frac{1}{2}$ miles of minimal pain and gain, the ascent stiffens, gaining 1,000 feet in the next $1\frac{1}{3}$ miles and reaching a junction.

❷ Trail Junction, Sunrise Lakes The trail to the three Sunrise lakes and the Sunrise Lakes High Sierra Camp, as well as to a junction with John Muir Trail, heads left (east).

Continue straight (south), dropping from the ridge top to the base of Sunrise Mountain. All too soon, you climb again, reaching another junction at the 5-mile mark. The left-branching trail is a connector leading to Sunrise Creek; the path also junctions the John Muir Trail.

❸ Summit Trail Tramp through thinning forest toward a rocky ridge. Just before the 7-mile mark, there's a junction, all right—signed, even—but not the most obvious of intersections. If you miss this turnoff to the summit of Clouds Rest, fear not, for the lower trail, used by stock, continues to a point where you can double-back and get up to the summit.

Any way you go, carefully climb the stacked layers of granite to the summit.

❹ Clouds Rest Clouds Rest is by no means in the center of the park, but it is in the middle of all the sights Yosemite visitors come to see.

From Clouds Rest, enjoy eye-popping up-close views of Half Dome and more distant vistas all the way to Matterhorn Peak. About the only features you can't see are Yosemite Valley's famed waterfalls.

Looking at Clouds Rest is like taking Glacier Geology 101, whereby granite is uplifted from deep within the earth by massive tectonics, then eroded by rains and rivers, then smoothed and polished by glaciers. We have glaciers to thank for sculpting the sheer faces in the granite that we so admire, particularly when water rushed over the top of them in the form of spectacular waterfalls. Clouds Rest is a truly epic expanse of granite; there's a 5,000-foot drop-off from the top of its northwest face to Tenaya Canyon.

CATHEDRAL LAKES

Difficulty rating: Moderate

Distance: 7.5 miles round trip to Lower Cathedral Lake

Estimated time: 4 hr.

Elevation gain: 1,000 ft.

Costs/permits: $20 national park entry fee

Best time to go: June to October

Website: www.nps.gov/yose

Recommended map: Trail map of the Yosemite High Country; Tom Harrison map of Yosemite Valley

Trail head GPS: N 37 52.396, W 119 22.965

Trail head directions: Parking is located on both shoulders of Hwy. 120 (Tioga Pass Rd.), 1½ miles west of Tuolumne Campground entrance or 24 miles east of White Wolf. In summer, you can ride the free shuttle bus to the trail head by leaving your car at the Tuolumne Meadows Wilderness Permit station or Tenaya Lake.

Many of John Muir's effusive descriptions of the High Sierra have a spiritual tone and refer to landscapes as sanctuaries, temples, and cathedrals. "This I must say is the first time I've been to church in California," wrote John Muir after visiting the lakes and making the first recorded ascent of Cathedral Peak in 1865.

When you reach the trail head, you'll first walk ¼ mile through the forest to a four-way junction. Proceed straight on steep John Muir Trail.

❶ John Muir Trail The John Muir Trail extends from Happy Isles in Yosemite Valley, some 210 miles through what some backpackers consider the most scenic high country in the U.S. There's a certain esprit de corps among hikers on particular lengths of the trail, such as the one leading toward Cathedral Lakes, as if the great naturalist is at our heels whispering, "Going to the wilderness is going home."

On a less lyrical note, the trail can be dusty (the path is heavily used by stock) and is steep going for the first ¾ mile. The trail mellows for a time, passing among lodgepole pine before climbing again.

About a mile out, Cathedral Peak pops into view. You traverse meadowland made soggy by Cathedral Creek and assorted creek-lets in the late spring and early summer. The trail curves from southwest to south, and you pass above a gurgling spring.

A bit more than 2 miles of ascent brings you to a forested saddle. And then the path begins descending. Now, Cathedral Peak appears on the skyline to your left. Three miles out, the trail divides.

❷ Trail Fork John Muir Trail leads another half-mile to upper Cathedral Lake and its shoreline campsites, handsomely back-dropped by craggy Cathedral Peak (10,911 ft.) in the east and 10,000-footers Echo and Tressider peaks rising above the south shore. Hike a few more minutes up the Muir Trail to Cathedral Pass and get a grand view of Cathedral Lakes Basin.

❸ Cathedral Lake Cathedral Lake is a popular weekend backpacker destination. A little too popular, perhaps. Even Yosemite's canny bears seem to know how many back-country campers come to the high country; they're positively ingenious at foraging for hiker's foodstuffs and thwarted only by the bear-proof food canisters all backpackers are required to use. Unless you're continuing to higher and farther destinations on the John Muir Trail, Cathedral Lake is best enjoyed as a day hike destination.

Around the lake, geologic history is written in the rocks. Lakeside granite slabs offer flat spots for sunning and picnicking. Near the lake are curious erratics: ice-transported boulders that were left here when the glaciers melted.

If you make your way to the far end of the lake and gaze westward, you'll get a bird's-eye view of Tenaya Lake, located just a mile away. Tenaya is not only a looker, it's hard to overlook. It's that big beauty you see right by Tioga Pass Road as you motor to Tuolumne Meadows. While you can see Tenaya Lake from the highway, you'll appreciate it all the more from on high.

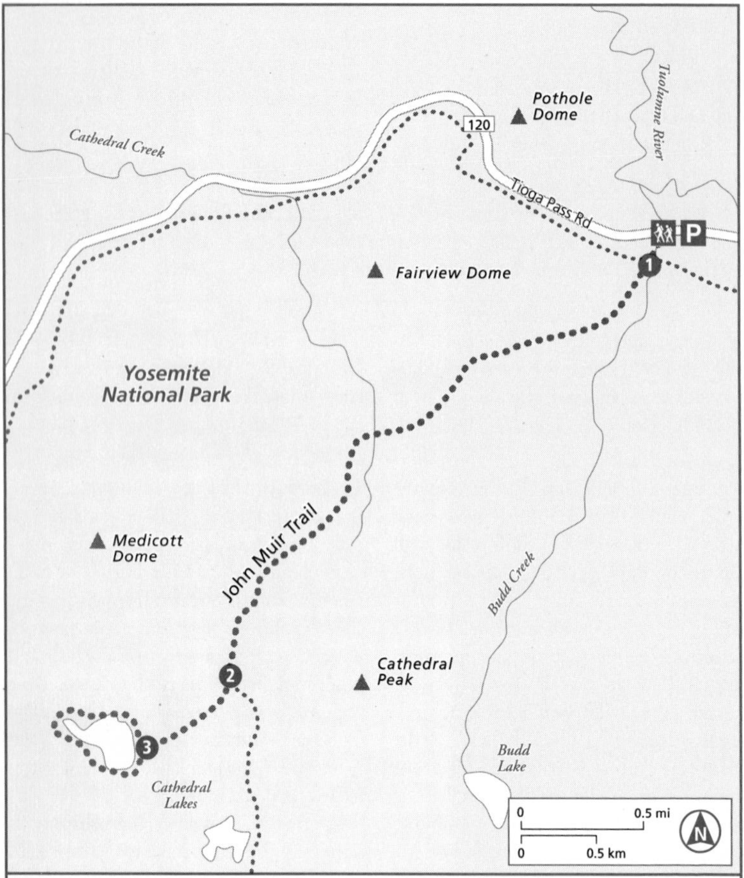

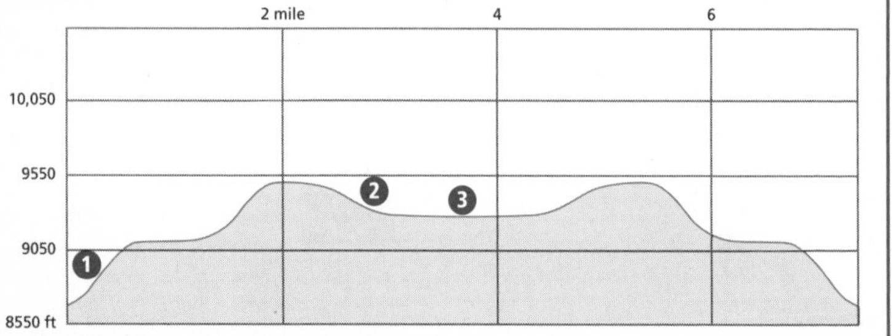

N 37 52.396, W 119 22.965 Trail head

1 N 37 52.333, W 119 23.010 (0.1 miles): Continue on John Muir Trail past four-way junction

2 N 37 50.929, W 119 24.918 (2.7 miles): Trail divides

3 N 37 50.683, W 119 25.294 (3.2 miles): Cathedral Lake

Tuolumne Meadows

Lush and lovely Tuolumne Meadow is likely the national park's best-known site outside of Yosemite Valley, and for good reason. Easily accessible by short trails, the High Sierra's largest sub-alpine meadow is a glorious, wildflower-splashed basin ringed by forested slopes, roundish domes, and sharp summits.

John Muir's first summer in the Sierra was spent as a shepherd, tending a flock of some 2,000 sheep pastured in Tuolumne Meadows. Muir's journals of that time are filled with the wonders of nature he observed, along with his first thoughts about the preservation of Yosemite. Muir soon realized that sheep, which he later characterized as "hoofed locusts," and other grazing animals could destroy an alpine meadow.

Today, a length of the John Muir Trail crosses the great naturalist's beloved Tuolumne Meadows. Other paths lead to Parsons Memorial Lodge, named for Edward Parsons, who fought alongside John Muir to preserve the park, Hetch–Hetchy Valley, and other wild lands during the early days of the Sierra Club. After Parsons—an accomplished photographer, outings leader, and early Sierra Club President—died in 1915, the Club constructed this lodge in his honor.

Parsons Lodge, long ago deeded to the National Park Service, has served as a reading room/library for generations of visitors. Many a hiker has found a cool retreat on a hot summer's day or taken refuge from an afternoon thunderstorm.

Interpretive signs posted sporadically along Tuolumne Meadows paths offer insights about Parsons, Muir, the old Tioga Road, and the Native American tribes who visited the meadows for so many centuries. For more information about the meadows, visit Tuolumne Meadows Visitor Center (open summer only).

One of my favorite little jaunts is the 1½-mile round trip walk from the visitors center to Parsons Lodge and Soda Springs. A wide path extends north across the meadows. Families linger along the bends of the Tuolumne River to fish or to enjoy one of the best picnic spots on the planet.

Cross the wooden bridge over the Tuolumne River, bend left along the river, and take the signed trail forking right to Parsons Memorial Lodge. From the lodge, follow the signed path very briefly east to Soda Springs, a muddy area where carbonated water percolates up from the ground.

The trail loops past some interpretive plaques, then angles back toward the bridge over the Tuolumne River. From here, you retrace your steps back to the trail head.

For those hikers looking for a longer return route, I heartily recommend returning to the John Muir Trail, ascending to Sunrise Camp, then looping over and down to Tenaya Lake.

This route is a total of 13 miles, and in summer, the park's shuttle bus service links the Cathedral Lakes Trailhead and Tenaya Lake.

LEMBERT DOME ★

Difficulty rating: Moderate

Distance: 4.5 miles round trip to Lembert Dome

Estimated time: 2 hr.

Elevation gain: 800 ft.

Costs/permits: $20 national park entry fee

Best time to go: June to October

Website: www.nps.gov/yose

Recommended map: Trail map of the Yosemite High Country; Tom Harrison map of Yosemite Valley

Trail head GPS: N 37 52.642, W 119 21.204

Trail head directions: From Tioga Rd. (Hwy. 120), head to the east end of Tuolomne Meadows; Lembert Dome parking area is on the north side of the road.

For the time-short (but not stamina-short) traveler, able to do only one quick hike in the Tuolomne Meadows area, this is the one to do. From atop the dome, located at the eastern end of Tuolumne Meadows, you'll have Tuolomne Meadows and Yosemite Valley at your feet, as well as a parade of peaks, from Cathedral Peak all the way to Mount Dana at Tioga Pass.

Leave behind the picnic area and restrooms, and head north from the Dog Lake/Lembert Dome trail head sign. The 9,450-foot dome looks absolutely impossible to scale when regarding it from the trail head, but fear not.

Traverse a rock slab to a fork in the trail at 1/4 mile. Continue north to a junction. Continue north toward Dog Lake, ignoring two more trails from the stables coming in from the left (west), and stay right (north) on the main path, ascending through lodgepole pine forest.

❶ Path to Dog Lake Just over a mile out, the path forks. The left fork ascends north to Dog Lake. Reach this destination by hiking 1/4 mile northeast to a junction. The main trail continues north toward Young lakes. Bear right (east) past some ponds to the southwest shore of Dog Lake. Stroll along the south shore, admire the view from the lake of Mount Dana, and take a swim. Dog Lake is good-sized but quite shallow, meaning it's one of Yosemite's warmest lakes.

❷ Onward to Lembert Dome The path to Lembert Dome soon passes a little pond perched in the shadow of the dome. At the 1 3/4-mile mark, you'll junction the signed 1/3-mile (with 350 ft. of elevation gain) summit trail to the dome.

❸ Summit Trail The path picks its way westward over a ridgeline—tree-spiked at lower elevation, treeless at higher elevation—gaining the granite-slabbed shoulder of the dome. The trail gives out, so choose among a couple of routes over the bare rock and zigzag your way to the top. (The south side is the least steep way to the summit.)

The summit is often very windy. Hold onto your hat and stay back from the edge!

Geologists say Lembert Dome is not a true dome (such as Sentinel Dome) but a *roche moutonée;* the French phrase "rock sheep" describes a glacier-carved formation recognized by its sheer front and sloping back.

The *roche moutonée* was named for shepherd/naturalist Jean Baptiste Lembert who worked for a decade in Tuolumne Meadows, beginning in 1885. An unsolved mystery to this day is who shot him dead in his cabin—and why—in 1896.

The summit views include grand vistas over the Tuolumne Meadows, Lyell Canyon, and the Cathedral Range. You can

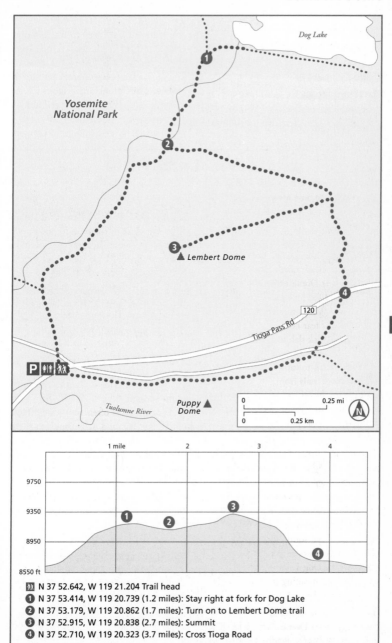

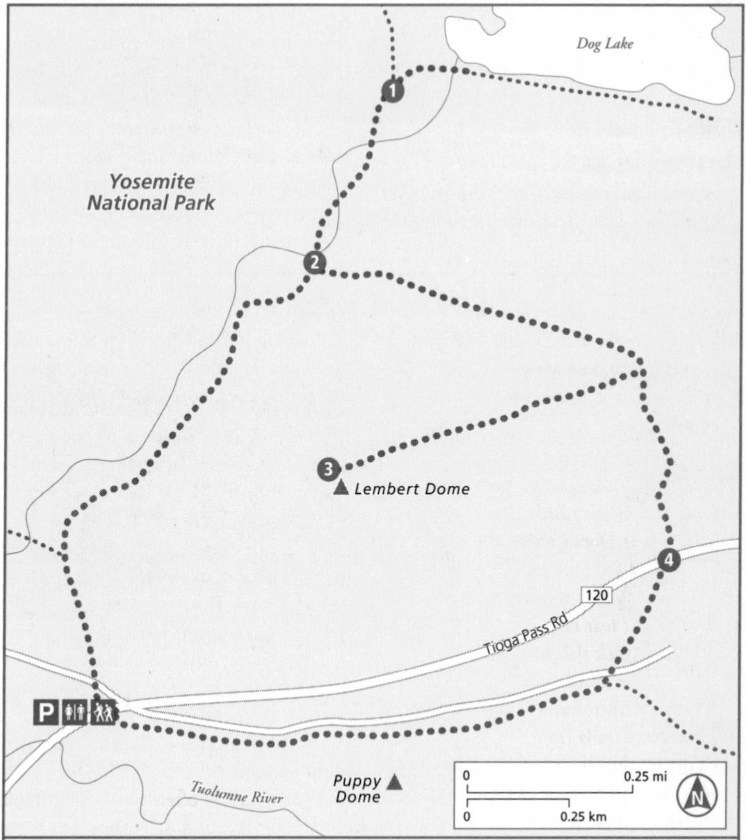

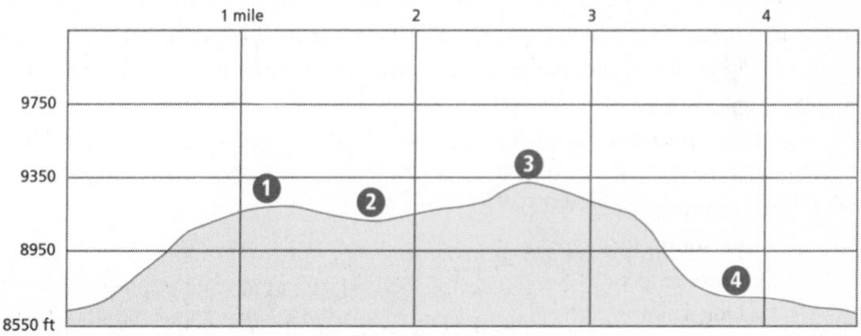

N 37 52.642, W 119 21.204 Trail head

1. N 37 53.414, W 119 20.739 (1.2 miles): Stay right at fork for Dog Lake
2. N 37 53.179, W 119 20.862 (1.7 miles): Turn on to Lembert Dome trail
3. N 37 52.915, W 119 20.838 (2.7 miles): Summit
4. N 37 52.710, W 119 20.323 (3.7 miles): Cross Tioga Road

identify the park's highest peaks, including Mount Florence (12,561 ft.) and Mount Lyell (13,114 ft.).

Backtrack on the summit path back to the main trail. Head right (south), switchbacking steeply downhill 3/4 mile to Tioga Road.

4 Tioga Road Carefully cross the road and hike 1/4 mile to a parking lot and the access road extending to Tuolumne Meadows Lodge. Cross this little road, and still heading south, you'll see a sign for John Muir Trail. Head west on a path that parallels the road from Tuolumne Lodge to the Wilderness Center—and also parallels Tioga Road—for about 3/4 mile, until it reaches a point opposite the parking area for Lembert Dome. Cross Tioga Road to return to the trail head.

SLEEPING & EATING

ACCOMMODATIONS

Lodging in the park is operated by the concessionaire, **DNC Parks & Resorts at Yosemite** (✆ **559/252-4848;** TTY 209/255-8345). Rooms can be reserved up to 366 days in advance. You can make reservation requests online at www.yosemiteparks.com. Reservations are also accepted by mail at **Yosemite Reservations,** 6771 N. Palm Ave., Fresno, CA 93704.

The Ahwahnee Elegance, luxury, and history converge in this exquisite hotel that has hosted queens, presidents, Hollywood legends, and sports stars. This soaring six-story stone structure offers views of the outstanding setting and provides supreme comfort in every room, nook, and cranny. Relax in your room after a tough hike or just visit the magnificent first-floor common areas.

Yosemite Valley, inside the park, CA 95389. ✆ **559/252-4848.** 118 rooms; 6 suites. $499–$984 double; from $1,301 suite. AE, DC, DISC, MC, V. Take the shuttle bus to stop 3. **Close to:** Yosemite Valley.

★ **Curry Village** Curry Village is best known as a mass of more than 400 white canvas tents tightly packed together on the valley's south slope. An economical place to crash, the village gives you the feeling of a camping vacation without the hassle of bringing all the gear. Curry Village also has just over 100 attractive wood cabins with private bathrooms; 80 wood cabins that, like the tent-cabins, share a large bathhouse; and a number of motel rooms. Landslides and rockfalls in 2008 destroyed some of the classic tent cabins and wood cabins. Check the park's website for updates.

9010 Curry Village Dr., Yosemite Valley, CA 95389. ✆ **559/252-4848.** Fluctuating number of units. $77 double tent-cabin; $90 double cabin without bathroom; $120 double cabin with bathroom; $147 double motel room. AE, DC, DISC, MC, V. Take the shuttle bus to stop 13A, 13B, 14, or 20. **Close to:** Yosemite Valley.

Housekeeping Camp All the fun of camping without bringing a tent. No-frills units include two single bunks and a double bed, as well as kitchen cupboard and table; each unit is fully electric—and includes lights. Utilitarian construction of cinder blocks, the units are topped with canvas roofs and set on concrete slabs to keep you dry and comfortable.

9005 Southside Dr., inside the park, CA 95389. ✆ **559/252-4848.** 266 units. All with shared restrooms and shower facilities $76 per site (up to 4 people; $5.25 per extra person). AE, DC, DISC, MC, V. Take the shuttle bus to stop 12. **Close to:** Vernal & Nevada falls.

Tuolumne Meadows Lodge A hiker's delight, this lodge is near many of the best trails in the park. Calling the place a lodge is a bit of a stretch; it's really a group of tent cabins made of canvas, featuring cozy wood-burning stoves and kitchen tables. Conveniences include stores, a restaurant, a post office, and a gas station.

Tioga Rd., inside the park, CA 95389. ✆ **559/252-4848.** 69 canvas tent-cabins, all with shared bathroom and shower house. $80 double; additional $10 per adult or $6 per child. AE, DC, DISC, MC, V. Closed in winter. From Yosemite Valley, take CA 120 east 60 miles (about 1½ hr.) toward Tioga Pass. **Close to:** Half Dome.

★ **Yosemite Lodge at the Falls** The prime attractions are the location near the falls and the abundance of wildlife that gather here. Pleasant rooms in a variety of sizes and shapes, most with patios or balconies from which to enjoy nature's ever-changing scene. Includes restaurants and a lounge, an outdoor pool, bicycle rentals, child-care programs, a general store, and an ice cream counter.

Yosemite Valley, inside the park, CA 95389. ✆ **559/252-4848.** 245 units. Apr–Oct $147–$177 double; additional charge of $10 per adult and $6 per child. Lower rates Nov–Mar. AE, DC, DISC, MC. Take the shuttle bus to stop 8. **Close to:** Vernal & Nevada falls.

Camping

Make your reservations early for scarce Yosemite Valley campsites. Reservations for park campsites are accepted beginning the 15th of each month and can be made up to 5 months in advance (✆ **877/444-6777;** www.recreation.gov). Additional campground information is available at ✆ 209/372-0200.

The busiest campgrounds in the park are in Yosemite Valley. All four of the following campgrounds are in Yosemite Valley, and have flush toilets and access to the showers nearby at Camp Curry ($2). Upper, Lower, and North Pines campgrounds require reservations. **Upper Pines** is pretty and shady, but you won't find peace and quiet here in the summer. Parking is available, or you can take the shuttle bus to stop 15 or 19. **Lower Pines Campground** is wide open with lots of shade but limited privacy. Still, it's a nice place with clean bathrooms, and it's bordered on the north by a picturesque meadow. Parking is available, or take the shuttle bus to stop 19. **North Pines** lies beneath a grove of pine trees that offers lots of shade but little privacy. The campground is near the river, roughly a mile from Mirror Lake. Parking is available, or take the shuttle bus to stop 18. **Camp 4** (also called Sunnyside Walk-In) has tent sites only. It's a small campground that's become a magnet for hikers and climbers taking off or returning from trips. It's situated behind Yosemite Lodge, near the trail head for Yosemite Falls and close to rocks frequently used by novice rock climbers. Pets are not permitted. Parking is available about 150 feet away, or take the shuttle bus to stop 7.

Elsewhere in the park, **Bridalveil Creek Campground,** at Glacier Point, is set along Bridalveil Creek, which flows to Bridalveil Fall—a beauty of a waterfall, especially after a snowy winter or wet spring. Near beautiful Glacier Point, and featuring flush toilets, this campground is away from the valley crowds but within a moderate drive to the valley sights. The campground can accommodate some pack animals; call for information. Take CA 41 (from either direction) to Glacier Point Road. The campground is about 8 miles down the road.

Among Yosemite's other campgrounds is **Tuolumne Meadows,** the biggest campground in the park and, amazingly, often the least crowded. Its location in the high country makes it a good spot from which to head off with a backpack. The site is also near the Tuolumne River, making it a good choice for anglers. In addition to standard

RV/tent sites, the campground has 25 walk-in spaces for backpackers and eight group sites; half of the sites require reservations. There are flush toilets, and showers can be bought nearby at Tuolumne Lodge. From Big Oak Flat Road, head east on Tioga Road for about 45 miles to Tuolumne Meadows.

RESTAURANTS

★ **Curry Village Pavilion** AMERICAN Buffet-style, all-you-can-eat for breakfast and lunch. No surprises, just good old American classics; load up pre- or post-hike for good taste at a good price.

Curry Village, Yosemite Valley, CA 95389. ✆ **209/372-0200.** Breakfast $9.50 adults, $7.50 children; dinner $12 adults, $10 children. DC, DISC, MC, V. Daily 7–10am and 5:30–8pm. Shuttle-bus stops 13A, 13B, 14, and 20. **Close to:** Yosemite Valley.

Curry Village Pizza Patio PIZZA Come for the pizza, stay for the fun. Indoors or outdoors, pizza is easy to order and fun to eat. Sports fans catch up with their favorite teams on the big screen; nature lovers stay outside and just enjoy the view. Very popular post-hike hangout for the whole family.

Curry Village, Yosemite Valley, CA 95389. ✆ **209/372-1000.** Pizza $8–$20. AE, DC, DISC, MC, V. Daily noon–9pm. Shuttle-bus stops 13A, 13B, 14, and 20. **Close to:** Yosemite Valley.

Degnan's Deli DELI Arrive early to grab some trail snacks at the market or a complete made-to-order lunchtime sandwich and salad, soup, and dessert at the deli to enjoy in the middle of the day. Or return to this convenient location to purchase some treats to enjoy—including beer and wine—back at camp.

Yosemite Village, in the valley, CA 95389. ✆ **209/372-8454.** Most items $3–$8. DC, DISC, MC, V. Daily 7am–7pm. Shuttle-bus stops 4 and 10. **Close to:** Yosemite Valley.

★★ **Mountain Room Restaurant** AMERICAN Great food with a view to match; Yosemite Falls is visible from every massive window. This is the place for healthy gourmet—even sticklers for organic. Entrees are accompanied by bread and veggies; there's an additional charge for salad or soup. Save room for tasty desserts. Lower cost alternative: order a la carte at the bar and lounge.

Yosemite Village, in the valley, CA 95389. ✆ **209/372-1274.** www.yosemitepark.com. Entrees $17–$34. AE, DC, DISC, MC, V. Daily 5:30–9pm. Shuttle-bus stop 8. **Close to:** Yosemite Valley.

★★ **Tuolumne Meadows Lodge** AMERICAN Situated in the heart of the high country, this is fine dining away from it all. Expect a selection of healthy breakfasts and delicious dinners—all a hiker needs, morning and night. The dinner menu varies but always includes vegetarian entrees, as well as a full complement of meats, fish, pasta, and seafood.

Tioga Rd., inside the park, CA 95389. ✆ **209/372-8413.** Reservations required for dinner. Breakfast $3.55–$6.95; dinner $10. AE, DC, DISC, MC, V. Daily 7–9am and 6–8pm. **Close to:** Half Dome.

Yosemite Lodge Food Court AMERICAN This place has something for everyone at food stations galore—better than a cafeteria, and more fun, too. The place is abuzz, especially after a tour bus arrives. Choose just what you want for basic breakfasts; tasty lunches; and an assortment of pastas, meats, and other entrees for dinner. Enjoy the spectacular view of Yosemite Falls.

Yosemite Village, in the valley, CA 95389. ✆ **559/252-4848.** Main courses $5–$14. AE, DC, DISC, MC, V. Daily 6:30–10am, 11:30am–2pm, and 5–8:30pm. Shuttle bus stop no. 8. **Close to:** Glacier Point, Yosemite Valley.

Sequoia & Kings Canyon National Parks

If you only drive through, you'll be disappointed: Sequoia and Kings Canyon have the superlative scenery and postcard views found in other national parks, but you have to hike to find them.

Naturally, the groves of sequoia are the primary draw to both namesake Sequoia and Kings Canyon national parks. Preserving these trees, the biggest on Earth, was the prime reason for the formation of the parks. The General Sherman, standing 274 feet tall and measuring 37 feet in diameter at the base of its massive trunk, is the largest of the large trees.

To begin a park visit with a walk among the big trees is sublime; to end your visit after a stop in the sequoias with the belief you've seen the parks is a notion bordering on the ridiculous. Auto travel is restricted to lower and middle elevations, so if you want to fully experience the park, you need to hike into the Sierra Nevada high country.

Trails explore a remarkable range of elevations from 1,600 feet to 14,000 feet, and a range of ecologies from Mediterranean to alpine. Kings Canyon is one of the continent's deepest canyons and 14,494-foot Mount Whitney is the highest peak in the continental U.S.

These national parks, which now boast such big attractions, started out rather small. Sequoia, the nation's second national park, totaled 50,000 acres when it was established in 1890. General Grant National Park, forerunner of Kings Canyon, was established a week after Sequoia and initially included only 2,560 acres.

But in 1860, people came to saw the big trees, not see them. Grove upon grove of giant sequoias were toppled and milled into lumber. John Muir's nature writing and newspaperman George Stewart, editor of the *Visalia Delta,* marshaled public opinion to form Sequoia and General Grant national parks.

Mount Whitney and adjacent high country was added to Sequoia National Park in 1926. Mineral King's valley, peaks, and alpine lakes became part of the park in 1978 after a lengthy battle between ski resort developers and conservationists led by the Sierra Club. A greatly expanded Kings Canyon National Park, incorporating the old General Grant National Park, was established in 1940.

The sequoias, reduced in number over millions of years by ecological and climatic changes, and further reduced by logging, survive today only in isolated groves on the Sierra Nevada's western slope. But sequoias are survivors. Some live 3,000 years or more, and many mature park specimens are 1,500 years old. A very thick (up to 2 ft.) bark resists insects, disease, and fire.

Where the road ends, an extensive trail system begins. Almost half of one of the great trails of the world—the 225-mile-long John Muir Trail—extends through Sequoia and Kings Canyon national parks. The trail ends (or begins, for a majority of long-distance hikers) at Mount Whitney. The famed High Sierra Trail extends east-west across Sequoia National Park.

The hiking season is a fairly short one. The middle elevations—4,000 to 8,000 feet—are often snow-covered from

November through May. I've selected the best hikes for a variety of scenery and for a range of abilities: memorable family walks among the big trees, pleasant excursions to lakes and waterfalls, and some challenging hikes high into the Sierra Nevada.

ESSENTIALS

GETTING THERE

By Air

Fresno–Yosemite International Airport (✆ **559/621-4500**), located 53 miles from the Big Stump Entrance in Kings Canyon, is the nearest major airport, with more than 100 flights daily. Airlines include Alaska, Allegiant Air, American/American Eagle, Continental, Delta, Express-Jet, Frontier, Hawaiian, Horizon, Mexicana, Northwest, United, and US Airways.

By Car

There are two entrances to the parks: CA 198 east, via Visalia and the town of Three Rivers, leads to the Ash Mountain Entrance in Sequoia National Park; CA 180 east, via Fresno, leads straight to the Big Stump Entrance near Grant Grove in Kings Canyon National Park. Both entrances are approximately 4 hours from Los Angeles and 5 hours from San Francisco.

By Bus

Greyhound (✆ **800/231-2222;** www.greyhound.com) serves Visalia and Fresno.

VISITOR INFORMATION

The National Park Service website (www.nps.gov/seki) has the most up-to-date information on the park, lodging, hikes, regulations, and the best times to visit. Much of the same information, plus road conditions, is available by phone (✆ **559/565-3341**). You can also get a variety of books and maps from the **Sequoia Natural History Association,** 47050 Generals Hwy. #10, Three Rivers, CA 93271 (✆ **559/565-3759;** www.sequoiahistory.org).

For lodging information and reservations at Wuksachi Lodge in the Giant Forest area of Sequoia National Park, contact Sequoia Lodge (✆ **866/807-3598** or 559/253-2199; www.visitsequoia.com). In Kings Canyon National Park, contact Sequoia–Kings Canyon (✆ **866/522-6966** or 559/335-5500; www.sequoia-kingscanyon.com) for lodging information at Grant Grove, John Muir, and Cedar Grove lodges.

Camping in Sequoia and Kings Canyon is often much easier than in Yosemite, as most of the 14 campgrounds operate on a first-come, first-served basis. To get up-to-date information, call the general Sequoia and Kings Canyon information line (✆ **559/565-3341**).

GETTING AROUND

Kings Canyon National Park bounds Sequoia National Park on the north and is nearest to Yosemite and Fresno. The main entrance (for all except Mineral King) is on CA 198, via Ash Mountain through Visalia and Three Rivers. From Sequoia's boundary, Visalia is 36 miles and Three Rivers is 7 miles.

You'll find the Big Stump Entrance (Kings Canyon National Park) via CA 180, and the Ash Mountain Entrance (Sequoia National Park) via CA 198, both from the west. Continuing east on CA 180 also brings you to an entrance near Cedar Grove Village in the canyon itself, which is open only in summer. To access the Mineral King area of

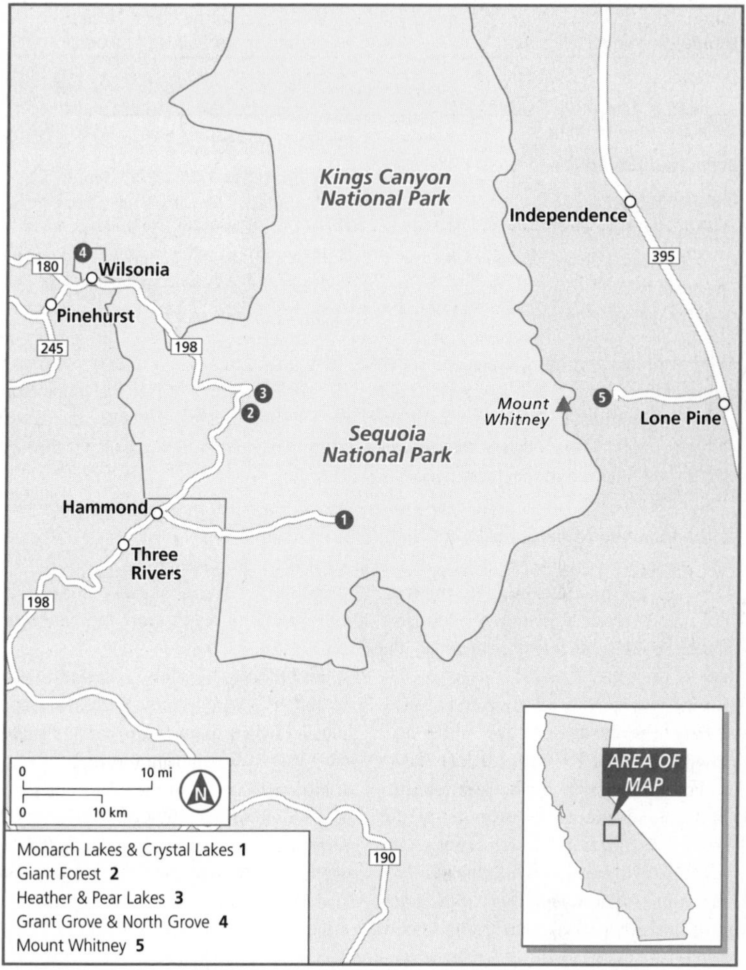

Sequoia National Park, take the steep, twisting Mineral King Road (closed in winter) off of CA 198, just a few miles outside the Ash Mountain Entrance.

ORIENTATION

Although it's impossible to drive through the parks from west to east—the High Sierra gets in the way—a north-south road, The Generals Highway, connects Grant Grove in Kings Canyon National Park with Giant Forest in Sequoia National Park. The highway runs 25 miles between two giant sequoias named for famous American generals—the General Grant Tree and the General Sherman Tree. Allow at least an hour to drive between the two on this slow, winding route.

MONARCH LAKES & CRYSTAL LAKES ★★

Difficulty rating: Strenuous

Distance: 8.4 miles round trip to Monarch lakes; 9.8 miles round trip to Crystal lakes; 11 miles to both

Estimated time: 5–7 hr.

Elevation gain: 3,000 ft.

Costs/permits: $20 national park entry fee; permit required only for overnight camping

Best time to go: June to October

Website: www.nps.gov/seki

Recommended map: Mineral King map

Trail head GPS: N 36 27.181, W 118 35.782

Trail head directions: From Hwy. 198, follow Mineral King Rd. 23 miles to Mineral King Ranger Station, then 1 mile to the Sawtooth trail head parking area. Both lakes share a common trail head and the first 3½ miles of the trail.

Mineral King, a gorgeous, avalanche-scoured valley ringed by rugged 12,000-foot peaks, is one of the most compelling areas in the High Sierra. For a great intro to this remarkable part of the national park, hit the trail to Monarch lakes and Crystal lakes, two superb sets of high-country lakes. High is the operative word here; lung-popping ascents through thin air are required to reach the lakes.

Right from the Mineral King trail head, this no-nonsense trail begins its steady ascent. A few hundred yards up the trail, look for a small waterfall on Monarch Creek. A side trail leads southeast to the base of the falls.

One reason Mineral King trails are so steep is because they follow routes used by miners in the 1870s to reach the silver mines. Miner paths, like those of their Native American predecessors, opted for beeline connections from Point A to Point B without switchbacks. Mineral King miners left behind their hillside diggings and some steep trails in their (vain) search for silver.

The trail to Monarch lakes is definitely an old mining route; the path to Crystal lakes, while more modern, is plenty steep, too. White Chief Peak and other stone ramparts are part of the fine view from the trail.

❶ Groundhog Meadow A half-mile out, you pass a junction with Timber Gap Trail and, after a mile, reach Groundhog Meadow. Marmots frolic in the meadow that's seasonally brightened by such wildflowers as Indian paintbrush, corn lily, and shooting star. At the meadow, you'll spot the abandoned Glacier Pass Trail leading off into the steep high country.

Groundhog Meadow is named for the abundant furry marmots—relatives of the woodchucks on the East Coast. Miners, not exactly finicky eaters, frequently ate them.

Marmots, not exactly finicky eaters themselves, may be exacting revenge: They have been known to eat the rubber hoses and fan belts of cars parked at the trail head.

❷ Monarch Creek Cross Monarch Creek and begin a steep ascent over slopes spiked with red fir and juniper. As you ascend switchbacks into the forest, enjoy those vistas of Mineral King Valley. The switchbacks end, but the vigorous climb continues to the ridgeline dividing the Monarch Creek drainage from Chihuahua Bowl. The grade lessens for a time, then switchbacks up to Monarch Lakes/Crystal Lakes Junction 3½ miles from the trail head.

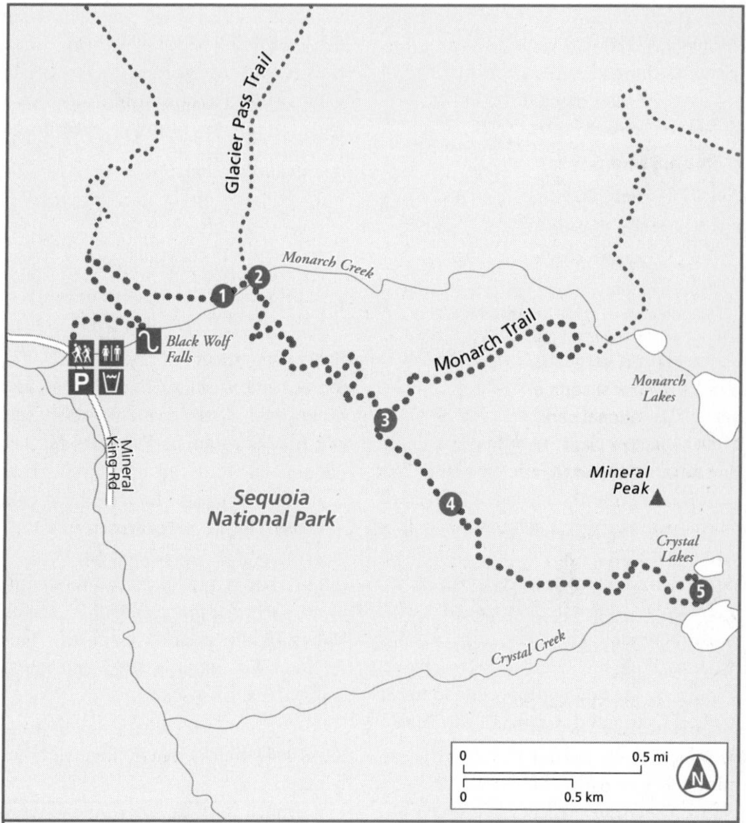

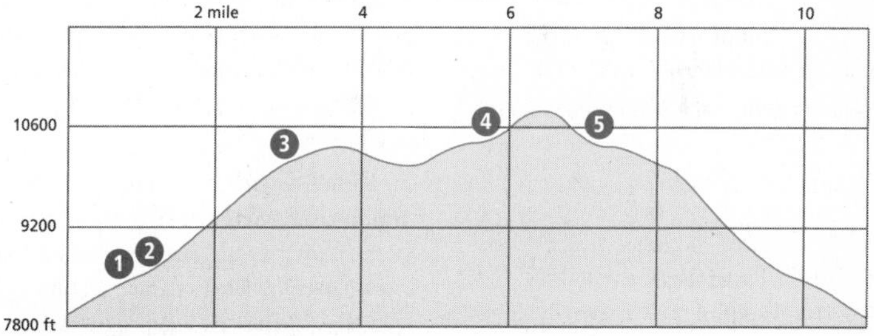

- N 36 27.181, W 118 35.782 Trail head
- ❶ N 36 27.286, W 118 35.263 (1.0 miles): Groundhog Meadow
- ❷ N 36 27.343, W 118 35.167 (1.2 miles): Cross Monarch Creek
- ❸ N 36 27.001, W 118 34.779 (3.0 miles): Trail divides to Monarch Lakes and Crystal Lakes
- ❹ N 36 26.782, W 118 34.566 (5.8 miles): Chihuahua Bowl
- ❺ N 36 26.636, W 118 33.810 (7.3 miles): Lower Crystal Lake

3 Monarch Lakes/Crystal Lakes Trail Junction **To Monarch lakes:** The ascent mellows some as you probe Monarch Canyon, where snow often lingers into summer.

> Look up ahead to towering, toothsome Sawtooth Peak (12,343 ft.) and the notch on its shoulder—Sawtooth Pass. After negotiating some shifting shale, cross Monarch Creek and arrive at the smaller of the two Monarch lakes. Looming over "Little" Monarch Lake is 11,615-foot Mineral Peak. Some rock-scrambling leads to the larger Monarch Lake.

Backpackers can continue past the Monarch lakes bound for Sawtooth Pass and the backcountry beyond. Experienced hikers, with map and compass, as well as cross-country travel skills, can make loop trips from Monarch lakes to Crystal Lake. From upper Monarch Lake, a rocky ravine leads to a saddle, the rocky ridge between Mineral Peak and Great Western Divide. From atop the ridge, you descend to upper Crystal Lake and the Crystal Lakes Trail.

4 Chihuahua Bowl Ascend the rugged path a severe 1/4 mile to rocky Chihuahua Bowl, an avalanche-scoured basin. Here, you'll find piled tailings, stone foundations, and the sealed entrance to Chihuahua Mine. The mine, a difficult-to-work operation (no water supply) failed to produce the volume of silver and gold its investors had hoped.

More climbing brings you to the foxtail pine–dotted ridge top, about 3/4 mile from the trail junction. Note diminutive Cobalt Lake below; after a short descent, you'll see an unsigned trail dropping down to it.

5 Crystal Lakes Crystal Lakes Trail contours along rocky slopes for a short while, then climbs again via some tight switchbacks to a junction with the short side trail that leads to Upper Crystal Lake. Continue straight for Lower Crystal Lake.

Lower Crystal Lake, nestled in a rocky bowl below some awesome peaks, beckons fishermen and day hikers. It's yet another Sierra lake made more reservoir-like by the Mount Whitney Power Company. From the lake's dam, built in 1903, enjoy excellent Mineral King vistas.

There is no maintained trail beyond the Crystal lakes.

GIANT FOREST ★ Kids

Difficulty rating: Easy to moderate

Distance: 2-mile loop on Congress Trail; 5.1-mile loop on Trail of the Sequoias

Estimated time: 1–3 hr.

Elevation gain: 500 ft.

Costs/ permits: $20 national park entry fee

Best time to go: April to November

Website: www.nps.gov/seki

Recommended map: Tom Harrison Sequoia–Kings Canyon National Park Recreation map

Trail head GPS: N 36 35.042, W 118 44.987

Trail head directions: From Generals Hwy., turn west on Wolverton Rd. and drive a half mile. Turn right for "Sherman Tree" and proceed 3/4 mile to the large parking lot.

Explore the John Muir–named Giant Forest, which holds the park's greatest concentration of sequoias. Sure, it's a tourist attraction, reached by the masses via a paved trail, but no visit to Sequoia National Park would be complete without a look at the General Sherman Tree, the world's largest living thing.

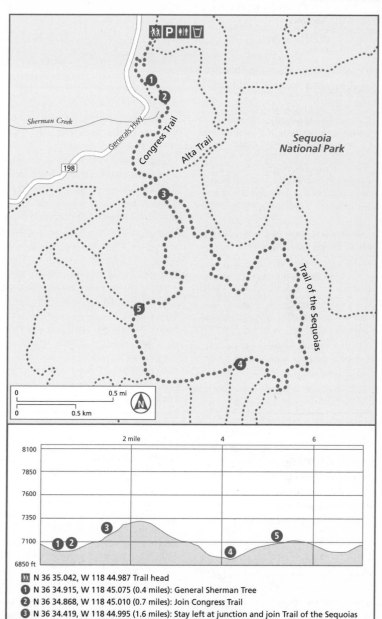

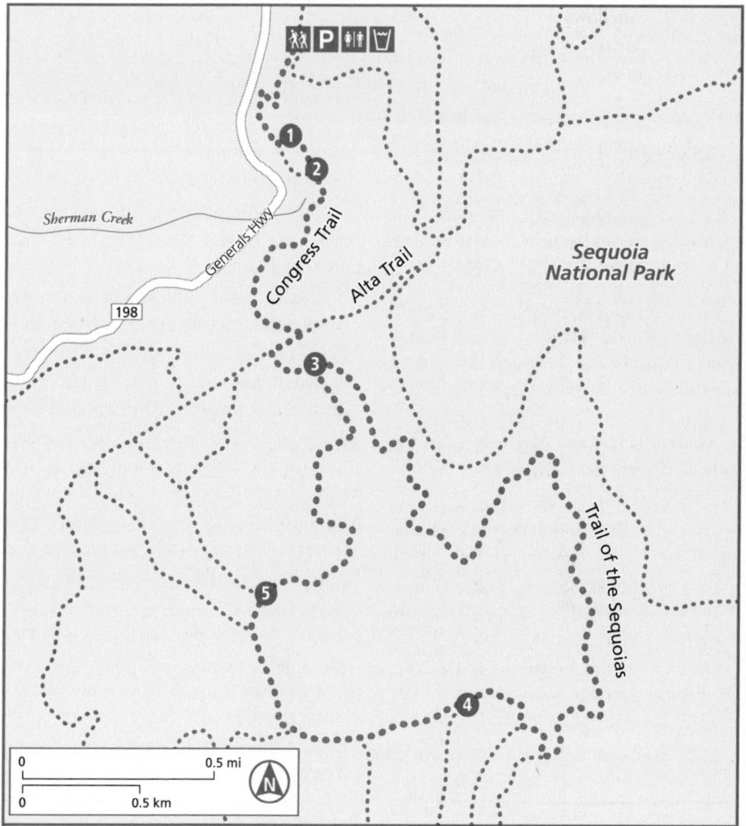

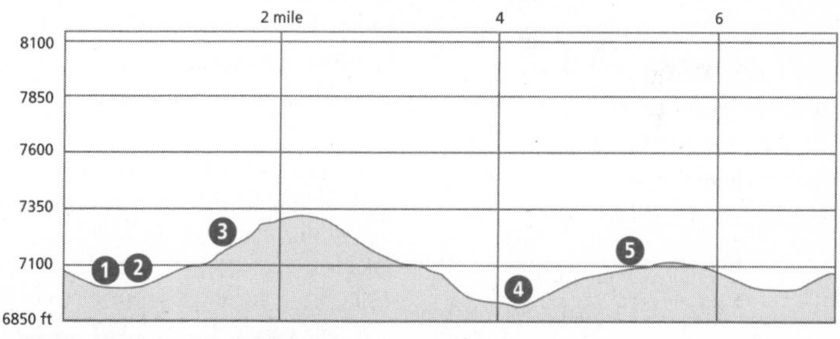

- N 36 35.042, W 118 44.987 Trail head
- ❶ N 36 34.915, W 118 45.075 (0.4 miles): General Sherman Tree
- ❷ N 36 34.868, W 118 45.010 (0.7 miles): Join Congress Trail
- ❸ N 36 34.419, W 118 44.995 (1.6 miles): Stay left at junction and join Trail of the Sequoias
- ❹ N 36 33.638, W 118 44.555 (4.3 miles): Tharps log cabin
- ❺ N 36 33.900, W 118 45.166 (5.3 miles): Turn right at junction to rejoin Trail of the Sequoias

Fun Fact **Presidential name-calling**

Hikers from near and far wonder why so many magnificent trees in Sequoia National Park are stuck with the names of politicos and obscure presidents. The Washington Tree, named for America's revered first president, seems appropriate. But the McKinley Tree? The Cleveland Tree?

Head down the paved path with many stairs, and most likely with lots of company, 1/3 mile to pay your respects to the General Sherman Tree.

1 General Sherman Tree The tree's vital statistics: 275 feet high, 102 feet in circumference, between 2,300 to 2,700 years old. General Sherman is some 52,500 cubic feet in volume and weighs an estimated 2.8 million pounds.

The tree was named for Civil War General William Sherman, then renamed the Karl Marx Tree for a time by the Kaweah colonists, who founded what they hoped would be a socialist utopia here in the forest.

Next, be thankful for what you don't see. Most of the buildings have been removed from Giant Forest, part of a decade-long National Park Service project. Tourist facilities and services have been relocated a few miles north to Wuksachi Village.

2 Congress Trail Join Congress Trail, which visits groups of trees named for the House and Senate, as well as trees named for presidents and assorted famous personages. It is an interpreted nature trail that loops through the Giant Forest, where four of the five largest trees dwell.

From the trail head close to Sherman Tree, join signed and paved trail. Cross Sherman Creek on a wooden bridge and begin your tour of the giant sequoias, including aptly named Leaning Tree and some fire-scarred old veterans.

As ancient the trees are, they're not frozen in time, and they display their individuality: Some lightning-struck sequoias have lost their crowns, others have been blackened by fire. Some long-dead specimens still stand.

The National Park Service has made a couple of major changes in its Giant Forest management policy. After many decades of fire suppression efforts, the agency has instituted a program of controlled burns designed to improve the forest's health and to reduce the risk by removing accumulated brush and thinning vegetation. (It's a bit disconcerting to some visitors when they see blackened tree trunks and don't realize that fire is a necessary element of forest ecology.)

About a mile out, you'll pass a junction with Alta Trail and soon reach an inspiring group known as The Senate. A short descent along the fern-filled forest path brings you to The House, another wondrous group. The path visits McKinley Tree and continues a final 1/2 mile back to Sherman Tree. You then return up the walkway and stairs back to the parking lot.

3 Trail of the Sequoias junction Trail of the Sequoias is a memorable half-day ramble through the Giant Forest and is a much-less traveled route.

Accompanied by visitors from around the world, march along paved Congress Trail a short mile to a junction along the Trail of the Sequoias. Join this path for a half-mile ascent to this hike's high point, then descend gradually 1 1/2 miles among more sequoias to Long Meadow.

4 Tharps Log cabin At the upper end of this meadow is Tharps Log, a cabin used for 30 summers until 1890 by cattle rancher Hale Tharp. From the cabin, you'll join Crescent Meadows Trail, passing the severely scarred but still standing Chimney Tree.

Four miles out, join Huckleberry Trail for a brief climb, then follow the signs to Circle Meadow, where shortly thereafter, you'll arrive at another trail junction.

5 Trail forks Trail of the Sequoias forks right (northeast), traveling a mile to the Senate group and then rejoining Congress Trail for the return to the General Sherman Tree trail head.

Don't look for the George Bush Tree or Barack Obama Tree anytime soon; the national park service abandoned the practice of naming big trees after World War II.

HEATHER & PEAR LAKES ★★

Difficulty rating: Moderate to strenuous

Distance: 8.4 miles round trip from Wolverton to Heather Lake; 10.5 miles round trip to Emerald Lake; 12.5 miles round trip to Pear Lake

Estimated time: 5–7 hr.

Elevation gain: 2,200 ft.

Costs/permits: $20 national park entry fee

Best time to go: June to October

Website: www.nps.gov/seki

Recommended map: Sequoia–Kings Canyon National Park Recreation map; Tom Harrison maps

Trail head GPS: N 36 35.800, W 118 44.050

Trail head directions: From Generals Hwy., 3 miles north of Giant Forest Village, take the Wolverton turnoff and proceed 1½ miles to the large parking area and signed Lakes Trail.

Lakes Trail delivers the promise in its name: Heather, Emerald, Aster, and Pear lakes. Many hikers consider it the best High Sierra backcountry hike in Sequoia National Park. The little lakes called tarns rest in rock bowls that were scoured by glaciers long ago. Named for the red heather growing nearby, Heather Lake, first along the way, is a worthy goal. With an early start, the ambitious hiker could visit all four lakes and return in a day.

From the parking lot, climb concrete steps to an information board, trail head, and signed Lakes Trail. In just ¼ mile, you'll meet a path leading to the Lodgepole area of the park. Keep on Lakes Trail and ascend a ridge amidst red fir forest.

A mile out, the trail climbs above Wolverton Creek and passes a lovely meadow. Curving southeast, the path meets signed Panther Gap Trail 1¾ miles from the trail head and, in another quarter mile, comes to a junction with Watchtower and Hump trails.

1 Junction of Watchtower and Hump trails Remember, both trails lead to Heather Lake and beyond.

Hiking over the Watchtower, an awesome granite formation, is a walk along the edge of the world—or, at least, along the edge of a precipitous cliff. Watchtower Trail was dynamited out of the rock by the Civilian Conservation Corps back in the 1930s and remains a stunning example of the trail builder's art. The path is dangerous when icy or covered with snow.

A less nerve-wracking alternative to the Watchtower is Hump Trail, which rises every bit as steeply as its name suggests.

Watchtower Trail: The path ascends moderately at first to a meadow, then more steeply with switchbacks up to The Watchtower, climbing onto the granite ledge.

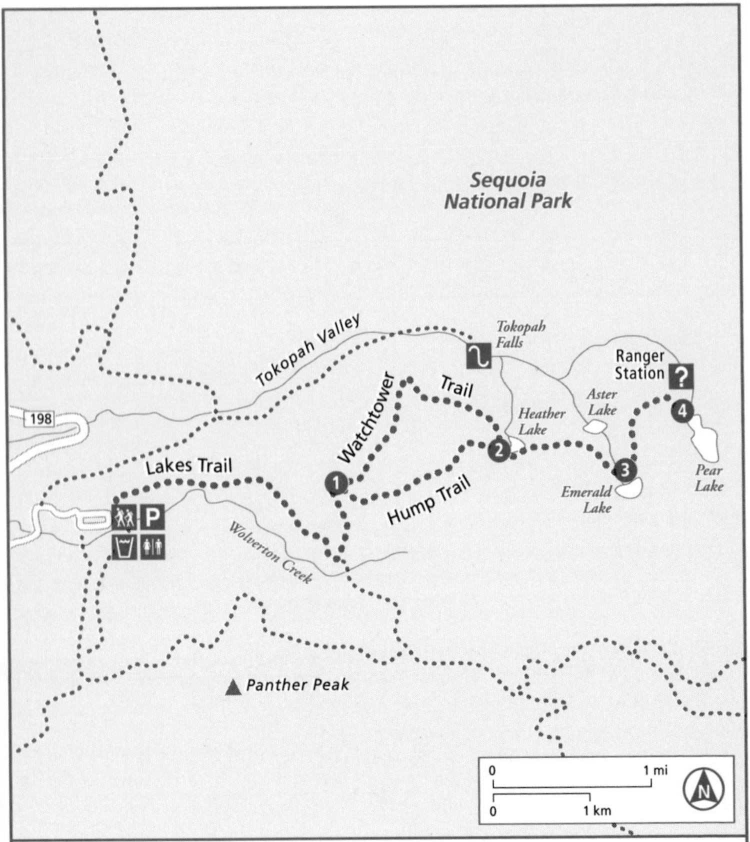

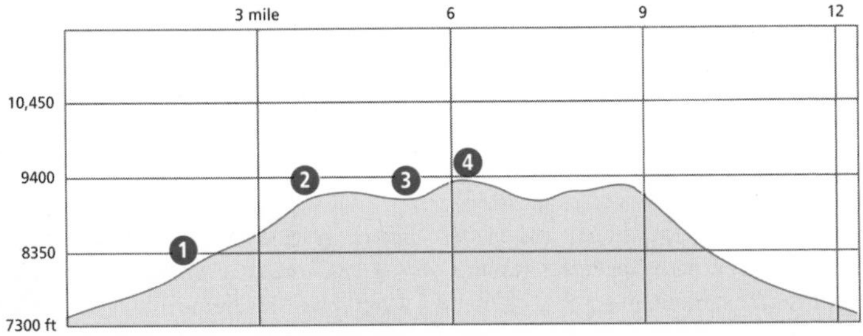

N 36 35.800, W 118 44.050 Trail head

1. N 36 35.932, W 118 42.607 (2.2 miles): Lake Trail divides into Watchtower and Hump Trails
2. N 36 36.130, W 118 41.500 (3.8 miles): Watchtower and Hump Trails reunite
3. N 36 35.959, W 118 40.632 (4.9 miles): Emerald Lake
4. N 36 36.204, W 118 40.137 (6.2 miles): Pear Lake

> Beyond the Watchtower, the dizzying path traces the cliff-face, far, far, above Tokopah Valley. Great views below if you dare take your eyes off the precipitous trail, which rejoins Hump Trail in another 3/4 mile.

Hump Trail: Begin a mile and a quarter grind, soon discovering what a hump this is to get over. You gain more than 1,000 feet in elevation in the first mile, ascending through red fir forest to a more rocky landscape. At the top of the hump, enjoy the views, then switchback down to meet Watchtower Trail.

❷ Reunion of Watchtower and Hump trails From the second meeting of Watchtower and Hump trails, and having now concluded that even without the lakes, Lakes Trail would be a compelling path, travel a mellow 1/4 mile to tranquil Heather Lake.

❸ Emerald Lake The trail then ascends and descends a foxtail pine–spiked ridge 1 1/4 miles to Emerald Lake. Like Heather, Emerald Lake is situated at about 9,200 feet in elevation. (Follow Emerald Lake's outlet creek downhill 1/4 mile to reach little Aster Lake.)

Towering above Emerald Lake and its campsites is 11,204-foot Alta Peak. Word to the Sierra Peak-bagger: Alta Peak and mighty Mount Whitney are the only major Sequoia National Park peaks reached by maintained trail. It's a 13.8-mile round trip (with 3,900-ft. elevation gain) to reach the peak via Lakes, Panther Gap, and Alta trails.

Lakeside campsites will probably all be occupied but not crowded. The path to the lakes is a popular backpacking trip, and so the National Park Service has placed a quota on backcountry camping.

Lakes Trail turns north and climbs another ridge, this one separating Emerald Lake from Pear Lake, and continues to a junction. A 1/4-mile-long side trail leads to the Pear Lake Ranger Station (staffed in summer).

❹ Pear Lake Stay with the right fork and ascend a short 1/2 mile to Pear Lake, largest of the lakes en route.

Enjoy the grandeur of the lake and its dramatic backdrop of gray granite cliffs streaked with vertical black bands. Pear Lake also boasts what many hikers report as the most stunningly situated solar toilet in all of the High Sierra.

While Pear Lake is the terminus of Lakes Trail, experienced off-trail hikers can hike onward and upward cross-country to an open area known as the Tablelands and visit Moose Lake, located 1,000 feet in elevation higher than Pear Lake.

GRANT GROVE & NORTH GROVE ★ Kids

Difficulty rating: Easy

Distance: 0.5 miles round trip on General Grant Trail; 3 miles round trip on North Grove Loop Trail

Estimated time: 1–2 hr.

Elevation gain: 300 ft.

Costs/permits: $20 national park entry fee

Best time to go: May to October

Website: www.nps.gov/seki

Recommended map: Sequoia–Kings Canyon National Park Recreation map; Tom Harrison maps

Trail head GPS: N 36 44.815, W 118 58.388

Trail head directions: From Hwy. 180 at the Kings Canyon National Park Big Stump entrance, take the Azalea Campground/Grant Tree turnoff and proceed

1 mile to the large parking lot. North Grove Trail begins at the far side of the recreational vehicle/bus parking area. If you happen to be staying at adjacent Azalea Campground, you can avoid the zoo-like Grant Tree parking lot by taking a connector trail to the trail head.

The world's third-largest tree is the showpiece of General Grant National Park, forerunner of Kings Canyon. Not far from the maddening crowd—just across the vast parking lot, in fact—tranquility, in the form of North Grove, awaits. Wander through a peaceful forest of sugar pine, white fir, and sequoia, the latter seeming all the more grand in the company of trees of lesser girth and stature.

In the General's neighborhood are many notable sequoias, which can be explored by an interpretive loop trail.

❶ Grant Grove Purchase a pamphlet from the self-serve donation box at the trail head if you wish and begin the 16-stop interpretive trail by taking the right fork of the paved path. You'll soon arrive at the Robert E. Lee Tree, ranked #13 on the Largest Sequoias List. Quite a number of sequoias and other Sierra features were named for Civil War and post Civil War–era famous personages because the region was explored and preservation efforts began during that period.

Continue past some young sequoias (planted in 1949) that range from 10 to nearly 90 feet in height; this height variation is an obvious example of the role of sunlight in stimulating the growth of individual trees. Also note the presence of the sequoia's forest companions: sugar pine, ponderosa pine, incense cedar, and white fir.

You can't miss trail namesake Grant Tree. Designated "the Nation's Christmas Tree" in 1926, Christmas services are still held beneath the boughs of General Grant Tree. Congress proclaimed the tree a National Shrine in 1956, a living memorial to the nation's war dead.

❷ General Grant Tree General Grant Tree is just plain big: 267 feet high, and an estimated 2,000 years old. While third in size, it's Number One in base diameter—more than 40 feet! Among the many attempts by park interpreters to help us realize just how darn big this tree is, are a couple of odd ones relating to autos. It seems the Grant trunk is wide enough to cover three lanes of a freeway. If the Grant Tree was hollow and filled with gasoline, do you know how far you could drive with a car getting 25 miles per gallon?

After finding out the answer to this question, continue on a dirt pathway that loops around the tree and perhaps take a side trail to the Vermont Tree Log, a 246-footer that had a Leaning Tower of Pisa lean before giving in to gravity in 1985.

Proceed to Gamlin Cabin, built by pioneer logging brothers Thomas and Israel in the late 1860s. The cabin later served as the first ranger station in General Grant National Park.

❸ Centennial Stump Centennial Stump is what remains of a 1,800-year old giant sequoia that was felled for display at America's 1876 Centennial Exhibition in Philadelphia. A 16-foot section was sliced off, split into sections, and reassembled at the exhibition. Attendees were disbelieving a tree could grow that large and branded it the "California Hoax."

Battered, burned, but unbowed, the California Tree is no hoax but was struck by lightning in 1967, and its crown caught fire. A park firefighter climbed a nearby fir with a fire hose and extinguished the blaze, saving the tree and perhaps others in the grove.

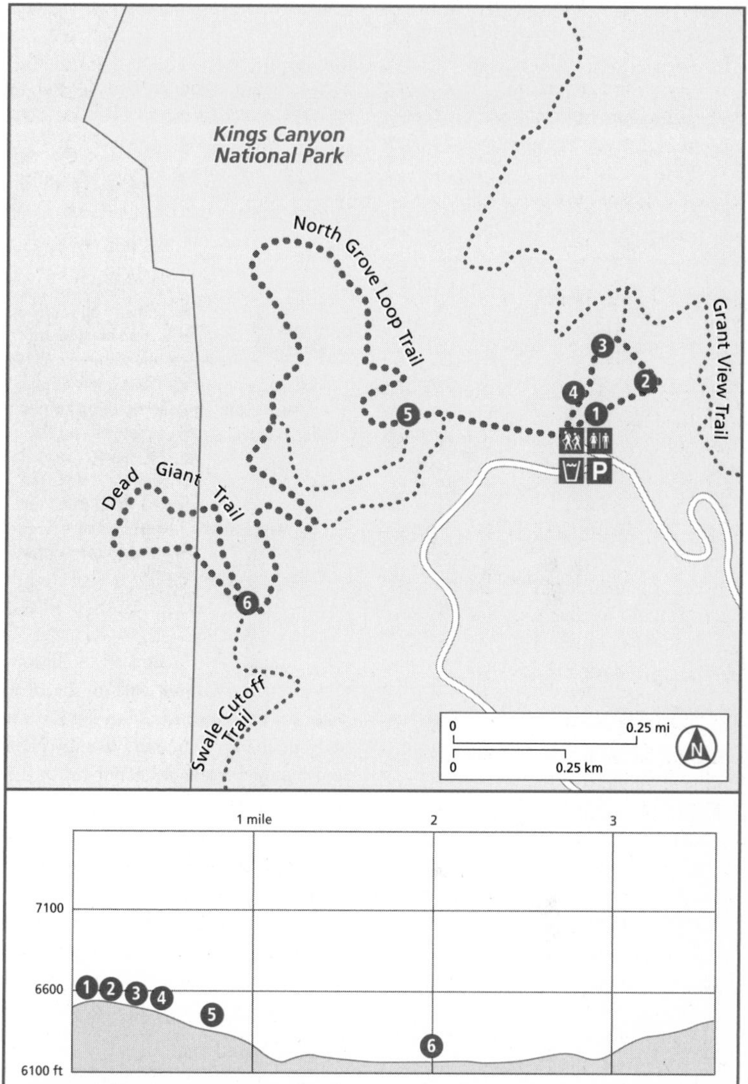

N 36 44.815, W 118 58.388 Trail head
1 N 36 44.831, W 118 58.348 (0.1 miles): Turn right on to General Grant Tree Trail
2 N 36 44.873, W 118 58.281 (0.2 miles): General Grant Tree
3 N 36 44.910, W 118 58.348 (0.3 miles): Centennial Stump
4 N 36 44.848, W 118 58.374 (0.4 miles): Fallen Monarch
5 N 36 44.836, W 118 58.621 (0.8 miles): Join North Grove Loop Trail
6 N 36 44.621, W 118 58.840 (2.0 miles): Turn right on to Dead Giant Trail

4 Fallen Monarch Fallen Monarch, a horizontal giant, was used as a hotel, saloon, and later as a stable for the horses of the U.S. Cavalry, who patrolled the national park in its earliest days.

Completing the loop, you pass Lincoln Tree and, as you approach the parking lot, look for two more Sequoia sights-to-see: On the west side of the lot, view Twin Sisters, two trees fused together, and on the east side, look for a grouping known as the Happy Family. Naturalists figure these specimens grew up together after a fire cleared out the area and gave them room to grow and grow and grow.

5 North Grove Start with a brief 1/4-mile descent on a paved road before veering right on signed North Grove Loop Trail. Your path, an old dirt road, descends 3/4 mile through a mixed forest of incense cedar, sugar pine, and sequoia to the bottom of a hill and a junction with Old Millwood Road. This now retiring road once extended to Millwood, an 1890s mill town from which sequoia logs were sent by flume down to the San Joaquin Valley town of Sanger, near Fresno. (It's far from my favorite hike, but those with a historic interest might like to trek the one-lane dirt road, which descends steeply 2 1/3 miles to the site of the old logging town.)

Past its junction with Millwood Road, North Grove Trail ascends south and east to a more distinct junction. Turn right and follow the road 1/4 mile around lovely Lion Meadow to intersect Dead Giant Trail, located about 1 1/4 miles from the trail head.

6 Dead Giant Trail Take the right (northwest), lower leg of the path that leads 1/4 mile to the Dead Giant, a towering, hollow, but still standing sequoia.

> The trail curves south then west to a signed side trail leading to a vista point overlooking Sequoia Lake. Now appearing as a brilliant blue gem, surrounded by pines, the lake was actually created as a reservoir in 1889 when the Sanger Lumber Company dammed Sequoia Creek. The lake stored and released water to fill the company's flume, which floated logs more than 50 miles down to the Central Valley town of Sanger.

Backtrack to the main trail and descend east through the forest back to the closed road. Bear left (north), following the road past junctions with both legs of North Grove Trail, back to the trail head.

MOUNT WHITNEY ★★★

Difficulty rating: Strenuous

Distance: 21.4 miles round trip from Whitney Portal to summit

Estimated time: 11–14 hr.

Elevation gain: 6,000 ft.

Costs/permits: $20 national park entry fee. See Trekking the Mount Whitney Trail sidebar for info on getting a wilderness permit.

Best time to go: July to September for milder weather and a (usually) snow-free trail

Website: www.nps.gov/seki

Recommended map: Mount Whitney High Country map; Tom Harrison maps

Trail head GPS: N 36 35.168, W 118 14.610

Trail head directions: From Hwy. 395 in Lone Pine, turn west on Whitney Portal Rd. and drive 12 miles to Whitney Portal.

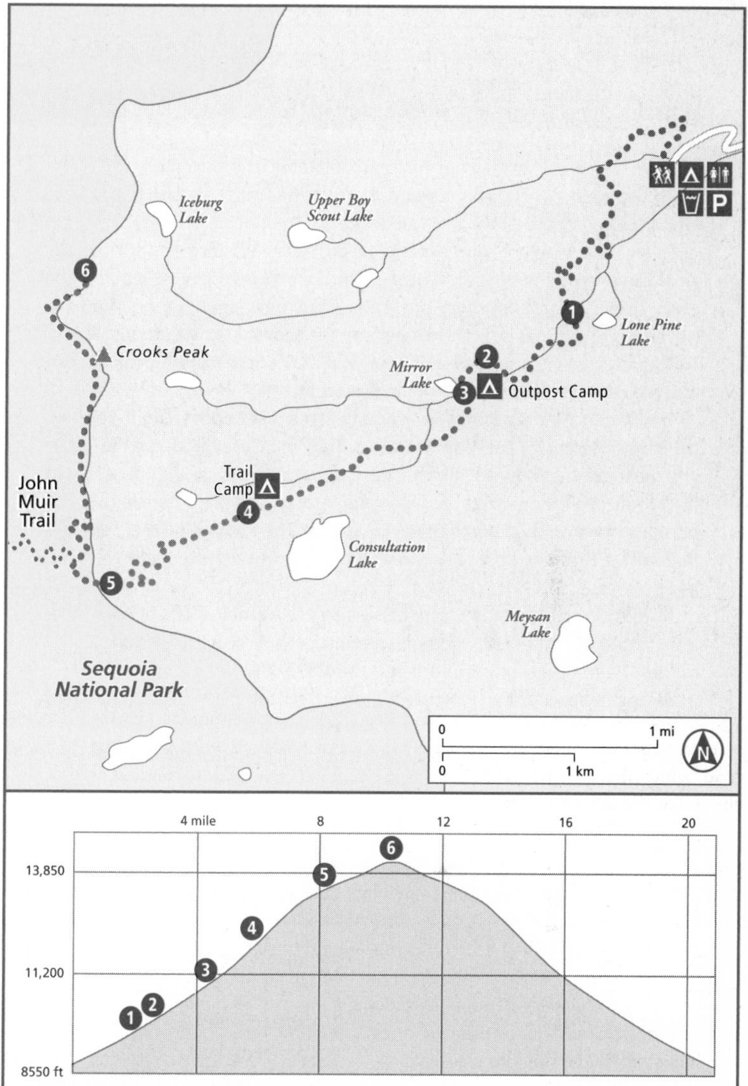

N 36 35.168, W 118 14.610 Trail head
1. N 36 34.626, W 118 15.062 (2.1 miles): Trail passes Lone Pine Lake
2. N 36 34.449, W 118 15.489 (2.7 miles): Outpost Camp
3. N 36 34.331, W 118 15.647 (4.3 miles): Mirror Lake
4. N 36 33.838, W 118 16.697 (6.0 miles): Trail Camp
5. N 36 33.577, W 118 17.390 (8.5 miles): Trailcrest Pass
6. N 36 34.779, W 118 17.539 (10.7 miles): Summit of Mount Whitney

Trekking the Mount Whitney Trail

Answering the call of science (astronomy and meteorology) and scientists, Lone Pine residents financed and constructed the Mount Whitney Trail in 1904. In 1909, a stone summit hut (which still stands today) was built by the Smithsonian Institute to study Mars.

Over the years, the trail has been rehabilitated and realigned, and stands today—graded switchbacks hewn out of granite walls—as one of the finest examples in America of the trail-builder's art.

To ensure a quality hiking experience on Mount Whitney and surrounding areas, known as the Mount Whitney Zone, the Forest Service requires that every hiker, year-round, must possess a wilderness permit. From May 1 to November 1, a quota of 60 hikers per day are allowed on the Mount Whitney Trail; quotas on the numbers of hikers who may approach the peak or come into the area from other trails are monitored, as well.

The Mount Whitney lottery in February is the first opportunity to reserve a wilderness permit for the Mount Whitney Trail. To be accepted into the lottery, you must use the Mount Whitney Lottery application available online. Search for "Mount Whitney permits" and navigate through the many details about the permit system on the Inyo National Forest site. The application must arrive by mail with a February postmark and include payment for reservation fees ($15 per person).

To request an application form be sent to you by mail or fax, or other questions about the lottery or wilderness permits, call the U.S. Forest Service's Wilderness Permit Reservation Office at ✆ **760/873-2483.**

All quota space for the Mount Whitney Trail can be filled by reservation. However, if the quota for a day has not been met or if there have been cancellations and permits are available, you can secure a permit at the **Eastern Sierra InterAgency Visitor Center,** located along Hwy. 395, 1 mile south of Lone

You can't get any higher than the 14,495-foot summit of Mount Whitney, highest of all peaks in the continental U.S., and a once-in-a-lifetime hiking experience. Hikers come from around the nation and from countries around the world to climb the fairly popular Mount Whitney Trail, which climbs the mountain's most accessible slopes. The summit, on the eastern boundary of Sequoia National Park, can be climbed by the most fit and least altitude-sickness-prone hikers in one day. Veteran hikers often make a before-dawn (3–4am) start for the climb to the peak.

From Whitney Portal, the path to Mount Whitney ascends open country dotted with Jeffrey pine and white fir. About 3/4 mile out, a path forks west—the famed Mountaineer's Route used by climbers who tackle the eastern slope of the great mountain. Mount Whitney Trail soon crosses the north fork of Lone Pine Creek and shortly thereafter enters the John Muir Wilderness.

Pine. There is no fee for these unreserved permits that will be issued to walk-in visitors starting at 11am the day before the entry date. Additionally, any permits that have been reserved, but are not confirmed or picked up, will be cancelled and made available to other parties on a walk-in basis.

When a permit is issued, the hiker also receives a list of dos and don'ts that must be signed. Hikers are issued free "Wag-bags" and expected to carry and use these human waste disposal bags; there are no toilets en route to Mount Whitney. All food must be secured in bear canisters, which can be rented for a small fee ($2, but with a $40 deposit) at the Whitney Portal Store.

Whitney Portal Store (open daily May–Oct) has camping equipment, replacement stove fuel canisters, and toiletries, plus an assortment of beer, sodas, munchies, ibuprofen, and other anti-inflammatory meds. If you want an "I hiked Mount Whitney" cap or other souvenir, this is the place to get it. The store has a grill and serves hot meals—a very limited menu with giant portions: The cheeseburgers are huge and delicious, as are the pancakes, which are nearly the size of small pizzas. Some Whitney-conquering hikers have been known to march quickly back to the trail head with the cadence: beer-burger-beer-burger.

Best months for a Whitney trek are July, August, and September, when the trail is (usually) clear of snow and daytime temperatures are usually mild. Depending on the snowfall, experienced hikers sometimes stretch the season from June to October.

By some estimates, about half the people who make a reservation reach the summit. Do not exceed your ability and level of condition by forcing yourself to make the top. The trail is absolutely stunning the whole way; your day won't be wasted if you turn around short of the peak. The mountain will be waiting for you when you return to try again.

❶ Lone Pine Lake Switchbacks, long and short, ascend nearly 2 miles over sun-drenched slopes to Lone Pine Lake, visible from the main trail. A short (200 yd. or so) side trail leads to the rock-walled lake. Perfect for a (cold) swim.

❷ Outpost Camp After another half mile of climbing, the path skirts the south side of Bighorn Park (a long meadow), ascending alongside Long Pine Creek and, after crossing the creek, reaches Outpost Camp. It's a pleasant enough camp but usually ignored by summit-bound hikers because it's too low and too far from the top.

❸ Mirror Lake Farther up the trail, 4¹/₃ miles from the trail head, is tiny Mirror Lake (10,640 ft.). Switchbacking above the lake, the trail passes some rather stunted foxtail pine and emerges above the tree line. The trail traverses Trailside Meadow, seasonally splashed with wildflowers.

❹ Trail Camp About 6 miles out, you climb to 12,000 feet and reach Trail Camp, the last (highest) place to camp on the mountain.

Now, tackle the famed switchbacks—96 of them. First, there are some longer ones, and then, about halfway along the $2\frac{1}{4}$-mile ascent to Trailcrest, you'll encounter a series of switchbacks fitted with handrails. If you're hiking this trail when it's icy, you'll know why the handrails were installed. Use them and appreciate them.

5 Trailcrest About $8\frac{1}{2}$ miles from the trail head, you'll reach Trailcrest, a pass located at 13,714 feet, at the boundary of Sequoia National Park. With nearly 100 switchbacks under your boots, you get a feeling of accomplishment when you look down at Trail Camp, seemingly so small and so far down the mountain.

The climb resumes as the path winds among large blocks of talus and between dramatic rock pinnacles. Enjoy stone-framed views of Owens Valley to the east. As for the western view, well, don't look if you're afraid of heights because there's quite a drop-off. Nevertheless, while an acrophobe's nightmare, the trail is plenty wide and distinct as it traverses the ridge.

6 Whitney Summit About 10 miles out, Whitney's summit pops into view, and you continue around to the southwest side of the peak. Choose among several steep summit routes marked with cairns. Gaining the summit, you'll find a register next to the mountaineers hut and the very highest point just east of the hut.

Oh, the view from all directions: To the north, the panorama of summits includes Mount Williamson (second-highest peak in the continental U.S.), and to the south, the procession of peaks includes Mount Langley and Mount Muir. To the west are the Sawtooth Peaks, the Kaweah Peaks, and a section of the Great Western Divide. And to the east, shimmering like some mirage far below, is the Owens Valley.

While it's tempting to want to linger on the summit for a long and well-deserved rest, be aware that hikers frequently underestimate the length of time required for the descent. You do not want to rush down the mountain on rubbery legs—that's how injuries occur—and you want to return to the trail head before dark. Enjoy your passage down the mountain, but remember to stay focused and watch your step.

It's somewhat fitting, somewhat not, that this highest of the High Sierra was named for geologist Josiah Dwight Whitney. At Whitney's urging, the California legislature founded and funded the California State Geological Survey in 1860 and placed him in charge.

In 1871, Whitney sent Clarence King, mountaineer extraordinaire and Geological Survey researcher, to the High Sierra for his second attempt (bad weather had hampered the first) at finding the highest peak. King reached what he thought was the highest peak and named it "Whitney." Alas, it was discovered a few years later that King had climbed the wrong peak (Mount Langley), located 6 miles south.

Before King could return to scale the right peak, some Lone Pine residents climbed it and named it Fisherman's Peak.

The last couple miles of trail to Whitney's summit is the climax of the John Muir Trail, which begins in Yosemite Valley; this meeting on the map of Muir and Whitney is ironic because Whitney really disliked the great naturalist.

Whitney had long insisted Yosemite Valley was the work of faulting. Upstart Muir advanced the then-revolutionary theory that Yosemite was carved by glaciers. "A mere sheepherder, an ignoramus," Whitney called Muir. "A more absurd theory was never advanced."

Unhappily for Whitney's place in geologic history, Muir's glaciation theory has proven to be largely correct. Still, Whitney's name remains at the top—elevation-wise, anyway, a few hundred feet higher than 14,015-foot Mount Muir, just south of Mount Whitney.

SLEEPING & EATING

ACCOMMODATIONS

★ **Grant Grove Cabins** The cabins range from back-to-nature shelter—no-frills, low-cost tent-cabins equipped with kerosene lanterns and no plumbing—to luxury in the woods—beautifully restored historic structures, complete with electricity, modern plumbing, and private baths. Linens are provided in all cabins, which are a short walk from the visitor center and restaurant.

CA 180, Grant Grove Village, inside the park, CA 93633. Send mail to Sequoia–Kings Canyon Park Services Company, 5755 E. Kings Canyon Rd., Ste. 101, Fresno, CA 93727. ✆ **866/522-6966** or 559/335-5500. www.sequoia-kingscanyon.com. 53 units (9 with private bathroom). $63–$91 cabin with shared bathroom; $129–$140 cabin with private bathroom. AE, DISC, MC, V. Register at Grant Grove Village Registration Center, between the restaurant and gift shop. **Close to:** Grant Grove.

John Muir Lodge Located in an idyllic forest, with stunning views, this classic national park lodge was built from logs in 1998. Rooms come with modern amenities, including private bathrooms and coffeemakers, and two queen beds (one room has a queen bed and a queen sleeper sofa).

CA 180, Grant Grove Village, inside the park, CA 93633. Send mail to Sequoia–Kings Canyon Park Services Company, 5755 E. Kings Canyon Rd., Ste. 101, Fresno, CA 93727. ✆ **866/522-6966** or 559/335-5500. www.sequoia-kingscanyon.com. 30 units. $170–$180 double. AE, DISC, MC, V. Register at Grant Grove Village Registration Center, between the restaurant and gift shop. Tram no. 9. **Close to:** Grant Grove.

★★ **Montecito Sequoia Lodge** The family-oriented, mountain lodge–style resort, near a small lake, provides a variety of seasonal activities, including water- and snow sports, and programs for children and teens. Accommodations vary from those sleeping two to eight; rooms have private baths. Buffet-style meals are served in the dining room. Also on site are a bar, a Jacuzzi, and a laundry room.

63410 General's Hwy, Kings Canyon National Park, CA 93633. ✆ **800/227-9900.** www.mslodge.com. 36 rooms, 14 cabins with shared baths. $99–$189 double. Rates include all meals. AE, DISC, MC, V. Take CA 180 into Kings Canyon National Park, turn right at the fork, and drive 8 miles south to the lodge entrance, turn right, and follow the road about 1/2 mile to the parking lot. **Close to:** Monarch Lakes.

Silver City Mountain Resort Book early January for best selection amongst three cabin choices in the woods: rustic, comfy cabins, and Swiss chalets. Relax by the wood-burning stove after a day on the trail. Guests must bring their own linens; refrigerators and barbeques provided for most units. A restaurant on site serves breakfast, lunch, and dinner Thursday through Monday.

Mineral King Rd, Three Rivers, CA 93271. ✆ **559/561-3223,** 805/461-3223 in winter. www.silvercityresort.com. 14 cabins, 7 with shared central bathhouse. $75–$395 cabin. Discounts June 1–15 and after Sept 18. MC, V. Closed Nov–May. Drive up Mineral King Rd. for 21 miles. **Close to:** Giant Forest.

Wuksachi Lodge Nestled in a setting of forest and mountains, this upscale lodge provides all the comforts of home. Rooms appointed in woodsy, Mission-style decor include king and queen beds, as well as sleeper sofas; some mini-suites are available. Other amenities include Wi-Fi, a restaurant, shops, and a relaxing lounge. The lodge is conveniently located near hiking trails and is minutes from the visitor center.

64740 Wuksachi Way, inside the park, CA 93262. ✆ **888/252-5757** or 559/253-2199. www.visitsequoia.com. 102 units. May–Oct $182–$252 double; Nov–Apr $89–$169 double. AE, DISC, MC, V. **Close to:** Giant Forest.

CAMPING

In Sequoia

Two National Park campgrounds—Dorst and Lodgepole—accept reservations up to six months in advance (✆ **877-444-6777;** www.recreation.gov); other park campgrounds are first-come, first-served.

The two biggest campgrounds in the park are in the Lodgepole area. The **Lodgepole Campground,** which has flush toilets, is often crowded, but it's pretty and near some spectacular big trees. Nearby backcountry trails offer some solitude. Close to the campground are a grocery store, restaurant, visitor center, children's nature center, evening ranger programs, and gift shop. From Giant Forest Museum, drive 5 miles northeast on the Generals Highway.

Dorst Campground, located 14 miles northwest of Giant Forest via the Generals Highway, is a high-elevation campground that offers easy access to Muir Grove and some pleasant backcountry trails. It has flush toilets and evening ranger programs. Group campsites are also available here by reservation.

The two campgrounds in the Mineral King area are open to tents only—no RVs or trailers. **Atwell Mill Campground** is a scenic, small campground near the East Fork of the Kaweah River, at Atwell Creek. It has pit toilets. From Three Rivers, take Mineral King Road east for 20 miles to the campground. **Cold Springs Campground,** which also has pit toilets, is a beautiful place to stay—it's just not very accessible. Once you get there, however, you'll be rewarded with stunning scenery. It's also a good starting point for many backcountry hikes, as it's near the Mineral King Ranger Station. From Three Rivers, take Mineral King Road east for 25 miles to the campground.

In Kings Canyon

All of the campgrounds in Kings Canyon are first-come, first-served only (reservations are not available), and all have flush toilets. Additional information can be obtained by calling the general Sequoia & Kings Canyon information line (✆ **559/565-3341**).

In the Grant Grove area, there are three attractive campgrounds near the big trees—**Azalea, Crystal Springs,** and **Sunset**—which have a nice woodsy feel, are close to park facilities, and offer evening ranger programs. To get to them from the Big Stump entrance, take CA 180 east about 1¾ miles.

RESTAURANTS

★ **Anne Lang's Emporium** DELI Grab a sandwich, salad, or box lunch to take into the park, or dine inside, instead. Selection includes daily soup specials and fresh-baked goods. Top your meal off with a smoothie, an Italian soda, a hot espresso drink, or some ice cream—and you're ready to hit the trail.

41651 Sierra Dr., Three Rivers, CA 93271. ✆ **559/561-4937.** Most items $2.95–$5.95. MC, V. Mon–Fri 10am–4pm, Sat–Sun 11am–4pm; store/ice cream parlor Mon–Fri 10am–5pm, Sat–Sun 11am–5:30pm. MC, V. **Close to:** Giant Forest.

★★ **Brewbaker's Restaurant Brewery** MICROBREWERY A post-hike indulgence of the highest order: Memorable microbrews and tasty soda pops are brewed right here. It's a great place to quaff your thirst and satisfy your hunger with burgers, chili, and pizzas—even fish and chips. Sit at the brass bar for cozy ambience or upstairs for a great view of the city.

219 E. Main St., Visalia, CA 93291. ✆ **559/627-2739.** Main courses $7–$21. Daily 11:30am–10pm. AE, DISC, MC, V. **Close to:** Giant Forest.

Grant Grove Restaurant AMERICAN The folks here keep it simple, down-home, and very tasty. This sit-down cafe provides a nice alternative to fast-food options in the busy part of the park. You can find standard breakfast and lunch choices available; dinner entrees include pasta, steaks, chicken, and more.

Grant Grove Village, inside the park, CA 93633. ✆ **559-335-5500.** www.sequoia-kingscanyon.com. Breakfast and lunch $4–$11; dinner $7–$25. AE, DISC, MC, V. Mid-May to Aug daily 7am–2pm and 5–9pm; Sept to mid-May daily 8am–2pm and 5–7pm. **Close to:** Grant Grove.

Hummingbirds AMERICAN In a world dominated by cookie-cutter chains, this diner prepares real, authentic American fare—fresh, flavorful, hearty, and homemade. The menu includes stick-to-the-ribs specials like country eggs Benedict, cornbread, burgers, steaks, and more. Do not miss the freshly baked desserts featuring locally grown fruits and berries—think pies, cobblers, and cakes.

35591 E. Kings Canyon Rd., Squaw Valley, CA 93675. ✆ **559/338-0160.** Menu items $4.25–$15. AE, MC, V. Daily 7:30am–8:30pm. 19 miles west of the Kings Canyon park boundary. **Close to:** Grant Grove.

Lodgepole Market DELI In the Lodgepole Market Center are two fast-food choices made-to-order. Watchtower Deli offers sandwiches, salads, and wraps, and Harrison BBQ & Grill serves up basic burgers, hot dogs, and pizza. Ice cream is also available for a sweet post-hike treat.

63204 Lodgepole Rd., inside the park, Sequoia National Park, CA 93262. ✆ **559/565-3301.** www.visit sequoia.com. Most items $3–$8. AE, MC, V. Daily 8am–8pm. Snack bar open year round; deli closed Nov–Apr. **Close to:** Giant Forest.

★ **Wuksachi Dining Room** AMERICAN With its warm, natural-wood ambience, including a gorgeous stone fireplace and striking views, this is the place to savor the moment while dining on deliciously prepared meals. Open for breakfast, lunch, and dinner—including meat, seafood, and vegetarian entrees—it's the perfect end to a perfect day outdoors.

Wuksachi Lodge, 64740 Wuksachi Way, inside the park, CA 93262. ✆ **559/565-4070,** ext. 608. Dinner reservations required. Sandwiches and salads $4–$12; main courses $17–$34. AE, DISC, MC, V. Daily 7–10am, 11:30am–2pm, and 5–10pm. **Close to:** Giant Forest.

10

Lake Tahoe

Lake Tahoe is easy to like, hard to know.

The lake's alpine grandeur sure is easy on the eye, but public access to the lakeshore is in short supply, hindering (but not halting) the kind of intimacy that hikers develop with other California scenic gems.

Fortunately for the hiker, there are ways to reach Tahoe's natural treasures. While highways and extensive lakeside properties ring much of the shore, significant parts of the shoreline and the nearby High Sierra backcountry are owned by California State Parks and the U.S. Forest Service. These public lands boast some terrific pathways along the lakeshore and in the Sierra Nevada rising above it.

The largest alpine lake in North America, Lake Tahoe measures 22 miles long and 12 miles wide, and has 72 miles of shoreline. About two-thirds of that shoreline is in California. The lake is mighty deep, too: 1,645 feet at its maximum depth, making it the second-deepest lake in the U.S., trailing only Oregon's Crater Lake.

From the Taylor Creek Visitor Center, trails radiate outward like spokes from a wheel. My favorite little walk is on Rainbow Trail (.5 mile round-trip) that leads from pine forest to a wildflower-strewn meadow to the Stream Profile Chamber, an underground viewing chamber that offers a fish's-eye view of Taylor Creek. Through the chamber's windows, you can see trout feed and watch other aquatic life. During early autumn, you can see the Kokanee salmon run.

Trail of the Washoe (.75-mile loop) tells the story of the Native Americans who called *Da ow a ga* (Lake Tahoe) home for thousands of years. The lake and environs have been (and still are) the geographical, indeed spiritual, focus of the tribe.

For me, the best part of hiking Lake Tahoe is walking along the lakeshore and observing "the three blues:" blue lupine, blue lake, and blue sky. I've selected a handful of trails, ranging from 2 to 12 miles long, that individually and collectively offer a great sampling of the Tahoe hiking experience.

The challenge for the hiker in Lake Tahoe is not finding a trail to hike, but coming up with a representative sampling of Tahoe trails that are memorable footpaths. (Hundreds of miles of trail crisscross the Tahoe Basin; however, many of these trails are better suited for mountain bicyclists and cross-country skiers.)

If you have 2 weeks to hike and want to circumnavigate the lake, head out on the 165-mile-long Tahoe Rim Trail. If you have 2 or 3 days to hike, enjoy my favorite lakeshore ramble, a walk in the ponderosa pines, and a great hike into the Desolation Wilderness.

"Three months of camp life on Lake Tahoe would restore an Egyptian mummy to pristine vigor; and give him an appetite like an alligator," wrote Mark Twain. I don't know about 3 months of camping, but I can promise that 3 days of hiking around Lake Tahoe will definitely be a restorative experience.

ESSENTIALS

GETTING THERE

By Car

It's a 4-hour drive from San Francisco. Take I-80 east to Sacramento, then U.S. 50 to the South Shore, or I-80 east to Hwy. 89 or Hwy. 267 to the North Shore. Be prepared for snow in the winter. During heavy storms, you won't be permitted to pass the CHP (California Highway Patrol) checkpoints without four-wheel-drive or chains. From Los Angeles, it's a 9-hour drive. Take I-5 through the Central Valley to Sacramento, and then follow the directions above.

By Plane

Reno–Tahoe International Airport (45 min. to North Shore, 90 min. to South Shore; www.renoairport.com) runs regular service by 10 major airlines, including American, Delta, and United. Rent a car or take a shuttle up to the lake: **North Lake Tahoe Express** (✆ **866/216-5222;** www.northlaketahoeexpress.com) serves the North and West shores, **South Tahoe Express** (✆ **866/898-2463;** www.southtahoeexpress.com) serves the South Shore (1-day advance reservations recommended).

By Bus

Greyhound Bus Lines (✆ **800/229-9424;** www.greyhound.com) serves both Truckee and South Lake Tahoe with daily arrivals from San Francisco and Sacramento.

By Train

Amtrak (✆ **800/USA-RAIL;** www.amtrak.com) stops in Truckee, 10 miles north of the lake. Public transportation (TART or Truce Trolley) is available from the train depot, or you can take a taxi to the North Shore.

VISITOR INFORMATION

The **Taylor Creek Visitor Center** (✆ **530/543-2674**) is a great place to get to know the lake, with interpretive displays, naturalist-led walks, and family-friendly trails. The paths offer a great introduction to the history and ecology of what Native Americans called "The Lake of the Sky." The center is located 3 miles north of South Lake Tahoe, off Hwy. 89. It offers a variety of maps, brochures, t-shirts, souvenirs, and other items available for purchase. You can also get wilderness permits (for forays into the Desolation Wilderness) and participate in interpretive programs. The visitor center is open daily 8:00am–5:30pm during the summer months, with shorter hours during October; the center is closed during the winter.

In Tahoe City, stop by the **Tahoe City Visitor Information Center,** 380 North Lake Blvd. (✆ **800/824-6348;** www.gotahoenorth.com). In Incline Village, go to the **Incline Village/Crystal Bay Visitors Center,** 969 Tahoe Blvd. (✆ **800/468-2463** or 775/832-1606). In South Lake Tahoe, go to the **Lake Tahoe Visitors Authority,** 1156 Ski Run Blvd. (✆**800/288-2463** or 775/588-5900; www.bluelaketahoe.com), or to the **South Lake Tahoe Chamber of Commerce,** 3066 Lake Tahoe Blvd. (✆ **530/541-5255;** www.tahoeinfo.com). Many other websites offer information about Lake Tahoe, including www.virtualtahoe.com, www.skilaketahoe.com, and www.tahoevacationguide.com.

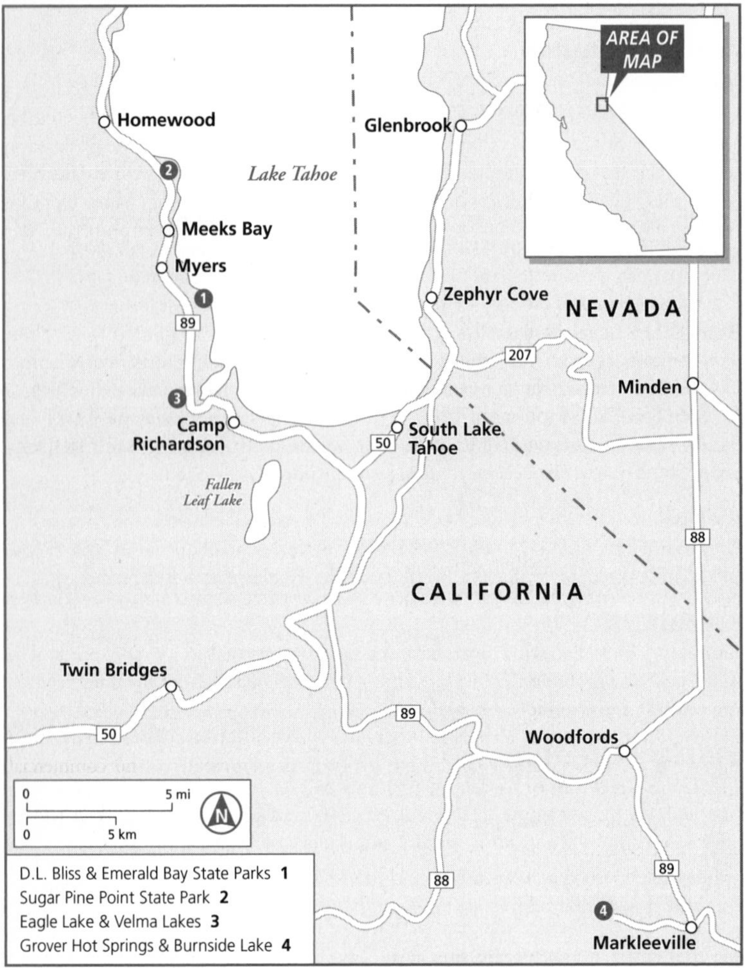

GETTING AROUND

To get to the lake, take U.S. 395 South to Route 431 for the North Shore or U.S. 50 for the South Shore. All the roads leading to the lake are scenic, but the panorama as you descend into Lake Tahoe Basin from Route 431 is particularly spectacular.

ORIENTATION

Before you visit Tahoe, it's important to understand the distinction between the North and the South shores. Don't let the "City" in the North Shore's "Tahoe City" fool you; you can drive through it in a couple of minutes. To the contrary, South Lake Tahoe brims

Tips A Tale of Two Shores

Before you visit Tahoe, it's important to understand the distinction between the North and the South shores. Don't let the "City" in the North Shore's "Tahoe City" fool you; you can drive through it in a couple of minutes. To the contrary, South Lake Tahoe brims with high-rise casinos, motels, and mini-malls. Where you choose to stay is important because driving from one end of the lake to the other takes an hour or more in summer and can be treacherous in winter.

So which side is for you? If you're here for gambling or entertainment, go south: The selection of casinos is better, with more action and more lodgings, often at better rates. If you seek a relaxing, outdoor retreat, head to the North Shore, which has a better selection of high-quality resorts and vacation rentals. The woodsy West Shore has the most camping spots, and the East Shore, protected from development, has no commercial activity.

Wherever you stay, you'll find plenty of water and mountain sports. The lake is crowded during summer and ski season, so plan far ahead. It's much easier to get reservations for the spring and fall, and rates drop significantly. Many vacation homes and condominiums are rentable; call the visitor-center bureaus or visit the websites below under "Visitor Information" for a list of rental agents.

with high-rise casinos, motels, and mini-malls. Where you choose to stay is important because driving from one end of the lake to the other takes an hour or more in summer and can be treacherous in winter.

So which side is for you? If you're here for gambling or entertainment, go south: The selection of casinos is better, with more action and more lodgings, often at better rates. If you seek a relaxing, outdoor retreat, head to the North Shore, which has a better selection of high-quality resorts and vacation rentals. The woodsy West Shore has the most camping spots, and the East Shore, protected from development, has no commercial activity.

Wherever you stay, you'll find plenty of water and mountain sports. The lake is crowded during summer and ski season, so plan far ahead. It's much easier to get reservations for the spring and fall, and rates drop significantly. Many vacation homes and condominiums are rentable; call the visitor-center bureaus.

D.L. BLISS & EMERALD BAY STATE PARKS ★

Difficulty rating: Moderate

Distance: 6 miles round-trip from Rubicon Point to Emerald Point; 9 miles round-trip to Vikingsholm

Estimated time: 4–5 hr.

Elevation gain: 400 feet

Costs/permits: $5 state park day-use fee

Best time to go: June to October

Website: www.parks.ca.gov

Recommended map: California State Parks D.L. Bliss & Emerald Bay State Parks map

Trail head GPS: Rubicon Point N 38 59.911, W 120 05.866; Vikingsholm N 38 57.175, W 120 06.409

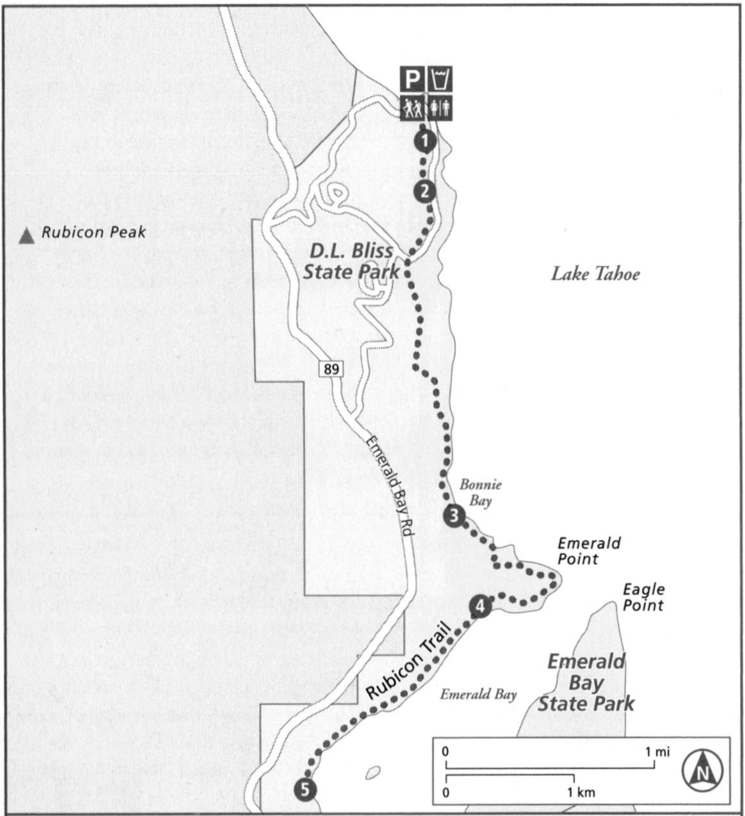

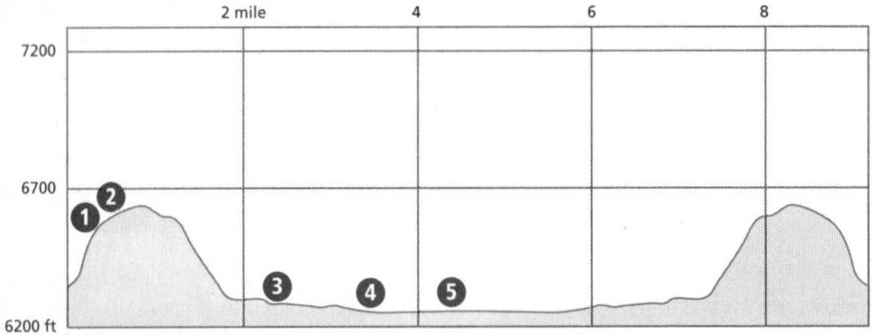

N 38 59.911, W 120 05.866 Trail head
1 N 38 59.805, W 120 05.743 (0.3 miles): Pass spur trail to old lighthouse
2 N 38 59.590, W 120 05.755 (0.5 miles): Balancing Rock
3 N 38 58.279, W 120 05.610 (2.3 miles): Trail reaches Bonnie Bay
4 N 38 57.898, W 120 05.454 (3.4 miles): Emerald Bay
5 N 38 57.175, W 120 06.409 (4.5 miles): Vikingsholm

Trail head directions: From South Lake Tahoe, drive 11 miles north on Hwy. 89 to the D.L. Bliss State Park entrance. If you're coming from Tahoe City, drive 16 miles south on Hwy. 89 to the park entrance. Follow the park road (Lester Beach Rd.) 2½ miles to its end at the parking area for Calawee Cove Beach. The trail begins at the east end of the lot. To reach the trail head for Vikingsholm from South Lake Tahoe, drive north 9 miles on Hwy. 89 to the Vikingsholm Overlook; a large parking area is on your right. If you're coming from Tahoe City, drive 18 miles south on Hwy. 89.

Adjoining state parks D.L. Bliss and Emerald Bay protect 6 miles of Lake Tahoe's shore. Even if the parks themselves weren't so splendidly scenic, they would still attract lots of visitors because they offer something in short supply around Lake Tahoe: public access to the lake. Rubicon Trail, a superb shoreline pathway, contours over shady slopes, linking the two parks and offering grand views of what Indians called the "Lake in the Sky." Keep an eye on the sky for osprey, canny fishing birds that dive toward the lake and perch in the shoreline trees.

Sunbathers hit the beach while hikers choose between two paths—an upper and lower trail—looping south. Take either; they rejoin in a bit more than a ¼-mile at the Old Lighthouse.

❶ **Old Lighthouse** The short spur trail leading to the lighthouse is hardly worth the effort; the lighthouse looks more like an outhouse. Surely, at one time, the lighthouse must have offered quite a view of the lake, but these days, conifers screen out much of the scene.

Rubicon Trail climbs gently south, soon offering much better views of Lake Tahoe. A steel cable along the most narrow and precipitous sections of trail offers the hiker something secure to hold.

Pause for a moment on the narrow path to give thanks to park namesake D.L. Bliss, a pioneering timber tycoon, railroad owner, and banker. The Bliss family donated the core of the park to the state park system in 1929.

A half-mile from the trail head, you'll arrive at some rock pinnacles. Kids will imagine that the natural stone sculptures resemble prehistoric animals and many more fanciful figures.

❷ **Balancing Rock** D.L. Bliss and Emerald Bay state parks share a shoreline and similar natural features, but only Bliss boasts a world-class boulder. Balancing Rock, 130 tons of granite, balances—precariously, it would seem—atop two fracturing and eroding stone pedestals. Sooner or later, the rock will roll, but in the meantime, you can photograph it from a ½-mile interpretive trail.

For the tree-loving hiker, Rubicon Trail offers plenty of arboreal companionship. You get in the Christmas spirit when you wander through stands of red and white fir. Joining the stately firs are ponderosa pine, Jeffrey pine, and incense cedar. "Leaf peepers" will certainly want to see how autumn colors Tahoe's aspen and maple trees.

Still, not all park foliage is 100 feet high. Bushes growing near the forest trees include manzanita, alpine prickly currant, and ceanothus. Monkeyflower, columbine, lupine, leopard lily, and many more wildflowers splash spring and summer color on the slopes.

❸ **Bonnie Bay** Continue your ascent into a white fir forest. Emerging from the trees, the path begins a 1-mile descent via switchbacks to the lakeshore at Bonnie Bay, a fine place to take a break.

Very soon after Bonnie Bay, the trail splits: The leftward branch meanders ¾ mile around Emerald Point to Emerald

Vikingsholm

Most park visitors come not to see flora's handiwork, but Lora's handiwork—Lora Knight, that is. In 1928, Knight commissioned Swede Lennart Palme to build her a 9th-century Norse Castle. A year later, Vikingsholm—turrets, towers, and 38 rooms—was completed. Knight, a Santa Barbaran, spent summers in her authentically furnished fortress until her death in 1945.

Guides give tours of Vikingsholm daily 10am to 4pm, every half-hour, from June through Labor Day, then only on the weekends for a few more weeks.

Even if you can't schedule a Vikingsholm tour, the 2-mile round-trip hike on Vikingsholm Trail (a road closed to vehicle traffic) to view the curious structure is well worth the effort. Just looking at the exterior of the castle (not a single tree was disturbed when it was constructed) in its lakeside setting is impressive.

Bay; the right branch, aptly named Bypass Trail, reaches Emerald Bay in 1/4 mile.

4 Emerald Bay Emerald Bay is not only beautiful to behold, it's also an officially designated underwater state park for its natural attractions, as well as 19th and 20th century artifacts resting on the bottom of the bay.

Wide Bypass Trail travels through impressive stands of large Jeffrey pine and incense cedar. After the trails rejoin, you cross the boundary from D.L. Bliss State Park into Emerald Bay State Park and hike another 1/2 mile among pine, fir, and incense cedar to the park's Boat Camp. This camp is an ideal lakeside picnic spot.

For its last mile, Rubicon Trail sticks close to shore, crossing a couple of bridges over small creeks and springs. Hikers make only a single foray inland to climb around Parson Rock, a fine perch for photographers.

5 Vikingsholm Picnic tables herald your arrival at Vikingsholm, the turnaround point, unless you've arranged to have transportation waiting for you at Vikingsholm parking lot, a 1-mile switchbacking ascent (with 400-ft. elevation gain) on paved Vikingsholm Trail.

Another reward at trail's end is Emerald Bay itself, one of Tahoe's best beaches. Swimmers can brave the bay's chilly waters, which warm only to the low 60s (low teens Celsius), even in mid-summer.

SUGAR PINE POINT STATE PARK (Kids)

Difficulty rating: Easy to strenuous

Distance: 4.5 mile loop to first bridge; 6.5 miles round-trip to Lily Pond; 14 miles round-trip to Duck Lake; 14.5 miles round-trip to Lost Lake

Estimated time: 2–7 hr., depending on hike

Elevation gain: 300–1,450 ft., depending on hike

Costs/permits: $5 California state park day-use fee per vehicle

Best time to go: May to October

Website: www.parks.ca.gov

Recommended map: Sugar Pine Point State Park map

Trail head GPS: N 39 03.437, W 120 07.287

Trail head directions: From Hwy. 89, drive 9 miles south of Tahoe City and 18 miles north of South Lake Tahoe; turn west onto the signed access road for Sugar Pine Point State Park and park your vehicle in the day-use lot located close to the entry station. Follow the paved pathway toward the campground. You'll soon spot a signed trail leading east to the lakeshore part of the park. Make a note to yourself to check out the park's 2 miles of lovely lakefront, including park namesake Sugar Pine Point, a forested promontory perched above the western shore of Lake Tahoe.

Sugar Pine Point names a forested promontory perched above the western shore of Lake Tahoe, as well as a state park that offers terrific hiking. Grand stands of sugar pine and lush mountain meadows here are ringed by aspen. Enjoy picnicking along General Creek, an escape from Tahoe crowds. Sugar Pine Point's trail system offers numerous options for hikers of all abilities and energy levels, with trails extending to the state park boundary, then into the El Dorado National Forest.

Turn-of-the-20th-century banker Isaias Hellman built "the finest High Sierra summer house in California"—a rustic, yet elegant three-story mansion overlooking the lake. Now known as the Ehrman Mansion (for a later owner), the house is now part of the state park and open for guided tours during the summer months. Exhibits about the natural history of the Tahoe Basin can be viewed in the park's nature center, located in the Ehrman Mansion's former power-generating plant.

❶ Campground Continue toward the campground and your rendezvous with General Creek Trail. Trailside interpretive panels point out the locale's history as a site for the Nordic skiing venue during the 1960 Winter Olympics. The paved path crosses the first campground access road (leading to sites 1–75), then leads to a second camp road (leading to sites 76–125). Past the road, join the dirt trail that swings left (south) and soon meets Creek Trail. Turn right and soon meet up with General Creek Trail, a dirt road.

The campground paths leading to General Creek Trail can be a bit confusing, so if you have any navigation issues at all, simply head for campsite 150, where you'll find the beginning of the trail.

❷ Bridge over General Creek The wide path leads west along the north bank of General Creek. At a signed junction, you'll spot a trail leading down to a bridge crossing the creek. This bridge, and another 2 miles farther along General Creek Trail, allow a pleasant loop trip without getting your feet wet.

The trail meanders through well-spaced stands of Jeffrey and sugar pine, and across meadowland seasonally sprinkled with lupine and aster. Sugar pines were once even more numerous. In the 1870s, there was a lot of logging in this part of the Tahoe Basin in order to supply Comstock Lode miners with lumber and firewood. One of Lake Tahoe's first permanent residents was "General" William Phipps, who homesteaded the land we now call Sugar Pine Point in 1860. Phipps protected his 160 acres from being logged.

Those granite boulders you see looking so out of place in the sylvan scene were left behind ages ago by a retreating glacier. Hikers with an interest in geology will enjoy glimpses of the two large lateral moraines that border the valley of General Creek.

❸ Footbridge A bit more than 2 miles along the trail, you'll reach a second footbridge. You can loop back to the trail

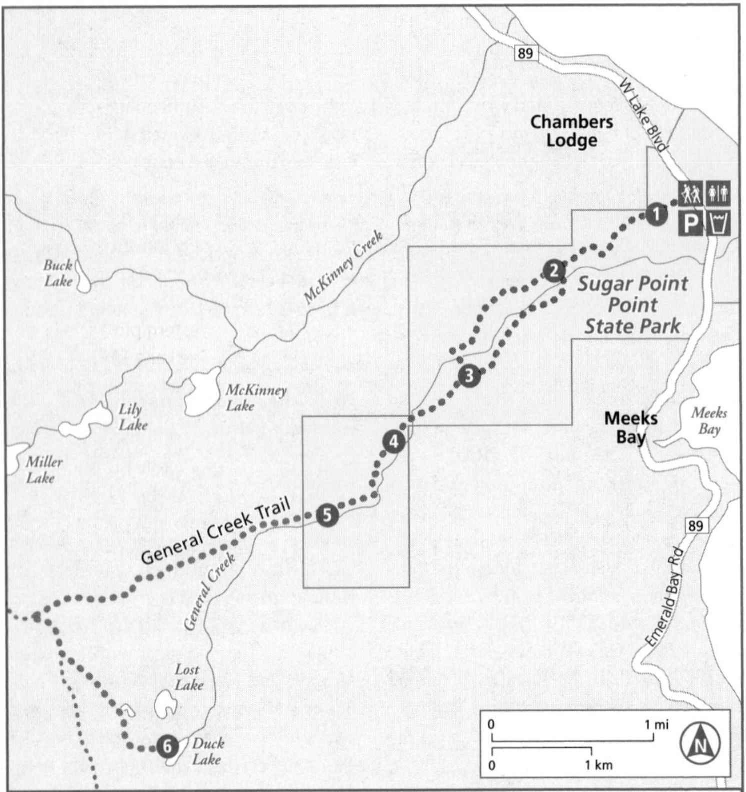

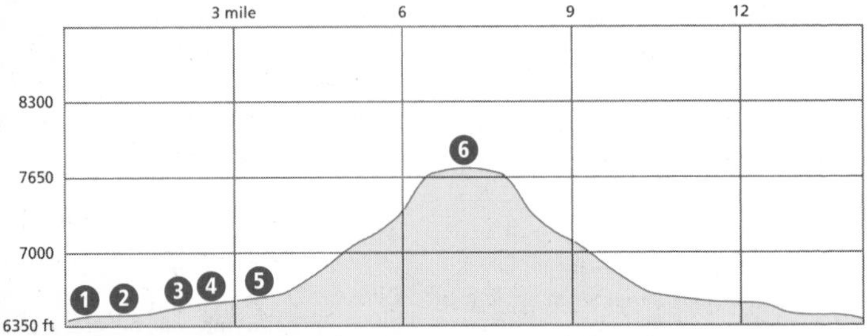

N 39 03.437, W 120 07.287 Trail head
1 N 39 03.358, W 120 07.429 (0.2 miles): Campground
2 N 39 03.019, W 120 08.163 (1.2 miles): Cross bridge over General Creek
3 N 39 02.551, W 120 08.751 (2.1 miles): Footbridge and turnaround point
4 N 39 02.176, W 120 09.313 (2.8 miles): Junction with Lily Pond Side Trail
5 N 39 01.825, W 120 09.762 (3.5 miles): Exit El Dorado National Forest
6 N 39 00.010, W 120 10.861 (7.2 miles): Duck Lake

Fun Facts The Sugar Pine

The great naturalist John Muir described the sugar pine as the "king of the conifers." Muir found the tree's sweet resin, which gives the tree its name, preferable to maple sugar. This tree is the largest species of pine, commonly growing from 130 to 200 feet tall, and with a trunk diameter of 5 to 8 feet. Its needles are in bundles of five. The sugar pine has long straight branches, weighed down at the tips by the cones. Sugar pine is notable for having the longest cones of any conifer (10–20 in. long).

The sugar pine, found in the mountains of California and Oregon, has been severely affected by white pine blister rot, a fungus accidentally introduced from Europe in 1909. Trees in the northern part of its range have been especially hard-hit. Fortunately for sugar pine and their admirers, the U.S. Forest Service has a program for developing rust-resistant sugar pine and their western pine relatives, and seedlings of these trees have been planted in the wild. The Lake Tahoe–based Sugar Pine Foundation has been particularly successful in finding disease-resistant sugar-pine seed trees and cooperating with the Forest Service to restore the species.

The ponderosa pine is also an attractive tree and can rather easily be distinguished from other pines with its distinctive bark: orange-ish colored, with black lining the crevices where the bark splits. Get close to these substantial pines, and you'll discover the needles grow in bundles of three and the bark smells like vanilla.

head via a path on the opposite side of General Creek. This makes for a fine family hike, as does the longer hike to Lily Pond, and leaves plenty of time for a visit to the lakeshore.

4 Lily Pond Side Trail junction Soon after passing the bridge, General Creek Trail dwindles to a footpath, and another half-mile's travel brings you to a signed junction with a side trail leading to Lily Pond; it's a 3/4-mile, heart-pounding ascent to the little pond. For families and those fully satisfied with a moderate hike, behold the pond lilies and head back to the trail head.

5 El Dorado National Forest Those bound for the lakes can retrace their steps to General Creek Trail and continue meandering above the creek. About 3 1/2 miles from the trail head, you'll exit the state park and enter El Dorado National Forest. The park is often used by long-distance hikers to gain access to the northerly part of the Desolation Wilderness, as well as to intersect the Pacific Crest Trail and other paths leading into the High Sierra backcountry west of Lake Tahoe.

After more meandering, the trail/dirt road crosses General Creek (no bridge this time), turns south, then east, and after a mile, crosses the creek fed by Lost Lake and Duck Lake.

6 Lost Lake and Duck Lake Now, the trail turns south again and climbs to the forested south shore of Lost Lake. Duck Lake is another 1/4 mile along the trail. Both scenic lakes offer good swimming.

Retrace your steps to the trail head. This time on the tree tour, keep an eye out for the stately white fir. In autumn, the black cottonwood and quaking aspen are something to behold.

EAGLE LAKE & VELMA LAKES ★

Difficulty rating: Easy to strenuous

Distance: 2 miles round-trip to Eagle Lake; 9 miles round-trip to Middle Velma Lake

Estimated time: 1 hr. to Eagle Lake; 4-5 hrs. to Velma

Elevation gain: 400–1,600 ft., depending on hike

Costs/permits: $5 day-use fee for parking at Eagle Falls Picnic area; wilderness permit (free and available at trail head) required

Best time to go: June to October

Website: www.parks.ca.gov

Recommended map: Desolation Wilderness Trail map

Trail head GPS: N 38 57.258, W 120 6.631

Trail head directions: From the junction of Hwy. 50 and Hwy. 89 in South Lake Tahoe, drive 9 miles north on Hwy. 89 to the signed turnoff on the left for Eagle Falls Picnic Area. If you're coming from Tahoe City, follow Hwy. 89 south 19 miles to the Eagle Falls Picnic Area. There is limited free parking alongside the highway. For a fee, you can park in the U.S. Forest Service lot. A picnic area is located just off the highway. The Tahoe City to Emerald Bay trolley makes a stop at the turnoff for the picnic area.

Desolation Wilderness, as it is called, at 12 miles long and 8 miles wide, is too popular with visitors to be considered desolate, and too close to Tahoe to be considered true wilderness, but it does offer a superb play land for anglers, swimmers, and hikers. One excellent Tahoe trail leads up dramatic, glacially sculpted Eagle Lake Canyon to a back-country basin containing the Velma lakes, as well as numerous lake-lets. Families with small children will enjoy the 1-mile climb through the forest to Eagle Lake. More experienced hikers should head for Lower, Middle, and Upper Velma lakes.

From the signed trail head, the path ascends up-canyon and soon splits. An upper leg ascends past interpretive panels describing the natural and human history of the region; the lower leg sticks closer to the river. The paths rejoin, and the path crosses Eagle Creek just above seasonal Eagle Falls on a sturdy steel footbridge.

❶ Upper Eagle Falls The upper Eagle Falls, located $^{1}/_{3}$ mile from the trail head, is pretty enough, but nowhere near as impressive as the lower falls, reached by a short walk descending from a trail head located on the lakeside of Hwy. 89.

The trail ascends a rock-strewn rise, enters Desolation Wilderness (marked by a sign), then reaches a second rise offering terrific views of Emerald Bay, Lake Tahoe, and the Carson Range.

❷ Side Trail to Eagle Lake Just short of a mile from the trail head is a junction. The right fork leads 200 yards to granite cliff–surrounded Eagle Lake, a perfect picnic spot. The lake, handsomely set in a glacial cirque below Maggie's Peak, was once nesting habitat for bald eagles and golden eagles—hence its name.

If you like Eagle Lake, consider that 100 lakes, both named and unnamed, are scattered like jewels in the Desolation

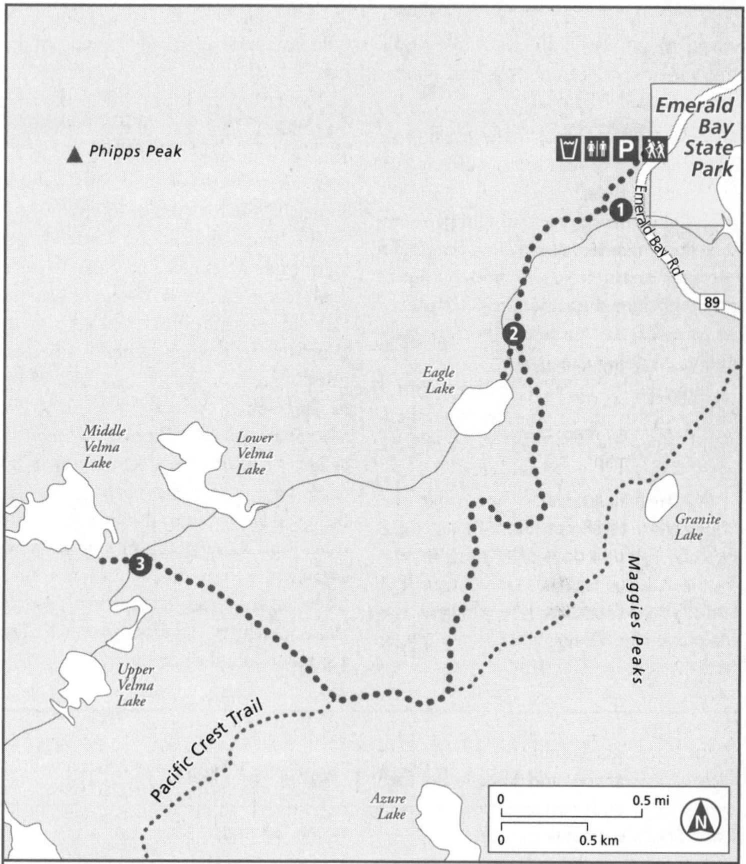

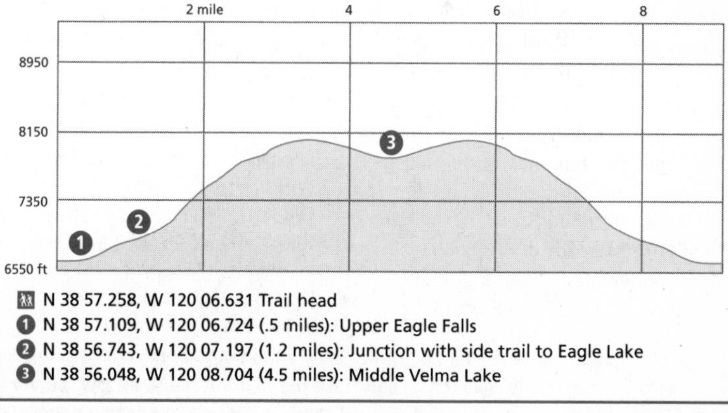

N 38 57.258, W 120 06.631 Trail head

❶ N 38 57.109, W 120 06.724 (.5 miles): Upper Eagle Falls

❷ N 38 56.743, W 120 07.197 (1.2 miles): Junction with side trail to Eagle Lake

❸ N 38 56.048, W 120 08.704 (4.5 miles): Middle Velma Lake

Wilderness. Aloha, Avalanche, Boomerang, Half Moon, and Hemlock are among the colorfully named lakes situated for the most part at about 8,000 feet in elevation and bordered with impressive and photogenic granite backdrops.

❸ Velma Lakes Trail After passing an unnamed lake on your left and crossing its outlet stream, you'll arrive at a trail junction. (The left-forking trail climbs south 1/3 mile to Upper Velma Lake.) Stay right and walk another quarter mile to a junction with famed Pacific Crest Trail. Stay right again and continue a short quarter-mile to Middle Velma Lake.

Sunbathe on the shore, swim out to a little rock island, try to catch a rainbow trout—the sprawling lake is a very mellow place to unwind.

For future reference, note that the Velma lakes are close to not one but three famous footpaths. In addition to the Pacific Crest Trail, the Tahoe Rim Trail and Tahoe Yosemite Trail traverse the Desolation Wilderness.

The Tahoe Rim Trail is a 165-mile long-distance hiking trail winding through the High Sierra and Carson Ranges of California and Nevada and looping around Lake Tahoe.

About 50 miles of trail above the lake's west shore are also part of the Pacific Crest Trail. First proposed in the late 1970s, the trail was completed in 2001, almost entirely through volunteer effort.

The Tahoe-Yosemite trail extends 185 miles from Meeks Bay at Lake Tahoe to Tuolumne Meadows in Yosemite National Park. It's not an official trail such as the John Muir Trail or Appalachian Trail; rather, its existence is due to a book, *Tahoe-Yosemite Trail*, written by trail author and *Wilderness Press* founder Thomas Winnett to describe a route long contemplated but never built across the High Sierra. The path, which receives no funding for maintenance and little governmental acknowledgement, is beloved by a cadre of Sierra hikers, who appreciate the volcanic terrain, handsome high elevation lakes and lush vegetation found along the trail.

GROVER HOT SPRINGS & BURNSIDE LAKE ★ Kids

Difficulty rating: Easy to strenuous

Distance: 3 miles round-trip to waterfall; 10 miles round-trip to Burnside Lake

Estimated time: 1½ hr. to waterfall; 56 hr. to Burnside Lake

Elevation gain: 2,100 ft.

Costs/permits: To use hot springs, $5 for adults, $3 for kids

Best time to go: May to October

Website: www.parks.ca.gov

Recommended map: California State Parks Grover Hot Springs State Park

Trail head GPS: N 38 41.760, W 119 50.596

Trail head directions: From Hwy. 89 in Markleeville (a half-hour drive from South Lake Tahoe), turn west on Hot Springs Rd. and drive 3½ miles to Grover Hot Springs State Park. Park in the lot just above the fence-enclosed hot springs. If you want to make the trip to Burnside Lake a one-way trip, you can drive to the lake. From the signed turnoff on Hwy. 88, drive 5½ miles down bumpy, dirt Burnside Rd. to road's end at the lake.

Nothing like a soothing soak in a hot spring after a long day on the trail. For the High Sierra visitor who wants to take a hike and "take the cure" in the same day, Grover Hot Springs State Park, located a bit south of Lake Tahoe, is the perfect destination. Enjoy a leisurely, family-friendly walk in the state park to a waterfall on Hot Springs Creek or a longer hike through the pines in Toiyabe National Forest to an alpine lake.

Join the signed Hot Springs Cutoff Trail through the park's large meadow. A bridge leads over Hot Springs Creek, a year-round watercourse. Some of the catchable trout planted in the creek are caught by campers for their suppers, though more serious anglers head for the nearby Carson River.

The quaking aspen fringing the meadow are particularly showy in autumn, when the fluttering leaves turn orange and gold. After $^{1}/_{3}$ mile from the trail head, you'll reach a junction with signed Burnside Lake Trail.

❶ **Burnside Lake Trail** Head left (west) about a half-mile, leaving the meadow behind and entering a thick forest.

❷ **Waterfall Trail** At a signed junction, the trail to the waterfall branches left, leading along Hot Springs Creek. Some minor rock climbing leads to an overlook above the small but vigorous falls. After admiring the falls, backtrack to the main trail. Burnside Lake Trail enters thicker forest and ascends, much more vigorously now, a mile to another junction. Charity Valley Trail heads south along Charity Valley Creek, but you stay with Burnside Lake Trail. The trail soon crosses Burnside Creek and climbs northwest, switchbacking up steep Jeffrey pine– and white fir–cloaked slopes. Near the top, you'll get a grand, over-the-shoulder view of Hot Springs Valley.

❸ **Burnside Lake** The last mile of this hike resembles the first mile—a walk through meadowland. The meadow below Burnside Lake is much wetter than the one in the state park, however, so take care to stay on the trail; you won't get your boots so wet, and you'll help protect the fragile meadow ecology.

Boulders perched above the lakeshore suggest fine picnic spots and inspiring places from which to contemplate pretty Burnside Lake.

Tucked in Hot Springs Valley, surrounded on three sides by Sierra Nevada peaks, Grover Hot Springs offers a soak in a setting as soothing as its waters. The granite peaks, including 10,023-foot Hawkins Peak to the northwest and 9,419-foot Markleeville Peak to the southwest, form an inspiring backdrop to an area that's been attracting visitors since the 1850s.

Don't expect a Baden-Baden–style, deluxe Euro-resort; Grover Hot Springs offers your basic soak—nothing more, nothing less. Bathers can sit in one hot pool (102°–105°F; 39°–41°C) fed by six mineral springs, and one cool pool. The two pools and the changing rooms are the extent of the state park facilities.

No, it's not the concrete pools, surrounded by a wooden fence (the effect is rather like a slightly seedy backyard swimming pool installed in the 1950s) but the setting that's inspiring in Grover Hot Springs.

At the park, true hot-springs aficionados can read up on the exact mineral content of Grover Hot Springs and find out just how many grams per gallon of magnesium carbonate and sodium sulfate the waters hold. Most bathers, even those without any interest in chemistry, will be happy to know that Grover, unlike most other hot springs, contains almost none of that nose-wrinkling sulfur.

Most visitors come to this out-of-the-way park for the waters, not the walking. Too bad, because the state park and surrounding national forest boast some inspiring footpaths.

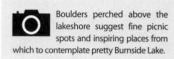

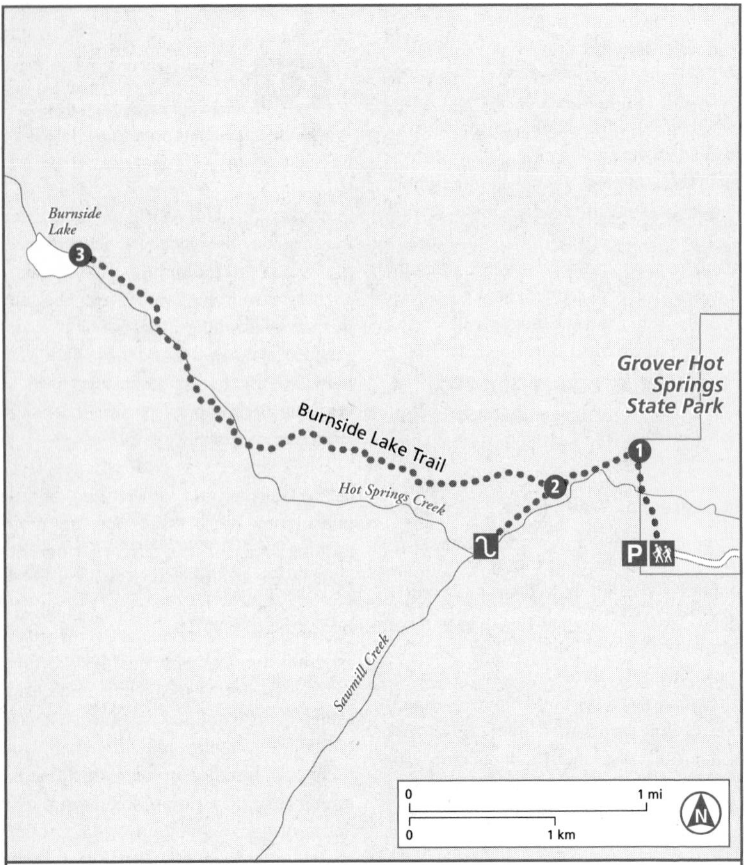

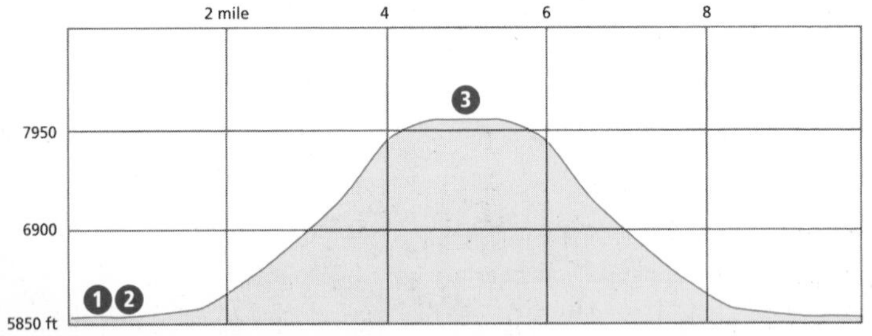

N 38 41.760, W 119 50.596 Trail head

1 N 38 42.083, W 119 50.760 (0.4 miles): Join Burnside Lake Trail

2 N 38 41.963, W 119 51.114 (0.8 miles): Follow spur trail to waterfall, then rejoin path

3 N 38 42.765, W 119 53.304 (5 miles): Burnside Lake

The "Heavenly Flyer" Zip-Line Thrill Ride

If you're looking to add some high-adrenaline thrills to your Lake Tahoe vacation, head over to the Heavenly Mountain Resort on the South Shore and take a ride on their new Heavenly Flyer, the longest zip line in the lower 48 states. Located at the top of the Heavenly Gondola's Adventure Peak, the Heavenly Flyer is sort of like a flying chair attached to a thick 3,100-foot-long cable that runs from the base to way up the mountainside. You buckle in at the take-off deck, and then descend 525 feet through the pine trees at an exhilarating 50 mph. Heck, the views of Lake Tahoe alone are worth the ride. The Heavenly Flyer is open year-round from 11am to 3pm daily, and a single-ride pass costs $30. For more information log on to **www.skiheavenly.com/mountain/heavenly_flyer**, or call the resort at ✆ **775/586-7000.**

SLEEPING & EATING

ACCOMMODATIONS

★★★ Camp Richardson Resort This is an outstanding full-service facility for short visits or group vacations; at its great location, beach and woods converge, and there's plenty of fun for all. Accommodations include campgrounds, an RV park, cabins, a hotel, and a beachside inn; many dining options, from deli lunches to elegant dinners; and organized activities and marina rentals. Book early.

1900 Jameson Beach Rd., Lake Tahoe, CA 96158. ✆ **800/544-1801** or 530/541-1801. www.camprichardson.com. $95–$195 double; $145–$250 cabins per day in winter, $745–$2,265 per week in summer; camping or RV hookup $20–$30 per day. Seasonal discount packages available on website. DISC, MC, V. **Close to:** D.L. Bliss & Emerald Bay State Parks.

★ Ferrari's Crown Resort It's been family first for decades around here. This no-frills motel has clean, comfortable rooms and a great lakefront location; some suites come with kitchenettes and fireplaces. Amenities include (seasonal) outdoor pools and Jacuzzis. Bargain rates off-season make this a year-round retreat filled with warmth and welcome.

8200 N. Lake Blvd., King's Beach, CA 96143. ✆ **800/645-2260** or 530/546-3388. www.tahoecrown.com. 72 units. $65–$139 double; $99–$235 2-bedroom suite or lakefront room. Rates include continental breakfast. Packages available. AE, DISC, MC, V. **Close to:** D.L. Bliss & Emerald Bay State Parks.

★★ The Resort at Squaw Creek Luxury abounds at this attractively appointed full-service, prize-winning, first-class resort and spa with every imaginable amenity available for true relaxation in a natural setting. You're close to many choices for dining, shopping, family, and business needs.

400 Squaw Creek Rd., Olympic Valley, CA 96146. ✆ **800/327-3353** or 530/583-6300. www.squawcreek.com. 403 units. $250–$395 double; $450–$1,900 suite. Packages available. AE, DC, DISC, MC, V. Valet parking $15. Free parking. **Close to:** Sugar Pine Point State Park.

The Shore House at Lake Tahoe All romance and nostalgia in this pretty bed-and-breakfast located on the lake. Cozy private rooms with individual entrances and fireplaces are made charming with knotty pine ambience and log-furnishings, and idyllic with featherbeds. Start the day with gourmet breakfast, enjoy nearby hiking trails, and relax at sunset in the outdoor hot tub by the lake.

7170 N. Lake Blvd., Tahoe Vista, CA 96148. ✆ **800/207-5160** or 530/546-7270. www.shorehouselaketahoe.com. 8 units, 1 cottage. $190–$250 double; $255–$290 cottage. Rates include full breakfast. DISC, MC, V. **Close to:** D.L. Bliss & Emerald Bay State Parks.

Sunnyside Lodge Located just steps from a gravel beach, water activities, and marina, this lodge is the stuff of dreams. A historic (1908) home transformed into a great, woodsy lodge with stone fireplaces and modern comforts. The Sunnyside Restaurant occupies the ground floor, but room service is also available. Ask for a lakefront room; a real treat with views and privacy.

1850 W. Lake Blvd., Tahoe City, CA 96145. ✆ **800/822-2754** or 530/583-7200. www.sunnysidetahoe.com. 23 units. $100–$295 double. Rates include continental breakfast. Packages available. AE, MC, V. **Close to:** Sugar Pine Point State Park.

★ **Tamarack Lodge** Hollywood history converges with North Shore ambience in this classic Tahoe hideaway. Accommodations include old-time cabins nestled in the pines, along with knotty-pine "poker rooms" once frequented by Clark Gable and Gary Cooper. Far less memorable are modern motel rooms—but the price is right and the location great.

2311 N. Lake Blvd., Tahoe City, CA 96145. ✆ **888/824-6323** or 530/583-3350. www.tamarackattahoe.com. 17 units, 4 cabins. $54–$145 double; $139–$379 cabin. DISC, MC, V. **Close to:** D.L. Bliss & Emerald Bay State Parks.

CAMPING

D. L. Bliss State Park, on the western shore (✆ **530/525-7277**), has 168 campsites, fine beaches, and hiking trails; campground is closed in winter. **Sugar Pine Point State Park,** open year-round on the western shore (✆ **530/525-7982**), has 175 campsites, a picnic area, beach, nature center, and cross-country skiing.

RESTAURANTS

★★ **Cantina Bar & Grill** MEXICAN California-Mexican fare with a fun-loving ambience. It's the place in Tahoe to grab a beer and a burrito, and watch the big game with a convivial group. Or enjoy an innovative, internationally influenced gourmet menu, along with classic southwestern specialties. Selection includes steak and fish, barbeque, chicken, sandwiches, and vegetarian entrees.

765 Emerald Bay Rd., South Lake Tahoe, CA 96150. ✆ **530/544-1233.** www.cantinatahoe.com. Main courses $9–$16. AE, MC, V. Daily 11:30am–10:30pm (bar until midnight). **Close to:** Grover Hot Springs & Burnside Lake.

★ **Ernie's Coffee Shop** DINER Not health food, but mighty good eatin'. This classic local diner has friendly atmosphere and a traditional menu that's a fine slice of Americana. Stoke up on a traditional, massive pre-hike breakfast to get up the most strenuous switchback. Arrive early; this is one of the most popular spots around—deservedly so.

1207 Hwy. 50, South Lake Tahoe, CA 96150. ✆ **530/541-2161.** www.erniescoffeeshop.com. Main dishes $5–$9. No credit cards. Daily 6am–2pm. **Close to:** Grover Hot Springs & Burnside Lake.

Fire Sign Café AMERICAN North Tahoe's legendary breakfast choice, for good reason; get here early for a pre-hike feast of authentic, homemade food, probably better than mom used to make. Or arrive in time for a post-hike salad, sandwich, or burger on the outdoor patio. Don't miss the smoked salmon, prepared on-site.

1785 W. Lake Blvd., Tahoe City, CA 96145. ✆ **530/583-0871.** Breakfast and lunch $4–$9. MC, V. Daily 7am–3pm. **Close to:** D.L. Bliss & Emerald Bay State Parks.

Rosie's Café AMERICAN Down-home eats in a comfortable setting with a casual, lodge-y atmosphere. Children are welcomed with their own menu and even rewarded with balloons. It's the place to take the entire family for lunch or dinner (or both!). Selections include salads, sandwiches, and burgers for lunch, and quality comfort food for dinner.

571 North Lake Blvd., Tahoe City, CA 96145. ✆ **530/583-8504.** www.rosiescafe.com. Reservations accepted for dinner. Main courses $5–$10 lunch, $10–$20 dinner. DISC, MC, V. Daily 6:30am–10pm. **Close to:** D.L. Bliss & Emerald Bay State Parks.

★★ **Yellow Sub** SANDWICHES American good taste and fine location in one great spot. Those in the know pick Yellow Sub as the best sandwich shop in Tahoe year after year. Fresh and filling subs and wraps, and the most substantial deli food on the South Shore, are conveniently located directly across from the popular El Dorado Campground.

983 Tallac Ave., at U.S. 50, South Lake Tahoe, CA 96150. ✆ **530/541-8808.** Sandwiches and wraps $3.20–$7.15. No credit cards. Daily 10:30am–9pm. **Close to:** D.L. Bliss & Emerald Bay State Parks.

11

Death Valley National Park

Death Valley National *Park?* The 49ers, whose suffering gave the valley its name, would have howled at the notion. "Death Valley National Park" seems a contradiction in terms, an oxymoron of the great outdoors.

Even the word "park" doesn't quite seem to evoke the area. Other four-letter words are more often associated with Death Valley: gold, mine, heat, lost, dead. And the four-letter words shouted by teamsters who drove the 20-mule-team borax wagons across the valley floor need not be repeated.

There is something about this desert, though, that at first glance seems the antithesis of all that park-goers find desirable. To the needs of most park visitors—shade, water, and easy-to-follow self-guided nature trails—Death Valley answers with a resounding "no."

The word "park" suggests a landscape under human control. In this great land of extremes, nothing could be farther from the truth. A bighorn sheep standing watch atop painted cliffs, sunlight and shadow playing atop the salt and soda floor, a blue-gray cascade of gravel pouring down a gorge to a land below the level of the sea—this territory is as ungovernable as its flaming sunsets.

In Death Valley, the forces of the Earth are exposed to view with dramatic clarity: a sudden fault and a sink became a lake. The water evaporated, leaving behind borax and, above all, fantastic scenery. Although Death Valley is called a valley, in actuality, it is not. Valleys are carved by rivers. Death Valley is what geologists call a graben. Here, a block of the Earth's crust has dropped down along fault lines in relation to its mountain walls. Americans looking for gold in California's mountains in 1849 were forced to cross the burning sands to avoid severe snowstorms in the nearby Sierra Nevada. Some perished along the way, and the land became known as Death Valley.

Many of Death Valley's topographical features are associated with hellish images—Funeral Mountains, Furnace Creek, Dante's View, Coffin Peak, and Devil's Golf Course—but the national park can be a place of serenity.

Death Valley celebrates life. A multitude of living things have miraculously adapted to living in this land of little water, extreme heat, and high winds. Two dozen Death Valley plant species grow nowhere else on Earth, including Death Valley sandpaper plant, Panamint locoweed, and napkin-ring buckwheat.

In spring, even this most forbidding of deserts breaks into bloom. The deep blue pea-shaped flowers of the indigo bush brighten Daylight Pass. Lupine, paintbrush, and Panamint daisies grow on the lower slopes of the Panamint Mountains, while Mojave wildrose and mariposa lily dot the higher slopes.

Two hundred species of birds are found in Death Valley. The brown whip-like stems of the creosote bush help shelter the movements of the kangaroo rat, desert tortoise, and antelope ground squirrel. Night covers the movements of the bobcat, fox, and coyote. Small bands of bighorn sheep roam remote slopes and peaks. Three species of desert pupfish, survivors from the last Ice Age, are found in the valley's saline creeks and pools.

At 3.3 million acres, Death Valley is the largest national park outside of Alaska. The very notion of hiking the desert, in general, and at a place like Death Valley, in particular, is a surprising one to some people—even to some avid hikers. The desert that seems so huge when viewed from a car can seem even more intimidating on foot.

Compared to forest or mountain parks, Death Valley has a limited number of signed footpaths; nevertheless, hiking opportunities abound because roads (closed to vehicles), washes, and narrow canyons serve as excellent footpath substitutes.

ESSENTIALS

GETTING THERE

By Car

Several routes lead into the park, all of which involve crossing one of the steep mountain ranges that isolate Death Valley from, well, everything. Perhaps the most scenic entry is via CA 190, east of CA 178 from Ridgecrest. Another scenic drive is by way of CA 127 and CA 190 from Baker.

For a first-time visitor, I recommend the road 1 mile north of Tecopa, marked to Badwater and Death Valley. It's longer and rougher, but you dip down from the hills into the valley and have the full approach into the region. Otherwise, for the shorter route, continue to CA 190, which will bring you into Death Valley Center. The $20-per-car entrance fee is valid for 7 days.

Note: Top off your gas tank in Tecopa—it's pricey but not as bad as in the valley.

By Air

The closest major airport is Las Vegas's **McCarran International Airport** (✆ **702/261-5211;** www.mccarran.com), which serves practically all major airlines. It's a 2½-hour drive from Las Vegas to Death Valley.

VISITOR INFORMATION

For camping and road information before you go, contact the Superintendent, **Death Valley National Park,** Death Valley, CA 92328 (✆ **760/786-3200** for road, camping, and weather information; www.nps.gov/deva). The **Furnace Creek Visitor Center & Museum** (✆ **760/786-3200**), 15 miles inside the eastern park boundary on CA 190, offers interpretive exhibits and an hourly slide program. Ask at the information desk for ranger-led nature walks and evening naturalist programs. The center is open daily 8am to 6pm in summer (8am–5pm in winter).

ORIENTATION

The distances across Death Valley are enormous. If you only have 1 day, stick around the Furnace Creek Visitor Center. Take in Harmony Borax Works, Badwater, and Dante's View, and hike the interpretive trail through Golden Canyon.

For the average hiker, there's a week or two's worth of hiking in the park, though you can get a fair sampling of this desert in 3 days. Although it's tempting, don't overschedule. Death Valley is vast, with an enormous number of sights to see and hikes to take.

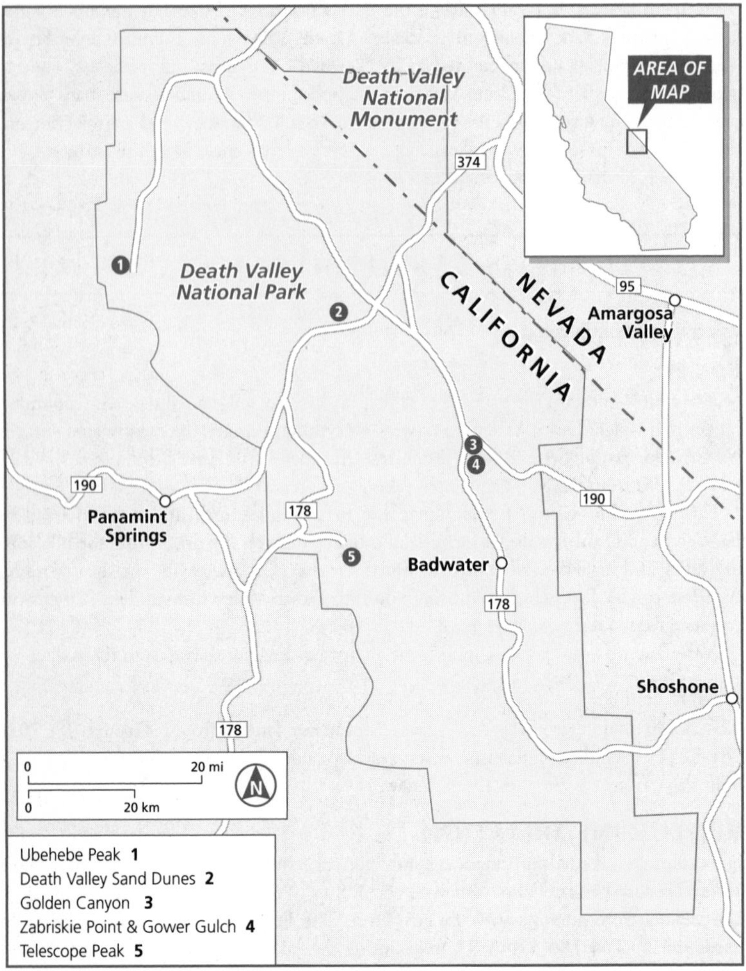

To see as much of the park as possible, choose a different entrance and exit highway. If you enter on CA 127 through Death Valley Junction, exit on the scenic byway through the Panamint Valley. If you entered from the Panamint side, take your leave of the park by following Badwater Road (CA 178) south from Furnace Creek, across the Black Mountains and Greenwater Valley, to intersect CA 127 at Shoshone.

UBEHEBE PEAK ★

Difficulty rating: Moderate

Distance: 3 miles round-trip to ridge crest

Estimated time: 1 1/2–2 hr.

Elevation gain: 1,300 ft.

Costs/permits: $20 national park entry fee

Best time to go: November to May

Website: www.nps.gov/deva

Recommended map: Death Valley National Park map; Tom Harrison maps

Trail head GPS: N 36 41.573, W 117 34.348

Trail head directions: From the Grapevine Ranger Station at the north end of the park, continue north (don't take the right fork to Scotty's Castle) 2 3/4 miles to the signed turnoff for Ubehebe Crater; turn here, and continue another 2 1/2 miles. The paved road ends with a left turn into the Ubehebe Crater parking lot, but you continue south 20 miles on the washboard-surfaced, occasionally rough Racetrack Valley Rd. to Tea Kettle Junction, colorfully decorated with tea kettles. Bear right, traveling another 5 3/4 miles to a turnout on the right (west) side of the road opposite the Grandstand and the Racetrack.

Marvelous vistas are the hiker's reward for climbing the steep trail to Ubehebe Peak, a remote summit in the equally remote Last Chance Range. The White Mountains Saline Valley and High Sierra are among the sights to be seen from the peak's crest of the ridge. To reach the very top of Ubehebe Peak requires some rock scrambling (Class 2–3); however, traveling only as far as the crest delivers equally good views.

The path begins a moderate ascent through a creosote-dotted alluvial fan, then soon steepens as it begins climbing higher over the desert-varnished shoulder of the peak. The old miners' trail that leads to the crest is in fairly good condition.

❶ **The Racetrack** You'll look out at the long mud flat known as the Racetrack. Rocks are pushed along the sometimes muddy surface by high winds, leaving long faint tracks. Most of the tracks you're likely to see on the playa are made by smaller rocks, but throughout the years, there have been reports of rocks weighing several hundred pounds skidding for a quarter-mile.

The amazing sliding rocks scooting across Racetrack Valley may just be the park's weirdest phenomena of all. While scientists have measured Badwater with great certainty and figured out how the pupfish endures in the middle of the desert, geologists have been unable to determine exactly how rocks migrate around the Racetrack.

An ancient lake bed, the Racetrack is a 2 1/2-mile-long, oval-shaped dry mud flat. A rock outcropping at the north end of the Racetrack is known as The Grandstand. Rocks of various sizes (baseball- to basketball-size) slide across the old lake bed, leaving tracks in their wake. These tracks (about 6 in. wide or so, depending on the size of the rock) are straight, curved, and even looped, and extend as much as 600 feet.

Prospectors first noticed the sliding rocks more than a century ago, earth scientists have studied them since the 1950s, and countless visitors have observed them. Sure, scientists have measured the rocks' location change, but no one—trained park naturalist or curious hiker—has ever seen the rocks actually move.

Scientists theorize that the rocks slide after rain moistens the top couple centimeters of the lake bed and a high wind (perhaps 70 mph or more) pushes them around the track.

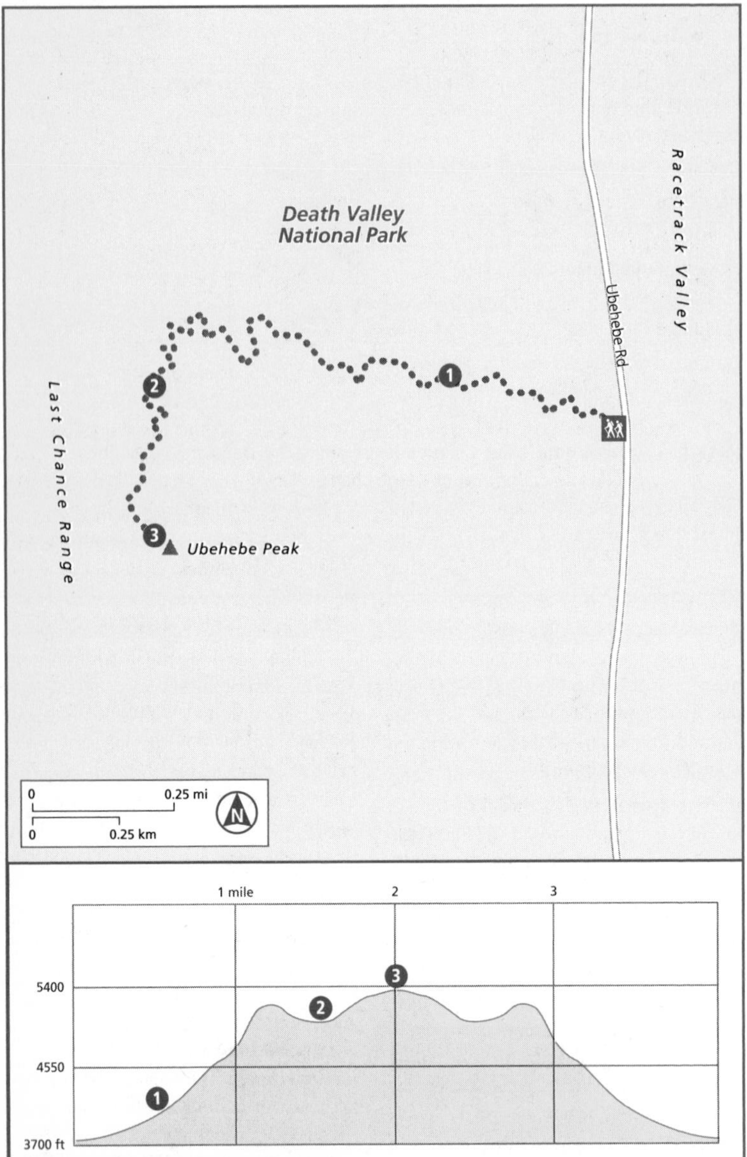

- Trail head icon: N 36 41.573, W 117 34.347: Trail head
- ❶ N 36 41.665, W 117 34.665 (0.4 miles):
- ❷ N 36 41.645, W 117 35.209 (1.5 miles):
- ❸ N 36 41.430, W 117 35.238 (2.0 miles):

Racetrack Valley

The amazing sliding rocks are not one of Death Valley's roadside attractions, so you'll have to take a short hike (a mile or two) to visit them. Even if you're not fortunate enough to be the first human to observe the rocks move, you'll have a great time tracing the rock tracks and playing on the playa.

Begin your sojourn to the rocks by heading due east across the old lake bed. Hiking straight across the valley from the sign is the quickest and most direct route to the rocks, though walking in other directions will also eventually deliver you to the rocks.

A half-mile of hiking brings you to the first rock tracks. If you keep hiking toward the mountains on the far side of the lake bed, you'll encounter more and more rocks and accompanying tracks.

Wind pushing rocks across a rain-slicked mud flat sounds like a plausible enough explanation for such movement, but does not explain why the rocks move in such peculiar patterns. Some rocks have made sudden right-angle turns, others have made complete loops and ended up almost exactly where they began.

❷ To the crest of the ridge Many a switchback brings you to the crest of the range, 1½ miles from the trail head. From the 5,000-foot crest, savor the panorama: the Inyo Mountains, the Racetrack, the Cottonwood Mountains, and the snow-capped peaks of the High Sierra.

❸ Ubehebe Peak *Ubehebe* means "big basket" in the Shoshone language; such a name seems more appropriate to Ubehebe Crater some 24 miles northeast of the rocky peak. If you want to bag the peak, follow the trail another mile (gaining 700 ft. in elevation) as it climbs steeply along the crest, switchbacks some more, and reaches a rocky shoulder, whereupon the trail fades away. You'll continue along the crest, dipping briefly, then rock scrambling up to the small summit area atop 5,678-foot Ubehebe Peak.

DEATH VALLEY SAND DUNES (Kids)

Difficulty rating: Easy

Distance: 2–4 miles round-trip

Estimated time: 1–2 hr.

Elevation gain: 100 ft.

Costs/permits: None

Best time to go: November to May, in the morning or late afternoon

Website: www.nps.gov/deva

Recommended map: Death Valley National Park map; Tom Harrison maps

Trail head GPS: N 36 36.330, W 117 06.648

Trail head directions: Take Hwy. 190 6 miles east of Stovepipe Wells village to the signed turnoff for the dunes. Turn north on the good dirt road and follow it a short distance to the dune picnic area.

A 14-sq.-mile field of dunes and some bizarre geology unfold around the Stovepipe Wells area of Death Valley National Park. Hiking the dunes is most fun in the cooler morning and late afternoon hours. At these hours, the dunes are at their most photogenic, too; the light is softer, the shadows longer.

Your hike into the dunes is exactly what you make of it—short or long, a direct or indirect route to the higher sand formations. Figure 4 miles max to climb up, down, and around the taller dunes, and return. Remember that doing the dunes means a two-steps-forward-one-step-backward kind of hiking, so pace yourself accordingly. Wear shoes; sand surfaces can be very hot.

Death Valley's dunes are formed in much the same way as those mega-dunes in the Middle East or North Africa. What nature needs to form dunes is fairly simple: a source of sand, wind to separate the sand from gravel, more wind to roll the sand along into drifts, and still more wind (perhaps in the form of a back draft) to keep the dunes in place.

The 1938 WPA Guide to Death Valley mentions the frequent winds that rearrange the dunes: "When the hot summer winds blow, the sand rises in a great swirling mass of yellow to fill the trough of Death Valley with a gritty fog that obscures sun and mountains."

Death Valley's dunes lie between Towne Pass on the west and Daylight Pass to the east; there's quite a sand-laden draft between the two passes.

"Dune Speak" is a colorful language, a vocabulary of windward and leeward faces, black patches, Chinese walls, blow sand, and sand shadows.

The slip face of the dunes (away from the wind) is very steep, but never steeper than 34 degrees, which is known as the angle of repose because at steeper than this angle, a slide occurs, thus reducing the angle a degree or three.

As you hike the dunes, you'll notice blow sand (loose, very fine particles) piled on the leeward side of plants; these piles are known as sand shadows.

Death Valley's dunes are sub-barchan, or crescent-shaped. The sand dunes are actually tiny pieces of rock, most of them quartz fragments.

Near the dunes are some weird natural features. Those surrealistic-looking corn stalks you see across Hwy. 190 from the dunes are actually clumps of arrow-weed. The Devil's Cornfield is perched on wind- and water-eroded pedestals.

Fringing the dunes are expanses of dry mud that have cracked and buckled into interesting patterns. These mud sink areas and the edges of the dunes themselves are good places to look for the tracks of the few desert creatures able to survive in the harsh environment—most notably rabbits and kangaroo rats.

If you enjoy these relatively accessible dunes and want an adventure, head for the often overlooked Eureka Valley, which holds many surprises, chief among them the Eureka Dunes.

> The Eureka Dunes occupy the site of an ancient lakebed, whose shoreline can be identified to the northeast of the dunes. The one-time flat lakebed northwest of the dunes sometimes captures a little surface water; this happenstance delights photographers who focus their cameras on the water and capture the reflection of the Inyo Mountains.

The neighboring Last Chance Mountains gets a fair share of the meager rains that fall in these parts—meaning the dunes are (relatively) well watered. Rain

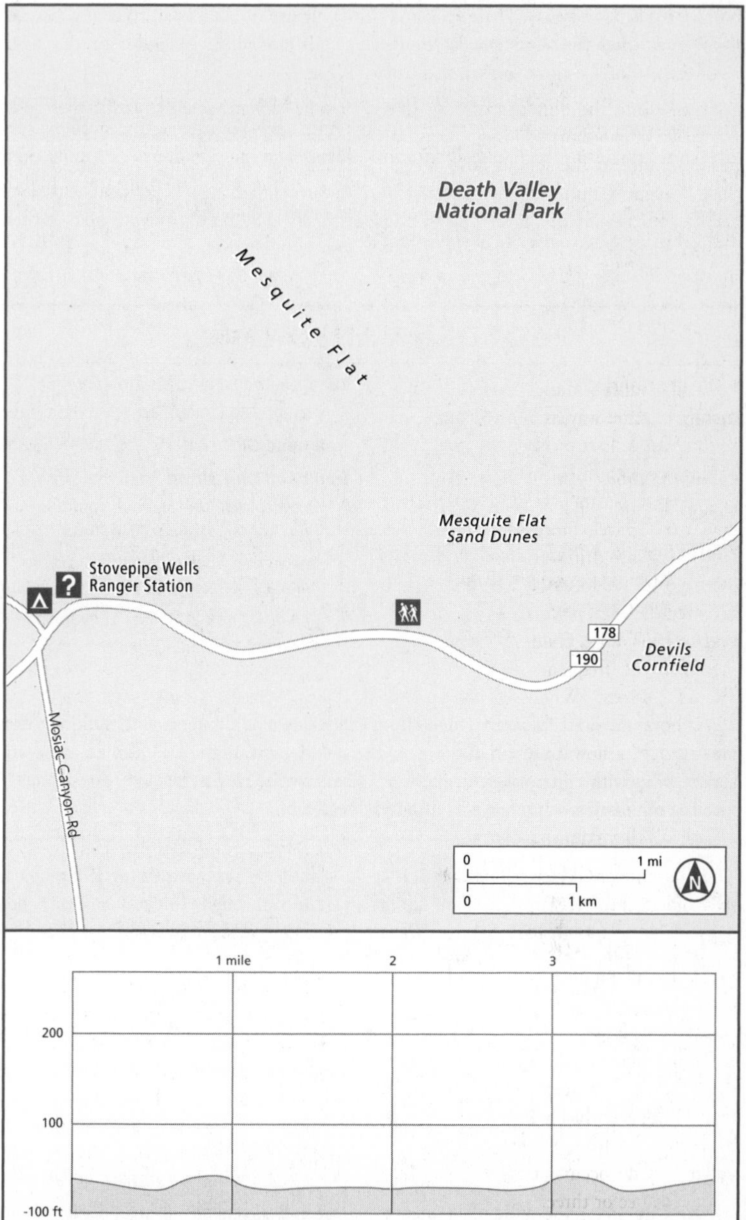

N 36 36.335, W 117 06.643: Trail head

percolates downward, the water later nurturing some fifty different dune plants even in the driest of years. Three species of flora occur nowhere else: Eureka dunes milkvetch, Eureka dune grass, and the showy, large white flowers of the Eureka Dunes evening primrose.

Like their cousins, the Kelso Dunes in Mojave National Preserve, the Eureka Dunes "boom." Low vibrational sounds are created when the wind-polished, well-rounded grains of sand slip-slide underfoot. The booming, which has been compared to the low-altitude airplane and a Tibetan gong, is louder in the Kelso Dunes.

However, it's not the noise of Eureka Dunes, but the silence that impresses the hiker. The massive dunes (3.5 miles long and .5 mile wide) are California's highest at nearly 700 feet high.

GOLDEN CANYON (Kids)

Difficulty rating: Easy

Distance: 2.8 miles round-trip to Red Cathedral

Estimated time: 1–2 hr.

Elevation gain: 400 ft.

Costs/permits: None

Best time to go: November to April, at sunrise or sunset

Website: www.nps.gov/deva

Recommended map: Death Valley National Park map; Tom Harrison maps

Trail head GPS: N 36 25.228, W 116 50.809

Trail head Directions: From the Furnace Creek Visitor Center, drive south on Hwy. 190, forking right onto Hwy. 178. The signed Golden Canyon Trail is on your left, 3 miles from the visitor center. The hike through Golden Canyon shares a common trail head with the longer excursion to Zabriskie Point.

The panoramic view of Golden Canyon from Zabriskie Point is magnificent, but don't miss getting right into the canyon itself—only possible by hitting the trail. Both sunrise and sunset, when the light is magical and fellow hikers are few, are particularly good times to hike the excellent interpretive trail through the canyon.

The first mile of Golden Canyon Trail is a self-guided interpretive trail. Pick up a copy of the National Park Service's *Trail Guide to Golden Canyon* pamphlet, available at the trail head for 50¢.

From the parking lot, hike up the alluvial fan into the canyon. Depending on the light, Golden Canyon can seem to glow gold, brass, yellow, or orange.

Marvel at the tilted, faulted rock walls of the canyon as they close in around you. Notice the ripple marks, created long ago by water lapping at the shore of an ancient lake.

Until the rainy winter of 1976, a road extended through Golden Canyon. A desert deluge washed away the road, and it's been a trail ever since.

Stops in the guide are keyed to numbers along the trail and may tell you more about Miocene volcanic activity, Jurassic granitic intrusion, and Precambrian erosion than you ever wanted to know; nevertheless, even the most casual student of earth science will gain an appreciation for the complex geology and the millions of years required to sculpt and color Golden Canyon. Aptly named Red Cathedral looms over the canyon in colorful contrast.

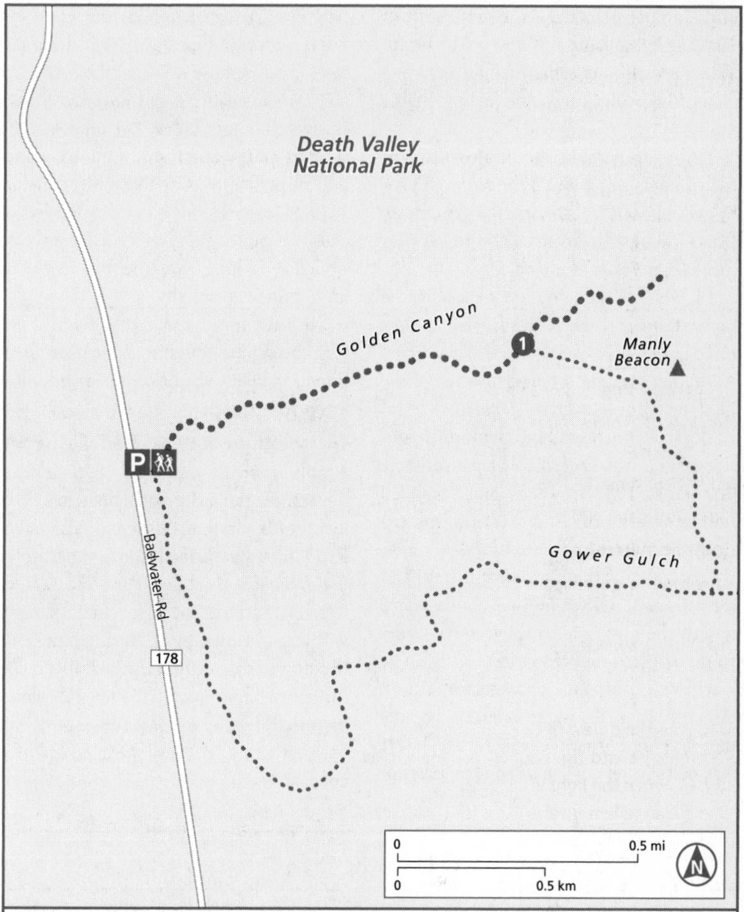

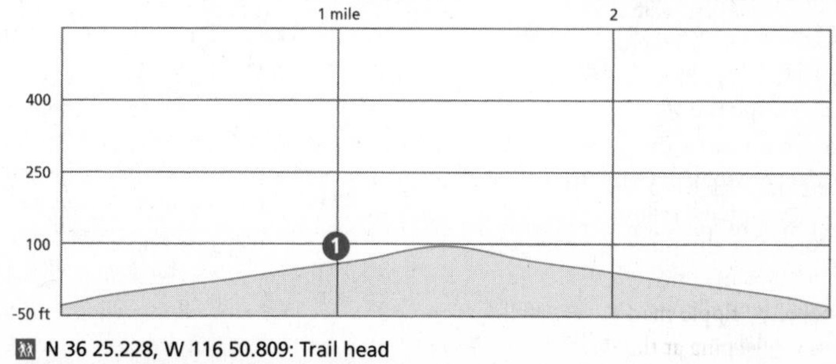

N 36 25.228, W 116 50.809: Trail head

1 N 36 25.474, W 116 49.912 (1.0 miles):

Deeper and deeper into the badlands you ascend. Watch for white crystalline outcroppings of borax—the same stuff of 20 Mule Team fame. "White gold," Death Valley prospectors called it. Not exactly a glamorous substance, but a profitable one.

Learn more about the intertwined stories of borax mining and the national park by hiking out to the nearby Harmony Borax Works—a rock salt landscape as tortured as you'll ever find.

In Death Valley, strangely enough, the borax story and the park story are almost inseparable. Borax super-salesman Stephen T. Mather became the first director of the National Park Service in 1916.

Borax is not exactly a glamorous substance, but has proved to be a profitable one. From 1883 to 1888, more than 20 million pounds of borax were transported from the Harmony Borax Works.

Transport of the borax was the stuff of legends, too. The famous 20-mule teams hauled the huge loaded wagons 165 miles to the rail station at Mojave.

Down-on-his-luck prospector Aaron Winters first discovered borax on the salt flats in Furnace Creek in 1881. He was ecstatic when San Francisco investor William Coleman purchased his rights to the borax field for $20,000. Coleman capitalized construction of the Harmony Borax Works, an endeavor that depended first and foremost on the labors of Chinese-Americans who gathered the fibrous clusters of borate called "cottonballs."

After purification at the borax works, the substance was loaded into custom 15-foot long wagons to be hauled by ten pairs of mules. The animals were controlled by a long jerk line and legendary mule-skinner profanity.

To learn more about this colorful era, visit the Borax Museum at Furnace Creek Ranch the park visitor center, also located in Furnace Creek.

❶ Junction, trail to Red Cathedral

A mile from the trail head, at the end of the nature trail, the path branches. One fork heads for Red Cathedral, also called Red Cliffs. Reach it by continuing up the main canyon 1/4 mile to the old Golden Canyon parking lot. The trail narrows, and you continue by squeezing past boulders to the base of Red Cathedral, a colorful natural amphitheater. The red color is essentially iron oxide—rust—produced by weathering of rocks with a high iron content.

ZABRISKIE POINT & GOWER GULCH ★

Difficulty rating: Moderate

Distance: 6.5-mile loop to Zabriskie Point with return via Gower Gulch

Estimated time: 3½ hr.

Elevation gain: 900 ft.

Costs/permits: None

Best time to go: November to April

Website: www.nps.gov/deva

Recommended map: Death Valley National Park map; Tom Harrison maps

Trail head GPS: N 36 25.228, W 116 50.809

Trail head directions: From the Furnace Creek Visitor Center, drive south on Hwy. 190, forking right onto Hwy. 178. The signed Golden Canyon Trail is on your left, 3 miles from the visitor center. The hike to Zabriskie Point shares a common trail head with the shorter excursion through Golden Canyon.

While it's true that you can drive to Zabriskie Point, you'll appreciate the view much more by sweating up those switchbacks on foot. The memorable panorama from Zabriskie Point includes a grand view of the valley, framed by the badlands just below and the Panamint Mountains to the west.

An engaging trail climbs through badlands to the point named for Christian Brevoort Zabriskie, one of the early heads of Death Valley borax mining operations. A return by way of Gower Gulch offers another perspective on this colorful desert land and enables hikers to make a loop.

➊ **Stop 10 Junction** Follow the Golden Canyon Interpretive Trail (see above) for 1 mile to stop 10, then take the signed fork toward Zabriskie Point. The path climbs into the badlands toward Manly Beacon, a pinnacle of gold sandstone. The trail crests at the shoulder of

Scotty's Castle

Scotty's Castle, the Mediterranean-to-the-max mega-hacienda in the northern part of the park, is unabashedly Death Valley's premiere tourist attraction. Visitors are wowed by the elaborate Spanish tiles, well-crafted furnishings, and innovative construction that includes solar water heating. Even more compelling is the colorful history of this villa in remote Grapevine Canyon.

Construction of the "castle"—more officially Death Valley Ranch—began in 1924. It was to be a winter retreat for eccentric Chicago millionaire Albert Johnson. The insurance tycoon's unlikely friendship with prospector-cowboy-spinner of tall tales, Walter Scott, put the $2.3-million structure on the map and captured the public's imagination. Scotty greeted visitors and told them fanciful stories from the early hard-rock mining days of Death Valley.

The 1-hour walking tour of Scotty's Castle ($11 adults, $9 seniors, $6 children 6–15, and free for kids under 6) is excellent, both for its inside look at the mansion and for what it reveals about the eccentricities of Johnson and Scotty. Tours depart about every 20 minutes (hourly in the winter and summer) from 9am to 5pm; they fill up quickly, so arrive early for the first available spots.

To learn more about the castle grounds, pick up the pamphlet at the castle visitor center, *A Walking Tour of Scotty's Castle,* which leads you on an exploration from stable to swimming pool, from bunkhouse to powerhouse.

Another walk is the short hike through Tie Canyon Wash, which supplied tons and tons of sand and gravel for the castle's construction. Mixed with cement, these raw materials went into the castle walls, and into the unique concrete fence posts, each bearing letters J and S—for Albert Johnson and Death Valley Scotty. Winters were cold in the canyon, and much wood was needed for the castle's many fireplaces. Johnson bought 70 miles worth of railroad ties from the abandoned Bullfrog–Goldfield railroad. The ties, thousands of which are still stacked in Tie Canyon, cost him about a penny a piece.

Windy Point Trail (.8 mile round-trip), which leads to a cross marking Death Valley Scotty's grave, is a self-guided path keyed to an interpretive pamphlet that gives an overview of the desert flora. Windy Point is, indeed, often windy but was actually named for Death Valley Scotty's dog, who lies buried next to his master.

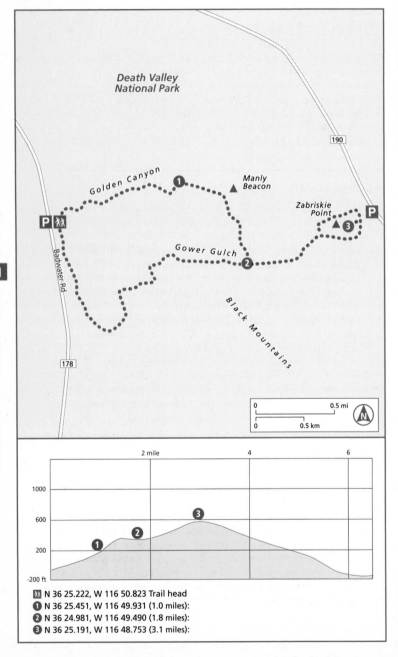

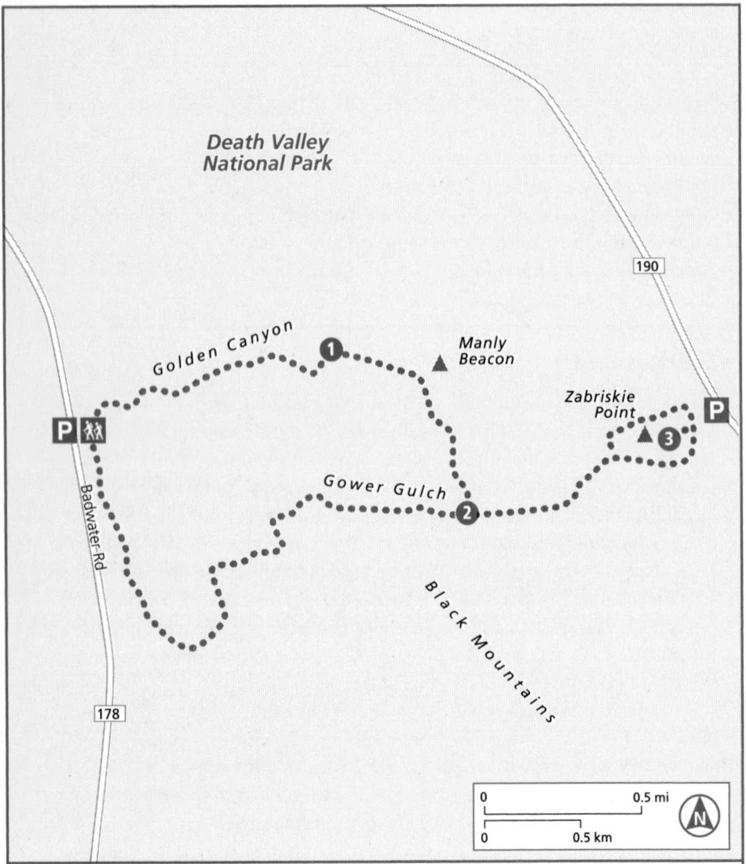

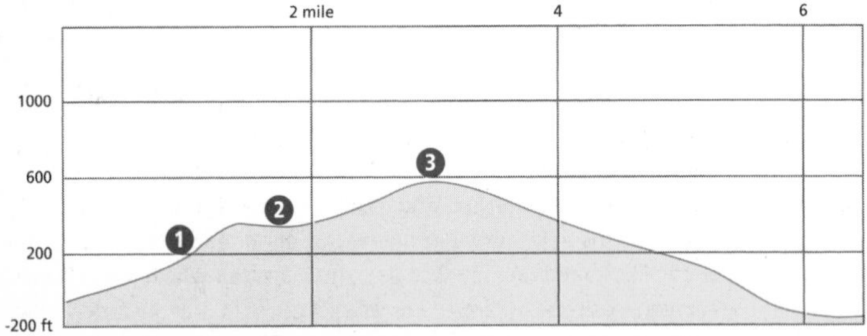

N 36 25.222, W 116 50.823 Trail head

1 N 36 25.451, W 116 49.931 (1.0 miles):

2 N 36 24.981, W 116 49.490 (1.8 miles):

3 N 36 25.191, W 116 48.753 (3.1 miles):

the beacon, then descends into the badlands and brings you to a junction $2\frac{1}{2}$ miles from the trail head.

❷ Junction with Gower Gulch Trail Go left (east) to Zabriskie Point. (The right fork is the return leg of your loop through Gower Gulch.)

Watch for Park Service signs to stay on the trail, which is a bit difficult to follow as it marches up and down the severely eroded silt-stone hills. After a mile, a final steep grade brings you to Zabriskie Point—or, more accurately, the parking lot.

❸ Zabriskie Point Step uphill to the point itself and savor the vast views of the eroded yellow hills below and the mountains across the valley.

> Before sunrise, photographers set up their tripods at Zabriskie Point and point their cameras down at the pale mudstone hills of Golden Canyon and the great valley beyond. The display of color from purple to gold as sun passes over Golden Canyon is memorable, to say the least.

Retrace your steps back to the trail fork.

❹ Junction with Gower Gulch Trail This time, you'll descend west into a wash. Wide, gray, and gravelly Gower Gulch has definitely felt the hand of man. The open mouths of tunnels and white smears on the gulch walls are reminders of the borax miners who dug up these hills. Gower Gulch has been altered considerably in order to protect Furnace Creek developments from flooding.

A bit more than a mile down the trail, the gulch narrows, and you'll suddenly encounter a 30-foot-high dry fall. Take the bypass footpath to the right. A final $1\frac{1}{4}$ miles of trail heads north along the base of the hills, on a route paralleling the highway, and leads back to the trail-head parking area at the mouth of Golden Canyon.

TELESCOPE PEAK ★★

Difficulty rating: Strenuous

Distance: 14 miles round-trip to Telescope Peak

Estimated time: 8 hr.

Elevation gain: 3,000 ft.

Costs/permits: $20 national park entry fee

Best time to go: Mid-May to November

Website: www.nps.gov/deva

Recommended map: Death Valley National Park map; Tom Harrison maps

Trail head GPS: N 36 13.867, W 117 04.036

Trail head directions: On Hwy. 178, drive 50 miles northeast of Hwy. 395 and Ridgecrest, turn right on Wildrose Canyon Rd., and follow it 9 miles to road's end at Mahogany Flat Campground. Park at the campground.

Most park visitors are content to stop their cars at Badwater, 282 ft. below sea level, and look up at Telescope Peak, the greatest vertical rise in the lower 48 states. For the serious hiker, however, the challenge of climbing 11,049-ft. Telescope Peak and looking down at Death Valley will prove irresistible. Views from Telescope Peak Trail include Badwater, low point of the continental U.S., and Mount Whitney, the continental high point.

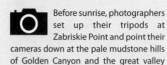

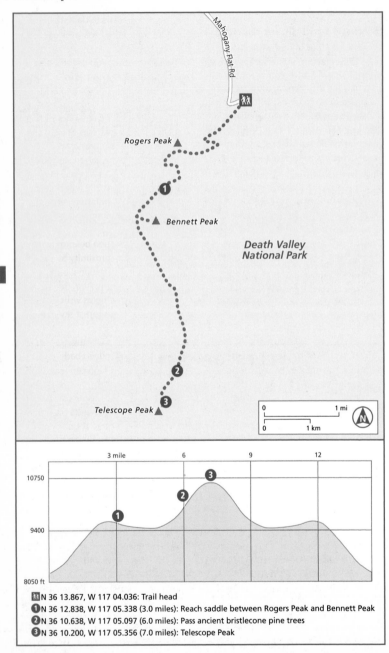

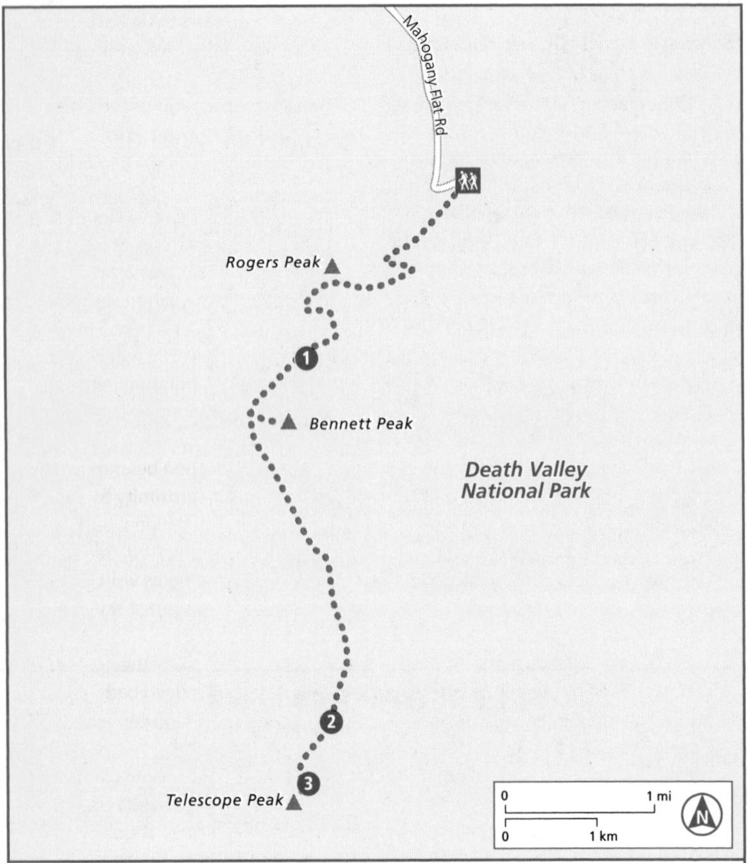

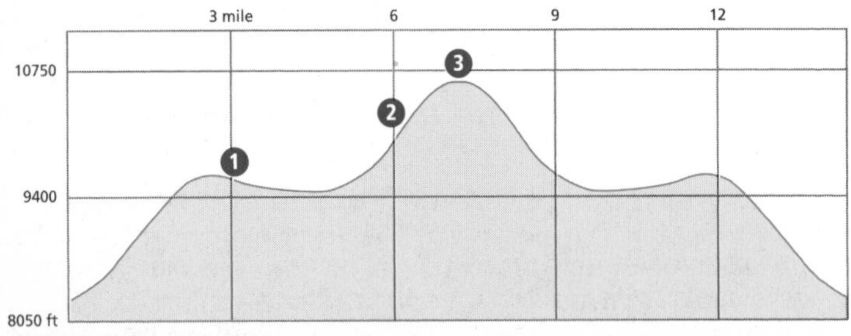

N 36 13.867, W 117 04.036: Trail head
1 N 36 12.838, W 117 05.338 (3.0 miles): Reach saddle between Rogers Peak and Bennett Peak
2 N 36 10.638, W 117 05.097 (6.0 miles): Pass ancient bristlecone pine trees
3 N 36 10.200, W 117 05.356 (7.0 miles): Telescope Peak

Badwater

Looking west from Badwater, the eye is drawn to what appears to be a shallow stream flowing across the valley floor. But this flow is a *trompe l'oeil,* a mirage caused by the strange terrain and deceptive colorings.

Light plays upon the valley floor, and the mind spins as though caught in a color wheel, from the gray and gold of sunrise to the lavender and purple of sunset. To say the least, visiting the lowest parts of Death Valley is often a colorful experience.

Badwater—and some of the nearby canyons off Badwater Road—offer object lessons of Death Valley geology in action, as well as shifting patterns of light and iridescent colors that make hikes in this part of the national parks ones to remember. A short hike (less than 1 mile round-trip) across the barren salt flats to Badwater may just be the definitive Death Valley experience. It's an excursion into extremes—the lowest point in the Western Hemisphere at 282 feet below sea level and one of the hottest places on Earth. Because temperature increases as elevation decreases, Badwater is no place to linger in the summer when temperatures of 120°F (49°C) are regularly recorded.

While Badwater is not the planet's lowest land (that distinction belongs to the Dead Sea, located some 1,290 ft. below sea level in Israel), its proximity to adjacent high country makes its lowness seem quite pronounced. National park highpoint Telescope Peak (11,048 ft.) is located fewer than 20 miles west of Badwater.

A "Sea Level" sign posted high on the cliffs above Badwater helps visitors imagine just what a depression 282 feet represents. These cliffs thrust skyward all the way up to Dante's View, 5,775 feet above sea level.

As the story goes, an early mapmaker named the briny pools "Badwater" when his mule refused to partake of the water. Badwater's water is indeed bad—as is most surface water in Death Valley—because of an extremely high concentration of salts; it is undrinkable, but not poisonous.

While Badwater's environmental conditions are hostile to life, some plants and animals manage to survive. Patches of grass and clumps of pickleweed edge the shallow pools, where water beetles and the larvae of insects frolic about.

A causeway leads out onto the salt flats. To really get a feel for the enormity of the valley floor, continue past the well-beaten pathway farther out onto the salt flats.

To get to Badwater, from the junction of Hwy. 190 and Hwy. 178, head south on Hwy. 178 (Badwater Rd.) for 17 miles to the signed Badwater parking area on the west side of the road.

During the colder months, Telescope Peak and much of the trail is covered in snow. Try to begin your hike at dawn, both to savor the sunrise and to allow sufficient time for the long journey.

The trail starts where most trails end—a mile and a half in the sky—and climbs a sagebrush- and pinyon pine–dotted hogback ridge to the pinnacle that is Telescope Peak.

The path climbs over pinyon pine–forested slopes and soon offers dramatic views of Death Valley and the Furnace Creek area. Sign in at the trail register located about a quarter-mile from the trail head. After 2 miles, the trail gains the spine of a ridge, and soon a second valley, Panamint, comes into view.

The well-maintained trails up Telescope Peak and Wildrose Peak offer a distinctly different hiking experience than other park trails which, for the most part, are of two types: nature/interpretive trails or cross-country routes through canyons or washes. In fact, these trails are the only substantial and well-engineered paths in the Death Valley wilderness backcountry.

❶ Rogers Peak and Bennett Peak Three miles of moderate climbing from the trail head bring you to a saddle between Rogers Peak and Bennett Peak. Typically, this part of the trail is snow-covered in the winter, and sometimes into the first weeks of May. You can strike cross-country to reach the antennae-crowned summit of Rogers Peak, which stands about 400 feet higher than the trail. To reach 9,980-foot Bennett Peak, continue on the main trail to a second saddle, about $4\frac{1}{4}$ miles from the trail head at an elevation of 9,500 feet, then ascend cross-country past stands of limber pine to the top.

❷ Ancient Bristlecone Pine Telescope Peak Trail's final third is steep and remarkable. The path zigzags up the peak's steep east side, ascending through a stunted forest of limber and bristlecone pine. About 6 miles out, at 10,500 feet, you'll pass some wonderfully statuesque bristlecones, ancients adjudged to be about 3,000 years old.

About a quarter-mile short of the peak, you'll reach the 11,000-foot mark and trek the windswept ridge over two bumps to reach a third, the summit promontory.

❸ Telescope Peak The 360-degree panorama inspired one W.T. Henderson, first to ascend the great mountain in 1860, to declare: "You can see so far, it's just like looking through a telescope."

> From atop the Telescope Peak, you can marvel at the magnificent vistas from the below-sea-level salt pans, including Badwater, to the more than 2-mile-high snowy summits of the Sierra Nevada. The far-reaching views also include the White Mountains to the north. Off in those two patches of purple haze are Las Vegas far to the east and the San Gabriel Mountains above Los Angeles to the southwest.

SLEEPING & EATING

ACCOMMODATIONS

★★ Amargosa Opera House and Hotel The hotel is part of a complex of Spanish Colonial–style buildings, including the opera house where owner Marta Becket performs on Saturday nights from October to May. The hotel is charming, clean, and filled with beautiful murals painted by Becket. For some, the hotel is the ideal desert retreat; others find it more than a little spooky.

CA 127 and State Line Rd., 30 miles east of Furnace Creek, Death Valley Junction, CA 92328. ✆ **760/852-4441.** www.amargosa-opera-house.com. 14 units. $67–$84 double. AE, MC, V. **Close to:** Death Valley Sand Dunes

El Portal Motel This family-style motel, located an hour's drive from the park's center, offers plain, spacious rooms with either one or two queen-size beds. ***Hint:*** Smoke-free rooms are available but are snapped up quickly. Restaurants, a steak house, a bakery, and an ice cream parlor are within walking distance of the motel.

420 Main St., two blocks from the junction of Rte. 374 and Hwy. 95, Beatty, NV 89003. © **775/553-2912.** www.elportalmotel.com. 25 units. $50 double. 35 miles northeast of Furnace Creek Visitor Center. MC, V. **Close to:** Golden Canyon

★★ **Furnace Creek Inn** Like an oasis in the middle of Death Valley, the inn's red-tiled roofs and sparkling blue mineral-spring-fed swimming pool hint at the elegance within. The hotel has equipped its 66 deluxe rooms and suites with every modern amenity while successfully preserving the charm of this 1930s resort. Stroll the palm-shaded gardens before sitting down to a meal in the elegant dining room, where the food is excellent but the formality a bit out of place. Reserve early: The inn is booked solid in winter with guests who appreciate a little pampering after a day in the park.

Hwy. 190, Death Valley, CA 92328. © **800/236-7916** or 760/786-2345. www.furnacecreekresort.com. 66 units. $260–$390 double; from $390 suite. Extra person $20. AE, DISC, MC, V. **Close to:** Golden Canyon

★ **Furnace Creek Ranch** Run by the same folks who maintain the elegant Furnace Creek Inn, the year-round Furnace Creek Ranch is more down-to-earth, with rustic cabin units and motel rooms that are great for families. Amenities include a naturally heated, spring-fed pool, the world's lowest 18-hole golf course (214 ft. below sea level), tennis and basketball courts, a playground, and a selection of dining options.

CA 190, adjacent to the Furnace Creek Visitor Center, Death Valley, CA 92328. © **800/297-2757** or 760/786-2345; 303/297-2757 for reservations. www.furnacecreekresort.com. 224 units. $116–$193 double. AE, DC DISC, MC, V. **Close to:** Golden Canyon

Panamint Springs Resort This privately owned resort, across the Panamint Range and about a 45-minute drive west of Furnace Creek, is a bit off the beaten path geographically and definitely off the tourist track. The charming rustic motel has plain rooms, as well as a full-service restaurant that serves traditional American fare at breakfast, lunch, and dinner.

CA 190, 30 miles west of Stovepipe Wells, Ridgecrest, CA 93555. © **775/482-7680.** www.deathvalley.com/psr. 14 units, 1 cottage. $79–$94 double; $149 cottage. MC, V. **Close to:** Death Valley Sand Dunes

Stovepipe Wells Village The truly budget-conscious opt for Stovepipe Wells Village, where the modest air-conditioned motel rooms (sans phones and TVs) surround a small pool. About 23 miles northwest of Furnace Creek, Stovepipe Wells has a general store, Internet kiosk, saloon, and dining room. Rooms have two twin beds, two double beds, or one king.

CA 190, at Stovepipe Wells, Death Valley, CA 92328. © **760/786-2387;** 800/297-2757 or 303/297-2757 for reservations. www.stovepipewells.com. 83 units. $91–$111 double. AE DC, DISC, MC, V. **Close to:** Death Valley Sand Dunes

CAMPING

The park's nine campgrounds are at elevations ranging from below sea level to 8,000 feet above sea level. In Furnace Creek, **Sunset** has 1,000 spaces with water and flush toilets. **Furnace Creek Campground** has 200 similarly appointed spaces. **Stovepipe Wells** has 200 spaces with water and flush toilets. For reservations call © **800/365-2267.**

RESTAURANTS

★★ **Furnace Creek Inn** CONTINENTAL Inside the elegant dining room here, the menu highlights several Continental and regional cuisines. The peaceful setting and attentive service can be a welcome (though pricey) treat during otherwise exhausting travels through the park. Breakfast, lunch, and dinner are served. The Sunday buffet brunch is truly decadent; reservations are necessary.

CA 190, adjacent to the Furnace Creek Visitor Center, Death Valley, CA 92328. ✆ **800/297-2757** or 760/786-2345. www.furnacecreekresort.com. AE, DC, DISC, MC, V. Mid-Oct to mid-May daily 7am–8:30pm. Closed mid-May to mid-Oct. **Close to:** Golden Canyon.

★ **Forty Niner Café** AMERICAN Here's a family-friendly diner with better-than-average food and a varied menu. The western Americana menu includes biscuits and gravy, omelets, hot cakes, burgers, fried chicken, hot and cold sandwiches, and even some vegetarian dishes. Great date shakes, as well. At the nearby Corkscrew Saloon, you can get a cold draft beer, along with pizza, hot dogs, and buffalo wings.

CA 190, adjacent to the Furnace Creek Visitor Center, Death Valley, CA 92328. ✆ **760/786-2345.** www.furnacecreekresort com. Main courses $6–$12. AE, DC, DISC, MC, V. Nov–Apr daily 7am–9pm; May-Oct daily 11:30am–9pm. **Close to:** Golden Canyon.

★ **The Mad Greek** GREEK/AMERICAN This blue-and-white-tiled, Greek kitsch-decorated oasis serves wonderful Greek specialties: souvlaki, gyros with homemade *tzatziki* sauce, calamari, spinach-and-feta spanakopita, a village salad laden with feta, baklava, and more. The huge menu also features burgers and all-American fare, as well as the best strawberry shake for hundreds of miles around.

72112 Baker Blvd., Baker(a gateway town to Death Valley), CA 92309. ✆ **760/733-4354.** Entrees $5–$9. MC, V. Daily. **Close to:** Golden Canyon.

The 19th Hole AMERICAN The veranda-style bar and grill offers stunning views of the Panamint Mountains. The emphasis is definitely on the bar, with its unique golf cart drive-up ramp. The grill menu features burgers, hot dogs, and sub sandwiches.

CA 190, adjacent to the Golf Pro Shop, Death Valley, CA 92328. ✆ **760/786-2345.** www.furnacecreekresort.com. Oct–May daily 11am–3pm. **Close to:** Golden Canyon.

★ **Toll Road Restaurant & Badwater Saloon** WESTERN AMERICAN Built from timbers from an old Death Valley mine, the restaurant features a full-service menu for breakfast, lunch, and dinner in a Western-style atmosphere. Hearty breakfasts include omelets, pancakes, and biscuits and gravy; lunches feature burgers and sandwiches; and the popular dinner choice is a steak and trip to the salad bar. Walk over to the Badwater Saloon for a cold one.

CA 190, at Stovepipe Wells, 23 miles northwest of Furnace Creek, Death Valley, CA 92328. ✆ **760/786.2387.** www.stovepipewells.com. Main courses $10–$20. AE, DC, DISC, MC, V. Daily 7am–9pm. **Close to:** Death Valley Sand Dunes.

Wrangler Steakhouse STEAKHOUSE This steakhouse serves an all-you-can-eat buffet for breakfast and a lunch buffet that offers a rotating menu of hot and cold entrees. The prices are higher than average, but the buffet is a good choice for families with hearty eaters. At dinnertime, the Wrangler offers table service, grilling steaks, ribs, and other satisfying specialties; the servings are generous, but the dinners are pricey.

CA 190, adjacent to the Furnace Creek Visitor Center, Death Valley, CA 92328. ✆ **800/297-2757** or 760/786-2345. www.furnacecreekresort.com. Main courses $15–$25. AE, DC, DISC, MC, V. Nov–Apr daily 6am–9am, 11am–2pm, and 5:30–9:30pm. May–Oct daily 11am–2pm only. **Close to:** Golden Canyon.

Appendix A: Fast Facts, Toll-Free Numbers & Websites

1 FAST FACTS: NORTHERN CALIFORNIA

AREA CODES The area code for the San Francisco area is 415 (if you're dialing locally, a preceding 1 is not necessary), although you may encounter the 510 code, which covers the East Bay, and 650, for the Peninsula south of town. Napa and Sonoma are in 707. To dial outside of the United States or Canada, dial 011 before the telephone number. Calls to numbers that begin with an 800, 866, 877, or 888 area code are toll-free.

AUTOMOBILE ORGANIZATIONS Motor clubs will supply maps, suggested routes, guidebooks, accident and bail-bond insurance, and emergency road service. The **American Automobile Association (AAA)** is the major motor club in the United States. If you belong to a motor club in your home country, inquire about AAA reciprocity before you leave. You may be able to join AAA even if you're not a member of a reciprocal club; to inquire, call AAA (✆ **800/222-4357**). AAA is actually an organization of regional motor clubs, so look under "AAA Automobile Club" in the White Pages of the telephone directory. AAA has a nationwide emergency road service telephone number (✆ **800/AAA-HELP**).

BUSINESS HOURS Offices are usually open weekdays from 9am to 5pm. Banks are open weekdays from 9am to 3pm or later, and sometimes Saturday mornings. Stores typically open between 9 and 10am and close between 5 and 6pm from Monday through Saturday. Stores in shopping complexes or malls tend to stay open late: until about 9pm on weekdays and weekends, and many malls and larger department stores are open on Sundays.

CAR RENTALS See "Toll-Free Numbers & Websites," p. 252.

CURRENCY The most common U.S. bills are the $1 (a "buck"), $5, $10, and $20 denominations. There are also $2 bills (seldom encountered), $50 bills, and $100 bills (the last two are usually not welcome as payment for small purchases). Coins come in seven denominations: 1¢ (1 cent, or a penny); 5¢ (5 cents, or a nickel); 10¢ (10 cents, or a dime); 25¢ (25 cents, or a quarter); 50¢ (50 cents, or a half dollar); the gold-colored Sacagawea coin, worth $1; and the rare silver dollar.

DRINKING LAWS The legal age for purchase and consumption of alcoholic beverages is 21; proof of age is required and often requested at bars, nightclubs, and restaurants, so it's always a good idea to bring ID when you go out. Supermarkets and convenience stores in California sell beer, wine, and liquor.

Most restaurants serve alcohol, but some only serve beer and wine—it depends on the type of liquor license they own. By law, all bars, clubs, restaurants, and stores cannot sell or serve alcohol after 2am, and "last call" tends to start at 1:30am. There are no county or calendar alcohol restrictions in California.

Do not carry open containers of alcohol in your car or any public area that isn't zoned for alcohol consumption. The police can fine you on the spot. And nothing will ruin your trip faster than getting a citation for DUI ("driving under the influence"), so don't even think about driving while intoxicated.

DRIVING RULES See "Getting There & Getting Around," p. 14.

EARTHQUAKES In the rare event of an earthquake, *don't panic.* If you're in a tall building, don't run outside; instead, move away from windows and toward the building's center. Crouch under a desk or table, or stand against a wall or under a doorway. If you're in bed, get under the bed, stand in a doorway, or crouch under a sturdy piece of furniture. When exiting the building, use stairwells, *not* elevators. If you're in your car, pull over to the side of the road and stop, but wait until you're away from bridges or overpasses, as well as telephone or power poles and lines. Stay in your car. If you're outside, stay away from trees, power lines, and the sides of buildings.

ELECTRICITY Like Canada, the United States uses 110–120 volts AC (60 cycles), compared to 220–240 volts AC (50 cycles) in most of Europe, Australia, and New Zealand. Downward converters that change 220–240 volts to 110–120 volts are difficult to find in the United States, so bring one with you.

EMBASSIES & CONSULATES All embassies are in the nation's capital, Washington, D.C. Some consulates are located in major U.S. cities, and most nations have a mission to the United Nations in New York City. If your country isn't listed below, call for directory information in Washington, D.C. (✆ **202/555-1212**) or log on to **www.embassy.org/embassies**.

The embassy of **Australia** is at 1601 Massachusetts Ave. NW, Washington, DC 20036 (✆ **202/797-3000;** www.visahq.com). There are consulates in New York, Honolulu, Houston, Los Angeles, and San Francisco.

The embassy of **Canada** is at 501 Pennsylvania Ave. NW, Washington, DC 20001 (✆ **202/682-1740;** www.canadainternational.gc.ca/washington). Other Canadian consulates are in Buffalo (New York), Detroit, Los Angeles, New York, and Seattle.

The embassy of **Ireland** is at 2234 Massachusetts Ave. NW, Washington, DC 20008 (✆ **202/462-3939;** www.embassyofireland.org). Irish consulates are in Boston, Chicago, New York, San Francisco, and other cities. See website for complete listing.

The embassy of **New Zealand** is at 37 Observatory Circle NW, Washington, DC 20008 (✆ **202/328-4800;** www.nzembassy.com). New Zealand consulates are in Los Angeles, Salt Lake City, San Francisco, and Seattle.

The embassy of the **United Kingdom** is at 3100 Massachusetts Ave. NW, Washington, DC 20008 (✆ **202/588-7800;** http://ukinusa.fco.gov.uk). Other British consulates are in Atlanta, Boston, Chicago, Cleveland, Houston, Los Angeles, New York, San Francisco, and Seattle.

EMERGENCIES Call ✆ **911** to report a fire, call the police, or get an ambulance anywhere in the United States. This is a toll-free call. (No coins are required at public telephones.)

If you encounter traveler's problems, call the Los Angeles chapter of the **Traveler's Aid Society** (✆ **310/646-2270;** www.travelersaid.org), a nationwide, nonprofit, social service organization that helps travelers in difficult straits. Its services might include reuniting families separated while traveling, providing food and/or shelter to people stranded without cash, and even emotional counseling.

GASOLINE (PETROL) At press time, in the U.S., the cost of gasoline (also known as gas, but never petrol), is abnormally high—about $2.50 per gallon at press time—and in California, it's typically more expensive than most other states. Taxes are already included in the printed price. One U.S. gallon equals 3.8 liters or .85 imperial gallons. Fill-up locations are known as gas or service stations.

HOLIDAYS Banks, government offices, post offices, and many stores, restaurants, and museums are closed on the following legal national holidays: January 1 (New Year's Day), the third Monday in January (Martin Luther King, Jr., Day), the third Monday in February (Presidents' Day), the last Monday in May (Memorial Day), July 4 (Independence Day), the first Monday in September (Labor Day), the second Monday in October (Columbus Day), November 11 (Veterans Day/Armistice Day), the fourth Thursday in November (Thanksgiving Day), and December 25 (Christmas Day). The Tuesday after the first Monday in November is Election Day, a federal government holiday in presidential-election years (held every 4 years, and next in 2012).

HOSPITALS **St. Francis Memorial Hospital** (900 Hyde St., btw. Bush and Pine; ✆ **415/353-6000**) operates emergency service 24 hours a day, and it also runs a physician referral service.

INSURANCE

Medical Insurance Although it's not required of travelers, health insurance is highly recommended. Most health insurance policies cover you if you get sick away from home—but check your coverage before you leave.

As a safety net, U.S. travelers may want to buy travel medical insurance. If you require additional medical insurance, try **MEDEX Assistance** (✆ **800/732-5309;** www.medexassist.com) or **Travel Assistance International** (✆ **800/821-2828;** www.travelassistance.com; for general information on services, call the company's **Worldwide Assistance Services, Inc.,** at ✆ **800/777-8710**).

Canadians should check with their provincial health plan offices or contact **Health Canada** (✆ **866/225-0709;** www.hc-sc.gc.ca) to find out the extent of their coverage and what documentation and receipts they must take home in case they are treated in the United States.

Travel Insurance The cost of travel insurance varies widely, depending on the destination, the cost and length of your trip, your age and health, and the type of trip you're taking, but expect to pay between 5% and 8% of the vacation itself. You can get estimates from various providers through **InsureMyTrip.com** (www.insuremytrip.com). Enter your trip cost and dates, your age, and other information for prices from more than a dozen companies.

U.K. citizens and their families who make more than one trip abroad per year may find an annual travel insurance policy works out cheaper. Check **www.moneysupermarket.com**, which compares prices across a wide range of providers for single- and multi-trip policies. The **Post Office** (✆ **080/0294-2292;** www.postoffice.co.uk) offers both annual and single-trip insurance coverage, which can be arranged online or at any post office counter.

Most big travel agents offer their own insurance and will probably try to sell you their package when you book a holiday. Think before you sign. **Britain's Consumers' Association** recommends that you insist on seeing the policy and reading the fine print before buying travel insurance. **The Association of British Insurers** (✆ **020/7600-3333;** www.abi.org.uk) gives advice by phone and publishes Holiday Insurance, a free guide to policy provisions and prices.

You might also shop around for better deals: Try **Columbus Direct** (✆ **087/0033-9988;** www.columbusdirect.net).

Trip Cancellation Insurance Trip-cancellation insurance will help retrieve your money if you have to back out of a trip or depart early, or if your travel supplier goes bankrupt. In the U.K., trip cancellation is normally included in travel insurance policies. Trip cancellation traditionally covers such events as sickness, natural disasters, and State Department advisories. The latest news in trip-cancellation insurance is the availability of **"any-reason"** cancellation coverage—which costs more but covers cancellations made for any reason. You won't get back 100% of your prepaid trip cost, but you'll be refunded a substantial portion. **TravelSafe** (✆ **888/885-7233;** www.travelsafe.com) offers both types of coverage. **Expedia** also offers any-reason cancellation coverage for its air-hotel packages. For details, contact one of the following recommended insurers: **Access America** (✆ 866/807-3982; www.accessamerica.com); **Travel Guard International** (✆ 800/826-4919; www.travelguard.com); **Travel Insured International** (✆ 800/243-3174; www.travelinsured.com); and **Travelex Insurance Services** (✆ 888/457-4602; www.travelex-insurance.com).

LEGAL AID If you are "pulled over" for a minor infraction (such as speeding), never attempt to pay the fine directly to a police officer; this could be construed as attempted bribery, a much more serious crime. Pay fines by mail or directly into the hands of the clerk of the court. If accused of a more serious offense, say and do nothing before consulting a lawyer. Here, the burden is on the state to prove a person's guilt beyond a reasonable doubt, and everyone has the right to remain silent, whether he or she is suspected of a crime or actually arrested. Once arrested, a person can make one telephone call to a party of his or her choice. International visitors should call their embassy or consulate.

LOST & FOUND Be sure to tell all of your credit card companies the minute you discover your wallet has been lost or stolen, and file a report at the nearest police precinct. Your credit card company or insurer may require a police report number or record of the loss. Most credit card companies have an emergency toll-free number to call if your card is lost or stolen; they may be able to wire you a cash advance immediately or deliver an emergency credit card in a day or two. Visa's U.S. emergency number is ✆ **800/847-2911** or 410/581-9994. American Express cardholders and traveler's check holders should call ✆ **800/221-7282.** MasterCard holders should call ✆ **800/307-7309** or 636/722-7111. For other credit cards, call the toll-free number directory at ✆ **800/555-1212.**

If you need emergency cash over the weekend when all banks and American Express offices are closed, you can have money wired to you via **Western Union** (✆ **800/325-6000;** www.westernunion.com).

MAIL At press time, domestic postage rates were 27¢ for a postcard and 42¢ for a letter. For international mail, a first-class letter of up to 1 ounce costs 94¢ (72¢ to Canada and Mexico); a first-class postcard costs the same as a postcard. For more information, go to **www.usps.com** and click on "Calculate Postage."

If you aren't sure what your address will be in the United States, mail can be sent to you, in your name, c/o General Delivery at the main post office of the city or region where you expect to be. (Call ✆ **800/275-8777** for information on the nearest post office.) The addressee must pick up mail in person and must produce proof of identity (driver's license, passport, and so on). Most post offices will hold your mail for up to 1 month, and are open Monday to

Friday from 8am to 6pm, and Saturday from 9am to 3pm.

Always include zip codes when mailing items in the U.S. If you don't know your zip code, visit www.usps.com/zip4.

PASSPORTS The websites listed provide downloadable passport applications, as well as the current fees for processing applications. For an up-to-date, country-by-country listing of passport requirements around the world, go to the "International Travel" tab of the U.S. State Department at **http://travel.state.gov**. International visitors to the U.S. can obtain a visa application at the same website. ***Note:*** Children are required to present a passport when entering the United States at airports. More information on obtaining a passport for a minor can be found at http://travel.state.gov. Allow plenty of time before your trip to apply for a passport; processing normally takes 4 to 6 weeks (3 weeks for expedited service) but can take longer during busy periods (especially spring). And keep in mind that if you need a passport in a hurry, you'll pay a higher processing fee.

For Residents of Australia You can pick up an application from your local post office or any branch of Passports Australia, but you must schedule an interview at the passport office to present your application materials. Call the **Australian Passport Information Service** at ✆ **131 232** or visit the government website at www.passports.gov.au.

For Residents of Canada Passport applications are available at travel agencies throughout Canada or from the central **Passport Office,** Dept. of Foreign Affairs and International Trade, Ottawa, ON K1A 0G3 (✆ **800/567-6868;** www.ppt.gc.ca). ***Note:*** Canadian children who travel must have their own passport. However, if you hold a valid Canadian passport issued before December 11, 2001, that bears the name of your child, the passport remains valid for you and your child until it expires.

For Residents of Ireland You can apply for a 10-year passport at the **Passport Office,** Setanta Centre, Molesworth Street, Dublin 2 (✆ **01/671-1633;** www.irlgov.ie/iveagh). Those under age 18 and over 65 must apply for a 3-year passport. You can also apply at 1A South Mall, Cork (✆ **21/494-4700**), or at most main post offices.

For Residents of New Zealand You can pick up a passport application at any New Zealand Passports Office or download it from the website. Contact the **Passports Office** at ✆ **0800/225-050** in New Zealand or 644/474-8100, or log on to www.passports.govt.nz.

For Residents of the United Kingdom To pick up an application for a standard 10-year passport (5-yr. passport for children 15 and under), visit your nearest passport office, major post office, or travel agency; or contact the **United Kingdom Passport Service** at ✆ **087/0521-0410** or search its website at www.ukpa.gov.uk.

POLICE For emergencies, call ✆ **911.** This is a free call (no coins required). For non-emergencies, call ✆ **311.**

SMOKING Heavy smokers are in for a tough time in California. Smoking is illegal in public buildings, sports arenas, elevators, theaters, banks, lobbies, restaurants, offices, stores, bed-and-breakfasts, most small hotels, and bars. That's right—as of January 1, 1998, you can't even smoke in California bars unless drinks are served solely by the owner (though you will find that many neighborhood bars turn a blind eye and pass you an ashtray).

TAXES The United States has no value-added tax (VAT) or other indirect tax at the national level. Every state, county, and city may levy its own local tax on all purchases, including hotel and restaurant checks and airline tickets. These taxes will not appear on price tags. Sales tax in California is generally around 8%. Hotel tax is charged on the room tariff only (which is not subject to sales tax) and is set by the city, ranging from 12% to 17% throughout California.

TELEPHONES Generally, hotel surcharges on long-distance and local calls are astronomical, so you're better off using your **cellphone** or a **public pay telephone.** Many convenience groceries and packaging services sell **prepaid calling cards** in denominations up to $50; for international visitors, these can be the least expensive way to call home. Many public phones at airports now accept American Express, MasterCard, and Visa credit cards. **Local calls** made from public pay phones in most locales cost either 25¢ or 35¢. Pay phones do not accept pennies, and few will take anything larger than a quarter.

Most long-distance and international calls can be dialed directly from any phone. **For calls within the United States and to Canada,** dial 1 followed by the area code and the seven-digit number. **For other international calls,** dial 011 followed by the country code, city code, and the number you are calling.

Calls to area codes **800, 888, 877,** and **866** are toll-free. However, calls to area codes **700** and **900** (chat lines, bulletin boards, "dating" services, and so on) can be very expensive—usually a charge of 95¢ to $3 or more per minute, and they sometimes have minimum charges that can run as high as $15 or more.

For **reversed-charge or collect calls,** and for person-to-person calls, dial the number 0, then the area code and number; an operator will come on the line, and you should specify whether you are calling collect, person-to-person, or both. If your operator-assisted call is international, ask for the overseas operator.

For **local directory assistance** ("information"), dial 411; for long-distance information, dial 1, then the appropriate area code and 555-1212.

Telegraph and telex services are provided primarily by Western Union. You can telegraph money, or have it telegraphed to you, very quickly over the Western Union system, but this service can cost as much as 15% to 20% of the amount sent.

Most hotels have **fax machines** available for guest use (be sure to ask about the charge to use it). Many hotel rooms are even wired for guests' fax machines. A less expensive way to send and receive faxes may be at stores such as **The UPS Store** (formerly Mail Boxes Etc.).

TIME California is on Pacific Standard Time (PST). The continental United States is divided into **four time zones:** Eastern Standard Time (EST), Central Standard Time (CST), Mountain Standard Time (MST), and Pacific Standard Time (PST). Alaska and Hawaii have their own zones. For example, when it's 9am in Los Angeles (PST), it's 7am in Honolulu (HST), 10am in Denver (MST), 11am in Chicago (CST), noon in New York City (EST), 5pm in London (GMT), and 2am the next day in Sydney.

Daylight saving time takes effect at 2am the second Sunday in March until 2am the first Sunday in November, except in Arizona, Hawaii, the U.S. Virgin Islands, and Puerto Rico. Daylight saving moves the clock 1 hour ahead of standard time. For the correct time, call "POPCORN" (✆ **767-2676**) in any California area code.

TIPPING Tips are a very important part of many workers' incomes, and gratuities are the standard way of showing appreciation for services provided. (Tipping is certainly not compulsory if the service is poor!) In hotels, tip **bellhops** at least $1 per bag ($2–$3 if you have a lot of luggage) and tip the **chamber staff** $1 to $2 per day (more if you've left a disaster area for him or her to clean up). Tip the **doorman** or **concierge** only if he or she has provided you with some specific service (for example, calling a cab for you or obtaining difficult-to-get theater tickets). Tip the **valet-parking attendant** $1 every time you get your car.

In restaurants, bars, and nightclubs, tip **service staff** 15% to 20% of the check, tip **bartenders** 10% to 15%, tip **checkroom attendants** $1 per garment, and tip **valet-parking attendants** $1 per vehicle.

As for other service personnel, tip **cab drivers** 15% of the fare; tip **skycaps** at airports at least $1 per bag ($2–$3 if you have a lot of luggage); and tip **hairdressers** and **barbers** 15% to 20%.

TOILETS You won't find public toilets or "restrooms" on the streets in most California cities (except San Francisco), but they can be found in hotel lobbies, bars, restaurants, museums, department stores, railway and bus stations, and service stations. Large hotels and fast-food restaurants are often the best bet for clean facilities. If possible, avoid the toilets at parks and beaches, which tend to be dirty; some may even be unsafe. Restaurants and bars in resorts or heavily visited areas may reserve their restrooms for paying customers.

VISAS For information about U.S. visas, go to **http://travel.state.gov** and click on "Visas." Or go to one of the following websites:

Australian citizens can obtain up-to-date visa information from the **U.S. Embassy Canberra,** Moonah Place, Yarralumla, ACT 2600 (✆ **02/6214-5600**), or by checking the U.S. Diplomatic Mission's website at **http://usembassy-australia.state.gov/consular**.

British subjects can obtain up-to-date visa information by calling the **U.S. Embassy Visa Information Line** (✆ **0891/200-290**) or by visiting the "Visas to the U.S." section of the American Embassy London's website at **www.usembassy.org.uk**.

Irish citizens can obtain up-to-date visa information through the **Embassy of the USA Dublin,** 42 Elgin Rd., Dublin 4, Ireland (✆ **353/1668-8777**), or by checking the "Consular Services" section of the website at **http://dublin.usembassy.gov**.

Citizens of **New Zealand** can obtain up-to-date visa information by contacting the **U.S. Embassy New Zealand,** 29 Fitzherbert Terrace, Thorndon, Wellington (✆ **6444/722-068**), or get the information directly from the "For New Zealanders" section of the website at **http://usembassy.org.nz**.

2 TOLL-FREE NUMBERS & WEBSITES

MAJOR U.S. AIRLINES

(*flies internationally, as well)

American Airlines*
✆ 800/433-7300 (in U.S. and Canada)
✆ 020/7365-0777 (in U.K.)
www.aa.com

Cape Air
✆ 800/352-0714
www.flycapeair.com

Continental Airlines*
✆ 800/523-3273 (in U.S. and Canada)
✆ 084/5607-6760 (in U.K.)
www.continental.com

Delta Air Lines*
✆ 800/221-1212 (in U.S. and Canada)
✆ 084/5600-0950 (in U.K.)
www.delta.com

JetBlue Airways
✆ 800/538-2583 (in U.S. and Canada)
✆ 801/365-2525 (in U.K.)
www.jetblue.com

Midwest Airlines
✆ 800/452-2022
www.midwestairlines.com

North American Airlines*
✆ 800/371-6297
www.flynaa.com

Northwest Airlines
✆ 800/225-2525 (in U.S. and Canada)
✆ 870/0507-4074 (in U.K.)
www.nwa.com

United Airlines*
✆ 800/864-8331 (in U.S. and Canada)
✆ 084/5844-4777 (in U.K.)
www.united.com

US Airways*
✆ 800/428-4322 (in U.S. and Canada)
✆ 084/5600-3300 (in U.K.)
www.usairways.com

Virgin America*
✆ 877/359-8474
www.virginamerica.com

MAJOR INTERNATIONAL AIRLINES

Air Canada
✆ 888/247-2262 (in North America)
www.aircanada.com

Air France
✆ 800/237-2747 (in U.S.)
✆ 800/375-8723 (in U.S. and Canada)
✆ 087/0142-4343 (in U.K.)
www.airfrance.com

Air India
✆ 212/407-1371 (in U.S.)
✆ 91 22 2279 6666 (in India)
✆ 020/8745-1000 (in U.K.)
www.airindia.com

Air New Zealand
✆ 800/262-1234 (in U.S.)
✆ 800/663-5494 (in Canada)
✆ 080/0028-4149 (in U.K.)
www.airnewzealand.com

Alitalia
✆ 800/223-5730 (in U.S.)
✆ 800/361-8336 (in Canada)
✆ 087/0608-6003 (in U.K.)
www.alitalia.com

American Airlines
✆ 800/433-7300 (in U.S. and Canada)
✆ 020/7365-0777 (in U.K.)
www.aa.com

bmi
✆ 087/0607-0555 (in U.K.)
✆ 133/264-6181 (outside U.K.)
www.flybmi.com

British Airways
✆ 800/247-9297 (in U.S. and Canada)
✆ 087/0850-9850 (in U.K.)
www.british-airways.com

China Airlines
✆ 800/227-5118 (in U.S.)
✆ 022/715-1212 (in Taiwan)
www.china-airlines.com

Continental Airlines
✆ 800/523-3273 (in U.S. and Canada)
✆ 084/5607-6760 (in U.K.)
www.continental.com

Delta Air Lines
✆ 800/221-1212 (in U.S. and Canada)
✆ 084/5600-0950 (in U.K.)
www.delta.com

EgyptAir
✆ 212/581-5600 (in U.S.)
✆ 020/7734-2343 (in U.K.)
✆ 09/007-0000 (in Egypt)
www.egyptair.com

El Al Airlines
✆ 972/3977-1111 (outside Israel)
✆ *2250 (from any phone in Israel)
www.elal.co.il

Emirates Airlines
✆ 800/777-3999 (in U.S.)
✆ 087/0243-2222 (in U.K.)
www.emirates.com

Finnair
✆ 800/950-5000 (in U.S. and Canada)
✆ 087/0241-4411 (in U.K.)
www.finnair.com

Iberia Airlines
✆ 800/722-4642 (in U.S. and Canada)
✆ 087/0609-0500 (in U.K.)
www.iberia.com

Icelandair
✆ 800/223-5500 ext. 2, prompt 1 (in U.S. and Canada)
✆ 084/5758-1111 (in U.K.)
www.icelandair.com

Japan Airlines
✆ 012/025-5931 (international)
www.jal.co.jp

KLM Royal Dutch Airlines
✆ 800/225-2525 (in U.S. and Canada)
✆ 087/1222-7474 (in U.K.)
www.klm.com

Korean Air
✆ 800/438-5000 (in U.S. and Canada)
✆ 080/0413-000 (in U.K.)
www.koreanair.com

Lufthansa
✆ 800/399-5838 (in U.S.)
✆ 800/563-5954 (in Canada)
✆ 087/0837-7747 (in U.K.)
www.lufthansa.com

Olympic Airlines
✆ 800/223-1226 (in U.S.)
✆ 514/878-9691 (in Canada)
✆ 087/0606-0460 (in U.K.)
www.olympicairlines.com

Quantas Airways
✆ 800/227-4500 (in U.S.)
✆ 084/5774-7767 (in U.K. and Canada)
✆ 13-13-13 (in Australia)
www.quantas.com

SAS Scandinavian Airlines
✆ 800/221-2350 (in U.S. or Canada)
✆ 087/1521-2772 (in U.K.)
www.flysas.com

Swiss Air
✆ 877/359-7947 (in U.S. and Canada)
✆ 084/5601-0956 (in U.K.)
www.swiss.com

United Airlines*
✆ 800/864-8331 (in U.S. and Canada)
✆ 084/5844-4777 (in U.K.)
www.united.com

US Airways*
✆ 800/428-4322 (in U.S. and Canada)
✆ 084/5600-3300 (in U.K.)
www.usairways.com

Virgin Atlantic Airways
✆ 800/821-5438 (in U.S. and Canada)
✆ 087/0574-7747 (in U.K.)
www.virgin-atlantic.com

BUDGET AIRLINES

Aegean Airlines
✆ 210/626-1000
www.aegeanair.com

Aer Arann
✆ 087/0876-7676 (in U.K.)
✆ 081/8210-210 (in Ireland)
✆ 353/8182-10210 (all others)
www.aerarran.com

Aer Lingus
✆ 800/474-7424 (in U.S. and Canada)
✆ 087/0876-5000 (in U.K.)
www.aerlingus.com

Air Berlin
✆ 087/1500-0737 (in U.K.)
✆ 018/0573-7800 (in Germany)
✆ 180/573-7800 (all others)
www.airberlin.com

Air Transat
✆ 020/7616-9187 (in U.K.)
www.airtransat.com

bmi baby
✆ 870/126-6726 (in U.S.)
✆ 087/1224-0224 (in U.K.)
www.bmibaby.com

easyJet
✆ 870/600-0000 (in U.S.)
✆ 090/5560-7777 (in U.K.)
www.easyjet.com

Flybe
✆ 087/1700-2000 (in U.K.)
✆ 1392/268-513 (outside U.K.)
www.flybe.com

flyglobespan
✆ 087/1971-1440 (in U.K.)
www.flyglobespan.com

JetBlue Airways
✆ 800/538-2583 (in U.S. and Canada)
✆ 801/365-2525 (in U.K.)
www.jetblue.com

Ryanair
✆ 353/249-7700 (in U.S.)
✆ 081/830-3030 (in Ireland)
✆ 087/1246-0000 (in U.K.)
www.ryanair.com

Southwest Airlines
✆ 800/435-9792
www.southwest.com

Thomson Airways
✆ 087/1231-4691 (in U.K.)
http://flights.thomson.co.uk

WestJet
✆ 800/538-5696 (in U.S. and Canada)
www.westjet.com

Wideroe
✆ 477/511-1111 (outside Norway)
www.wideroe.no

CAR RENTAL AGENCIES

Advantage
✆ 800/777-5500 (in U.S.)
✆ 021/0344-4712 (outside U.S.)
www.advantage.com

Alamo
✆ 800/462-5266 (in U.S.)
✆ 087/0400-4562 (in U.K.)
www.alamo.com

Avis
✆ 800/331-1212 (in U.S. and Canada)
✆ 084/4581-8181 (in U.K.)
www.avis.com

Budget
✆ 800/527-0700 (in U.S.)
✆ 800/268-8900 (in Canada)
✆ 087/0156-5656 (in U.K.)
www.budget.com

Dollar
✆ 800/800-4000 (in U.S.)
✆ 800/848-8268 (in Canada)
✆ 080/8234-7524 (in U.K.)
www.dollar.com

Easycar.com
✆ 087/1050-0444 (in U.K.)
www.easycar.com

Enterprise
✆ 800/261-7331 (in U.S.)
✆ 514/355-4028 (in Canada)
✆ 012/9360-9090 (in U.K.)
www.enterprise.com

Hertz
✆ 800/645-3131 (in U.S.)
www.hertz.com

National
✆ 800/227-7368 (in U.S.)
✆ 087/0400-4581 (in U.K.)
www.nationalcar.co.uk

Thrifty
✆ 800/367-2277 (in U.S.)
✆ 918/669-2168 (international)
www.thrifty.com

Best Western International
© 800/780-7234 (in U.S. and Canada)
© 0800/393-130 (in U.K.)
www.bestwestern.com

Clarion Hotels
© 800/CLARION or 877/424-6423 (in U.S. and Canada)
© 0800/444-444 (in U.K.)
www.choicehotels.com

Comfort Inns
© 800/228-5150 (in U.S.)
© 0800/444-444 (in U.K.)
www.ComfortInnChoiceHotels.com

Courtyard by Marriott
© 888/236-2427 (in U.S.)
© 0800/221-222 (in U.K.)
www.marriott.com/courtyard

Crowne Plaza Hotels
© 888/303-1746 (in U.S.)
www.ichotelsgroup.com/crowneplaza

Days Inn
© 800/329-7466 (in U.S.)
© 0800/280-400 (in U.K.)
www.daysinn.com

Doubletree Hotels
© 800/222-TREE (800/222-8733) (in U.S. and Canada)
© 087/0590-9090 (in U.K)
www.doubletree.com

Econo Lodges
© 800/55-ECONO (800/552-3666) (in U.S.)
www.choicehotels.com

Embassy Suites
© 800/EMBASSY (800/362-2779) (in U.S.)
www.embassysuites.hilton.com

Fairfield Inn by Marriott
© 800/228-2800 (in U.S. and Canada)
© 0800/221-222 (in U.K.)
www.marriott.com/fairfieldinn

Four Seasons
© 800/819-5053 (in U.S. and Canada)
© 0800/6488-6488 (in U.K.)
www.fourseasons.com

Hampton Inn
© 800/HAMPTON (800/426-4766) (in U.S.)
www.hamptoninn.hilton.com

Hilton Hotels
© 800/HILTONS (800/445-8667) (in U.S. and Canada)
© 087/0590-9090 (in U.K.)
www.hilton.com

Holiday Inn
© 800/315-2621 (in U.S. and Canada)
© 0800/405-060 (in U.K.)
www.holidayinn.com

Howard Johnson
© 800/446-4656 (in U.S. and Canada)
www.hojo.com

Hyatt
© 888/591-1234 (in U.S. and Canada)
© 084/5888-1234 (in U.K.)
www.hyatt.com

InterContinental Hotels & Resorts
© 800/424-6835 (in U.S. and Canada)
© 0800/1800-1800 (in U.K.)
www.ichotelsgroup.com

La Quinta Inns and Suites
© 800/642-4271 (in U.S. and Canada)
www.lq.com

Loews Hotels
© 800/23LOEWS (800/235-6397) (in U.S.)
www.loewshotels.com

Marriott
© 877/236-2427 (in U.S. and Canada)
© 0800/221-222 (in U.K.)
www.marriott.com

Motel 6
© 800/4MOTEL6 (800/466-8356) (in U.S.)
www.motel6.com

Omni Hotels
✆ 888/444-OMNI (888/444-6664) (in U.S.)
www.omnihotels.com

Quality
✆ 877/424-6423 (in U.S. and Canada)
✆ 0800/444-444 (in U.K.)
www.QualityInn.ChoiceHotels.com

Radisson Hotels & Resorts
✆ 888/201-1718 (in U.S. and Canada)
✆ 0800/374-411 (in U.K.)
www.radisson.com

Ramada Worldwide
✆ 888/2-RAMADA (888/272-6232) (in U.S. and Canada)
✆ 080/8100-0783 (in UK)
www.ramada.com

Red Carpet Inns
✆ 800/251-1962 (in U.S.)
www.bookroomsnow.com

Red Lion Hotels
✆ 800/RED-LION (800/733-5466) (in U.S.)
www.redlion.rdln.com

Red Roof Inns
✆ 866/686-4335 (in U.S. and Canada)
✆ 614/601-4075 (international)
www.redroof.com

Renaissance
✆ 888/236-2427 (in U.S.)
www.marriott.com

Residence Inn by Marriott
✆ 800/331-3131(U.S.)
✆ 800/221-222 (in U.K.)
www.marriott.com/residenceinn

Sheraton Hotels & Resorts
✆ 800/325-3535 (in U.S.)
✆ 800/543-4300 (in Canada)
✆ 0800/3253-5353 (in U.K.)
www.starwoodhotels.com/sheraton

Super 8 Motels
✆ 800/800-8000
www.super8.com

Travelodge
✆ 800/578-7878
www.travelodge.com

Vagabond Inns
✆ 800/522-1555
www.vagabondinn.com

Westin Hotels & Resorts
✆ 800/937-8461 (in U.S. and Canada)
✆ 0800/3259-5959 (in U.K.)
www.starwoodhotels.com/westin

Wyndham Hotels & Resorts
✆ 877/999-3223 (in U.S. and Canada)
✆ 050/6638-4899 (in U.K.)
www.wyndham.com

Appendix B: Other Sports & Activities in Northern California's National Parks

1 DEATH VALLEY

BIKING Cycling is allowed on the 1,000 miles of dirt and paved roads used by motor vehicles in the park, but not on hiking trails or anywhere else. Weather conditions between May and October make bicycling at the lower elevations dangerous at times other than early morning. There are no bike rentals available in the park, and given the park's isolation, the only practical option is to bring your own. You'll need a pretty rugged mountain bike to do most of these routes. Good choices are Racetrack (28 miles one-way), Greenwater Valley (30 miles one-way, mainly level), Cottonwood Canyon (20 miles one-way), and West Side Road (40 miles one-way, fairly level with some washboard sections). Artists Drive is 9 miles long, paved, with some steep uphill stretches. Other favorites include Titus Canyon (28 miles on a one-way hilly road—it has some very difficult uphill and downhill stretches) and Twenty-Mule Team Canyon Road (a one-way 2¾-mile graded gravel road through colorful badlands).

2 POINT REYES NATIONAL SEASHORE

BIKING As most ardent Bay Area mountain bikers know, Point Reyes National Seashore has some of the finest mountain-bike trails in the region—narrow dirt paths winding through densely forested knolls and ending with spectacular ocean views. A trail map (available free at the Bear Valley Visitor Center) is a must, because many of the park trails are off-limits to bikes. Note: Bicycles are forbidden on the wilderness area trails, and plotting a course exclusively on the bike trails can be tricky, so plan your route well in advance. Check at the visitor center to find out which trails are currently open to bikes.

BIRD-WATCHING Point Reyes National Seashore boasts one of the most diverse bird populations in the country, with over 490 different species sighted. Popular bird-watching spots are Abbotts Lagoon and Estero de Limantour. You can hang out with the pros at the **Point Reyes Bird Observatory–Palomarin Field Station (© 415/868-0655;** www.prbo.org), one of the few full-time ornithological research stations in the United States, at the southeast end of the park on Mesa Road. This is where ornithologists keep an eye on the myriad feathered species that call the seashore home. Admission to the visitor center and nature trail is free, and visitors are welcome to observe the tricky process of catching and banding the birds. The observatory is open daily sunrise to 5pm (banding hours vary; call for exact times).

HORSEBACK RIDING Equestrian activities are very popular at Point Reyes, where all of the trails (save Bear Valley Trail on weekends and holidays) are horse-friendly. A good resource is **Five Brooks Ranch** (✆ **415/663-1570;** www.fivebrooks.com), located at the Five Brooks Trailhead, 3½ miles south of Olema on Highway 1. The ranch offers guided trail rides (horses provided) at prices ranging from $50 for an hour-long ride to $220 for a 6-hour beach ride. Horse boarding is available.

KAYAKING **Blue Waters Kayaking** (✆ **415/669-2600;** www.bwkayak.com) offers kayak trips, including 3-hour sunset outings, 3½-hour full-moon paddles, yoga tours, day trips, and longer excursions. Instruction and clinics are available, and all ages and skill levels are welcome. Prices start at $68 for tours. Four-hour rentals begin at $45 for one person, $70 for two. Basic skill classes last a full day and run $99. There are no waves to contend with in placid Tomales Bay, a haven for migrating birds and marine mammals. The launching point is on Calif. 1 at the Marshall Boatworks in Marshall, 8 miles north of Point Reyes Station.

WHALE-WATCHING Each year, gray whales (the barnacles make them appear gray) migrate from their winter breeding grounds in the warm waters off Baja California to their summer feeding grounds in Alaska. You can observe them as they undertake their 10,000-mile journey from just about anywhere in **Point Reyes National Seashore.** The most popular vantage point is the **Point Reyes Lighthouse.** During peak season (Dec–Mar), you might see dozens of whales from the lighthouse, and the Lighthouse Visitor Center offers great displays on whale migration and maritime history. During this period, the Park Service runs a shuttle from Drakes Beach to the Point Reyes Lighthouse ($5 adults, free for children under 17), where watchers have been known to see as many as 100 whales in a single afternoon. Even if the whales don't materialize, the lighthouse itself, a fabulous old structure teetering high above the sea at the tip of a promontory, is worth a visit. Two other spots, Chimney Rock, east of the lighthouse, and Tomales Point, at the northern end of the park, offer just as many whales without the crowds.

3 REDWOOD NATIONAL & STATE PARKS

BEACHES The park's beaches vary from long white-sand strands to cobblestone pocket coves. The water temperature is in the high 40s to low 50s (single digits to 10s Celsius) year-round, and it's often rough out there. Swimmers and surfers should be prepared for adverse conditions. **Crescent Beach** is a long, sandy beach just 2 miles south of Crescent City that's a popular destination for beachcombing, surf fishing, and surfing. Just south of Crescent Beach is **Enderts Beach,** a protected spot with a hike-in campground and tide pools at its southern end. Picnickers alert: The Crescent Beach Overlook, along Enderts Road (off U.S. 101 about 4 miles south of Crescent City), is one of the prettiest picnic sites on the California coast. Pack a picnic lunch from Good Harvest Cafe (see "Where to Dine," below), park at the overlook, lay your blanket on the grass, and admire the ocean view from atop your personal 500-foot bluff. 1.3 miles one-way. Moderate. Access: End of Tall Trees Access Rd., off Bald Hills Rd. Permit required.

BICYCLING Most of the hiking trails throughout the **Redwood National and State Parks** are off limits to mountain bikers. However, **Prairie Creek Redwoods State Park** has a fantastic 19-mile mountain-bike trail through dense forest, elk-filled meadows, and glorious mud holes. Parts of it are difficult, though, so beginners should sit this one out. Pick up a 25¢ trail map at the **Elk Prairie Campground Ranger Station.**

A few other mountain-bike loops are about 20 miles long, but they are serious thigh burners and make the one above look easy. These loops are the Holter Ridge Trail and Little Bald Hills. Also, mountain biking is permitted on the old U.S. 101, now the Coastal Trail within **Del Norte Coast Redwoods State Park.** The park recently completed the Davison Trail, which connects the Prairie Creek bike trails and the Newton B. Drury Scenic Parkway with U.S. 101 and the Holter Ridge Trail.

FISHING The Redwood Coast's streams are some of the best steelhead trout and salmon-breeding habitat in California. Park beaches are good for surfcasting, but you should be prepared for heavy wave action. A California fishing license (available at local sporting goods stores) is required. Be sure to check with rangers about closures or other restrictions, which seem to change frequently. **Rivers West Outfitters** (✆ **707/482-5822** or 707/465-5501; www.riverswestoutfitters.com) offers guide service for around $150 per person per day.

HORSEBACK TRAIL RIDES Equestrians can go on a variety of guided trail rides, including lunch and dinner trips, with **Redwood Trails Horseback Riding** (✆ **707/498-4837**), at the **Redwood Trails Campground,** 5 miles south of Orick on U.S. 101. Riders should be less than 230 pounds. Rates range from $20 for a half-hour ride to $250 for a 6-hour ride with lunch.

JET-BOAT TOURS Tours aboard a jet boat take visitors 22 miles upriver from the **Klamath River Estuary** to view bear, deer, elk, osprey hawks, otters, and more along the riverbanks. It's about $40 for a 45-mile scenic trip, $35 for seniors. Kids pay half-price, and children under 4 ride free. Meals are not included. Tours run May through September. Contact **Klamath River Jet Boat Tours,** Klamath (✆ **800/887-JETS** or 707/482-5822; www.jetboattours.com).

WHALE-WATCHING & BIRD-WATCHING High coastal overlooks such as **Klamath Overlook** and **Crescent Beach Overlook** make great whale-watching outposts during the December–January southern migration and the March–April return migration. The northern sea cliffs also provide valuable nesting sites for marine birds such as auklets, puffins, murres, and cormorants. Birders will also love the park's coastal freshwater lagoons, which are some of the most pristine shorebird and waterfowl habitats left and are chock-full of hundreds of different species.

WILDLIFE VIEWING One of the most striking aspects of **Prairie Creek Redwoods State Park** is its herd of Roosevelt elk, usually found in the appropriately named Elk Prairie in the southern end of the park. These gigantic beasts can weigh up to 1,000 pounds. The bulls carry huge antlers from spring to fall. Elk are also sometimes found at **Gold Bluffs Beach**—it's an incredible rush to suddenly come upon them out of the fog or after a turn in the trail. Nearly 100 black bears also call the park home but are seldom seen. Unlike those at Yosemite and Yellowstone, these bears avoid people.

4 SEQUOIA & KINGS CANYON NATIONAL PARKS

CROSS-COUNTRY SKIING There are 35 miles of marked backcountry trails in the parks. Call park concessionaires for information (© **559/335-5500** in Grant Grove and © 559/565-4070 in the Wuksachi Lodge area). The **Pear Lake Ski Hut** is open to the public for backcountry accommodations in Sequoia from mid-December through April. Call © 559/565-3759 for more information.

FISHING A section of the south fork of the Kings River, the Kaweah drainage, and the parks' lakes are open all year for trout fishing—rainbow, brook, German brown, and golden. Most other waters are open for trout fishing from late April through mid-November, and open for other species year-round. California fishing licenses (available at stores in the park) are required for anglers 16 and older, and you should also get a copy of the National Park Service's fishing regulations, available at visitor centers.

HORSEBACK RIDING Concessionaires in both parks and the adjacent national monument offer guided horseback and mule rides and overnight pack trips during the summer. In Kings Canyon, **Cedar Grove Pack Station** (© **559/565-3464** summer, 559/337-2314 winter) is about 1 mile east of Cedar Grove Village, and **Grant Grove Stables** (© **559/335-9292** summer, 559/337-2314 winter) is near Grant Grove Village. In Giant Sequoia National Monument, **Horse Corral Pack Station** is on Big Meadows Road, 10 miles east of Generals Highway (© **559/565-3404** summer, 559/564-6429 winter; www.horsecorralpackers.com). The pack stations offer hourly rides as well as overnight treks. The stables offer day rides only. Rates range from $30 to $35 for a 1-hour ride to $100 to $200 for a full day in the saddle; call for rates for pack trips.

SNOWSHOEING On winter weekends, rangers lead introductory snowshoe hikes in **Grant Grove** (© **559/565-4307**) and **Giant Forest** (© **559/565-4436**). Snowshoes are provided, and a $1 donation is requested.

WHITE-WATER RAFTING The Kaweah and Upper Kings rivers in the parks are not open to boating, but several companies run trips just outside the parks. The thrilling roller-coaster ride through the rapids is a great way to not only see but also to experience these scenic rivers. Offering trips on the Kaweah, Kings, Merced, and other rivers is **Whitewater Voyages** (© **800/400-RAFT;** www.whitewatervoyages.com), with rates that range from $89 to $219 for half- and full-day trips, and multi-day trips are also available (call for rates). **Kings River Expeditions** (© **800/846-3674** or 559/233-4881; www.kingsriver.com) specializes in rafting trips on the Kings. For 1-day trips they charge $90 to $150 in spring, and $130 to $199 from mid-May until the season ends. Overnight trips are also available (call for rates).

5 YOSEMITE NATIONAL PARK

BICYCLING Twelve miles of designated bike trails cross the eastern end of Yosemite Valley, which is the best place to ride because roads and shuttle bus routes are usually crowded and dangerous for bicyclists. Children under 18 are required by law to wear helmets. Single-speed bikes are for rent by the hour ($7.50) or the day ($25) at **Curry**

Village (✆ **209/372-8319**) in summer only, and at **Yosemite Lodge** (✆ **209/372-1208**) year-round. Bike rentals include helmets for all ages.

CROSS-COUNTRY SKIING The park has more than 350 miles of skiable trails and roads, including 25 miles of machine-groomed track and 90 miles of marked trails in the Badger Pass area. Equipment rentals, lessons, and day and overnight ski tours are available from **Badger Pass Cross-Country Center and Ski School** (✆ **209/372-8444;** www.yosemitepark.com).

FISHING Several species of trout can be found in Yosemite's streams. Guided fly-fishing trips are available from **Yosemite Guides** (✆ **877/425-3366** or 209/379-2231; www.yosemiteguides.com) for $275 for two for a full day. California fishing licenses are required for those 16 and older; information is available from the **California State Department of Fish and Game** (✆ **559/243-4005;** www.dfg.ca.gov). Village Sport Shop in Yosemite Valley has fishing gear and sells fishing licenses. There are also special fishing regulations in Yosemite Valley; get information at the visitor centers.

GOLF The park has one golf course, and several others are nearby. **Wawona** (✆ **209/375-6572**) is a 9-hole, par-35 course that alternates between meadows and fairways. Just outside the park, the 18-hole **Sierra Meadows Golf Course** (✆ **559/642-1343**) is in Oakhurst. Call for current greens fees and other information.

HORSEBACK RIDING Several companies offer guided horseback rides in and just outside the national park, with rates starting at about $25 for 1 hour, $40 for 2 hours, and $75 for a half day. **Yosemite Stables** (✆ **209/372-4386**) offers mule rides from several locations, including Yosemite Valley and Wawona, and leads multiday pack trips into the backcountry (call for details). **Yosemite Trails Pack Station** (✆ **559/683-7611;** www.yosemitetrails.com) offers riding just south of Wawona. **Minarets Pack Station** (✆ **559/868-3405;** www.highsierrapackers.org) leads day trips to Yosemite and the Ansel Adams Wilderness.

ICE-SKATING The outdoor ice rink at **Curry Village,** with great views of Half Dome and Glacier Point, is open from early November to March, weather permitting. Admission is $8 for adults, $6 for children; skate rental costs $3. Call ✆ **209/372-8319** for current hours.

RAFTING A raft-rental shop is located at **Curry Village** (✆ **209/372-4386**). Daily fees are $21 for adults, $14 for children under 13. Fees include a raft, paddles, mandatory life preservers, and transportation from Sentinel Beach to Curry Village.

Swift currents and cold water can be deadly. Talk with rangers and shop people before venturing out to be sure you're planning a trip that's within your capabilities.

ROCK CLIMBING Yosemite is considered one of the world's premier playgrounds for experienced rock climbers and wannabes. The **Yosemite Mountaineering School** (✆ **209/372-8344;** www.yosemitemountaineering.com) provides instruction for beginning, intermediate, and advanced climbers in the valley and Tuolumne Meadows from April through October. Classes last anywhere from a day to a week, and private lessons are available. Rates vary according to the class or program. All equipment is provided.

SKIING Yosemite's **Badger Pass Ski Area** (✆ **209/372-8430;** www.yosemitepark.com) is usually open from Thanksgiving through Easter, weather permitting. The small resort 22 miles from Yosemite Valley was established in 1935. There are 10 runs, rated 35% beginner, 50% intermediate, and 15% advanced, with a vertical drop of 800 feet from its highest point of 8,000 feet. There are five lifts—one triple chair, three double chairs, and a cable tow. Full-day adult lift tickets cost $38, and full-day lift tickets for kids 7 to 12 are $15; half-day tickets are $28 and $11, respectively. The ski area has several casual restaurants, a ski shop, ski repairs, a day lodge, and lockers. There's also an excellent ski school, thanks to "Ski Ambassador" Nic Fiore, a Yosemite ski legend who arrived in the park in 1947 to ski for a season and never left. Fiore became director of the ski school in 1956, and park officials credit Fiore with making Badger Pass what it is today—a family-oriented ski area where generations have come to ski.

INDEX

See also Accommodations and Restaurant indexes, below.

General Index

audio may not be returned, but can be exchanged only for the same title if defective.

After 14 days or without a sales receipt, returns or exchanges will not be permitted.

Magazines, newspapers, and used books are not returnable. *Product not carried by Barnes & Noble or Barnes & Noble.com will not be accepted for return.*

Policy on receipt may appear in two sections.

Return Policy

With a sales receipt, a full refund in the original form of payment will be issued from any Barnes & Noble store for returns of new and unread books (except textbooks) and unopened music/DVDs/audio made within (i) 14 days of purchase from a Barnes & Noble retail store (except for purchases made by check less than 7 days prior to the date of return) or (ii) 14 days of delivery date for Barnes & Noble.com purchases (except for purchases made via PayPal). A store credit for the purchase price will be issued for (i) purchases made by check less than 7 days prior to the date of return, (ii) when a gift receipt is presented within 60 days of purchase, (iii) textbooks returned with a receipt within 14 days of purchase, or (iv) original purchase was made through Barnes & Noble.com via PayPal. Opened music/DVDs/ audio may not be returned, but can be exchanged only for the same title if defective.

After 14 days or without a sales receipt, returns or exchanges will not be permitted.

Magazines, newspapers, and used books are not returnable. *Product not carried by Barnes & Noble or Barnes & Noble.com will not be accepted for return.*

Policy on receipt may appear in two sections.

Return Policy

With a sales receipt, a full refund in the original form of payment will be issued from any Barnes & Noble store for returns of new and unread books (except textbooks) and unopened music/DVDs/audio made within (i) 14 days of purchase from a Barnes & Noble retail store (except for purchases made by check

Barnes & Noble Booksellers #2703
1851 Fountain Drive
Reston, VA 20190
703-437-9490

STR:2703 REG:009 TRN:9417 CSHR:Ken C

BARNES & NOBLE MEMBER EXP: 10/31/2010

Fodor's Northern Califor	
9781400008056 T1	
(1 @ 18.95) Member Card 10% (1.90)	
(1 @ 17.05)	17.05
Frommer's Best Hiking Tr	
9780470159910 T1	
(1 @ 19.99) Member Card 10% (2.00)	
(1 @ 17.99)	17.99
Subtotal	35.04
Sales Tax T1 (5.000%)	1.75
TOTAL	**36.79**
VISA DEBIT	**36.79**
Card#: XXXXXXXXXXXX7290	
MEMBER SAVINGS	3.90

Thanks for shopping at
Barnes & Noble

V101.19 03/22/2010 01:11PM

CUSTOMER COPY

Accommodations

Restaurants

NOTES

NOTES